DELEUZE AND THE SCHIZOANALYSIS OF FEMINISM

Schizoanalytic Applications

Schizoanalysis has the potential to be to Deleuze and Guattari's work what deconstruction is to Derrida's—the standard rubric by which their work is known and, more importantly, applied. Many within the field of Deleuze and Guattari studies would resist this idea, but the goal of this series is to broaden the base of scholars interested in their work. Deleuze and Guattari's ideas are widely known and used but not in a systematic way, and this is both a strength and weakness. It is a strength because it enables people to pick up their work from a wide variety of perspectives, but it is also a weakness because it makes it difficult to say with any clarity what exactly a 'Deleuzo-Guattarian' approach is. This has inhibited the uptake of Deleuze and Guattari's thinking in the more willful disciplines such as history, politics, and even philosophy. Without this methodological core, Deleuze and Guattari studies risk becoming simply another intellectual fashion that will soon be superseded by newer figures. The goal of the Schizoanalytic Applications series is to create a methodological core and build a sustainable model of schizoanalysis that will attract new scholars to the field. With this purpose, the series also aims to be at the forefront of the field by starting a discussion about the nature of Deleuze and Guattari's methodology.

Series editors: Ian Buchanan, David Savat, and Marcelo Svirsky

Other titles in the series:

DELEUZE AND THE SCHIZOANALYSIS OF RELIGION,
edited by Lindsay Powell-Jones and F. LeRon Shults

DELEUZE AND THE SCHIZOANALYSIS OF LITERATURE,
edited by Ian Buchanan, Tim Matts and Aidan Tynan

DELEUZE AND THE SCHIZOANALYSIS OF VISUAL ART,
edited by Ian Buchanan and Lorna Collins

DELEUZE AND THE SCHIZOANALYSIS OF FEMINISM

ALLIANCES AND ALLIES

Editors
Janae Sholtz
Cheri Lynne Carr

BLOOMSBURY ACADEMIC
LONDON • NEW YORK • OXFORD • NEW DELHI • SYDNEY

BLOOMSBURY ACADEMIC
Bloomsbury Publishing Plc
50 Bedford Square, London, WC1B 3DP, UK
1385 Broadway, New York, NY 10018, USA

BLOOMSBURY, BLOOMSBURY ACADEMIC and the Diana logo are trademarks
of Bloomsbury Publishing Plc

First published in Great Britain 2019

Cover image: *It's important to revisit traumas...*, 2018, mixed media on canvas © Jeanne Hamilton

A catalogue record for this book is available from the British Library.

A catalog record for this book is available from the Library of Congress.

ISBN: HB: 978-1-3500-8041-6
ePDF: 978-1-3500-8042-3
eBook: 978-1-3500-8043-0

Series: Schizoanalytic Applications

Typeset by Newgen KnowledgeWorks Pvt. Ltd., Chennai, India
Printed and bound in Great Britain

To find out more about our authors and books visit www.bloomsbury.com
and sign up for our newsletters.

For Lynette and Velita

CONTENTS

Contents

ILLUSTRATIONS

INTRODUCTION: ALLIANCES AND ALLIES

Janae Sholtz and Cheri Lynne Carr

This collection explores the myriad ways that Gilles Deleuze and Félix Guattari's schizoanalytic methodology can align with contemporary feminist concerns and practices to generate mutually productive insights for future directions within these fields. The volume creates spaces for positive encounters between Deleuze and feminism that enhance and inform contemporary feminist perspectives and concerns and sharpens the focus of this engagement by specifically considering how Deleuze and Guattari's collaborative project proposed in *Anti-Oedipus*, developed and transformed through their later, subsequent work together can be an ally to various forms of feminist methodology. Thus, its thematic focus on schizoanalysis constitutes an innovative and unique intervention into the already rich discussions which have transpired over the last decades with regard to feminist responses to Deleuzoguattarian philosophy. Thus, this is a project is about alliances—exploring how the methods, concepts, and practices that evolve out of Deleuze and Guattari's vision for philosophy can be allies to feminist projects of critique, revaluation, and reimagining of the philosophical, ethical, aesthetic, and political fields. The overarching questions we explore are: Between schizoanalysis and feminism, what alliances have been formed or can be imagined? What can schizoanalysis do for feminist theory? What would a feminist schizoanalysis look like, or, rather, what can feminism do for schizoanalysis? We hope to create a space to unleash new ideas, new desires, and new imaginings—a feminist delirium.

As a whole, this collection highlights the strength, richness, and diversity of feminist perspectives and prerogatives. Issues of reconceiving desire, theorizing embodiment and materiality, interrogating the status of sexuality and difference, the project of decentering feminist practice to be inclusive of transnational and de-colonial concerns, critiques of binary logic and gender from materialist or LGBTQA perspectives, intersectional and transversal analyses, posthumanist and ecological concerns, and the need for new political visions in light of advanced capitalism, are all points of connection. The creative intervention that this book offers operates with two guiding assumptions: (1) To forge an alternative alliance between feminism and Deleuze and Guattari's work, we have to locate the particular invocations of sexuality and the feminine within the broader conceptual concerns of their work and recognize that any decontextualized emphasis on certain concepts often eclipses the possibility of engaging their project. Thus, we hope to broaden the engagement of Deleuze and Guattari's corpus through rigorous attention to the scope and breadth of schizoanalysis as a methodology that extends throughout their work. Though the focus may seem to be narrowed in this manner, we actually think that the effect will be the opposite: schizoanalysis represents the theoretical and methodological foregrounding of the concepts like becoming-woman, rhizomatics, and deterritorialization central to *A Thousand Plateaus* and returns us to the locus of their transformative theory of desire which is at the center of their understanding of both individual subjectivity and social collectivities, ethics and politics. We hope to avoid some of the pitfalls of excising particular problematic concepts from their milieus and, by doing so, look at some of these issues with fresh eyes. (2) Such a focus also provides an opportunity to return to the necessity of critiquing our contemporary social and economic frameworks from both the local and global perspective and to address the motivations and origins of fascistic tendencies that lead to and solidify oppressions, as these are central problematics that schizoanalysis addresses. The aim, then, is to see how schizoanalysis can help address some of the pressing problems and concerns for feminism today. In order to do this, we have striven for diversity of perspectives, thematically and geographically.

1. Why Now?

In the past, Deleuze and feminism have enjoyed what might be considered a rocky relationship. It is safe to say that the centrality of the issues of sexuality and desire to the process of desubjectification, the implication that their reconceptualization of desire as impersonal and machinic demands the dispersal of sexuality into a generalized becoming, as well as Deleuze and Guattari's explicit use of language that invokes feminine constructs, such as becoming-woman and the figure of Alice as a paradigm of paradoxical becoming, have met with skeptical responses from feminists. So, it is not surprising that a number of the initial responses and critiques by feminists to Deleuze and Guattari's work evince a certain adversarial or protective tenor, implying a reluctance to give over a certain space to the engagement, and perhaps rightly so, as the suspicion that Western European male philosophers have either neglected, appropriated, or made use of concepts concerning women for their own theoretical purposes has considerable merit. Yet, with the publication of *Deleuze and Feminist Theory* (2000), we see a notable desire for more positive engagements with Deleuze's philosophy. These essays provide some of the clearest examples of how to put Deleuzian concepts to work within and alongside feminist theory, as well as providing accounts of the positive stakes involved in thinking Deleuze alongside feminist figures such as Luce Irigaray, Julia Kristeva, and Hélène Cixous. Even while acknowledging the anxiety that Deleuze's philosophy has evoked within feminism,[1] the overall spirit of the book is one of affirmation, to produce an encounter between the two that "might give feminist thought a new way of proceeding" (Colebrook 2000: 15) and to explore potential overlaps between Deleuzian thought and feminist prerogatives. If it is the case that Deleuze's philosophy and feminism share a mutual tendency to understand the general purpose of philosophy as practical and generative rather than merely reactive and oppositional (see Colebrook 2000), then the question that both Deleuze and feminists have in common is what can philosophical concepts *do*? Further, what types of interventions are necessary and what can philosophy (or feminism, or subjectivity) become? Given this prerogative, it is easy to see why feminists have primarily focused on the concept of becoming (woman) in Deleuze and Guattari's work. Indeed, this is one of the recurrent interests of many of the contributions to this original volume, and rightly so. There are contributors in our collection who certainly address this crucial concept (such as Kit Sze Chan in Chapter 10 and Mackenzie in Chapter 15), but we also envision that by insisting on the guiding theme of schizoanalysis, this collection can add a new trajectory to these discussions.

Almost two decades later, it is time to revisit this relationship in light of the important developments within feminism itself. It is clear that feminism has provided crucially important critiques of phenomenology, ontology and epistemology through the insertion of concerns for materiality, embodiment, intersubjectivity, the environment, and sexuality, and that it has been at the forefront of these discussions. This has led to an enormous proliferation of theoretical applications, which have been invoked and developed under the auspices of the relatively new disciplines such as new materialism, posthumanism, affect studies, and de-colonial and global feminisms. Many of these theoretical innovations were just being digested at the beginning of the new millennia, and our contributors are responding to, critiquing, and expanding questions, themes, and problems that have arisen in light of them.

It is also the case that the reception of Deleuze's philosophy has become increasingly more positive, sometimes concerning just those issues that were once sticking points. For instance, in a 2012 interview, Braidotti insists, "Deleuze's work is of high relevance for feminism: not only does he display a great empathy with issues of difference, sexuality and transformation, but he also invests the site of the feminine with positive force" (Dolphijn and van der Tuin 2012: 23). The concerns of many feminist scholars for embedded and embodied accounts of post and nonhuman subjectivity also provide potential sites of alliance with a Deleuzoguattarian philosophy of immanence and materialist vitalism.[2] In fact, the mechanics of transformation implied in Deleuze and Guattari's ontology of becoming aligns with the feminist imperative of exploring the potential for new forms of subjectivity that privilege relationality, becoming, and materiality rather than identification, representation, and linguistic performativity. The implications of a pre-personal and molecular desire also align with posthumanist feminist philosophies that seek to expand our understanding of our relation to the environment and our ultimate imbrication within the web of impersonal and cosmic becomings.[3] Deleuze and Guattari's concept of assemblage has been used to enhance discussions of relationality and to assess different modalities of experience and, in fact, assemblage theory has become another point of alliance for creative and critical feminist enterprises.[4] Moreover, many transnational feminists propose the transgression/crossing of borders, both theoretical and literally, as a central to their practice,[5] and the Deleuzoguattarian language of deterritorialization could be a powerful theoretical tool (ally) in clarifying and conceptualizing how border theories expose and detach from Western European prerogatives and constrictive territorialities) (see Sholtz's Chapter 8). This volume provides a space for many new scholars to encounter Deleuze and Guattari's work through the lenses of these proliferations in feminist philosophy and to revisit these initial positions, in light of the various transformations and developments. Finally, it is important to consider the increased interest in Deleuze and Guattari's work over the last several decades, which has spawned an enormous explosion of commentaries that have increased awareness and understanding of their philosophical project. All of these reasons lead us to the conclusion that the time is right for this intervention, one that we might call a creative repetition, as it traverses the familiar territory of the reception of Deleuze and Guattari, but with a difference.

2. Why Schizoanalysis?

The recent emphasis on the methodology presented in *Anti-Oedipus*, in relation to issues of visual art, cinema, literature, and religion through the *Schizoanalytic Applications* series, as well as the recent publication of the English translation of Guattari's *Schizoanalytic Cartographies* (2013) has led to increased interest in how schizoanalysis can be applied to contemporary issues and its relevance for critically oriented and socially engaged philosophical approaches.[6] Its relevance to feminist theorists can be similarly situated in providing a new lens for critical and social engagement, and the question that this book addresses is what would this new encounter yield?

In *Anti-Oedipus*, Deleuze and Guattari propose schizoanalysis as a new framework for analyzing "how things work" in terms of their machinic, productive, and transversal natures. It is a methodology born from a critical engagement and rethinking of the fields of psychoanalysis, phenomenology, and Marxism, wherein they reconceive the dynamics of desire and its manifestations within the social field in a way that destroys the paradigms of essentiality, identity, and universality in order to open up our thinking to reality as comprised by connectivity, interrelations, dynamic and creative flows and processes that have potentially revolutionary implications. Though Deleuze and Guattari say, "[T]he task of schizoanalysis goes by way of destruction," it is a methodology that is firmly oriented toward the future; their theory of creativity relies on the double negation of reactivity and the productive forces that arise out of that destruction. The threefold task of schizoanalysis set out in *Anti-Oedipus* is, thus, both destructive and productive: (1) Destruction of Oedipal constraints on the unconscious—to destroy the illusion of the ego and the law of castration, which also implies a critique of the molar, binary categories of sexuality (male and female). (2) Discovering in a subject the nature, formation or functioning of his/her desiring-machines, independently of interpretations; as Deleuze and Guattari put it, "[W]hat are they, what do you put into these machines, how does it work, what are your nonhuman sexes" (Deleuze and Guattari 1983: 322). Discovering desire as delirium/schizophrenic implies the pluralization of sexuality and unmoors it from its anthropocentric constraints. (3) Distinguish the unconscious libidinal investment of group or desire of the social field from the preconscious investments of class and interest. The latter has to do with selections of flows and particular codes representing particular interests. The former has to do with the regime of desiring-production and degree of development of forces or energies. This final task provides the possibility of moving from repressive to revolutionary unconscious: "Desiring production as an overthrown power on the bodywithoutorgans" (Deleuze and Guattari 1983: 347). These tasks are left largely obscure in *Anti-Oedipus*, primarily because the elaboration of these tasks cannot be presented as a theoretical constant and their application must always be situated, contextual, and nuanced. Thus, this methodology is diagrammatic, rather than comprehensively descriptive, which is also why it rife with such a range of potentialities.

In *Schizoanalytic Cartographies* (2013), Guattari provides some clarification as to how this analysis can be conducted by providing a schizoanalytic cartography, as a fourfold structure through which to analyze individual and collective subjectivity: (1) finite existential territories (feelings of familiarity and belonging), (2) virtual universes of value (world of senses and feeling), (3) concrete and abstract machinic phylums (realm of knowledge and ideas), and (4) material, energetic, and semiotic fluxes (libidinal, geological, economic, linguistic, and semiotic).[7] Territories, which are the main molar structures that guide our experience, are brought to life through incorporeal universes of value, but this experience is always subject to the fluctuating external factors, first, of the realm of knowledge and ideas which is always involved in processes of production and, second, a machinic phylum of material and semiotic flows—a plane of consistency. This multivalent mode of analysis poses an interesting parallel to the intersectional approach embraced by feminism. In both cases, multiple elements must be considered simultaneously for their differential relations in order to provide a nuanced perspective that takes into consideration significant differences in experience, context, and situatedness. Analyzing the relations between these elements is central to the methodology of schizoanalysis as a descriptive tool but also illuminates the revolutionary potential within any given assemblage/system, whereby the confrontation with the larger flows of this machinic phylum and the movements of knowledge/ideas can open up existential territories to new potentials and transformations. This is the process of deterritorialization that Deleuze and Guattari identify as a revolutionary force. Schizoanalysis involves bringing to light each of these components in any given situation, to understand the interactions between these heterogeneous domains. We are interested in how the multilevel analysis indicated by schizoanalysis intersects with contemporary feminist concerns and how the application of schizoanalysis can produce new and innovative encounters and ideas.

Schizoanalysis extends from Deleuze and Guattari's revolutionary theory of desire; this theory of desire stands at the base of their realizations concerning subjectivity, social collectivity, and sexuality. They posit a model of desire as desiring-production, through which they conclude that production as process overtakes all idealistic categories and constitutes a cycle whose relationship to desire is that of an immanent principle (Deleuze and Guattari 1983: 5). They describe this immanent principle as a materialist field of partial objects, molecular and positively dispersed, as the foundation of the unconscious. This energy of desire, now conceived as desiring-production, causes flows and breaks flows, in a cycle of production and product. Production is an immanent principle without intent, goal or signification; it is non-representative and it is pre-personal. Therefore, desiring-production is not confined to individual. Rather, its connections organize the social field and the constitution of subjects. Schizoanalysis, most basically, is a project of revealing this level of desire-production and anticipating the potential revolutionary effects of liberating this desire. Unfortunately, this aim is constantly disrupted by the nature of desiring-production and its inherent tendency toward its own repression.

Therefore, one of the goals of schizoanalysis must be to reveal this tendency toward repression and root it out, the recognition of which is extremely useful in analyzing the particularities of oppression and their persistence in order to come up with practical solutions that take into consideration the affective and unconscious depth at which these phenomenon instantiate themselves: "[T]o analyze the specific nature of the libidinal investments in the economic and political spheres, and thereby to show how, in the subject who desires, desire can be made to desire its own repression" (Deleuze and Guattari 1983: 115). Yet, Deleuze and Guattari also seek to distinguish the legitimate versus the illegitimate uses of the synthesis of production in order to reveal that, though there is both a reactive/repressive potential within desiring production, there is also a revolutionary potential. Moving closer to identifying the kinds of repression that desire undergoes through conscious and unconscious desires (collectively and socially as well as individually) is the method of transforming said desire toward its revolutionary potential. It is a methodology of "denouncing the illegitimate use of the synthesis of the unconscious as found in Oedipal psychoanalysis, so as to rediscover a transcendental unconscious defined by the immanence of its criteria, and a corresponding practice that we shall call schizoanalysis" (1983: 75). This is why Deleuze and Guattari insist that schizoanalysis must proceed by way of destruction, whereby they mean, particularly, the destruction of the Oedipal structure that has constricted and routed the full range of desire available to individuals and the social collective. The Oedipal structure is the primary pseudo-form of the unconscious that has installed itself in our collective social understanding, and Deleuze and Guattari's main objective is to show how this transcendental illusion actually represents a particular repressive investment of desire that has become entirely bound up with the economic prerogatives of capitalism, prerogatives which themselves must be understood as desire's unconscious investments of the social field. Oedipal structures of desire reduce the expression of sexuality and generate specific symbols and structures that restrict bodies and connections. This is the infamous "theft of the body" that is related to the figure of the girl and, ultimately, relates the prioritization of becoming-woman that has been the subject of much debate in feminist circles.

There are two important implications here that have been acknowledged to various degrees in feminist theory: (1) First, in showing how the Oedipal structure represents a particular construction rather than an origin of unconscious desire, Deleuze and Guattari also reveal that Oedipal structures can become decoded and that those molar categories which accrue to them are themselves constructs that must be interrogated. Where the nuclear Oedipal family and its insistence on heterosexuality, patriarchy, and the normativity of binary sexual categories is articulated and re-instantiated as natural and inevitable is exactly where we must recognize "the degree of disfiguration it implies and brings to bear on desiring-production" (1983: 175). Thus, these normative ideals are no longer seen as foundational. (2) Second, if it is the case that this molar, binary sexual difference reduces the expression of desire and sexuality, the liberation of desire could produce new forms of gender and sexuality by and through investments of desire that are directly plugged into social organization and disorganization (163), a thousand tiny sexes that are materially embedded in relational assemblages.

Their account of desire as positive, proliferative, and pre-personal is one of the most novel contributions of schizoanalysis, one which could be productively mobilized in the re-evaluations of desire, gender, and sexuality.[8] Yet, the deconstruction of the categories of sexuality in favor of an infinite proliferation of desire at the molecular level with a concomitant multiplication of sexualities has led to deep anxieties among feminists concerning both the possible incommensurability between Deleuzian multiplicity of sexual desire and sexual difference and the dissolution of subjectivity that accompanies this vision of desire/s. Certainly, there are several feminists who have sought to work through or with Deleuze and Guattari's concept of desire to conceptualize sexual difference as fluid and morphological (Olkowski 2000), by suspending the ontological question in favor of epistemological or practical ones (Colebrook 2003), or re-envisioned sexual difference as a force of differing, which could accommodate the proliferation of sexualities, at a materialist, embodied level (Braidotti 2002, 2003). We hope to extend these considerations and provide a selection of novel approaches that speak to the constant evolution of thought, theory, and experience within both fields of this alliance.[9]

This focus on re-conceiving desire and sexuality is all the more relevant given the contemporary controversies and debates related to the struggles for recognition and voice of transsexual, intersexed, and transgender people. The growing awareness of these issues reflect the changing terrain and status of these terms in our own social fields and the need for new language and concepts. These emerging discussions could benefit from schizoanalysis approach that reveals how normative associations can be restrictive and damaging with respect to these issues. Interrogating this new terrain is the subject of Hannah Stark and Tim Laurie's contribution (Chapter 7) on the potential for transfeminism in Deleuze and Guattari. From the schizoanalytic perspective, we must persistently assess how all manifestations of sexuality reflect certain investments of desire, as Nir Kedem does in his chapter on queer theory (Chapter 6).

Schizoanalysis is oriented toward liberation, thus its utopian aspirations. It is never merely a matter of descriptive analysis but a way of identifying the restrictive mechanisms that capture and direct these flows and occlude recognition of the range of potentials that exist in order to create new conditions, both politically and aesthetically, and socially/economically, as is the case with Heidi Samuelson's piece (Chapter 9). On a political level, this practice concerns the passage from "subjected groups," which are alienated and controlled by social forces and transcendent ideals, to "subject groups," which can access and explore desires and flows within the social field to create new assemblages and to enact social transformations. Schizoanalysis, as a methodology, loosens the grips of social and ideational territorializations which produce an aura of totalization; it is with this in mind that we consider the truly transformative nature of becoming—that this transformation challenges both sides of the alliance to become and to free intensities that have become entrenched or routinized. A particular challenge to feminism from the schizoanalytic perspective might be what are the libidinal investments guiding the refusal to relinquish certain prerogatives, such as the duality of sexuality? Can we imagine a world of impersonal individuations and pre-individual singularities that does justice to feminist concerns? Tamsin Lorraine (Chapter 4) and Audronė Žukauskaitė (Chapter 2) respectively address these questions through the issues of the dissolution of binary sexed subjectivity and becoming-imperceptible. Janae Sholtz (Chapter 8) will address issue of feminism's own libidinal investments from a different tack, framing the discussion in terms of Western epistemic imperialism and postcolonial critiques, and asking the reader to consider performing a schizoanalysis of feminism itself in order to imagine how schizoanalysis could lend itself to a new political vision for feminism. Samuelson (Chapter 9) also emphasizes the importance of a transnational feminist outlook from an economic purview. Amy Chan Kit-Sze (Chapter 10) continues to deterritorialize feminism's geographical and epistemic boundaries by incorporating prerogatives and figures from Chinese culture into considerations of a posthuman feminist future. As the conjunction of theory and practice has always been a hallmark of feminist reflection, the desire to envision a new politics that extends from these philosophical reflections is yet another point of alliance that our contributors draw upon. For instance, Erinn Cunniff Gilson (Chapter 3) adroitly navigates the criticisms of Deleuzian desubjectivization to suggest a new political direction, while Katja Čičigoj (Chapter 5) argues for a particularly political and materialist understanding of sexual difference itself and Claire Colebrook (Chapter 1) gives voice to pressing political realities of white privilege and sexism in some of their most recent manifestations.

Many of these themes are most intensely expressed through the medium of aesthetics. Deleuze considers artworks transformative encounters *par excellence;* it is significant that many feminists have been drawn to Deleuze and Guattari through their contributions to aesthetics or the various literary characters and references to which they refer. Celiese Lypka (Chapter 12) embraces the Deleuzoguattarian idea of literature as a desiring-machine, combines Sara Ahmed's work on affect with Deleuze and Guattari's challenges to psychoanalysis to bring about a reorientation of feminine anxiety toward the generation of productive encounters and affects, and positive alliances. Fernanda Negrete (Chapter 13) presents an enticing new perspective on the figure of Alice by incorporating the strikingly fluid and powerful work of Horn's multimedia *Wonderwater.* Both Austin Sarfan (Chapter 14) and Chrysanthi Nigianni (Chapter 11) focus on aspects of literature and writing, the former conducting a precise analysis of Chris Kraus in order to bring elucidation to the idea of becoming-imperceptible and the latter taking a more theoretical/political approach to interrogate how the praxis of writing as a form of becoming-minoritarian becomes a form of radical critique and open up spaces of resistance. Hollie Mackenzie brings a particularly artist-oriented perspective, calling for transformational art practices that are inspired by an Irigarayan-inspired labial metaphoricity.

3. Why Alliance?

Deleuze and Guattari understand alliance as supporting the process of becoming, a term which itself indicates heterogeneous encounters and operates by elevating ideas of difference and mutual transformation rather than the tendencies toward assimilation and identity associated with filiation: "Becoming produces nothing by filiation; all filiation is imaginary. Becoming is always a different order than filiation. It concerns alliance. If evolution includes any veritable becomings, it is in the domain of symbioses that bring into play beings of totally different scales and kingdoms" (Deleuze and Guattari 1987: 238). This conjunction of alliance, difference, and becoming aligns with particular lineages within feminism itself and speaks to the desire for mutual recognition and eschewal of appropriation that has been an ongoing priority for feminists. Valentine Moulard-Leonard speaks to this alignment in her article, "Moving beyond Us and Them? Marginality, Rhizomes, and Immanent Forgiveness," where she connects alliance to the legacy of bell hooks's desire to establish solidarity on the basis of a shared experience of the spaces of resistance—dislocation, marginality, self-recovery[10] and, with respect to Deleuze and Guattari, as a mode of becoming that engages us at the level of our differences rather than identifications, our affects and regions of intensity rather than our affiliations. Thus, alliance indicates a mode of engagement that eschews assimilation or mere identification, and in this respect, it speaks to the concerns that feminists have had concerning the necessity of visibility and recognition. Alliance indicates the willingness and potential for a thoroughgoing creative transformation. For Moulard-Leonard, to establish alliances means forming necessary, if only momentary and unlikely, communities, and depends on the activity of sharing marginal spatiality, temporality and nomadic history, rather than shared lived experience. It is wish to facilitate encounters, unlikely encounters, which necessitate what she calls a peculiar spatiality—integral spatiality or the spatiality of integrity, "whose parts do not fit in with one another, or whose connection is not predetermined; a migratory space whose territories must be mapped and remapped following decentralized lines of communication between margins and center ... [a] mapping of flows and migrations, rather than the internalized image of a certain (imperialist) order of the world" (Moulard-Leonard 2012: 831).

The possibility of an alliance between schizoanalysis and feminism reveals a project: to interrogate the relation between feminism and a practice of schizoanalysis; to ask what are the resistances and impasses that arise; to contemplate how we can mobilize unconscious desire for resistance; to imagine how schizoanalysis and the concept of machinic assemblage can be utilized in defining anti-essentialist feminist projects. But it also invites a reconsideration of Deleuze and Guattari's work, through the interrogation of its blind spots, omissions, and unthought lines of flight. This volume is an invitation to open up our collective imaginations and to think about the future of feminism and the future of philosophic engagements in ways that liberate rather than foreclose the fields of desire and forces within which we find ourselves.

4. Our Feminist-Schizoanalytic Alliances

The volume is organized into four major sections, I. Realigning Methodology, II. Rethinking Sexuality and Subjectivity, III. Deterritorializing Feminist Praxes, and IV. Redrawing Aesthetic Alliances. Each section presents a different mode of alliance between Deleuze and Guattari and feminism, and, as the titles suggest, emphasizes the potential of transformation made possible through alliance/becomings that operate according to the paradigm of encounter outlined above.

In the first section, Realigning Methodology, our authors lay out much of the conceptual terrain of our volume, doing so with a particularly feminist attention to practical considerations and real experiences and concerns of women. In each instance, there is an acknowledgment of the way that looking at feminist concerns through schizoanalysis opens up new avenues for methodological intervention—in areas of political resistance to sexism and racism, of reconceiving subjectivity, and of strategies for addressing the evolution of feminism itself. The first chapter, "White Analogy: Transcendental Becoming-Woman and the Fragilities of Race and Gender," is written by Claire Colebrook. Given the key role that Colebrook has played in developing the scholarship in this area, we believe that her contribution is a fitting beginning to our volume, one that seeks to contemporize this relationship and connect theory to the practical and social conditions of our time—an aptly feminist-Deleuzian endeavor. She proposes not only rethinking feminism in light of schizoanalysis, but also rethinking schizoanalysis in light of some of the most current debates in feminism, including the #metoo movement, white privilege, and the problematic of analogizing transgender issues and race (the "Tuvel affair"). Colebrook's contribution re-aligns methodology in ways that circumvent some of the stalemates in contemporary feminist theory and shows how the integration of feminist prerogatives can yield a new conception of schizoanalysis. As such, it is an excellent launching point for our theme of alliance.

In Chapter 2, "Deleuzian Notion of Becoming-Imperceptible and New Postfeminist Strategies," Audronė Žukauskaitė provides a solid reading of Deleuze and Guattari's redefinition of such concepts as schizophrenia and desire in *Anti-Oedipus* and desiring production as becoming in *A Thousand Plateaus*. She shows how schizoanalysis productively intervenes on recent debates in feminist theory and lays out some of the historical transformations in the uptake of Deleuze and Guattari's work within feminist circles. Aligning with Colebrook, Žukauskaitė also points to the recent #MeToo movement, illustrating how a Deleuzian understanding of multiple levels of desire can help feminists formulate more potent mechanisms of resistance/revolutionary behavior and (even internal) critique. Engaging the work of prominent feminist foremothers such as Braidotti and Grosz, Žukauskaitė articulates the framework for a vision of feminist schizoanalysis that understands becoming-imperceptible as a viable, non-exclusionary feminist strategy. Finally, Žukauskaitė explores the potential of imperceptibility for feminism by analyzing the works of the artist and forensic pathologist, Teresa Margolles, and Lithuanian artist, Kristina Inčiūraitė, "[W]ho while being associated with feminist art, detach themselves from defined forms of identity and follow the transformations of corporeal elements, such as substances, particles, and haecceities."

In Chapter 3, "Undoing the Subject: Feminist and Schizoanalytic Contributions to Political Desubjectification," Erinn Gilson explicitly invokes the feminist critique of Deleuze's desubjectification, which is particularly important given that one of the intentions of this volume is to address these presumed impasses. Gilson posits an alliance between feminist positions on subjectivity and Deleuzoguattarian desubjectification based on the idea of this alliance as a form of becoming in which both are pushed beyond their limits, yielding a discussion of a radicalized relational self that enables a reevaluation of molar identity and identity politics. Gilson shows how the discussion of dissolution of the self can be brought into alignment with the real political and social concerns of those identifying as a "woman," "Black," "trans," "white," "queer," and so on, explaining how past feminists concerns that Deleuze's desubjectification is really a privilege of the masculine subject can be overcome in the process. Gilson's piece provides a new framework for thinking political critique and methodology, but in doing so, she provides a nuanced account of the sometimes fraught relationship between feminism's contextual and practical politics (the need for political representation/identification) and Deleuzoguattarian imperatives for dissolution.

This focus on desubjectification as a key political methodology serves as a bridge to the next section of the volume, Rethinking Sexuality and Subjectivity. One of the key areas of alliance between schizoanalysis and feminism comes from their mutual recognition of the need to redefine desire, sexuality, and subjectivity. Schizoanalysis presents a materialist theory of desire that both disrupts entrenched normative paradigms and returns attention to the material relations between bodies. These prerogatives have not been lost of feminists, many of whom have found this renewal of materialist concerns quite fecund for feminist theorizing. Yet, the issue of the dissolution of the subject has also been one of the stumbling blocks for feminists to truly embrace Deleuze's position. Moreover, the issues of the multiplication of desires and sexuality—a thousand tiny sexes—have led to many questions about the fault lines between feminism, gender and queer studies, and transfeminism. The next four chapters tackle these issues, asking what forms of subjectivity and sexuality are possible and desirable within this Deleuzoguattarian/feminist alliance.

In the first piece of this section, Chapter 4, "Schizoanalyzing Anoedipal Alliance," Tamsin Lorraine reads Deleuze's schizoanalysis as opening a fault line for new transversal connections that speaks to the demands of our times. Her diagnosis of contemporary problems being related to a destructive desire for completeness (i.e., Lacanian subject) opens the door for us to consider how schizoanalysis calls attention to sex and gender as a fault line that can rather be opened to heterogeneous connections. Thus, rather than view Deleuze and Guattari's dissolution of binary sexed subjectivity as a threat, Lorraine conceives it positively as a way to eradicate some of those destructive tendencies related to the integration of everything under capitalist homogeneity, allying Deleuze and Guattari to feminist critiques of global capitalism and its multiple forms of (sexed) violence. Engaging the Warren meme, "nevertheless she persisted," Lorraine connects the idea of persisting to the constant unfolding of a never-ending series of moments that constitute an anoedipal subjectivity, one that is neither active nor passive, where personal identity falls away in lieu of a multitude of embodied individuals. Lorraine argues against the idea of Deleuze exploding or destroying the subject, to give a nuanced account of a subject in transformation, that stabilizes in different ways around different configurations but whose very persistence is predicated on the ability to transform and morph and is able to facilitate a fictioning of self.

In Chapter 5, "The Alliance between Materialist Feminism and Schizoanalysis: Toward a Materialist Theory of Sexed Subjectivity," Katja Čičigoj extends considerations of methodology by problematizing the tendency to ontologize schizoanalysis rather than focusing on its political applications, while applying these methodological considerations to the key feminist issues of sexual difference and subjectivity. We think that this chapter will provide an interesting counter-perspective, as Čičigoj offers a critical reading of the appropriation of Deleuze and Guattari's work in feminist new materialisms and the postfeminist theory of queer multitudes of Paul Preciado. Čičigoj argues that both rely upon some common politically dangerous misreadings of Deleuze and Guattari. By invoking the lineage of French materialist feminisms—Christine Delphy, Monique Wittig, and Simone de Beauvoir—Čičigoj proposes to read Deleuze and Guattari's schizoanalysis against the metaphysical reification of an affirmation of sexual difference or multiple differences. The proposed rereading of Deleuze and Guattari underscores the fact that a political grappling with Oedipalization and patriarchy does not reside in valuing difference over identity; rather the beginning of a political analysis starts with asking: how do we conceptualize a particular political difference? She argues that, upon such a politicized analysis of sexual difference, the only viable political aim for feminism is the orientation toward an androgynous "becoming-imperceptible" of sexual difference, which Deleuze and Guattari's work, read through materialist feminism, might help us conceptualize.

In Chapter 6, "To Have Done with Sexuality: Schizoanalysis and the Problem of Queer–Feminist Alliances," Nir Kedem asks, "What would constitute a queer–feminist alliance from a schizoanalytic viewpoint," proposing that the answer lies in a common taste for becoming-revolutionary, which takes the form of a charge against the very notion of sexuality and relies on the particular the dual function of destruction and creation indicative of a Deleuzoguattarian critique which corresponding to schizoanalysis. Under the schizoanalytic lens, sexuality becomes an obstacle for a queer–feminist alliance for it marks the limit of queer theory's image of thought or, more extensively, its illegitimate uses of the three syntheses of desire. Kedem argues that if schizoanalysis works to rediscover and perpetuate the revolutionary nature of desiring-production that informs both individual and collective ways of thinking and living, then schizoanalysis will result in a radical desexualization of queer theory, yet in a very specific sense—it does not operate as a reactionary call for asexual ascesis, nor as a denial of sexual pleasures, practices, politics, and lifestyles, but rather as an insistent refusal of sexuality inasmuch as it is conceived as a privileged analytical category and an exclusive foundation of political praxes of resistance. Kedem provides critical analysis of particular American milieu that originated queer theory, including the work of Butler, while emphasizing the fundamental desexualized component of David M. Halperin's concept of queer and its prime example: the activist movement ACT UP—The AIDS Coalition To Unleash Power, offering this queer movement's schizophrenic coalitional logic as a model for inclusive disjunction and queer–feminist alliance.

Continuing the project of reconceptualizing and widening our understanding of the potentials of sexuality, Hannah Stark and Tim Laurie, in Chapter 7, "Deleuze and Transfeminism," look at the latent potential for transfeminism in Deleuze and Guattari's work. They bring this into dialogue with contemporary debates as they manifest in the work of Jack Halberstam, Paul Preciado, and Maggie Nelson. Arguing that "intersecting transitions have always posed an important problem for feminist philosophy," they seek to find resources within feminism to make alliance with trans communities and trans activists, utilizing Deleuze and Guattari's model of becoming to facilitate a new understanding of the commonality of transition as a consistent and overarching quality of subjective existence. Stark and Laurie present a positive, productive view of Preciado's work, along with that of Nelson, in order to dramatize the political potential of Deleuze and Guattari's work and in order to articulate the positive, transformational power of *trans, opening up ambivalent, creative spaces for non-cisgendered identities and new forms of alliance and interaction.

Deterritorializing Feminist Praxes is the third section of our volume. These chapters emphasize different kinds of (feminist) praxis and how a feminist/ schizoanalytic lens either disrupts or transforms them or provides a new basis for action—thus referring to feminist praxes that are deterritorializing forces. Second, one will find that there is an emphasis on transnational and global feminism, thus this section deterritorializes feminism away from a primarily Western European focus. In Chapter 8, "Schizoanalysis and the Deterritorializations of Transnational Feminism," Janae Sholtz conceives deterritorialization both in terms of geographical location and epistemological focus, advocating that Western feminism must perform its own schizoanalysis, to open itself to its seething borders and its refusals, and that this is necessary in order to understand the nuance of larger global women's issues as well as be a corrective to the colonizing effects of Western feminism. Thus, the intent of this chapter is to widen the scope of feminist concerns through an alignment with Deleuzoguattarian methodology. Sholtz argues that a schizoanalytic approach that emphasizes the micrological level of desiring production is better suited to nuanced understanding of complex social, economic, and political issues as they intersect with feminism and examines how schizoanalysis opens up new ways of conceiving community and identity by emphasizing shifting localities and alliance through minorization. Thus, this chapter uses schizoanalysis to interrogate the molar within feminism discourse itself in order to form alliances with non-Western and transnational feminisms. Sholtz highlights particular practices of non-Western women, such as Islamic veiling and Filipina diasporic migration, in order to emphasize the necessity of critiquing the imperializing forces of globalization and capitalism. Sholtz argues that this engagement is crucial given the current state of our social and political fields, the intensification of control mechanisms, the mobilizations of unconscious desire and affective labor that Deleuze and Guattari could only anticipate but that contemporary feminism is in the process of critically negotiating.[11]

In Chapter 9, "Microrevolutions in Feminist Economics: A Schizoanalytic Response to "Third Way" Identity Production," Heidi Samuelson focuses on economic praxes and feminist concerns about types of traditionally viewed women's work, and, particularly, on Deleuze and Guattari's analysis of the economic conditions of late Capitalism vis-à-vis an appropriation of Marxist materialist critique. Samuelson is also interested in deterritorializing feminism by expanding considerations to global economics and the conditions of women beyond its primarily Western focus. She (re)introduces the traditional feminist issue of unpaid reproductive labor to illuminate how Deleuze and Guattari diverge from Marx and to suggest how their schizoanalysis can better address contemporary exacerbations of gendered economic inequality on a global scale. Samuelson wonders if Deleuzian multiplication of perspectives through microrevolutions gives us a better means to preserve the resistance to molar organization than the Marxist model for revolution. Thus, Samuelson's piece continues our theme of alliances and allies, as she offers an example of how schizoanalysis amplifies and allies with feminist economic praxes and critiques.

In Chapter 10, "Bodhisattva Avalokiteśvara as a Symbol for the Posthuman Future in the Anthropocene," Amy Chan Kit-Sze evokes several senses of deterritorializing praxes, in that she is interested in how feminist praxes can address the Anthropocene, how Chinese symbology advances certain feminist theoretical and practical concerns in light of the Anthropocene, and, ultimately, how feminist praxis must move away (deterritorialize itself) from anthropocentric prerogatives and become-with other species. Chan discusses how Deleuze and Guattari's theory of schizophrenia, especially in the aspect of family and Oedipalization, sheds light on the development of feminism in the Anthropocene. The thrust of her chapter is to bring an important figure in Chinese culture, that is, Bodhisattva Avalokiteśvara into the scene, in order to highlight the possibility of being-with a multitude of others—animals, insects, trees, plants, and nature. She suggests Bodhisattva Avalokiteśvara as an alternative symbol to Haraway's cyborg in order to continue the particularly feminist praxis of envisioning new conceptual personae for a posthuman future.

In Chapter 11, "Writing Difference: Toward a Becoming Minoritarian," Chrysanthi Nigianni explores the potential variances of deterritorialization through writing, drawing out implications of a minoritarian praxis and style of writing for feminism. Nigianni suggests that becoming-minoritarian is a political gesture as well as a grammatical gesture that invites us to turn the fixity of the noun into the intensity of the verb, to resist the various ways that -isms (Marxism, Calvinism, communism) tend toward closure and consequent fixity. Her critical position is that Feminist scholarship has not escaped such closure and has come to constitute such a doctrine characterized by master methodologies (e.g., intersectionality, poststructuralism) and master concepts, and that feminist writing as a practice seems to conform to the prerogatives of the neo-liberal university, a standardized and increasingly regulated academic writing. Thus, she argues for a kind of methodological deterritorialization of feminism through writing praxes oriented by becoming-minoritarian.

Our fourth, and final, section, Redrawing Aesthetic Alliances, is dedicated to creative, aesthetic alliances. It is well known that Deleuze understands art as a kind of encounter that has transformative potential. Read through a schizoanalytic framework, we can say that art practices provide a means to liberate desires and create new machinic connections and flows of desire. The four contributions included herein illustrate how this potential can be directed to particular social relations and feminist concerns; the first three chapters offer some examples of creative, minoritarian writing practices—intervention to which Nigianni alludes in the prior section, while the fourth and final chapter develops a specifically feminist schizo-revolutionary theory of artist practice. In the first chapter of the section, "Affective Alliances: A Feminist Schizoanalysis of Feminine Anxiety, Dis/orientation, and Affect Aliens" (Chapter 12), Celiese Lypka reorients our understanding of the role of literature, looking at the way that literature is a desiring-machine that creates affective relations and contagions. What is unique to Lypka's analysis is her invocation of affect theory, primarily through the work of Ahmed, from whom she takes the idea of affective alienation as a form of positive intervention or generative force. Schizoanalytic understanding of literary machine forms an alliance with feminist affect, leading Lypka to consider how to harness the power of feminine marginality to disrupt the social order, in turn returning us to a thoroughly schizoanalytic aim to release a revolutionary [now feminine] desire. Hers is an attempt to *reorient* the anxiety attached to the female body toward a mobilizing affect. Importantly, Lypka provides nuance to the idea of alliance, suggesting that hers is not a matter of Deleuzian feminism—as some sort of master-discourse to build a better feminism. Rather, she attempts to read the echoes and alliance that might be built between schizoanalysis and Ahmed's work on feminism and affect theory, noting the similarity between Deleuze and Guattari's schizoanalysis as a process of interrogating norms and creating new becomings as a process of world making and Ahmed's view of feminist theory as world-making.

Fernanda Negrete's piece, "Alice in Wonderwater: Hysteria, Femininity, and Alliance in Clinical Aesthetics" (Chapter 13), connects Deleuze's aesthetics to schizoanalysis through the concept of the aesthetic clinic, then connecting this concept to an underlying feminine desire. To illuminate this feminine desire, Negrete explores the literature of female writers, aligning this analysis with feminist theorists who also consider the implications of female writing (Claire Colebrook, Cixous). Negrete's essay is valuable in moving beyond theorizing about art, either through feminism or schizoanalysis, to addressing how contemporary feminist art (Horn's multimedia *Wonderwater*) can be an example. Her reading of Horn's *Wonderwater* is inspired, truly illustrating the creative proliferation of affect and ideas that is possible when alliances, or creative becomings, are formed. Chapter 14, "Asceticism and Impersonality in Spiritual Aversion from Schizoanalysis to Chris Kraus," continues the alliance of schizoanalysis and feminist literary artists, with the intent to connect to yet go beyond Deleuze (reminiscent of Gilson's desire in Chapter 3 for a creative alliance/becoming that pushes both sides beyond their limits). Austin Sarfan analyzes Chris Kraus's literary form as related to the impersonal, vis-à-vis her own invocation of Deleuze. The claim is that schizoanalysis moves toward impersonality, and this impersonality of life manifests itself through processes of estrangement to which Deleuze's reading of Anglo-American literature is especially indebted, which is complicated by considering the female-gendered subject. This is interesting because it takes a different entry point into schizoanalysis beyond the well-trodden "becoming-woman" issue for feminism. The concept of impersonality is reminiscent of Žukauskaitė's piece advocating a feminist interpretation of becoming-imperceptible, thus adding resonance to our volume.

In Chapter 15, "A Schizo-Revolutionary Labial Theory of Artistic Practice," Hollie Mackenzie aptly points toward futural artistic practices. Mackenzie's forceful essay allies Deleuzoguattarian aesthetics to Irigaray's concept of the undifferentiated, expressed through the material form of the labial lips, to form a specifically feminist schizo-revolutionary theory of artist practice. Mackenzie's piece is appropriately aspirational, sweeping us up in the possibility of connecting with the infinite possibilities of the cosmos through the emancipation of female imagination, pleasure, and expression. Mackenzie wants to explore how this schizo-revolutionary artistic process can be sustained as a form of feminist resistance that can engender *becomings woman*. Her essay is an excellent example of the way that Deleuze claims art can open us to other possible worlds, and we like the idea of ending our volume with a piece that inspires new ways of thinking about our relationality to the cosmos and new ways of expressing embodiment—a truly Deleuzo-feminist prerogative.

It is with gratitude, humility, and eagerness that we present this volume. It has been a work of love and labor, which has taught us to be more sensitive to the intellectual bonds and debts that make new paths for thinking possible. Through this collection, we do not purport to have assembled all the perspectives or wonderful work that has been done on these subjects. What we hope to have done is allow voices of the past, the present, and the often unheard to shine forth in a new light. Many thanks for the time and dedication of our contributors, whose willingness to push the boundaries of thought, present new ideas, and address difficult questions—of ourselves and our disciplines—has truly inspired us.

Notes

1. Such as the fear of propagating a masculine point of view at the expense of the erasure of the feminine voice or whether feminism should embrace or reject a conceptual apparatus that relied so heavily on the deconstruction of molar sexuality. See early criticisms by Irigaray ([1977] 1985), Jardine (1985), Butler (1987), Spivak (1988), and Braidotti (1994).

2. Although we do not purport to place these thinkers in any 'one camp,' they are loosely connected by their concerns for re-envisioning the interactions and relations between beings along an immanent axis and have been variously inspired by Deleuze and Guattari's work. The Deleuzian ontological model, with its emphasis on relations and assemblages of bodies, forces, and partial objects, has been incorporated into the feminist new materialist premises of univocal or egalitarian material existence and seen as foregrounding the conceptualization

of vital matter. See, for instance, Braidotti (2002), Barad (2007), Bennett (2010), Dolphijn and van der Tuin (2012).

3. See Grosz (2005), Braidotti (2013), Tsing (2015), Thiele (2016), Sheldon (2016).

4. For feminist usage of assemblage theory, see Currier (2003), Puar (2011), Ringrose and Coleman (2013), Ringrose and Renold (2014), Bogic (2017), Hickey-Moody (2019).

5. See Mohanty (2003), Anzaldúa (1987).

6. Jessica Ringrose's research is particularly relevant, as she (often with collaborators) uses Deleuzian models to contextualize the sociological experience of childhood and girlhood within contemporary problematics of sexual harassment, bullying, rape culture, and educational environments (see Ringrose 2013; Ringrose and Coleman 2013). Likewise, Anna Hickey-Moody's applications of Deleuze to issues of pedagogy and youth, as well as the importance of socially engaged art-based research should be noted (see, for instance, 2013, 2017, 2019).

7. See Holmes's 'Guattari's Schizoanalytic Cartographies or, the Pathic Core at the Heart of Cybernetics' for summary and chart of this Guattarian cartography. https://brianholmes. wordpress.com/2009/02/27/guattaris-schizoanalytic-cartographies/#sdfootnote39anc (accessed April 17, 2019).

8. Beckman (2013) extends these questions by both critically assessing the residual masculinity in Deleuze's conception of pleasure and exploring the latent potential of revolutionary desire to break these masculinist constraints.

9. We, of course, would like to acknowledge the lineage of feminists who have creatively engaged with Deleuzoguattarian theories of desire, sexuality, and becoming, opening the way for an opportunity to reconceive sexual difference and move to more nuanced accounts of materiality, temporality, and embodiment. On the subject of becoming (woman), for instance, see Gatens (1996, 2000), Conley (2000), Grosz (2005), Pisters (2003), Braidotti (2003), Colebrook (2003), Burchill (2010).

10. "The self not as a signifier of one 'I' but the coming together of many 'I's, the self as embodying collective reality past and present, family and community" (hooks 1989: 31).

11. The urgency of these interventions cannot be overstated given the concrete political situation in the United States wherein fascist tendencies have gained center stage and on the global stage, where capitalist expansion has violently deterritorialized entire populations.

References

Anzaldúa, G. (1987), *Borderlands/La Frontera: The New Mestiza*, San Francisco, CA: Aunt Lute Books.

Barad, K. (2007), *Meeting the Universe Halfway: Quantum Physics and the Entanglement of Matter and Meaning*, Durham, NC: Duke University Press.

Beckman, F. (ed.) (2011), *Deleuze and Sex (Deleuze Connections)*, Edinburgh: Edinburgh University Press.

Beckman, F. (2013), *Between Desire and Pleasure: A Deleuzian Theory of Sexuality*, Edinburgh: Edinburgh University Press.

Bennett, J. (2010), *Vibrant Matter: A Political Ecology of Things*, Durham, NC: Duke University Press.

Bogic, A. (2017), "Theory in Perpetual Motion and Translation: Assemblage and Intersectionality in Feminist Studies," *Atlantis* 38 (1): 138–49.

Braidotti, R. (1994), *Nomadic Subjects: Embodiment and Sexual Difference in Contemporary Feminist Theory*, 111–23, New York: Columbia University Press.
Braidotti, R. (2002), *Metamorphoses: Towards a Materialist Theory of Becoming*. Oxford: Blackwell.
Braidotti, R. (2003), "Becoming Woman: Or Sexual Difference Revisited," *Theory, Culture, & Society* 20 (3): 43–64.
Braidotti, R. (2013), *The Posthuman*, Cambridge: Polity Press.
Buchanan, I., and C. Colebrook (eds.) (2000), *Deleuze and Feminist Theory, Deleuze Connections EUP*, Edinburgh: Edinburgh University Press.
Burchill, L. (2010), "Becoming-Woman: A Metamorphosis in the Present Relegating Repetition of Gendered Time to the Past," *Time & Society* 19 (1): 81–97.
Butler, Judith (1987) *Subjects of Desire*, New York: Columbia Press.
Colebrook, C. (2003), "Introduction," in B. Ali and A. Ivanchikova (eds.), *theory@buffalo 8: Deleuze and Feminism*, 3–9, Buffalo, NY: SUNY Department of Comparative Literature.
Coleman, R. (2008), "The Becoming of Bodies: *Girls*, Media Effects and Body Image," *Feminist Media Studies* 8 (2): 163–79.
Conley, V. (2000), "Becoming Woman Now," in I. Buchanan and C. Colebrook (eds.), *Deleuze and Feminist Theory*, 18–37, Edinburgh: Edinburgh University Press,.
Currier, D. (2003), "Feminist Technological Futures: Deleuze and Body/Technology Assemblages," *Feminist Theory* 3: 321–38.
Deleuze, G., and F. Guattari (1983), *Anti-Oedipus Capitalism and Schizophrenia*, trans. R. Hurley, M. Seem, and H. R. Lane, Minnesota: University of Minnesota Press.
Deleuze, G., and F. Guattari (1987), *A Thousand Plateaus: Capitalism and Schizophrenia*, trans. B. Massumi, Minneapolis, MN: University of Minnesota Press.
Dolphijn, R., and I. van der Tuin (eds.) (2012), *New Materialism: Interviews and Cartographies*, Ann Arbor, MI: Open Humanities Press.
Gatens, M. (1996), *Imaginary Bodies: Ethics, Power, and Corporeality*, London: Routledge.
Gatens, M. (2000), "Feminism as 'Password': Rethinking the 'Possible' with Spinoza and Deleuze," *Hypatia* 15 (2): 59–75.
Gilson, E. C. (2011), "Responsive Becoming: Ethics between Deleuze and Feminism," in Daniel Smith and Nathan Jun (eds.), *Deleuze and Ethics*, 63–88, Edinburgh: Edinburgh Press.
Grosz, E. (2005), *Time Travels: Feminism, Nature, Power*, Australia: Allen & Unwen.
Guattari, F. (2013) [1989], *Schizoanalytic Cartographies*, trans. Andrew Goffey, London: Bloomsbury Press.
Hickey-Moody, A. (2013), *Youth, Arts, and Education: Reassembling Subjectivity through Affect*, London: Routledge.
Hickey-Moody, A. (2017), "Arts Practice as Method, Urban Spaces, and Intra-active Faiths," *International Journal of Inclusive Education* 21: 1083–96.
Hickey-Moody, A. (2019), *Deleuze and Pedagogy of Gender: Masculinity and Methodology*, United Kingdom: Palgrave Macmillan.
hooks, b. (1989), *Talking Back: Thinking Feminist, Thinking Black*, Boston, MA: End Press.
Irigaray, L. ([1977]1985), *This Sex Which Is Not One*, trans. C. Porter and C. Burke, Ithaca, NY: Cornell University Press.
Jardine, A. (1985), *Gynesis: Configurations of Woman and Modernity*. Ithaca, NY: Cornell University Press.
Marrati, P. (November 2006), "Time and Affects: Deleuze on Gender and Sexual Difference," *Australian Feminist Studies* 21 (51): 313–25.
Mohanty, C. (2003), *Feminism without Borders: Decolonizing Theory, Practicing Solidarity*, Durham, NC: Duke University Press.

Moulard-Leonard, V. (Fall 2012), "Moving Beyond Us and Them? Marginality, Rhizomes, and Immanent Forgiveness," *Hypatia* 27 (4): 828–46.

Olkowski, D. (1999), *Gilles Deleuze and the Ruin of Representation*, Ithaca, NY: Cornell University Press.

Olkowski, D. (2000), "Body, Knowledge and Becoming-Woman: Morphologic in Deleuze and Irigaray," in I. Buchanan and C. Colebrook (eds.), *Deleuze and Feminist Theory*, 86–109, Edinburgh: Edinburgh University Press.

Pisters, P. (2003), Chapter 4: "Conceptual Personae and Aesthetic Figures of Becoming-Woman," in *The Matrix of Visual Culture: Working with Deleuze in Film Theory*, 106–40, California: Stanford University Press.

Puar, J. K. (2011), "I Would Rather Be a Cyborg than a Goddess: Intersectionality, Assemblage, and Affective Politics," European Institute for Progressive Cultural Policies, http://eipcp.net/transversal/0811/puar/en (accessed April 18, 2019).

Ringrose, J. (January 2013), "Beyond Discourse? Using Deleuze and Guattari's Schizoanalysis to Explore Affective Assemblages, Hterosexually Striated Space, and Lines of Flight Online and at School," *Educational Philosophy and Theory* 43 (6): 598–618.

Ringrose, Jessica, and Emma Renold (2014), "F**k Rape!": Exploring Affective Intensities in a Feminist Research Assemblage," *Qualitative Inquiry* 20 (6): 772–80.

Ringrose, Jessica, and R. Coleman (2013), "Looking and Desiring Machines: A Feminist Deleuzian Mapping of Bodies and Affects," in Ringrose and Coleman (eds.) *Deleuze and Research Methodologies*, 125–44, Edinburgh: Edinburgh University Press.

Sheldon, R. (2016), "Matter and Meaning," *Rhizomes: Cultural Studies in Emerging Knowledge* 30: np.

Spivak, G. C. (1988), "Can the Subaltern Speak?," in Cary Nelson and Lawrence Grossberg (eds.), *Marxism and the Interpretation of Culture*, 271–313, Chicago: University of Illinois Press.

Thiele, K. (2016), "Of Immanence and Becoming: Deleuze and Guattari's Philosophy and/as Relational Ontology," *Deleuze Studies* 10 (1): 117–34.

Tsing, A. L. (2015), *The Mushroom at the End of the World: On the Possibility of Life in Capitalist Ruins*, Princeton, NJ: Princeton University Press.

PART ONE
REALIGNING METHODOLOGY

Figure 1.1 *"#59", 2018, watercolor, ink, chalk, and salt on paper, Fredrica Introne*
Photo taken by the artist.

CHAPTER 1
WHITE ANALOGY: TRANSCENDENTAL BECOMING-WOMAN AND THE FRAGILITIES OF RACE AND GENDER
Claire Colebrook

In this essay I want to draw together two recent, apparently only vaguely related, cases of sexual politics: the *Hypatia*/Tuvel case (or affair or scandal)[1] and the social media #metoo campaign. Both events were more significant in their aftermath than they were in their original occurrence because both seemed to create a whole series of problems for whatever was left of a shared theoretical political lexicon. Both events, in different ways, expose the oddly robust (while fragile) politics of identity, and—I will argue—require a reassessment of what one might possibly mean by becoming-woman. The #metoo movement seemed to revive the possibility of a general women's movement, at the same time as it brought attention to the privileged voices that were able to speak out against sexual violence. Identity seems to be a necessary strategy for resistance at the same time as any claims for political identity draw attention to both the privileges and impossibilities of identity. Not all women have the power to declare "#metoo"; not all those who have suffered violence are women, and some forms of suffering take the form of having one's identity denied. Being able to declare "#metoo" is at one and the same time to have felt harm because of one's sexual identity—in a gender system that seems to entitle some men to enjoy violence with impunity—and to be able to enjoy an identity. Not only were the first women to voice their claims women of white privilege, the campaign that followed—like the much smaller Tuvel/*Hypatia* social media event—raised the problem of the positions of power required to feel aggrieved. In both cases the dominant voices were those of white women, in a world where women of color and transgendered persons are rarely granted the identity and recognition required to voice a complaint. In both cases those who called out abuse or voiced objections were accused of engaging in a witch hunt (Berlinski 2017; Magness 2017; Singal 2017), as though the revolt against oppression was becoming oppressive in turn, filled with a new self-righteousness that still left those without power and recognition on the losing side of the identity politics game.

Yet, even if there are those who always lose in struggles over identity, the ways in which identity is questioned or refused *are not analogous*. Arguing that women who object to the widespread and systemic nature of sexual predation is a warlock-hunt, or that objecting to a practice of philosophy that continually silences women of color is a witch hunt, forecloses the possibility of identifying an antiblackness and masculine supremacy that is so constitutive of thinking that its removal would seem to be catastrophic. Here, one might understand the forms of "panic" that accuse outrage over white supremacy as unreasonable and too extreme as stemming from just how deeply intertwined philosophical reasonableness is with whiteness and gender normalization. That is, there is a violence already in the ways in which identity, being, and reasonableness have been secured. As Fred Moten argues, "The state is a mechanism for the monopolization of violence, its placement in or under reserve, in and as the strict regulation of generativity. And western thought and culture has been the place where this monopolization is theorized and defended, in the name and by way of sovereignty, self-possession, and self- determination" (2017: 224). What I want to do in this essay is look at blackness and transgender as forces that are an affront to the violence of analogical reason (Bey 2017); so resistant are they to the calm of cool reason that their affirmation can only provoke outrage. In brief, arguing—supposedly philosophically—that one ought to consider the legitimacy of transracial identity because one has already admitted the legitimacy of transgendered identity must assume that identity is something like a detachable, equivalent and comparable predicate, something that attaches to a subject. Here I am as a unique individual who may, (or may not) claim to be *a*, *b*, *c*. In the case of the #metoo movement it seemed, once again, that something like "woman" would create one grand, unifying, solidarity-generating cause that could be defined against patriarchy, as though being able to say "me too" could unite movie stars, journalists, Walmart employees, women of color. In both cases there is an underlying substrate—the self who can make a claim to "a" race or "a" gender—and, then, it seems objections were made regarding the ways in which identity occluded complexity.

Rather than see a tension between identity and complexity, we can turn to Deleuze and Guattari's quite specific conceptualization of individuation to see identity as made possible by intensive complexity. This is not a complexity where one adds more and more predicates to be the unique individual one claims to be, as in some notions of intersectionality, but an identity-complexity where relations among forces transform what each force is. For Deleuze and Guattari encounters among forces pulverize the "I" and this is because the "collective" is not a "we" given through a shared long-circuit of reading and history, but a far more anonymous crowd. The "we" is not a plural "I" or "me" but a "they" insofar as everything that composes us is not ours:

Desiring-production and machines, psychic apparatuses and machines of desire, desiring-machines and the assembling of an analytic machine suited to decode them: the domain of free syntheses where everything is possible; partial connections, included disjunctions, nomadic conjunctions, polyvocal flows and chains, transductive breaks; the relation of desiring-machines as formations of the unconscious with the molar formations that they constitute statistically in organized crowds; and the apparatus of social and psychic repression resulting from these formations—such is the composition of the analytic field. And this subrepresentative field will continue to survive and work, even through Oedipus, even through myth and tragedy, which nevertheless mark the reconciliation of psychoanalysis with representation. The fact remains that a conflict cuts across the whole of psychoanalysis, the conflict between mythic and tragic familial representation and social and desiring-production. (Deleuze and Guattari 1983: 300)

Put more simply, Deleuze argues that the "I" and self are possible because of the way in which humans as a species have taken on a certain type of individuation. There has to be individuation before there can be individuals, and this in turn means that other modes of individuation might *not* lead to the "I" or "humanity":

> For the I and the Self are perhaps no more than indices of the species: of humanity as a species with divisions. The species has undoubtedly reached an implicit state in man. As a result, the form of the I can serve as a universal principle for recognition and representation, whereas the specific explicit forms are recognised only by means of this I, and the determination of species is only the rule of one of the elements of representation. The I is therefore not a species; rather—since it implicitly contains what the species and kinds explicitly develop, in particular the represented becoming of the form—they have a common fate, *Eudoxus* and *Epistemon*. Individuation, by contrast, has nothing to do with even the continued process of determining species. Not only does it differ in kind from all determination of species but, as we shall see, it precedes and renders the latter possible. It involves fields of fluid intensive factors which no more take the form of an I than of a Self. Individuation as such, as it operates beneath all forms, is inseparable from a pure ground that it brings to the surface and trails with it ... Turning over the ground is the most dangerous occupation, but also the most tempting in the stupefied moments of an obtuse will. For this ground, along with the individual, rises to the surface yet assumes neither form nor figure ... The individual distinguishes itself from it, but it does not distinguish itself, continuing rather to cohabit with that which divorces itself from it. It is the indeterminate, but the indeterminate in so far as it continues to embrace determination, as the ground does the shoe. Animals are in a sense forewarned against this ground, protected by their explicit forms. Not so for the I and the Self, undermined by the fields of individuation which work beneath them, defenceless against a rising of the ground which holds up to them a distorted or distorting mirror in which all presently thought forms dissolve. (Deleuze 1994: 152)

There is a long history of seeing women and non-whites as less than human, although in different ways: the feminine is man's enigmatic complementary other, differing in degree, while blackness is the negation of humanity *tout court*, which threatens the very stability of personhood precisely required for gender normativity. Sometimes this alterity is imagined nostalgically, as in Freud's notion of woman as the "dark continent"—when even knowing what women might want is elusive given the feminine capacity to remain neither fully determined nor differentiated from the ground of intensities from which humanity proper ought to emerge (Freud 1926: 211). One might think of becoming-woman as the "key to all becomings" *not* because another relatively stable assemblage of forces negates the supposed unity of "man," but rather because what becomes known and lived as "man" (the "I," self or individual) emerges from individuation. More specifically, "woman" is not the marked or inflected form that differs from the ground or generic subject of "man." Similarly, but not analogously, "blackness" is not the marked form that is defined against generic whiteness. Quite the contrary, "woman" or "becoming-woman" would be a movement away from the individual toward individuation—all those intense forces through which we become who "we" are. Blackness differs again in being that which does not come to own itself (Hartman 1997: 25).

In what follows I hope to make the following three points. First, it is illegitimate to think of race and gender analogously, as predicates that mark an otherwise neutral subject who is the ground for various identities or acts of identification. Second, sexual identity— being male *or* female—is possible because of a far more complex field of individuation. The human species has become what it is, capable of saying "I" because of its particular modes of individuation: its living in common, in sexual relations, and bearing a relation to a past and future of desire. It may, however, *not* accede to that becoming "I"; it is this possibility of not being singular that Deleuze and Guattari embrace. Third, racial identity operates by a different historical logic from forms of gender identity, or by a different relation to individuation. For Deleuze and Guattari both sexual and racial individuation have a history that happened to result in what now passes for race and gender. Race is not the discrimination of the human, the marking of differences in an otherwise universal humanity. Rather, the "intense germinal influx" of life generates assemblages of bodies, such as tribes or packs, but these become deterritorialized when a part of that assemblage governs of stand for the whole (Deleuze and Guattari 1983: 170). In deterritorialization a punishing despot sets a law of the body outside the body political. It is in reterritorialization that a universal "we" becomes possible: the socius is not seen as the result of a coming-into-relation of differences, but as the effect of an underlying commonality (humanity) that is then inflected differently in each one of us. "Race" is the effect of imagining a common humanity within which there are differences or identifying markers. Deleuze and Guattari will argue that the very notion of "the human" is possible only because one has occluded delirium. "Man" emerges because one has repressed differences in order to achieve the human race. Accordingly, "becoming-woman" and "racial-delirium" are two very different events in *Anti-Oedipus* and *A Thousand Plateaus*, even if both move away from the individual who is able to claim "a" race or a gender. "Becoming-woman" is the beginning of a movement toward becoming-imperceptible, the taking up of more and more intensive traits that will end in the dissolution of the self's capacity to be defined by the exclusive disjunction of male *or* female. Racial delirium is the global and historical dimension of every sexualized subject: I become dependent on the male/female disjunction because of a history in which colonization and imperialism subjected complex social assemblages to a single power, increasingly contracting the nexus of power-desire to the notion of "a" humanity—all defined through the oedipal complex where "I" internalize the authority of the father in opposition to the seeming indistinction of maternal plenitude. For Deleuze and Guattari, "the father" becomes a figure of generic human authority only after a long history of despots, lords, tyrants, colonizers, police, and kleptocrats. In the beginning is not the social contract—an agreement to live in common for our private security—but the seizing of excess that allows a single body to appear to be the law of all. It is the event of plunder that produces authority and the figure of humanity. It follows that what is plundered is not another, lesser, marked or sub-humanity, but nothing more than the (black) property through which man comes to be. The forming of "a" human race becomes possible first through races, which in turn become possible only through the seizing of power that creates a sovereign body. When that sovereign body becomes "humanity," that which is seized, held, used, and sold is not even less than human; blackness is therefore bound up with but utterly distinct from the logic of the sexual binary.

The oedipal family is at the end of a history of violence and theft that passes from despotism to humanism. On the one hand, one might say that race precedes and makes possible the relation of sexual difference: there cannot be a mother-father-child triangle unless tribes have assembled to form polities that eventually enable the great family of man that imagines itself as a subject, necessarily lining up with the male/female binary. Deleuze and Guattari describe the emergence of the despot that begins with one body engaging in excessive consumption, as though he were the divine law of the earth; that body then becomes an abstracted principle of law and eventually the "man" of modernity, a figure of authority because the family is a contraction of a broader history of colonization:

> We believe that this is also true in the case of the family-society relationship. There is no Oedipal triangle: Oedipus is always open in an open social field. Oedipus opens to the four winds, to the four corners of the social field (not even 3 + 1, but 4 + n). A poorly closed triangle, a porous or seeping triangle, an exploded triangle from which the flows of desire escape in the direction of other territories. It is strange that we had to wait for the dreams of colonized peoples in order to see that, on the vertices of the pseudo triangle, mommy was dancing with the missionary, daddy was being fucked by the tax collector, while the self was being beaten by a white man. It is precisely this pairing of the parental figures with agents of another nature ..., that keeps the triangle from closing up again, from being valid in itself, and from claiming to express or represent this different nature of the agents that are in question in the unconscious itself. (1983: 95)

On the other hand, one might say that race is the effect of sexual difference: in the beginning are desiring relations among forces, with bodies being the effect of encounters in which what something *is* results from the stabilization of an assemblage of affects. It is only with the formation of bodies into territories, and the desiring relation among those bodies (by way of collective investments in scarring, tattooing, painting, dancing, singing) that something like a tribe can be formed. Everything begins with desire—pre-personal intensities *from which* something like the sexed body emerges. But whether sex or race come first is a false problem. The gender binary is an effect of a sexual difference that goes well beyond human sexes and bodies; the male/female binary of modern man is an effect of colonization and capitalism that has also coded the "intense germinal influx" into the seeming difference of races. Becoming-woman would be a way of thinking sexual difference *not* in terms of gender identity but in all the modes of attraction and intensification that create bodies; the self is an effect (not the ground) of desires. "Racial delirium" would be a quite distinct intuition that situates the isolated (gendered) individual within a historical field, in which "man" emerged from a history of violence.

For Deleuze and Guattari a seemingly revolutionary desire can be structured by entirely reactionary investments. To demand recognition according to *who I am*, for all its manifest rebellion, nevertheless leaves the supremacy of the subject in place—supremacy of "the subject" is *always* white supremacy, given that the very figure of "man" is the result of a history of imperialist plundering. Desire is revolutionary when it opens out to a history in which "man" is dispersed, seen to be an effect of an inhuman history:

> We define the reactionary unconscious investment as the investment that conforms to the interest of the dominant class, but operates on its own account, according to the terms of desire, through the segregative use of the conjunctive syntheses from which Oedipus is derived: I am of the superior race. The revolutionary unconscious investment is such that desire, still in its own mode, cuts across the interest of the dominated, exploited classes, and causes flows to move that are capable of breaking apart both the segregations and their Oedipal applications—flows capable of hallucinating history, of reanimating the races in delirium, of setting continents ablaze. No, I am not of your kind, I am the outsider and the deterritorialized, "I am of a race inferior for all eternity … I am a beast, a Negro." There again it is a question of an intense potential for investment and counterinvestment in the unconscious. Oedipus disintegrates because its very conditions have disintegrated. The nomadic and polyvocal use of the conjunctive syntheses is in opposition to the segregative and biunivocal use. Delirium has something like two poles, racist and racial, paranoiac-segregative and schizonomadic. (Deleuze and Guattari 1983: 105)

Quoting Arthur Rimbaud, Deleuze and Guattari argue for a blackness that is not one of affirmation and identification, but far closer—and this makes sense given their reading of Fanon—to a destructive negativity. One could not then align the dissolution of the gendered subject into a thousand tiny sexes that begins with becoming-woman with the racial delirium that opens the history that subtends "man." Race and sex—or the races and sexes that have emerged from the intense germinal influx—are different modes of stratification. Sexual difference becomes subjectified and rendered binary through an exclusive disjunction: one is either male *or* female, and this is because being a subject requires lining up beneath one or the other identity. Gaining a form of recognizable humanity requires being determined as, living as, embodied as *a gender*. Transgendered individuals do not choose another sex as if one's sexuality were added on to being human; one's sexuality *is* one's humanity, and it then follows that trans becomes a quite singular form of violence done to the propriety of man. Race and Oedipus are intertwined (but not aligned) in the "segregative use of the conjunctive synthesis." As soon as one imagines that there are whites *and* blacks—distinct peoples and their kind— then it becomes possible to see blackness and whiteness as symmetrical, and as different ways of thinking about an underlying humanity. That underlying generic humanity—cut up into distinct races, nations and families— enables a gender system such that male and female also become ways of differentiating humanity. Deleuze and Guattari see the very concepts of "humanity," "gender," and "race" as the result of a history of desire. Gender and race are not ways of differentiating a generic humanity, such that we might think of these as identifiers that mark out differences among us; rather, that sense of a common "us" or "we" follows from a history that produced the subject as white, male, and average:

> Why are there so many becomings of man, but no becoming-man? First because man is majoritarian par excellence, whereas becomings are minoritarian; all becoming is a becoming-minoritarian. When we say majority, we are referring not to a greater relative quantity but to the determination of a state or standard in relation to which larger quantities, as well as the smallest, can be said to be minoritarian: white-man, adult-male, etc. Majority implies a state of domination, not the reverse. (1987: 291)

Let's turn back to the politics of Tuvel's article where she proposed—with all the rigors that philosophy demands—that we consider transracialism alongside transgenderism. As the social media furor that followed the article's publication demonstrated, there were many political components that made up the article's capacity to cause offense. I want to leave aside several very important problems that were raised by those who objected to the article's publication and focus on the possibility of making the claim itself. Tuvel's use of terminology, apparent dead-naming, and paucity of citation of critical race theory are distinct and important issues. What I do want to focus on is why it was possible, philosophically, to ask the type of question Tuvel posed, *and* why the *philosophical* question created such outrage. In so doing I want to argue that there is something quite distinct about the way philosophy deals with race, as opposed to sexuality, and that this should alert us to a broader philosophical problem regarding what it might mean to ask a question—and to ask a question about race, gender, and their relation. Tuvel's defense of her article was that she was simply doing what philosopher's do, asking a question, posing a possibility, following through on logical consequences if we accept certain premises. This is a particular mode of philosophy in which we have components—sex, race, identity, bodies—with questions being formed by asking how those components cohere. It would make sense on this model to say that if we think it's legitimate to change one's sex on the basis of one's felt identity, then it would also be legitimate to do so at the level of race: "[I]f some individuals genuinely feel like or identify as a member of a race other than the one assigned to them at birth—so strongly to the point of seeking a transition to the other race—we should accept their decision to change races" (Tuvel 2017: 264). The philosopher looks at two bodies—the body that makes a claim regarding sexual identity and the body that makes a claim regarding racial identity—and recognizes a formal equivalence. Interestingly, in order to make her claim Tuvel draws upon Sally Haslanger's notion of racial membership on the basis of racial treatment (Haslanger 2012).

The #metoo movement also created a unity by way of a common experience of mistreatment, and at least one theory of blackness as slavery defines this specific event of race as given through a common relegation of blackness to nonbeing (Wilderson 2010: 89). It would seem that there *are* similarities across quite divergent experiential and theoretical domains. Yet, it is the difference between similarities that makes all the difference, and this is why it is worth noting the distinct ways in which "treatment" might seem to create an identity and a legitimate claim to identity. In the case of gender—at least as it was played out in the #metoo movement— one might say that there is an embedded system of sexual harassment, sexual violation, and sexual assault that *in general* allows those in power (usually men) to sexualize relations that would ostensibly be intellectual, collegial, commercial, professional, or pedagogical. For this reason, it made sense that some men could also claim to have been violated, and that some women may have made enough progress up the corporate, political, or professional ladder to be on the offending side of sexual violence. It is worthwhile to think about the ways in which #metoo appears to be revolutionary but operates by way of a reactionary unconscious investment. What happened as a result of the campaign was a series of high-profile resignations and shamings, as though the playing out of violence among men and women was a case of men behaving badly, rather than thinking about the very system of gender and humanization as itself violent. In the case of blackness being produced by negation the commonality of mistreatment is not the same at all. It is not that some humans are granted less respect than others because of their race, and this is because blackness is not a way of differentiating some humans from others but is a radical negation of being. There are different ways in which this blackness as negativity of being (rather than mistreatment of *one's being*) might be thought. The first would be to see blackness as intertwined with, *but not reducible to,* a world in which those who endure states of injury generate a commonality that is outside community. Fred Moten undertakes a long exploration of the relation between a dispossession created by antiblackness that nevertheless does not have a secure identity:

> Perhaps identities forged in severe injury might have something to do with a kind of persistent resistance to (states of) power and to taking power that not only will have clearly borne a deep attraction to those who remain excluded from power, especially when others have taken power in their names (i.e., the general constitution of what is called the postcolonial), but also will have served well the task of forming the genuinely new comportment, the out-from-the-outside thing, that is the aim and object of musical and political fantasy. Such fantasy constitutes and is constituted by rigorous analysis of the relation between blackness and the politics and aesthetics of a certain claim on dispossession that will have animated

the range of musical homelessness with which I have here been concerned. (2017: 117)

The second would be to see blackness not as one injured state among others, even in its unique relation between an American and diasporic mode, but as a necessary negativity that has always underpinned whiteness: "[A]nti-Blackness subsidizes Human survival in all its diversity" (Wilderson 2010: 141). What is important in these different ways of thinking about blackness is a relation to nonbeing, even when non-belonging might intimate some outside of belonging. By contrast, one must have a gender; one must be male *or* female. So rather than say black is to white as man is to woman it would be more accurate to say that *male/female and whiteness* are inextricably intertwined in ways that generate blackness as a negativity, *and* that preclude any possibility of the transition from male to female as being simply analogous to choosing to be white or black. Further, to see such transitions as events of choice and identification is to assume the normative and stably gendered subject as an unquestioned ground. In quite different ways transgender and black bodies destroy the ground of the type of subject who can ask questions about race and gender as though they were qualities added on to an unqualified being. Blackness is not a predicate that is donned or abandoned within the structure of "man." "Man" has been constituted through antiblackness. Transgenderism, by contrast, is at once refused by the normative oedipal binary of male and female, even as that same system of normality demands that one must have "a" gender. This is why one of the main objections to any comparison between transgenderism and transracialism is that race and sex are not analogous; to treat them as such is to be negligent, to refuse to consider the histories that compose race and gender (including the fact that there can be a trans community *because* of the compulsion to line up with a normative gender binary, while there is no transracial community precisely because race plays out as the belonging of whiteness) (Borck 2017).

Further, the mode in which racial and sexual questions are posed philosophically is not only negligently analogous, but the very possibility of analogy presupposes a normative conception of the subject—a subject who, in its most elevated mode, would be a philosophical subject. To make this a little clearer, think about the way in which the philosophical practice of thought experiments operates: imagine you are a slave chained in a cave or a brain in a vat, that you are creating society from behind a veil of ignorance or that you wake up one day as a giant insect. When Rawls asks us to think about the "veil of ignorance" (1999), we are any subject whatever, and *who we are* would seem to be transportable to and from any possible position in the society imagined. Plato asks us to imagine being those slaves *from the point of view of the un-enslaved*—the point of view of one who can transpose his "self" into other bodies and worlds, *because he has a self that is lived as not determined by the world.* You can only wonder if you are a brain in a vat, or whether the body and world you think of as your own is real if your world is already composed such that you have the experience of a private, detached, interior, and abstracted self. The conditions that go into making up the Cartesian subject are the conditions of race and empire; only after centuries of colonization and expropriation where some bodies are isolated and privatized to the point that they can conclude that it is interior "thinking" that composes the self: "I think, therefore I am," is made possible by the global production of others as nonbeing. Or, as it is narrated in *Anti-Oedipus,* the production of privacy was made possible when collective investments of bodies grouped together were deterritorialized by investment in a single transcendent body.

Such experiments were diagnosed artfully in Franz Kafka's *Metamorphosis*: a world in which you can only wake up one day in the body of an insect is a world in which self and body have been lived as distinct entities, with the spaces across which the self moves being nothing more than a simple exterior. When Deleuze and Guattari theorized becoming-animal it was not anything like imagining what it's like to be a bat but rather the dissolution of the imagining self. This is the trajectory of Kafka's story: from a world in which there is an isolated self—a mind in a body—to a conclusion where the movements of fleeing, being beaten, suffering, and crying in the style of an insect are destructive of the subject (Deleuze and Guattari 1986: 5). The difference between the thought experiment of imagining oneself behind a veil of ignorance, or as a brain in a vat, or as a slave in a cave, and "becoming-animal" is that one's self is not transported into another body, but the experience of movements, affects, manners, and sounds renders whatever the self was into a machine. Why use the term machine? Whereas an organism is imagined to be a bounded whole, with each part contributing to overall coherence, a machine is an assemblage of forces without center, without overarching identity, and in which the operation of any single force is capable of transforming every other force's functioning:

> A writer isn't a writer-man; he is a machine-man, and an experimental man (who thereby ceases to be a man in order to become an ape or a beetle, or a dog, or mouse, a becoming-animal, a becoming-inhuman, since it is actually through voice and through sound and through a style that one be-comes an animal, and certainly through the force of sobriety). A Kafka-machine is thus constituted by contents and expressions that have been formalized to diverse degrees by unformed materials that enter into it and leave by passing through all possible states. To enter or leave the machine, to be in the machine, to walk around it, to approach it—these are all still components of the machine itself: these are states of desire, free of all interpretation. The line of escape is part of the machine. (Deleuze and Guattari 1986: 7)

Here we can start to think two distinct modes of trans*. The first would be a transitivity of analogy. The "I" that now exists in the body of a white man might imagine itself as the same but in the body of a black woman; just as selves migrate across space, so they can migrate across genders or races (Brubaker 2016). Such a transitivity is possible if the space and bodies of one's world are what they are, and *then* engage in movement. One would be a self, and then capable of imagining one's world "as if" one were otherwise. To move across space, to shift from one body to another, would be possible, and one's self would either remain intact *or* it could claim that such a shift was required by the very nature of one's true self. The second mode would be a transitivity of intensity and disequilibrium. The space and bodies of one's world are neither equal nor simply different. Some bodies have emerged from a history of sexualization, privatization, colonization, imperialism, slavery, marriage, and domestic labor relations to move, feel, speak, and see their way in the world as if it were their own, as if changing places would be just that—changing places. This is why there is no becoming-man; the formation of man is one in which analogy is the perfect trope. One's world is there to be viewed, and one's self is stable enough that it can be transported elsewhere (imaginatively). Other bodies, however, would always have been more porous, where each movement, affect, touch, gaze, step, cry, or call reconfigures body, space, and self. From *psycho*analysis, where questions are oriented to who the self is, one would shift toward *schizo*analysis, or all the events, encounters, manners, styles, and movements that continually pulverize the self. These intensive encounters are not rearrangements of qualities, where white, black, male, and female are predicates that can be added or subtracted: blackness, femaleness, trans-ness, and whiteness are different modes of composition. The assemblage that forms race and blackness is stretched across history and empire, colonization, and enslavement; the formation of maleness/femaleness takes place on a different plane—through the production of privacy and interiority. The experience of blackness is that of nonbeing, a formation generated through a "humanity" created through antiblackness. The experience of trans* follows from a compulsory yet impossible belonging—to be male *or* female. Whereas the history of sexuality has tended toward privatization, identification, belonging, and having "a" sexuality, the history of race has been a history of a supposedly global humanity, ever more inclusive, and achieved by the negation of blackness.

To say that becoming-woman is a "key" to becomings might be thought by way of analogy *or* by way of another trope, perhaps that of metonymy *or* catachresis. One could think of transgenderism and transracialism *as if* one were the same person but now inhabiting another body. But such identifications would be majoritarian and reactionary: one would still be a sovereign subject and still blessed with the type of analogical reason that is enabled by a history of assuming the world as so much matter to be adapted to one's will. Alternatively, becoming-woman would not have a subject *who* becomes; the taking on of traits, manners, styles, movements, and desires would generate a temporality *as if* there had been an agent who preceded the events that composed one's being. That claim—of an ideal dissolution of sexual identity in favor of becoming—would seem to violate the deeply and painfully felt experience of those who are refused an identity: it's easy to affirm becoming-woman from the point of view of a philosophical subject for whom the task of writing becomes one of becoming-imperceptible. It would seem that becoming-woman would begin this journey in order to depart from the subject for whom becoming is something that one does as opposed to an event that transforms subjectivity and ontology. The stakes of this claim could be revolutionary or banal. The practice of philosophy, theory, the academy—the conditions of labor that make possible what counts as philosophical thinking—rely on authorship, copyright, owning one's ideas, the consecrations of one's ideas by way of citations and prestige publications, and an increasingly subtle relationship to a gendered and racialized history of proper names. Citing canonical philosophical names is at once imperative in order to have a voice in the conversation, and yet what counts as canonical and worthy of citation may, and should, have a role in the ontology and subjectivity of citational economies. If one takes Deleuze and Guattari seriously, "becoming-woman" should not be a metaphor; it should transform philosophical writing and modes of philosophical subjectivity—to the point of becoming-imperceptible.

Here, I want to return to the two conundrums that opened this essay: the problem of an analogy between transracialism and transgenderism, and the #metoo movement. In both cases one could think of becoming-woman as a trope: just as all seemingly stable genders emerge from a multiplicity far too intensive to be captured by the binary of male and female, so we might see becoming-woman as a figure or metaphor that would shift from segregative conjunction (men *and* women) to inclusive disjunction (I am male and female and black and white). We could pass from an original sexual transitivity, where male *or* female are contractions from a far more complex and plural field, to a general transitivity where races are similarly less differentiated assemblages that emerge from marking out in extensive space the intense germinal influx. The #metoo movement would begin with those who are clearly identified as women, but just as women have been defined by way of sexual objectification and use in relation to man, so we might extend this structure to others who have been harassed, assaulted, raped, and abused because of a general structure of silencing sexual violence: "we" would all be "metoo." Another possibility is to see tropology, analogy, and metaphor as inherently normalizing modes of philosophical thinking whereby the thinking subject can shift predicates around as if qualities existed in extensive space: as man is to woman, so white is to black.

Deleuze and Guattari were not the only thinkers of the twentieth century to challenge the logic of metaphor: to say that x is like y is to erase the complex formations of sense that allow "x" and "y" to emerge as stable terms. To think of metaphor as an "army of anthropomorphisms" is itself a metaphor; it's a metaphor that situates violence, conquering and the formation of man as the seeming foundation for what will count as thinking. What if the formation of "x" were not at all the same as the formation of "y"? What if "man" were formed by a process of exclusive disjunction (man *or* woman) while race were generated by segregating conjunction (black *and* white, where blackness is not the other of man but its negation)? The practice of metaphor—Freud's claim that women are the "dark continent"—would seem to suggest a likeness: just as Africa is a foreign and unknowable terrain, so woman. ... And yet, it is this unknowability that destroys metaphor: to liken woman to Africa as a site of mystery is to disclose the extent to which Africa stands for a hole in being, a figure which is then transferred to other sites to make sense of what cannot be rendered sensible. Similarly, to see women as an entity formed by violation—such that #metoo creates a post-essential non-natural kind, unified by mistreatment—erases the ways in which mistreatment operates differentially. There are not simply differences in degree of mistreatment, such as class and race, where one might be exposed to heightened degrees of vulnerability, but forms of being defined by mistreatment: in addition to those who have argued that blackness is constituted through an absolute violence, where whiteness constitutes itself as a right of man through antiblackness, there's the quite different *demand for being* placed upon transgendered bodies where one must be "a" sexual kind.

If we *apply* Deleuzoguattarian philosophy to these problems, as I have suggested we ought to do, then we have a two-stage or two-strata approach that was already suggested when Deleuze and Guattari argued that while there needed to be a women's movement, a revolutionary subject capable of arguing in its name, there also needed to be a becoming-woman that would open the way to becoming-imperceptible. Why, though, would one say that becoming-woman is the key to all becomings? Does this suggest that *sexual difference* is foundational, and that this foundational difference begins with male or female? In the current terrain of gender politics and normativity it is certainly the case that an exclusive disjunction operates: be male or female or fall back into the dark night of psychosis. By contrast racial identity works in an opposing, but not opposite, direction: we are all the same, one great family of man, and if you try to insist that black lives matter I'll tell you that *all* lives matter. Sexual identity seems to impose itself with a strict difference, while racial identity seems everywhere to be erased. Deep down there is one race—the great white family of man—and this one race finds itself happily sorted into two distinct sexes. Becoming-woman would appear to have a metaphoric value, as one would find some space outside the normativity of man who has always been the white, bourgeois man of reason. Already, approaching forms of trans* politics, such a claim is fraught with political problems. To see gendered identity as having philosophical value only insofar as it departs from "man,"—moving away from identity altogether—would appear to valorize sexual indifference. It is easy for the avant-garde philosopher to embrace a task of writing and thinking that destroys the rigidity of identity for the sake of a becoming-molecular, and in doing so to appropriate those writers (from Frantz Fanon to Antonin Artaud and Jean Genet) whose lives were painfully constituted through the experience of nonbeing. Yet, a closer reading ought to yield the contrary. Becoming-woman, despite its ostensible value in regarding sexual identities as expressions of a more profound difference that would ultimately be indifferent to man or woman, provides a new way of thinking about philosophy's relation (or non-relation) to sexuality. To do philosophy would require departing from man, the thinking being who surveys a field, sees relations among components, notes similarities and concludes: A is to B, as C is to D. Or, "race and sex are forms of identity; if I can assert a different sexual identity, I can assert a different racial identity." Man is a being who is set apart from the questions he poses; he is a being for whom sex and race can be questions. By contrast, becoming-woman is part of a series of maneuvers that sexualizes philosophy's mode of composing questions. Rather than survey components from a position of detached abstraction, one would be transformed by the problems one poses. To look at an animal would not be to ask what it is like to be an animal, nor would it be to act like or imagine the animal's being; something about relating to an animal, perceiving its movements, would transform one's mode of perceiving and questioning. To question sexual identity, to question sexual bodies, would amount to a transformation of what it is to question, of what it is to think, of what it is to perceive a problem. Here one would move beyond a reason of analogies toward a desire that cannot be likened to anything precisely because it is through desire that a field with possible likenesses emerges. Once one acknowledges that intensive mode of desire, one might also admit that desire is as constitutive of identities as it is destructive, and that a radical antiblackness can be discerned in a history of nonidentity.

Let us then proceed from becoming-woman to "becoming-trans*." This would not entail an affirmation of transgenderism and then transracialism, but a transgenderism that takes seriously the transitivity of desire—that gender emerges from a more complex field than can be captured by the figure of "man." Race, in turn, would be the broader logic of negation that allowed man to emerge as an animal with a sexually binary nature. If the philosophical subject had been composed as a subject for whom the world is a field of components to be calculated, arranged, questioned, and logically rendered into like and unlike, then becoming-woman would be the first stage in transforming philosophical questions. What would happen if this analogical point of view (or way of writing) did not exist? What would happen if asking a question or posing a problem generated *who* one is? This would then mean one would shift from questions of the type: "What *is* woman?" or "What do women want?" to "What happens to questions when they are oriented toward sexed bodies, to bodies that are not subjects distinct from the world they perceive and judge?" Sexual questions are transitive questions, where the identity of the questioner comes into being in relation to the questions and problems contemplated. This, at least, was how Deleuze and Guattari deployed becoming-woman, not so much as a concept within philosophy but as a new philosophical relation. More concretely, it would no longer be possible to look at a body and ask about the relation of identity to that body. Identity is neither something a body takes on or sloughs off, nor is identity something a philosopher can discern as a property, natural, nonnatural, or otherwise. What something is emerges from the questions it poses, and the problems that capture it. Freud's question of what women want enabled something like a subject to emerge as the purveyor of sexual difference, whereas becoming-woman strives to think sexual difference as a question, as part of a problematic field. More concretely, one might note a rather naïve transcendental trans-ness in Deleuze and Guattari's work where the genuine experience of philosophy, or of writing, moves in the direction of erasing binaries and fixed forms, and of being at odds with whatever one is recognized to be. Such a valorization pays no heed to the embedded problems of social recognition and normativity, but it does not dismiss the urgent affect of being trans*. To become other than what is recognized as being, to perceive sexuality as a problem, to desire to become through the way one lives and feels the world—this is one way of living philosophically.

One cannot say the same thing about race, and not only because race and sex are not only not socially, politically, or even philosophically analogous, but because philosophy (after becoming-woman) is counter to all analogy. To say that philosophy is sexual is to say that the desires through which questions are posed are formative of the entire plane of concepts and problems, and formative of one's own being. This is not to say that one creates oneself or one's sexuality through philosophy; on the contrary, the sexuality or desire of philosophy is what takes hold of anyone who poses a question. To have "a" sexuality is to be seized hold of by desire, a desire one negotiates but never fully owns. One cannot say, *in the same way,* that philosophy is racial. Both race and sex have been coded and deterritorialized as forms of human identity, and—as I have argued— philosophers have treated race and sex as properties or markers that one might render analogous, or that might form the basis for arguments of equality. When Deleuze and Guattari argue for life as desire, as the way in which forces enter into relation in order to become what they are while also generating potentials to be otherwise, they also offer a model of philosophy. As a form of questioning, philosophy transforms itself by way of the problems it poses. Race plays quite a different role in their thought. Let us say that they try and bring philosophy back to desire, to the forces that allow problems to emerge. Crucial to this endeavor is overcoming that white face which is at once "the" subject of philosophy, as well as a certain way of thinking. The white face is a screen with eyes that are the window to the soul. In short, whiteness is not a race, but a way of forming a logic of race where "a" human can read the being of the other. Race is that which exists beneath the skin, the skin that's the sign or exterior of an inner life. Without this logic of reading life, without this white face that looks out on the world and discerns its logic, there is no race and no racism. The binary of sex is an entirely different parsing of difference than the stratification of race. In gendered Oedipal difference "the human" is read as that which must be subjected to a recognizable structure of sexual desire, as a lining up of relations. In racial difference a broader logic of life is deemed to be operative and given through the signs of the skin, signs that are read by a whiteness that is not identified with the skin, or the body, but with a capacity to decode.

Not only can there be no analogy between racial difference and sexual difference, both race and sex would be occluded—in different ways—by analogy. If we follow Deleuze and Guattari here, we can see that sexual difference in its heteronormative form is tied to an oedipality that goes well beyond sexuality in the everyday sense. In order to have the masculine/feminine kinds that are organized in a family triangle, there must have been a contraction of complex social forms and relations into the unity of the family. The family, in turn, comes with its own fantasy of biology: the human subject who replicates and extends himself through the lines of genetic sameness. What has been repressed in figure of the family is the differential complexity—the intense germinal influx. What come to be known as sex and race are both effects of a repression of a difference. The white man of reason who views the world as a plane of comparable and analogous difference is already the effect of a racial delirium that is sexual in nature. In order to become the "I" who conducts the detached thought experiments that reduce race and sex to predicates one must first have had the formation of territories in order to produce organized bodies; the modern subject is the effect of a long history of social formations, following a deterritorialization that subjects the relation of bodies to an external law, and then a reterritorialization that allows any one of those bodies to internalize that law as one's own. Rather than see personal identities as composed from a long history of figures—such that the capacity to be "man" is the result of a whole history of despots, authorities, and elevated bodies—modern subjects see social authorities as projections of our own very private familial fantasy. Only on the basis of that modern delusion can one imagine that one could take one's race or gender on and off in the way one makes other personal decisions of belief.

We can begin to draw some preliminary conclusions. First, the notion that one might regard race and sex as analogous predicates that one might add and subtract from a subject who precedes and decides those qualities relies upon the figure of white man, the self who is apart from the world, who compares, contrasts, surveys, and decides upon who he really is. Second, this would then entail that selves who experienced themselves as (say) female while nevertheless being designated as male at birth would not be *choosing* a different identity but expressing one of the (many) complex ways in which bodies and persons are sexed, beyond oedipal identifications. Third, because sexuality has been parsed by way of an oedipal history—moving from larger social units toward the family, in order to arrive at "man"—it is illegitimate to align the formations of race with that same (though related) history. Abstractly, one would need to consider the different stratifications, violences, and inscriptions that produce bodies as having "a" race and sex. Again, this is not social construction, as though differentiation were imposed from above, but stratification and machination: whiteness is produced through the production of man as the subject of reason; he who surveys the world as so many qualities in need of organization and management. Race is originally formed through bodies being subjected to global markets but becomes increasingly—as a result of that history of exchange and commodification—a signifier of a fantasized history of humanity, with blackness marking that which cannot be reckoned with in the history of the human. In short, while sexuality is formed through a long history of social formations that results in the family and an oedipal figure of "man," race is formed through a history of global networks and trades that results in something like "the human" that operates by occluding the racializing history that made it possible. The two planes of history are related but neither the same nor reducible to each other, and together result in a figure of the modern subject who is deemed to be recognized by way of a single private sexuality *and* deemed to be of no race whatsoever. To be human is to be male *or* female, *and* to be "white" where whiteness stands for an imaginative capacity to be race-free *and to think of race and sexuality as analogous, as identities one may experience as private affairs and objects of choice.* There are only two genders and only one race: the race that has no race, or the race that can imagine race as a detachable quality.

Note

1. Trysh Travis, "Teaching Moments from the Hypatia Controversy," *Inside Higher Ed*, June 2017, https://www.insidehighered.com/views/2017/06/30/instructor-analyzes-how-discuss-hypatia-controversy-her-grad-students-essay (accessed December 31, 2017); Meryl Altman, Timothy Burke, and Claire Potter, "What Happened at Hypatia?," *Public Seminar*, May 2017, http://www.publicseminar.org/2017/05/what-happened-at-hypatia/ (accessed December 31, 2017); Daniel Engber, "Are Angry Mobs on Facebook Taking Over Academia?," *The Slate*, May 2017, http://www.slate.com/articles/health_and_science/science/2017/05/rebecca_tuvel_amy_cuddy_and_bullying_in_academia.html (accessed December 31, 2017).

References

Berlinski, C. (2017), "The Warlock Hunt," *American Interest*, https://www.the-american-interest.com/2017/12/06/the-warlock-hunt/ (accessed January 1, 2018).

Bey, M. (May 2017), "The Trans*-ness of Blackness, and the Blackness of Trans*-ness," *TSQ: Transgender Studies Quarterly* 4 (2): 275–95. DOI 10.1215/23289252-3815069.

Borck, C. R. (November 2017), "Negligent Analogies," *TSQ: Transgender Studies Quarterly* 4 (3–4): 679–84. DOI 10.1215/23289252-4190064.

Brubaker, R. (2016), *Trans: Gender and Race in an Age of Unsettled Identities*, Princeton, NJ: Princeton University Press.

Deleuze, G. (1994), *Difference and Repetition*, trans. P. Patton, New York: Columbia University Press.

Deleuze, G., and F. Guattari (1983), *Anti-Oedipus: Capitalism and Schizophrenia*, trans. R. Hurley, M. Seem, and H. R. Lane, Minneapolis: University of Minnesota Press.

Deleuze, G., and F. Guattari (1986), *Kafka: Toward a Minor Literature*, trans. D. Polan, Minneapolis: University of Minnesota Press.

Deleuze, G., and F. Guattari (1987), *A Thousand Plateaus: Capitalism and Schizophrenia*, trans. Brian Massumi, Minneapolis: University of Minnesota Press.

Freud, S. (1926), "The Question of Lay Analysis," in J. Strachey (ed.), *The Standard Edition of the Complete Psychological Works of Sigmund Freud, Volume XX (1925–1926)*, 177–258, London: Hogarth.

Hartman, S. V. (1997), *Scenes of Subjection: Terror, Slavery, and Self-making in Nineteenth-century America*, New York: Oxford University Press.

Haslanger, S. (2012), *Resisting Reality: Social Construction and Social Critique*, New York: Oxford University Press.

Magness, C. (2017), "It's Time to Stop the Sexual Witch Hunt and Take a Hard Look at Ourselves," *The Federalist*, http://thefederalist.com/2017/12/12/time-stop-sexual-witch-hunt-take-hard-look/ (accessed January 1, 2018).

Moten, F. (2017), *Black and Blur: Consent Not to Be a Single Being*, Durham, NC: Duke University Press.

Rawls, J. (1999), *A Theory of Justice*, 2nd ed., Cambridge: Harvard University Press.

Singal, J. (2017), "This Is What a Modern-Day Witch Hunt Looks Like," *New York*, http://nymag.com/daily/intelligencer/2017/05/transracialism-article-controversy.html (accessed January 1, 2018).

Tuvel, R. (2017), "In Defense of Transracialism," *Hypatia* 32 (2): 263–78.

Wilderson, F. B. (2010), *Red, White and Black: Cinema and the Structure of U.S. Antagonisms*, Durham, NC: Duke University Press.

CHAPTER 2
THE DELEUZIAN NOTION OF BECOMING-IMPERCEPTIBLE AND POSTFEMINIST STRATEGIES
Audronė Žukauskaitė

Deleuze and Guattari's notion of schizoanalysis, formulated in their seminal work *Anti-Oedipus*, offers enormous potential for contemporary feminism. Although feminist thinkers, for instance, Rosi Braidotti and Elizabeth Grosz, were quite critical about Deleuze and Guattari's project of schizoanalysis and its implications for feminism in the last decade of the twentieth century (Braidotti 1994; Grosz 1994), their subsequent research reveals how strongly they are influenced by Deleuze and Guattari's philosophy. Deleuze and Guattari's project of schizoanalysis and desire production, as well as their ontology of becoming suggest a radically different account of identity, sexuality, and subjectivity. As a result, many questions formulated in the so-called second wave feminist agenda, such as sexual difference and the quest for specific feminine identity and its recognition, are reformulated in contemporary theory. In this essay I will concentrate on Deleuze and Guattari's redefinition of such concepts as schizophrenia and desire in *Anti-Oedipus*, and their subsequent elaboration of the idea of desire-production in the form of becoming in *A Thousand Plateaus*.

Deleuze and Guattari's project of schizoanalysis is important for feminist thinkers for several reasons: first, desire is defined not as a lack but as a productive force which produces the real. In contrast to Lacanian psychoanalysis, which is organized around the processes of identification taking place in the realms of the Imaginary and the Symbolic (and having no access to the Real), Deleuze and Guattari's schizoanalysis functions in the real and produces the real. In other words, schizophrenic desire is oriented not toward the imaginary realm of fantasy but toward real social change. Second, for Deleuze and Guattari desire is an unlimited process of transformation, which produces not identities but schizo-flows, becomings, and multiplicities. Psychoanalysis defines the processes of identification, which result in creating imaginary or symbolic identity and integrating the newly created subject into the social order; in contrast, schizoanalysis describes the unlimited process of desire production, desire as endless becoming which ends up in disintegrating the social and the dissolution of any identity into the becoming-imperceptible. Third, desire works not in the register of signification or representation but in the mode of expression, experimentation, and affectivity. Psychoanalysis is based on the model of interpretation and seeks the reconstruction of lost meaning, whereas schizoanalysis examines affects and intensities, physical and psychical forces, defining our activity.

Thus, schizoanalysis intervenes into the recent debates in feminist theory, which relate feminism either to the creation of new subjectivity and identity, or to the politics of the impersonal, which relies not on identity but on becoming. The identity model is based on performative identification, which needs the recognition of the Other. As a consequence of this, as Grosz (2002) has pointed out, the politics of identity and recognition gets stuck in the Hegelian master and slave dialectics. In contrast to identity politics, Grosz argues for the "politics of imperceptibility," which is based not on the concept of subjectivity but on inhuman and impersonal forces. Thus, the psychoanalytical model of identification is replaced by a schizophrenic flux of becomings, expressions, and affections. Following from Friedrich Nietzsche and Deleuze, Grosz defines force as becoming and qualitative multiplicity. In this sense it is not the master's recognition, but material and qualitative becoming, which engenders political change. This essay will explore Deleuze and Guattari's notion of becoming-imperceptible in the context of contemporary feminist theory and contemporary art, and, in this way, it will seek to outline new postfeminist strategies.

1. Feminism and Schizoanalysis

Deleuze and Guattari's project of materialist and machinic schizophrenia is clearly opposed to the metaphysics secretly underlying Freudian and Lacanian psychoanalysis. Deleuze and Guattari invent a new register of desiring-production which relates and connects libidinal economy and political economy, libidinal forces and labor power. Instead of having two separate realms, such as inward, private and unconscious desire, and the social field of labor and production, Deleuze and Guattari suggest one type of desiring-production that is at the same time social-production. As they point out,

> Desire produces reality, or stated another way, desiring-production is one and the same thing as social production. It is not possible to attribute a special form of existence to desire, a mental or psychic reality that is presumably different from the material reality of social production. Desiring-machines are not fantasy-machines or dream-machines, which supposedly can be distinguished from technical and social machines. Rather, fantasies are secondary expressions, deriving from the identical nature of the two sorts of machines in any given set of circumstances. (2004a: 32)

In other words, similarly as labor produces social reality, desire produces social reality in its own way, by investing it with unconscious drives. The model of psyche here has to be imagined not as a theater of representation but as a factory, which does not represent but functions, produces, and expresses. Therefore, desire is organized not around a lack, as was presumed from Plato to Freud and Lacan, but is an expression of forces, both human and inhuman. "Desire does not lack anything; it does not lack its object. It is, rather, the *subject* that is missing in desire, or desire that lacks a fixed subject; there is no fixed subject unless there is repression" (Deleuze and Guattari 2004a: 28). Desire is not locked in a bounded subject; desire is not individual, it is collective. In this sense desire is seen not as individual and idiosyncratic but as a collective assemblage of social forces.

In other words, libidinal investment is simultaneously a social investment, impregnating the social and political field. This helps Deleuze and Guattari to explain the "irrational" investments which appear in such social delirium as fascism. The social investment oscillates between two major types: the paranoiac fascisizing pole or type, which invests into a fixed and final identity, and the schizo-revolutionary pole or type, which "breaches the wall and causes flows to move" (Deleuze and Guattari 2004a: 305). These oscillations from one pole of libidinal-social investment to the other is seen as the major object of schizoanalysis. However, the opposition between the paranoiac desire for fixed identity and schizophrenic desire for nomadic, fluctuating multiplicity cannot be interpreted as a simple opposition between the individual and the collective. The collective can be equally impregnated by the same oscillations between the paranoiac pole (the fixed aggregates and persons) and the schizophrenic pole (the molecular multiplicities, partial objects and flows). This is the opposition between so-called subjugated groups and subject-groups, between a socius as a full body and its limit, the body without organs, or between molar aggregates and molecular multiplicities. Thus, the task of schizoanalysis is to break the socius and its aggregates, to invent molecular multiplicities of singularities, to open the lines of escape and follow the schizo-flows, which are molecular, microphysical, and material.

What kind of perspective does this model offer for feminism? First, schizoanalysis radically changes the focus of critique because desire is regarded not as merely anthropological phenomenon but as a human and nonhuman libidinal investment. Desiring-machines express libidinal investments and tensions not only between different sexes and genders but also between different classes or ethnic groups, between powers of sovereignty, and the suppressed groups. Libidinal investments define the relationships with social aggregates and institutions: It is "the way a bureaucrat fondles his records, a judge administers justice, a businessman causes money to circulate" (Deleuze and Guattari 2004a: 332). Sexuality is derived from the social and not the other way around: "Desiring-machines are the nonhuman sex, the molecular machinic elements, their arrangements and their syntheses, without which there would be neither a human sex specifically determined in the large aggregates, nor a human sexuality capable of investing these aggregates" (Deleuze and Guattari 2004a: 324). As such, schizoanalysis detaches sexuality from sexual difference and human subjectivity, and establishes it as a general principle of social organization (or disorganization in terms of molecular multiplicities of singularities).

Desiring-machines or the nonhuman sex: not one or even two sexes, but *n* sexes. Schizoanalysis is the variable analysis of the *n* sexes in a subject, beyond the anthropomorphic representation that society imposes on this subject, and with which it represents its own sexuality. The schizoanalytic slogan of the desiring-revolution will be first of all: to each its own sexes. (Deleuze and Guattari 2004a: 325)

Thus, feminism cannot choose female identity as its goal, unless it is guided by paranoiac investments. As Eugene Holland points out,

> Women's liberation is not possible as long as the concept of *woman* itself is not disseminated in a polyvalent multiplicity of different roles and orientations, but remains locked in a bi-polar opposition to man, based on illegitimate uses of the syntheses of connection, registration, and consummation. By contrast, legitimate uses of the syntheses … produce subjects that are fluid, ambivalent or polyvalent, open to change; that are continually being made, unmade, and remade. (1999: 119–20)

Thus, to retain its schizo-revolutionary potential, feminism has to withdraw from any sexual, individual, or personal identity.

However, this task is not so easy to achieve. Even if Deleuze and Guattari assert that the task of schizoanalysis is to investigate the oscillations between the paranoiac and the schizophrenic poles, this opposition is much more complicated than it seems. This opposition is complicated by introducing a division between the preconscious libidinal investment of interest and the unconscious libidinal investment of desire. As Deleuze and Guattari point out, "[W]hat is reactionary or revolutionary in the preconscious investment of interest does not necessarily coincide with what is reactionary or revolutionary in the unconscious libidinal investment" (2004a: 380). If we take as an example a schizo-revolutionary investment, it can have a double direction: a preconscious libidinal investment may seek a new power, a new form of socius and social organization, whereas an unconscious libidinal investment may continue to invest in the former body, the old form of power. As Deleuze and Guattari point out, "[E]ven when the libido embraces the new body—the new force that corresponds to the effectively revolutionary goals and syntheses from the viewpoint of the preconscious—it is not certain that the unconscious libidinal investment is itself revolutionary. For the same breaks do not pass at the level of the unconscious desires and the preconscious interests" (2004a: 381). In the case of preconscious revolutionary investment, the break is between two forms of socius, in other words, it produces a new social arrangement, whereas in the case of unconscious revolutionary investment the break is within the socius itself. The unconscious libidinal desire pushes the socius to its limit and disorganizes it into what Deleuze and Guattari call the body without organs. The preconscious revolutionary investment creates a new socius, a new social body and a new power, whereas the unconscious revolutionary desire overthrows power and dissolves socius on the body without organs.

What do these complications of schizoanalysis mean to feminist theory? Here we come to the second task of schizoanalysis to distinguish between preconscious feminist investments and unconscious feminist desires. Feminist schizoanalysis should be very careful by examining those preconscious libidinal investments, which seek to overthrow the old patriarchal powers and create new socius and new arrangements of power, which will end up by establishing new political identities. Even in keeping its schizo-revolutionary potential, the preconscious libidinal investment might stick to the old hierarchies and get involved into power relationships. For example, the recent activist movement #MeToo, to which Colebrook and Kedem refer in Chapters 1 and 6 respectively, is revolutionary in its attempt to overthrow power, to liberate women from their subordinated and sexualized position; it definitively aims at creating a new social body with a different distribution of equality and rights. On the other hand, it may happen that at the level of unconscious desire, it still continues to invest into the old forms of power based on social ostracization and exclusion. Deleuze and Guattari have this internal contradiction in mind when they argue,

> It is, of course, indispensable for women to conduct a molar politics, with a view to winning back their own organism, their own history, their own subjectivity... But it is dangerous to confine oneself to such a subject, which does not function without drying up a spring or stopping a flow. The song of life is often intoned by the driest of women, moved by *ressentiment*, the will to power. (2004b: 304)

Thus even revolutionary in its preconscious interests, such activist practices are reactionary in their unconscious desire to embrace the old forms of powers.

To become revolutionary both at the level of preconscious interest and the level of unconscious desire, such practices should lead to the disorganization of power on the plane of the body without organs. Instead of investing into revengeful practices of will to power, feminists should invest into the flows of desire and the constitution of the body without organs understood as a model of dis-organization. That would mean to break with the old forms of socius and the question of rights and power. As Cora Diamond argues, the question of rights is concerned not with justice but with the system of entitlement and with the issue of how much someone gets in this system (2001: 121). Thus, instead of participating in this system of power, schizo-revolutionary activism should invent new forms of cohabitation, new assemblages as bodies without organs, which could include not only human but also nonhuman forces. Schizoanalysis for Deleuze and Guattari is a strategy of getting away from the socius as the model of power and engaging into the unlimited becoming which strives toward becoming-imperceptible. For example, here we can recall Donna Haraway's desiring becomings, such as becoming-cyborg, becoming-dog, or even becoming-critter, which do not rest on the old forms of femininity but engage into different forms of cohabitation with nonhuman other.

Here it is important to point out that different forms of investment do not exclude each other but pass into one another. As Deleuze and Guattari point out,

> A revolutionary group at the preconscious level remains a *subjugated group*, even in seizing power, as long as this power itself refers to a form of force that continues to enslave and crash desiring-production ... A *subject-group*, on the contrary, is a group whose libidinal investments are themselves revolutionary; it causes desire

to penetrate into the social field, and subordinates the form of power to desiring-production. (2004a: 382)

In other words, a subject-group may derive from a subjugated group through a rupture and vice versa: a subjugated group may break with the circuit of power and become a subject group. Thus, Deleuze and Guattari are constructing a fluid ontology where molar identities are coupled with molecular becomings, social stratification is resisted by social destratification, and the plane of organization is struggling with the plane of consistency. In this sense we can see a clear continuity between *Anti-Oedipus* and *A Thousand Plateaus*: both volumes explore the same opposition between the paranoiac drive for identity and the schizophrenic desire of becoming. Identity is established by means of exclusion and always works at the expense of someone else, whereas becoming is multiple and inclusive, starting from becoming-woman and ending with becoming-imperceptible.

Deleuze and Guattari argue that all kinds of becoming begin with and pass through becoming woman. However, this is only the first stage in the general process of becoming which should move toward becoming-animal, becoming-molecular, becoming-imperceptible. As Deleuze and Guattari explain, "Becoming-imperceptible means many things. What is the relation between the (anorganic) imperceptible, the (asignifying) indiscernible, and the (asubjective) impersonal?" (2004b: 308). The quest for the imperceptible, the indiscernible, and the impersonal is precisely what schizoanalysis is striving for: it is the deconstruction of identity, signification, and subjectivity. We can presume that to become imperceptible means to reject the notion of individual identity and replace it with the flux of particularities or haecceities; to dismantle the system of signification and interpretation and replace it with (indiscernible) affectivity; to erase person and subjectivity and replace it with impersonal forces. Deleuze and Guattari argue that becoming-imperceptible leads to a reduction of personal and individual identity, simultaneously reassembling the residues of this subjectivity in new connections and correlations with the surrounding world: "Such is the link between imperceptibility, indiscernibility, and impersonality – the three virtues. To reduce oneself to an abstract line, a trait, in order to find one's zone of indiscernibility with other traits, and in this way enter the haecceity and impersonality of the creator" (Deleuze and Guattari 2004b: 309). Becoming-imperceptible is the process of dissolving the subjective identity into qualities, particularities, intensities, and affects.

Becoming is imperceptible in the sense that it is not perceived by human consciousness, it goes beyond the system of signification. Becoming is movement and movement is by nature imperceptible: "Movements, becomings, in other words, pure relations of speed and slowness, pure affects, are below and above the threshold of perception" (Deleuze and Guattari 2004b: 309). Thus becoming-imperceptible might be interpreted in several ways. For example, Rosi Braidotti discusses the notion of becoming-imperceptible in the context of death, where the individual self is about to disappear and merge with the general flow of becoming (2006b: 153; 2013: 136). In this sense the subject literally becomes posthuman by connecting to the inorganic world. However, Deleuze and

Guattari point out the creative force of becoming-imperceptible, which is achieved when becoming is unleashed from organization, signification, and subjectification. As Holland interprets this, "[B]ecoming augments our ability to act and our mutual enjoyment of affecting and being affected by others" (2013: 114). We can presume that what escapes perception is precisely an affect, which is not convertible into function and meaning, conventional and recognizable signification. In this respect we can argue that to become imperceptible means to become-affective, to become intense, and to get involved into the general economy of corporeal forces.

2. Feminist Schizoanalysis

Deleuze and Guattari's theory and especially their notion of becoming provoked very diverse feminist reactions. In 1994 both Rosi Braidotti and Elizabeth Grosz published books in which they closely examined Deleuze and Guattari's philosophy and its implications for feminist thought. In *Nomadic Subjects*, Braidotti was quite critical about the implications of Deleuze and Guattari's philosophy for feminism. On the one hand, she interpreted the theory of becoming as a conceptual possibility engendering new forms of feminine subjectivity; on the other hand, she was wondering if this theory is not another male fantasy, seeking to recuperate specific feminist territories. Braidotti points out that the Deleuzian theory of becoming is very ambivalent, because, on the one hand, the becoming-woman is posited as a potentiality of the new philosophical subjectivity, and, on the other hand, feminists are conscious that not all the forms of this process of becoming are equivalent. Thus, "[T]he becoming-woman is a privileged position for the minority-consciousness of all" and, in this way, women again are positioned as the privileged figure of otherness (Braidotti 1994: 114). Is it possible to conceptualize feminist subjectivity without recourse to sexual difference and sexual dualism?

Braidotti also seemed to be quite unconvinced by Deleuze and Guattari's call for the dissolution of feminine subjectivity and sexuality into an impersonal, multiple, molecular flow. For example, Braidotti argued,

> One cannot deconstruct a subjectivity one has never controlled. Self-determination is the first step of any program of deconstruction. I concluded that Deleuze gets caught in the contradiction of postulating a general "becoming-woman" that fails to take into account the historical and epistemological specificity of the female feminist standpoint. A theory of difference that fails to take into account sexual difference leaves me as a feminist critic in a state of skeptical perplexity. (1994: 117)

It seems that at this point she is not ready to give up a territory that feminism never completely possessed–a territory of autonomous subjectivity. In a very similar way, Grosz argued in *Volatile Bodies* that "what becoming-woman means or entails for men is different than for women. For men, it implies a de- and restructuring of male sexuality ... bringing into play the microfemininities of behaviors, the particles of another sexuality, or many sexualities ... But exactly what this means for women remains disturbingly unclear" (1994: 177). Grosz was concerned that the process of becoming-woman actually leads to the abandoning of the very struggles by which feminists had sought to create new social places and values for women (ibid.). In other words, even if feminists express emancipatory or revolutionary preconscious libidinal investments, they still seek to maintain the old differences and divisions between sexes at the level of unconscious desire. The unconscious libidinal desire might be reactionary in the sense that it is attached to one or another form of identity, which simultaneously reverses and mirrors the existing power relationships. But, for Deleuze and Guattari, it is precisely identity, or molar stratification (the division between classes, races, and sexes) that creates the conditions of domination and power. As far as feminist theory cannot conceptually distance itself from standard forms of identity and cannot break the poisonous circuit of revenge and *ressentiment*, it still operates within the framework of power.

However, in their more recent works, both Braidotti and Grosz have reconsidered Deleuze and Guattari's theory in a much more positive way. For example, in *Metamorphoses* (2002) and *Transpositions* (2006a) Braidotti, even repeating all her reservations expressed in *Nomadic Subjects*, argues that the theory of becoming opens "alternative patterns of desire." Following the Deleuzian critique of psychoanalysis, Braidotti points out that one of the most important implications of this theory is the new interpretation of desire: desire is defined not in terms of negativity and lack but in terms of productive and creative forces. Desire is not repressed but produced and expressed in new collective assemblages:

> Desire is for me a material and socially enacted arrangement of conditions that allow for the actualization (that is, the immanent realization) of the affirmative mode of becoming. Desire is active in that it has to do with encounters between multiple forces and the creation of new possibilities of empowerment. (Braidotti 2002: 99)

Another important point is that becoming presupposes temporality, duration, endurance and has the power to enact a qualitative change:

> Temporally speaking, a body is a portion of living memory that endures by undergoing constant internal modifications following the encounter with other bodies and forces ... As such, desire and yearning for interconnections with others lies at the heart of Deleuze's vision of subjectivity. (Braidotti 2002: 99)

Similarly, Grosz points out that Deleuzian notions of becoming, duration, and virtuality are crucial in trying to conceptualize change and to introduce this change into our social and political reality: "This understanding of virtuality as the impetus for incipient action is itself a dynamizing concept, one which may serve feminist, anti-racist and other political movements by making clear that there is always a leap, an unexpectedness that the new brings with it, and that it is the goal of politics to initiate such leaps" (2000: 228–9). In this regard some unconscious libidinal investments may appear revolutionary even if they do not express any political interests or goals. Thus, feminist schizoanalysis should be very careful in examining these oscillations between preconscious and unconscious, revolutionary and reactionary investments. In more recent debates in feminist theory we can also discern the same opposition between the desire to create new stratification and the desire to dissolve into a general flux of becoming. As Grosz argues, in contemporary feminist practices we have a twofold choice:

> Either we ascribe to a theory of the subject that strives to have its identity affirmed through relations, especially relations of desire, but also relations of identification, with other subjects, a subject that seeks the recognition of others and a place as a subject within culture … or we ascribe to a theory of the impersonal (and ultimately a "politics of imperceptibility," the opposite of identity politics, a politics of acts, not identities), in which inhuman forces, forces that are both living and non-living … are acknowledged and allowed to displace the centrality of will and consciousness. (2002: 470)

The first theoretical choice, in Grosz's view, is guiding Judith Butler's theory of performativity, because performativity is enacted and supported only through the recognition of other subjects. Grosz points out that Butler's notion of subject-formation is deeply indebted to the Hegelian master and slave dialectics and the Lacanian model of identification with the Other. On the one hand, the individual has to gain his or her identity via the processes of identification with the Other, on the other hand, this identity has to be recognized by the Other. In this sense every plea for recognition gets involved in a Hegelian master and slave dialectics. Here we come to the question: Who is this Other with whom we want to identify? Isn't this model of identification just a more intelligent means of submission, which is internalized by the subject? As Grosz points out,

> In place of the desire for recognition as the condition for subjective identity, we need to begin with different working assumptions, which may cover some of the same issues as those conceived by identity politics … In place of the desire for recognition … we could place an account of subjectivity, identity, or agency at the mercy of forces, energies, practices, which produce an altogether different understanding of both politics and identity. (2002: 468)

Thus, instead of waiting for the master's patronizing recognition or "tolerance," we should invent new concepts and strategies for feminist politics. The most important point here is that political space does not have to be organized around individual identity and can be seen as a field of forces which are not necessarily human and identity oriented. As Grosz argues, "[p]olitics can be seen as the struggle of imperceptible forces, forces in us and around, forces in continual conflict; it is a useful fiction to imagine that we as subjects are masters or agents of these very forces that constitute us as subjects, but misleading" (2002: 471).

Contrary to identity politics, Grosz is trying to formulate what she calls "a politics of imperceptibility," based both on the Nietzschean notion of force and on Deleuze and Guattari's notion of becoming. For Nietzsche force is an agency, which is both human and nonhuman, quantitative and qualitative, active and passive. Force is always engaged in becoming; it seeks its own multiplication and expansion. As such, the Nietzschean force by nature is very close to the Deleuzian notion of becoming discussed earlier. The multiplication of forces, intensities, and becomings is also the main task of feminist schizoanalysis. Instead of engaging into reactionary investments related to the question of identity, production of meaning or subjectivity, feminist theory should invest into the processes of becoming, which connect and reconnect active and reactive, human and nonhuman, psychic and physical forces. As Grosz points out,

[I]t is no longer a subject that takes before it a subject with whom to identify, and an object on which to enact its desire or will; rather forces act through subjects, objects, material and social worlds without distinction, producing ... relations of intensity and force. They constitute an inhuman, sub-human field, a field of "particles" or elements of force which are only provisionally or temporarily grouped together in the form of entities and actions. (2002: 469)

In this respect feminist theory should seek not for identity and recognition but for expansion and multiplication of forces, which can connect with other forces. Thus becoming-imperceptible refers not to disappearance, self-annihilation or death, as Braidotti points out, but to connection with the world and its worldly forces.

Here we have to explain that the quest for becoming-imperceptible does not deny or exclude other feminist strategies. It is obvious, that, in a certain social or political situation, women have to regain their bodies, their speech, and their sexuality. However, once a feminine identity is conceptualized, it should be replaced by another goal or strategy. As Grosz points out, "[T]his future feminine may render itself obsolete or the object of profound and even inhuman (or imperceptible) becomings rather than rest itself on the forms of femininity as they have been represented and idealized within sexual indifference, within patriarchy as it has existed up to now" (2005: 177). The problem that we encounter here is that the quest for feminine subjectivity and identity is reactionary because it mirrors the relations of power which ground patriarchal and colonialist hierarchies. The feminist fight for women's rights and recognition temporarily changes the balance of power but does not change the existing social stratification. As Grosz explains,

Instead of a politics of recognition, in which subjected groups and minorities strive for a validated and affirmed place in public life, feminist and postcolonial politics should, I believe, now consider the affirmation of a politics of *imperceptibility*, leaving its traces and effects everywhere, but never being able to be identified with a person or an organization. It is not a politics of visibility, of recognition and of self-validation, but a process of self-marking that constitutes oneself in the very model of that which oppresses and opposes the subject. The imperceptible is that which the inhuman musters, that which the human can sometimes liberate from its own orbit but not control or name as its own. (2002: 471)

Jami Weinstein, interpreting Grosz, in a similar vein argues that "the ultimate goal of human becoming is becoming imperceptible," though being quite conscious that "feminists would also be hesitant about, if not completely antagonistic to, the idea that a fully successful feminist strategy is to aim for its own eradication" (2008: 25).

In her more recent book *Becoming Undone* (2011) Grosz argues that at least three feminist issues should be reformulated and reframed—first, the notion of identity and the plea for its recognition; second, the concern with the epistemological instead of ontological; and third, the concern with binary sexual difference instead of multiple becoming. The first issue was discussed already in this section—the idea to establish a feminist subject seeking recognition of others is seen as reactionary, going against the grain of schizoanalysis and contemporary philosophy. Grosz deconstructs the psychoanalytic model of recognition, revealing that it is useless for emancipatory politics:

Feminism ... cages itself in the reign of the "I": who am I, who recognizes me, what can I become? ... The subject seeks to be known and to be recognized, but only through its reliance on others, including the very others who function to collectively subjugate the subject ... And once the subject is recognized as such, what is created through this recognition? (Grosz 2011: 84)

In other words, instead of being fixed on the psychoanalytic model of recognition, we should create, invent, and experiment, which would enable new modes of existence. Here we come to the second point, that instead of raising epistemological questions (of what we are able to know), feminists should pose "questions of the nature and forces of the real, the nature and forces of the world, cosmological forces as well as historical ones" (Grosz 2011: 85). These are the forces of desire production, which reshape and invent new social relations, new assemblages, and connections. Here we come to the third point, that by producing schizo-flows which are real and make the real, feminism necessarily has to place the problem of sexual difference into the broad context of a "thousand tiny sexes," which may be human and nonhuman (animal), or human and inhuman (machinic). "Sexual difference is an invention of life itself which the human inherits from its prehuman past and its animal connections here and now ... In other words, feminism needs to direct itself to questions of complexity, emergence, and difference that the study of subjectivity shares in common with the study of chemical and biological phenomena" (Grosz 2011: 86). Human subject is part of a larger process of nonhuman evolution, therefore it should be analyzed in a much broader context of animal and molecular becoming, up to becoming-imperceptible at the level of matter itself. Here again we come to the conclusion that becoming-imperceptible is not the dissolution of the subject, but its connection with human and nonhuman forces, organic and inorganic materials.

3. Becoming-Imperceptible in Contemporary Art

The notion of becoming-imperceptible is very important in discussing contemporary art. While more conventional art forms rely on the representation of already existing time and space relationships, new forms of art invent new relationships between different modalities of time and space, thus creating the conditions for qualitative change. The practice of becoming-imperceptible can be seen as a practice of experimentation working on several levels: first, it is an attempt to abandon the anthropomorphic forms and defined gender identities and replace them with molecular transformations; second, it is an attempt to abandon the old forms of representation and open a space for non-anthropocentric imagery and virtual images. In this section I will analyze the works of female artists, which, while being associated with feminist art, detach themselves from defined forms of identity and follow the transformations of corporeal elements, such as substances, particles, and haecceities.

The first artist I would like to discuss is Teresa Margolles, working in Mexico City, and closely examining the life of bodies after their actual death. Margolles is a forensic pathologist, working in a morgue in Mexico City for many years. This explains why the protagonists of her works are unidentified bodies, the victims of drug-related crimes, military violence, or extreme poverty. Having in mind the social and political circumstances of this violence, the conventional artistic strategy would be to confront their death and disappearance with the action of identification. The victims of genocide or the Holocaust usually are commemorated by scrupulously reestablishing their identities and names. However, Margolles uses a different strategy: instead of reestablishing identities, she dissolves them into evanescent substances. For example, in *En el aire* (2003) we encounter a machine, blowing bubbles in an empty room, where they float elegantly and burst on visitor's heads. However, the reception of this work changes when the visitors realize that the bubbles are made of water which was collected after cleaning the bodies in a morgue. A similar strategy is used in *Aire* (2004), where the water taken from a morgue is used to humidify the room. In this case the water is evaporating in the air and filling the visitor's lungs. In both cases the molecules of dead bodies, contained in the water, are transformed into new substances, such as a bubble or a vapor, and continue their lives by entering into contact with other human bodies. Desirable or not, this contact forces the audience to reflect about the political and social circumstances causing the deaths of those bodies.

Other works by Margolles also consist of substances which were in close contact with unidentified bodies. In *Papeles* (2004) the artist uses the sheets of paper to make the imprints of body liquids which remain when the bodies are washed after autopsy. The imprints not only contain the real substances of dead bodies but also create a specific gallery of portraits of death. In *127 Bodies* (2006) she presents 127 surgical suture threads which were used to sew up the bodies after autopsy, and knots them into a string, stretched out in an empty gallery space. In these and many other works the artist relies not on the modes of identification, memory, and representation but on physical affectivity and direct contact. Margolles is not concerned whether these bodies were identified and recognized; she does not speak in terms of victims and perpetrators. Instead she invents the processes of molecular transformation, which allow these body particles to continue their lives postmortem in some inhuman but highly aesthetic and elegant form. In this sense the human body becomes impersonal, indiscernible, and imperceptible, but still existing in some virtual form—as a bubble, a vapor, or a liquid on an imprint. The body here is transformed into an abstract line, a trait, and enters into the general flow of becoming-imperceptible.

The second example is the work by the Lithuanian artist Kristina Inčiūraitė who regularly deals with gender issues. Inčiūraitė provides another strategy of becoming-imperceptible because she works not with bodies or substances but with mental images. Inčiūraitė's videos usually depict female characters in their specific social environment, but these female characters are not visible on the screen. In other words, the visible and perceptible dimension is suspended in order to demonstrate mental relations between what is visible and what remains invisible. For example, the video *Bathhouse* (2003) is constructed in such a way that it makes a contrast between the virtual image, which inspired the story, and the actual perception, which in its turn is split between visible and audible perception. The video was inspired by Gustav Machatý's film *Ecstasy* (1933), starring the Austrian actress Hedy Lamarr. In this movie the young actress performed naked in a swimming scene that lasted ten minutes. The video by Inčiūraitė, by contrast, depicts the bathhouse in Innsbruck that was opened in 1927. The video captures the empty premises of the bathhouse. The visual images are accompanied by interviews with students of the Innsbruck school of actors. They discuss such questions as performing nude, and the relationship between eroticism and shame. Although the interview is focused on the naked body and eroticism, the young female narrators are not visible, only imagined. What we actually see are the images of the bathhouse which traditionally is conceived as a place where nude bodies are exposed.

In this respect the video *Bathhouse* creates imagery which functions on three different levels: the first level is a virtual image of Hedy Lamarr performing naked in a swimming scene, which engenders the mainstream representation of a naked female body; the second level is an actual narrative by young female actresses, discussing eroticism and subjective bodily experience, although the actresses themselves remain invisible; the third level is the actual perception of the bathhouse images which show the traditional place where naked bodies are exposed without actually showing any body. This specific example reveals the force of becoming-imperceptible, when gender and sexual identities are dissolved into different layers: the virtual and the actual, the real and the imaginary, the visual and the audible. A certain politics of imperceptibility leaves behind the habitual visual scenario according to which the woman is represented as an erotic object: instead of scopic pleasure we are confronted with haecceities without subjectivities—with the cold images of water and ceramic tiles.

The more recent work by Kristina Inčiūraitė, *Nameless Hour* (2014), contains many cinematic references and also a participatory performance enacted by an LGBT group. As a starting point it takes the 1948 crime drama *Sorry, Wrong Number*, directed by Anatole Litvak. The film presents a female character, played by Barbara Stanwyck, who is confined to her bed. A woman is imprisoned in her bedroom, with no chance of escaping, and is eventually killed. This situation of absolute passivity is contrasted with the avant-garde film *Hand Movie* by Yvonne Rainer (1966). In *Hand Movie* the director Yvonne Rainer, being confined to a hospital bed while recovering from an operation, performs a hand dance in front of the camera. In this sense passive affects and forces are transformed into an active and creative action. These cinematic influences create the backdrop for the project's protagonist—members of a basketball team of the Lithuanian LGBT community. Contrary to our expectations, the protagonists of this project are not striving for recognition of their identities or struggling for their rights. Instead, they create a certain "politics of imperceptibility," a certain collective sensitivity, which is conceptualized as a "nameless hour"—it is a virtual extension of time, in which transformation becomes possible. The protagonists of this project have tried to collect their own negative experiences by referring to certain locations, situations, smells, that have a negative effect on them. All these collective experiences are visible in the film called *Nameless*, which refers not to subjects or individuals, but to qualities, particularities, intensities, nonhuman, or inhuman forces. In this sense the "politics of imperceptibility" can be interpreted not as vanishing or disappearance, but as an active medium for transformation. In this vein, the film *Nameless* is followed by other collective actions and gestures: for example, the helpless gestures of the female victim from the film *Sorry, Wrong Number* are repeated but also altered by the basketball players, which are trying to re-play these gestures in the trajectories of a basketball game. The sound of this basketball game is recorded in an audiovisual work *Barbara* (2014), which expresses the metamorphosis from passive and desperate gesture into a joyful action. The basketball players are also trying to repeat the gestures from Yvonne Rainer's film, in this way trying to extend and intensify their creative potential.

Thus the "politics of imperceptibility" is not an escape from visibility or a drive toward annihilation but a new conceptual strategy for postfeminist theory and contemporary art: becoming-imperceptible enables new material forces, both human and nonhuman, active and passive, qualitative and quantitative. Of course, some thinkers and artists might have reservations about this strategy, saying that becoming-imperceptible leads to abandoning the struggles of minority or subjugated groups which they conduct in seeking recognition and visibility. But the most important thing here is to remember and enact positive tasks of schizoanalysis: the first task is to detach oneself from the old logic of representation and identitarian thinking and move toward the flux of molecular becoming which can engender bodily modifications, political changes, and artistic innovations. The second task of schizoanalysis is to distinguish between preconscious libidinal investments and unconscious libidinal desires, which may be reactionary and seek the reconstruction of old power relationships. The third task of schizoanalysis is to examine desire not merely as an anthropomorphic phenomenon but as both a human and nonhuman (or posthuman) libidinal investment, as a desire which is immanent to the materiality of molecular becomings. And the last task of schizoanalysis is to create the sensitivity for what is not perceived and discerned by human consciousness: movement and affect. However, the "politics of imperceptibility" is not a defined program and it does not necessarily lead to a successful postfeminist strategy. On the one hand, it can disintegrate into chaos. On the other hand, it can make an unforeseen and unpredictable leap into a new social and political order.

References

Braidotti, R. (1994), *Nomadic Subjects: Embodiment and Sexual Difference in Contemporary Feminist Theory*, New York: Columbia University Press.

Braidotti, R. (2002), *Metamorphoses: Towards a Materialist Theory of Becoming*, Cambridge: Polity Press.

Braidotti, R. (2006a), *Transpositions: On Nomadic Ethics*, Cambridge: Polity Press.

Braidotti, R. (2006b), "The Ethics of Becoming-Imperceptible," in C. V. Boundas (ed.), *Deleuze and Philosophy*, 133–59, Edinburgh: Edinburgh University Press.

Braidotti, R. (2013), *The Posthuman*, Cambridge: Polity Press.

Deleuze, G., and F. Guattari (2004a), *Anti-Oedipus. Capitalism and Schizophrenia*, trans. R. Hurley, M. Seem, and H. R. Lane, New York: Continuum.

Deleuze, G., and F. Guattari (2004b), *A Thousand Plateaus: Capitalism and Schizophrenia*, trans. B. Massumi, London: Continuum.

Diamond, C. (2001), "Injustice and Animals," in Carl Elliott (ed.), *Slow Cures and Bad Philosophers: Essays on Wittgenstein, Medicine, and Bioethics*, 118–48, Durham, NC: Duke University Press.

Grosz, E. (1994), *Volatile Bodies: Toward a Corporeal Feminism*, Bloomington: Indiana University Press.

Grosz, E. (2000), "Deleuze's Bergson: Duration, the Virtual and a Politics of the Future," in I. Buchanan and C. Colebrook (eds.), *Deleuze and Feminist Theory*, 214–34, Edinburgh: Edinburgh University Press.

Grosz, E. (2002), "A Politics of Imperceptibility: A Response to 'Anti-racism, Multiculturalism and the Ethics of Identification,'" *Philosophy and Social Criticism* 28 (4): 463–72.

Grosz, E. (2005), *Time Travels: Feminism, Nature, Power*, Crow's Nest, Australia: Allen & Unwin.

Grosz, E. (2011), *Becoming Undone: Darwinian Reflections on Life, Politics, and Art*, Durham, NC: Duke University Press.

Holland, E. W. (1999), *Deleuze and Guattari's Anti-Oedipus: Introduction to Schizoanalysis*, London: Routledge.

Holland, E. W. (2013), *Deleuze and Guattari's A Thousand Plateaus*, London: Bloomsbury.

Weinstein, J. (2008), "Introduction Part II," in C. Colebrook and J. Weinstein (eds.), *Deleuze and Gender, Deleuze Studies* 2 (supplement), 20–33, Edinburgh: Edinburgh University Press.

CHAPTER 3
UNDOING THE SUBJECT: FEMINIST AND SCHIZOANALYTIC CONTRIBUTIONS TO POLITICAL DESUBJECTIFICATION

Erinn Cunniff Gilson

Feminist, critical, psychoanalytic, and post-structuralist theories, and combinations thereof, have for the last fifty years or so regularly postulated and analyzed the undoing of coherent sovereign subjectivity. The modern subject, as both a metaphysical and a political entity, has been theorized as, among other things, nonidentical, divided, opaque, ecstatic, layered, and formed through processes both habitual and structurally arranged. Such visions of the subject include theories of psychic complexity, in particular those of unconscious dimensions of the self; feminist contestation of the sovereign masculine subject and articulation of subjectivity's grounding in relations of dependency and otherness, specifically feminine otherness; post-structuralist deconstruction of notions of unitary, self-same identity in terms of its constitutive relation with difference; and critical theories of the disillusionment of modern subjectivity concomitant with the fragmentary conditions of contemporary political and social life.

Accordingly, there are many ways to understand what it means to undo subjectivity: to emphasize its construction through difference, its non-sovereignty defined in terms of dependency or multiplicity, the centrality of interconnection and constitutive relationality, our own opacity to ourselves and thus our inability to know ourselves fully and determine our own actions willfully, and so on. All accounts of the undone subject, however, contrast such subjectivity with the supposition of a masterful, atomistic, coherent, self-transparent, freely willing and acting, and implicitly masculine, able-bodied, white, and colonizing subject. To undo the subject is often conceived as a project of destabilizing this form of subjectivity or, when it is conceded that such sovereign masterful subjectivity never actually existed nor could exist, this *ideal* of subjectivity. Sovereignty or pretensions to it are taken as a target while asserting its illusoriness or falsity.[1] Indeed, the very language of decentering and destabilizing presumes that there is a stable *something* at the center of subjectivity and that subjectivity itself lies at the center of our feelings, thoughts, and actions. What has been taken as a main target, therefore, has been a fiction. When acknowledged as a fiction, sovereign subjectivity is parsed as merely a mode of experience, an illusion or guise, rather than an ontological reality. Even then, however, it is still taken to be central. Proportionally less attention has been paid to examining the many and varied modes of the undoing with which we live: How is the subject constitutively undone? How can different modes of undoing best be described? What are the implications of diverse ways of being undone? Is subjectivity really constructed as a veneer of coherence despite its fragmentary constitution? How might it be undone strategically? And to what ends?

Both feminist theory and Deleuzoguattarian schizoanalysis have interrogated conceptions of subjectivity and theorized subjectivity's undoing or destabilization. As such, both are approaches that can deepen our understanding of what it means for the subject to be undone and whether and how such an undoing can contribute anything of significance to emancipatory movements. Accordingly, the project of this chapter is to work through the different ways of parsing the complexity of non-sovereign subjectivity specifically from feminist and Deleuzoguattarian perspectives. Subsequently I inquire into how subjectivity might productively be undone for transformative or emancipatory ends and, more to the point, what productively undoing subjectivity might entail given the challenges of contemporary neoliberal capitalism, in particular its tendency to co-opt counter-movements, transgressions, and modes of resistance. Thus, the two core questions of the chapter are (1) What does it mean to undo the subject?—the focus of sections 1 and 2; and (2) How might undoing the subject be central to contesting capitalism and oppression?—addressed in section 3.

More specifically, the chapter explores what Deleuze and Guattari's work, in particular their method of schizoanalysis, can contribute to feminist thinking concerning the subject and what a broadly anti-oppressive feminism can contribute to the deployment of the schizoanalysis of the subject. Throughout the two volumes of *Capitalism and Schizophrenia*, Deleuze and Guattari invoke processes of desubjectification and deindividualization, alternately and simultaneously describing these as inevitable, irrepressible movements and as processes strategically undertaken in resistance to dominant norms. This point in the Deleuzoguattarian corpus has provoked the strong critique from feminist quarters that such calls for desubjectification emerge, suspiciously and problematically, only after women have begun to claim their own political subjectivity.[2] The secondary aim of the chapter, therefore, is to forge an alliance between Deleuzoguattarian and feminist thought by transforming each beyond its own comfort in order to disturb and undermine the limiting and oppressive structures of contemporary capitalism and its expression in neoliberal logics.[3] I do so by weighing the value of desubjectification—an undoing of the self—for radical politics.

Before turning to some feminist approaches to the undoing of the subject, I distinguish some of the different senses in which the subject could be said to be undone. To undo the subject refers both to an alternative ontology of the subject, namely one that runs counter to a metaphysics of substance and to a project undertaken with the aim of subjective undoing. We can distinguish three forms of undoing. These forms overlap and interrelate rather than being wholly separable either in their theoretical sources or their concrete implications.

First, there is an *ontological* or ontogenetic undoing in which the subject is conceived as divided, split within itself, fragmented, and/or multiple. This form of undoing is an outgrowth of a developmental and processual understanding of ontology, and refers to the ways the self is formed through relations with others although the nature of this relationality differs: psychoanalytic accounts emphasize the constitutive quality of early relations with caregivers; post-structuralist accounts attend to the power and its expression in social norms as the mediating milieu in which relations with others take place; Black and Latina feminism articulate identity as intersectional and characterized by multiplicity.[4] The common thread, however, is that the subject is not unified, uniform, or necessarily coherent. The subject is relational in two interrelated senses: in the sense that the subject is always in the making, in process, rather than a terminal point or ultimate achievement, and in the sense that it is composed of pieces that are more or less known and more or less synthesized. These pieces of the self include corporeal gestures and comportment, affects, ideas and beliefs, modes of response and engagement, and so on, all of which are produced via various specific relations and modes of connection. Such relational dimensions of the subject can be both habitual, sedimented through repetition, and intermittent, occasional or spontaneous in expression. In these two ways, undoing the subject is a challenge to traditional substance metaphysics: the subject is neither unified nor an enduring entity.[5]

Second, and subsequent, there is what we might call an *epistemic undoing* in which the knowing subject is decentered and destabilized. This kind of undoing stems from critiques of the centrality of reason and conscious awareness, of the partiality and bias of the perspectives of dominant subjects (white, cis-gender, heterosexual, able-bodied, male, colonizing), and of the assumption that the subject is transparent to itself and thus intentional in its beliefs and actions.

Third, there is a *politico-ethical undoing* that takes the form of a deindividualization, indeed a desubjectification, of the subject, a turning away from the quintessential idea of the individual as the locus of experience, thought, value, and action. Such a deindividualization is a hallmark of schizoanalysis. Here it suffices to note that this form of undoing can be described as politico-ethical even as it is rooted in the supposition of an ontological undoing because it is conceived both as having ethico-political implications and, when undertaken strategically, as being an ethico-political move itself. In what follows, I consider how these forms of undoing are elaborated in feminist theories before turning in section 2 to Deleuze and Guattari's schizoanalytic approach.

1. Feminist Reframings of the Subject

Contra the conventional views of the subject within the history of philosophy—the oft referenced atomistic self as an isolated, independent individual—feminist theorists have centered attention on elements of the subject that have been overlooked, devalued, or denied: embodiment, emotion, dependency on others, and the particularity of social location. In particular, feminist thinkers have reconstructed an understanding of the subject that centered on relationality. This vision of the self is a developmental one, countering the mythic Hobbesian man who emerges ex nihilo like a mushroom from the ground. Against that notion of sovereign subjectivity, the subject is conceived as unavoidably interdependent and interconnected; it develops only through relationships and is relationally constituted. Such a view amounts to an undoing of subjectivity insofar as it departs from the presumptions of unity, coherence, self-transparency, and rational volition that characterize an ideal of sovereign subjectivity. The idea of relational subjectivity, however, is elaborated in distinct ways.

One idea of a feminist relational subject focuses on how the defining qualities and capacities of the self are relationally produced. By shifting attention to relations of dependency and care that sustain us, a feminist idea of relational subjectivity shows that these relations are formative because they are a precondition for developing a sense of self and the capacities that come to define us as selves. Feminist theorists of relational autonomy take this tack.[6] They displace masculinist assumptions about the independence and self-sufficiency of the subject and establish that autonomy is grounded in relationality rather than being in opposition to it. On this kind of view, the role of relationality is that of a backdrop for a developmental view of the subject; we cannot do without relations because it is in the context of such relations that we are nurtured and delivered into the world as more capable beings. Yet, such "prevalent Western [feminist] views ... of self-identity commonly invoke a tale of early dependency upon the family and the eventual achievement of autonomy through narratives of separation and virtues of independence and self-determination" (Willett et al. 2016). That is, this kind of account may lend itself to the imposition of teleological narratives of normal or ideal development, and thus stipulation of proper forms of relationality for distinct stages of development (less and less dependency, more and more autonomy).

Another perspective takes the centrality of relations of care and dependency to have implications for the kinds of subjects we are: more fragile, more dependent, and less self-sufficient beings than we might have thought we were or desired to be. Given this reality, the ethical and political conclusions we draw from our stipulations about our "nature" ought to change. Eva Kittay proposes that "our societies should be structured to accommodate inevitable dependency within a dignified, flourishing life ... [and, further,] if we see ourselves as always selves-in-relation, we understand that our own sense of well-being is tied to the adequate care and well-being of another" (2011: 54). Policy, social structure, and ethical norms need to change to recognize and respond to the fact of dependency and the care-giving and care-receiving relationships that accompany it, as do our attitudes toward our selves so that we acknowledge rather than disavow our interdependent existences, our intertwined selves and fates.

Judith Butler's approach to relational subjectivity takes the ontological undoing of the subject further. The subject just is how it has been affected by others, the environment, and the norms of the social world and how it has engaged and responded to them. Emphasizing the constitutive nature of relational subjectivity leads to the conclusion that we are fundamentally dispossessed of ourselves. Our traits, capacities, our very subjectivity are not *ours* per se, not proprietary. They only ever come into existence as part of us by way of our being affected by others. Butler's conception of ec-static subjectivity expresses this idea, "To be ec-static means, literally, to be outside oneself," which entails that "I cannot be who I am without drawing upon the sociality of norms that precede and exceed me. In this sense, I am outside myself from the outset, and must be, in order to survive, and in order to enter into the realm of the possible" (2004: 20,

32). Butler's rendering of the undone subject foregrounds a kind of vulnerability that is constitutive of the self. We are vulnerable to others and the social milieu in which we find ourselves as both embodied and social beings. Our emergence as selves is conditioned by the publicity of the body—its visibility and openness to touch—and the way in which we can only develop a sense of ourselves through recourse to social norms, the forms of intelligibility offered us by our social world. An epistemic undoing follows: ec-static subjectivity entails that one cannot know oneself fully and that attempts to understand and account for one's desires, intentions, and impulses are beset by failure from the start. Our opacity to ourselves hinders our ability to narrate our lives and more specifically the reasons for our actions, suggesting the need for "another ethical disposition in the place of a full and satisfying notion of narrative accountability" (Butler 2005: 40). Consequently, there is a fundamental ambivalence to subjectivity: the norms that underlie subject formation are often as constraining as they are productive.

Other feminists thinkers inspired by Friedrich Nietzsche and Michel Foucault elaborate the ambivalent bind of subjectivity—in a nutshell, its simultaneously enabling and constraining effects—and the fundamental non-unitariness that is a condition for this bind. Premised on the fragmented or divided nature of the subject, the critiques of subjectivity offered by Wendy Brown and Dianna Taylor provide insight into the challenges facing a notion of relational subjectivity. Rather than regard the relational subject as an ideal with which to counter the sovereignty of the masculine subject, they reckon with the ambivalence of subjectivity itself.

Taylor analyzes Foucault's genealogy of hermeneutical subjectivity, that is, the form of subjectivity that entails that the self has an essence, an internal truth that is discoverable through processes of interpretation. This "hermeneutical self-relation [that begins in early Christianity] … characterizes modern Western subjectivity. Modern subjectivization as he sees it thus inherits and continues to be characterized by a power relation that is clearly normalizing" (Taylor 2013: 91). Taylor argues that subjectivity is a normalizing form of self-relation because it retains and is rooted in self-renunciation and obedience. To relate to oneself as an interpretable being and to seek to know the truth of oneself, one must submit to the frameworks for intelligibility that guide and govern this hermeneutic posture. In early Christianity these frameworks for interpretation were external and one had to verbalize one's obedience via confession to authorities who possessed the requisite knowledge of them. In modernity, however, the Kantian notion of enlightenment required renouncing immaturity through adherence to the subject's own use of reason, which amounts to an internalization of the relation of obedience: one gives the law to oneself rather than submitting to another's law. What is at stake in modernity, therefore, is not overt obedience but conformity through normalization and, on the Foucaultian account, a conformity that finds its way into our relation to ourselves to the extent that increased capacity is continually tied to increased obedience to norms (as in the achievement of greater rationality, self-determination, and self-control). Thus, Taylor maintains, subjectivity continues to be a "renunciation of ourselves"; moreover, its very structure impedes our ability to perceive both the tie between conformity and capacity and the self-renunciation embedded in our relation to ourselves (2017: 46).

Taylor thus demonstrates the historical longevity of the non-unitary subject. Self-renouncing subjectivity requires that the subject is not one with itself: there must be pieces of the self to bring to consciousness, to confess, to control, and ultimately to repudiate. Modern forms of self-renunciation, however, produce the paradigmatic ideal of sovereign subjectivity: the rational, masculine, sovereign lawgiver. This subject must renounce "the most repugnant part of" itself, namely, the facets of itself that would prevent it from achieving masterful autonomy: its passive, weak, obedient, conformist aspects (Taylor 2017: 46). Yet it does so in the context and as a consequence of normalization, paradoxically repudiating obedience out of an (ostensibly self-imposed) obligation to obey. Accordingly, Taylor concludes that subjectivity itself is a particularly harmful mode of self-relation for women, for whom obedience and self-renunciation are often both regarded as natural and prescribed: "When we merely assert our-selves as subjects, we thereby keep in play the dynamic of obedience and conformity that subjectivity, construed in terms of autonomous and rational agency, is supposed [but fails] to overcome—which of course makes us assert ourselves as subjects all the more vigorously" (2013: 91). The bind of subjectivity, thus, is deeper than we might have thought.

Whereas Taylor focuses on the structure of subjectivity, Brown identifies problems with how this structure manifests in modern liberal political subjectivity. In a now oft-cited essay, "Wounded Attachments," Brown critically analyzes contemporary identity politics of race, gender, and sexuality in liberal democracies. Although these identities emerge as politicized, they are depoliticized by liberalism, which renders political identity as "essentialized private interest," and by disciplinary power, which shapes it as "normativized identity manageable by regulatory regimes" (Brown 1993: 393). Paired with the absence of continued critique of capitalism, she argues that identity politics have become "tethered to a formulation of justice which, ironically, reinscribes a bourgeois ideal as its measure" (ibid.: 394). Although identity politics protest exclusion from a form of justice that is conceived as universal, and seek inclusion within it, in so doing they are premised upon status quo bourgeois norms (ibid.). Brown suggests that this ideal is retained especially insofar as "the injuries suffered by these identities are measured by bourgeois norms of social acceptance, legal protection, relative material comfort, and social independence" (ibid.).

The contradictory structure of subjectivity that Taylor identifies, one in which the subject eschews its submissiveness and conformity but engages in self-renunciation on the basis of the imperatives of normalization, also underlies Brown's analysis. In a Nietzschean assessment, Brown concludes that the ideal of liberal individualism and self-reliance produces *ressentiment* for all subjects given their inevitable failure in relation to this ideal and the power it has to mask the conditions under which subjects are becoming: "[I]t is their situatedness within power, their production by power, and liberal discourse's denial of this situatedness and production that casts the liberal subject into failure, the failure to make itself in the context of a discourse in which its self-making is assumed, indeed, is its assumed nature" (Brown 1993: 401). Thus, the subject either internalizes his own abjection or casts blame outward in a resentful projection, or some combination thereof. The identities of identity politics are also structured by such resentment and are relationally defined in opposition to dominant identities. Since they are invested in the norms of (neo)liberalism, they are invested in their own subjection to such norms. A resentful attachment to and identification with one's woundedness—that is, one's identity qua excluded and marginalized—manifests in a focus on censure, blame, and punishment. Although Taylor focuses on *self*-renunciation rather than externalized blame, Brown's conclusion is consonant with her assessment that subjectivity is premised upon a twinned self-renunciation and self-assertion: the political subject can become resentful only because its relation to itself is one of self-renunciation, a repudiation of that which is abject, namely, failure in relation to (neo)liberal ideals.

What these analyses bring to the fore is the problematic structure of subjectivity and the reactive, self-repudiating movement of attachment that defines modern subjectivity at its heart. From a feminist Foucaultian perspective, a core problem with subjectivity is not its unitariness or sovereignty but rather how the divisions internal to subjectivity are deployed to conceal the processes through which it is continually constructed: subjectivity's "situatedness within power," the coproduction of conformity and capacity. The fragmentary structure of subjectivity becomes cruel, harmful, and restrictive because it is enmeshed in normalizing power relations that require self-denial. This harm and constriction is maintained because we don't see how we are produced as subjects. The constitutive relationality of subjectivity, thus, is not an antidote to masculine sovereignty but an ambivalent underpinning and the notion of a relational subject does not undo subjectivity per se but points to the problems it raises.

Involvement in normalizing power relations, however, requires subjectivity's attachment not only to particular traits, norms, and forms of identity (e.g., race, gender, sexuality) but also, perhaps more fundamentally, to subjectivity itself. Subjectivity requires identification with itself and, in the contemporary capitalist social world, with the self as an individual: the individual subject as the locus of desire and interest, intention and action, and thought and experience.[7] Butler's account of dispossession and Taylor's critique of the structure of subjectivity altogether lead in an alternative direction: away from a reformulated subject to a desubjectified self. We find in Deleuze and Guattari an account of such a self, a thoroughly depersonalized subject.

2. Schizoanalytic Undoings of the Subject

Deleuze and Guattari's ontological account of the undone subject construes the subject as process and a movement. Specifically, it is the residuum of processes of interaction between desiring-machines and social formations. As process, the subject may be a movement of traversal, "on the periphery, with no fixed identity, forever decentered, *defined* by the states through which it passes," just as well as a process that consolidates identity through redundancy and territoriality (Deleuze and Guattari 1983: 20). As such, the subject might be nomadic, schizo, a bourgeois private individual, and so on, but in all cases is what it is in virtue of the mutable relations between its desiring-machines and the social formation. This section considers first Deleuze and Guattari's analysis of how desire is colonized in order to construct the subject within the social machine that is capitalism, producing the private individual. Then it turns to the critical work of schizoanalysis and their expressions of an egoless, nomadic subject. Given their ontology of process, both figurations are instances of non-sovereign subjectivity.

Although the critical analysis of *Anti-Oedipus* revolves around the Oedipal complex and the way it corners and captures desire, the critique has broader implications. The problem they pose, as Foucault puts it in the preface to the text, is "the fascism in us all, in our heads and in our everyday behavior, the fascism that causes us to love power, to desire the very thing that dominates and exploits us" (1983: xiii). Schizoanalysis aims to address this problem of micro-fascism, the basis for our actual desire for subjugation, which requires analyzing the co-implication of desire and the social domain. If "*social production is purely and simply desiring-production itself under determinate conditions*" and desiring-machines and social machines only ever exist as mutually affecting, then we must identify these determinate conditions and how they shape desire (Deleuze and Guattari 1983: 29). The Oedipal complex is central to this analysis not just because of the fact that it corrals desire but because of how it does so. In the Freudian paradigm, "[d]esiring-production is personalized, or rather personologized" (55). Oedipus, latent within prior social formations, both sets the stage for and comes to fruition in capitalism. The Oedipal complex enables capitalism precisely because it is defined by the personalization, interiorization, and privatization of desire: the movement of desire "must reverberate in the pure and private element of interiority, of interior reproduction ... [and desire] will have to experience this extreme affliction of being turned against itself" (217). The Oedipal frame privatizes desire by interpreting it as detached from its animating social conditions and context, locating it within an individual unconscious and thus denying the salience of group or collective desire, fantasies, and dynamics (the flows of the social world). Desire and the social, however, are always co-implicated in one another and, thus, desire is never purely individual. Therefore, the critique of Oedipus is not just a critique of desire as lack but, even more fundamentally, of the individualization that is the condition of the possibility for the micro-fascist investments of desire that enable capitalism, and which need not only or primarily be expressed in Oedipus.

On Deleuze and Guattari's account, capitalism is defined by decoding, freeing flows of desire from the delimited codes for social use and meaning to which they were subjected. Thus, it destabilizes the qualities attributed to things, opening them to other uses and meanings. By decoding in this way, this movement of deterritorialization both enables these flows to be subordinated to the capitalist quantifying axiomatic, its rule of quantification, and opens space for reterritorialization: what modern societies "*deterritorialize with one hand, they reterritorialize with the other*" (Deleuze and Guattari 1983: 257). By freeing flows of desire from code, capitalism, on the one hand, produces schizophrenia as both a syndrome and a movement of unruly energy in response to capital. On the other hand, since this movement is capitalism's absolute limit and ultimate undoing, it is also one "against which it brings all its vast powers of repression to bear" (34). As a consequence, "[e]verything returns or recurs: States, nations, families" and "ancillary apparatuses, such as government bureaucracies and the forces of law and order, do their utmost to reterritorialize" (34). For these reasons, capitalism and its effects on desire and the subject are profoundly ambivalent.

Deleuze and Guattari specify that capitalist decoding takes two forms: (1) privatization, as in the privatizing function of property, and (2) abstraction, as in commodity production in which the abstract quantity that is money replaces the qualities involved in particular patterns of use (140). These forms of decoding and the quantifying axiomatic that comprises capitalism's essential movement entail that capitalism can accommodate, co-opt, anything: "[I]ts axiomatic is never saturated" and it creates new axioms to incorporate anything and everything, especially whatever would undermine it (250). For persons to "become 'private' in reality" is for them to be rendered fungible as abstract quantities because they are abstracted away from the specific kinds of collective functions and meanings (codes) that demarcated what was possible for them; they are made concrete again "in the becoming-concrete of these same quantities" (251). Thus, the individual subject is just those abstract quantities, labor or capital, fit into an axiom. Privatization, however, does not mean that persons are abstracted away from social roles but rather that the social is subordinated to economic axioms, concretized therein. Accordingly, "[I]ndividual persons are social persons first of all, i.e., functions derived from the abstract quantities," preordained to be workers, consumers, capitalists, and so on (Deleuze and Guattari 1983: 263–4). Given that persons amount to abstract quantities—"the capitalist as personified capital," "the worker as personified labor capacity"—they "are an illusion, images of images" (264).

The conditions necessary for capitalism – privatization, individualization, and interiorization – make possible a subject of bad conscience, a repressed subject for whom desire is lack and in whom "desire lets itself be caught" (266). The classic expression of bad conscience—"the double direction given to *ressentiment*, the turning back against oneself, and the projection against the Other"—is mobilized by capital and its "ancillary apparatuses" (269). Directing desire inward, or inward then back outward, prevents desire from overrunning, undermining, and disrupting the capitalist machine. In this way, "[T]he colony becomes intimate and private, interior to each person," and subjects become desirous of their own subjugation: beings who identify with their subjectivity as image, and whose desire is consolidated around that image and the images—father, mother, racialized Other, sexualized Other, and so on—that circulate with it (269). The bourgeois capitalist subject thus constructed is also a narcissistic one: "the little ego of each person ... is truly the center of the world" (265). Micro-fascism requires this kind of subject: one that is split through the creation of interiority, one that is individualized as an abstract quantity, one that identifies with and through those abstract quantities represented as images.

In summation, on this account, the subject in general is a continually reconstituted product of complicated processes. Process, Deleuze and Guattari propose, means, first, that "[e]verything is production," including what we conceive as consumption or social formation; second, that there is no difference between human and natural production or between producer and product; and third, that processes of production do not constitute ends in themselves, are discrete and have their own duration rather than constituting movements that must be indefinitely extended and intensified (Deleuze and Guattari 1983: 4–5). The interlacing of desiring machines and social machines is process. Desiring machines move and produce through flows that diverge from one another, by objects that are detached from these flows, and finally, by generating a subject as a residuum. The subject "consumes and consummates each of the states through which it passes, and is born of each of them anew, continuously emerging from them as a part made up of parts" (41). As such, it lacks a center or core; it is not an entity, an ego as a locus of experience, that moves through these states but is a residual accumulation that happens in virtue of the movement of production (21). Although the subject is always processual, processes differ in virtue of the dynamics of the flows involved and the objects connected and broken-off from these flows. Thus, the individualized, personalized subject is neither pregiven and essential nor coherent and centered, but a residuum of trapped, redundant desire. In contrast, the nomadic, decentered schizo subject is one for which the traversal movement continues as a free and "inclusive disjunction ... in drifting from one term to another" rather than returning over and again to the same molar terms or the same representative images. This subject is a process marked by "the loss of the Ego" is depersonalized rather than individualized (77, 84).

Thus, the desubjectified subject of schizoanalysis amounts to a radicalization of the relational self elaborated by some feminist theorists. The processual nature of the Deleuzoguattarian subject is unremitting. Again, it is not an "I" that moves through states and relations that affect it, but a residual accumulation that simply learns "the habit of saying 'I' " through the repetition of certain kinds of relational connections (Deleuze 1991: x). Moreover, whereas many feminist accounts retain a relational subject as a locus of intention and volition, action and experience, the nomadic subject as residuum might be understood, on the one hand, as basically asubjective in its depersonalization and, on the other hand, as fundamentally processual and thus always open to change. Deleuze and Guattari's vision of the subject might thus advance feminist theories further. A main question of the next section is to what extent this radicalization enables emancipatory change. Deleuze and Guattari's account also helps us understand not only how the subject can desire its own subjection, an analysis also offered by Foucaultian feminists, but how the relational subject in particular does so. That is, they expose how the subject as process, as relationally constituted, becomes micro-fascist and how its processual nature is, fundamentally, ambivalent. Thus, Deleuze and Guattari's analysis of the ambivalence of the movement of decoding and deterritorialized, and its effects on subjectivity, gives us cause to rethink assumptions about the revolutionary power of the freed flows of desire. In response to the colonization of desire in capital, schizoanalysis entails both a theoretical project of discovering and analyzing the investments that conduce subjects to desire their own exploitation and a practical project of *reversion* to process as an unknown, potentially joyous becoming (Deleuze and Guattari 1983: 112). These two projects are necessarily conjoined. Given the tendency of capital both to check and to co-opt deterritorialized flows, the free reign of the flow of process in and of itself may be futile, fascistic, or destructive. Avoiding haphazard, catastrophic deterritorialization requires careful, "very deliberate analysis," and it is on this point that feminist concerns valuably complement this project of desubjectification (116).

3. Convergences Contra Capital

Whereas the two prior sections elaborated what it means for the subject to be undone and what it looks like to begin with processes and relations rather than an assumption of a coherent, dominant, sovereign subject that needs to be decentered, this concluding section turns to the question of how to undo the subject in ways that contest capitalism and the forms of normalization and oppression that characterize the contemporary social world. Amidst this examination, I also assess the worry of feminist critics that the desubjectification and destabilization of the subject advanced by Deleuze and Guattari is perilous for feminist politics. As I suggested in an earlier essay, a major tension between the Deleuzoguattarian perspective and a sympathetic feminist one lies in the fact "that many feminists espouse the need to pay heed to the experience[s] of women qua women while Deleuzian becoming dismantles molar identities such as that of 'woman'" (Gilson 2011: 75). Desubjectification may be premised on dismantling molar identities but might also reconfigure how the terms of so-called molar identities are experienced and thought. I argue that desubjectification need not be perilous, especially if we understand undoings of the subject to be as momentary as any subjective formation and potentially strategic rather than total. To make this assessment, I consider the pressing problems to which feminism must respond contemporarily and some of the traps to which feminism has and is falling prey.

Three common traps for feminism can be summarized as neoliberal or "choice" feminism, representational feminism, and carceral or disciplinary feminism. Although initially a manifestation of classical liberal feminism, the appellation "choice" feminism, or "lifestyle feminism" as defined by bell hooks, is now a hallmark of neoliberal feminism.[8] It declares that any choice made by a woman is a feminist choice because women are assumed to be autonomous, volitional, free, and sovereign subjects, and neoliberal permutations place additional weight on the significance of these choices by rendering all choices as opportunities to maximize women's human capital through calculation in accordance with capitalism's quantifying axiomatic. As Catherine Rottenberg notes, the neoliberal feminist shift away from a critical feminist "attempt to alter social pressures towards interiorized affective spaces that require constant self-monitoring is precisely the node through which liberal feminism is rendered hollow and transmuted into a mode of neoliberal governmentality" (2013: 424). Representational feminism accompanies choice feminism as a relic of liberalism: it entails a focus on the symbolic representation of women both in visible positions of power and prestige and as visible in statistically salient numbers. "Carceral feminism" describes the tendency of the mainstream feminist movement to rely on state intervention to attempt to prevent and respond to violence against women, thus reinforcing the violent logics and action of the State and the vulnerabilities of those who are most marginalized by it, women of color in particular. With a broader lens, carceral feminism is one manifestation of a disciplinary and corrective ethos within feminism, one animated by the tendencies to blame, judgment, and policing that Brown eschews.

These modes of feminism involve a range of errors. Choice feminism deepens the interiorization, individualization, and privatization that characterize capitalism and so diverts feminist attention from broader conditions of social, economic, and political inequality, encouraging both self-disciplining and normalization and greater depoliticization. Representational feminism assumes the bourgeois, white male norm— the power and status of the CEO or the political representative—and that visible representation of women in such positions of power will alter beliefs, attitudes, and habits, as well as altering structural conditions for the rest of women and other marginalized people. Yet, such representation is merely symbolic and remains disconnected from material change to remedy inequality and oppression. A disciplinary and corrective ethos amounts to fascist tendencies within feminism. Such an ethos impedes collaborative alliances, checking dissent and requiring diverse constituents to toe the party line. All in all, these errors show how implicated certain varieties of feminism are in capitalist machinery and the accompanying resentful structure of subjectivity.

These errors are especially harmful in light of pressing contemporary problems to which feminism must respond for emancipatory ends. Two prominent problems are of special concern since they call the politics of identity into question and have recently been thrown into relief: first, the ability of disparate groups to achieve collectivity (e.g., so-called populist political groups); second, the proliferation of specific politicized affects that enable collectivity (such as fear, anger, resentment, and hatred). Political mobilization via affective resonance is brought to the fore in the context of increasingly complex political-economic systems: affectively charged anti-immigrant rhetoric, for instance, binds resentful white people in the United States across socioeconomic classes and circulates as a way of avoiding the actual complexity of a globalized economic structure. Feminism and other movements countering oppression must deal with and respond to those increasingly complex and multilayered politico-economic systems and the injustices embedded within and obscured by them, as well as to the possibility for political mobilization through affect.

In light of these traps and these pressing problems, does desubjectification pose a threat or constitute a resource for emancipatory feminist politics? One way to answer this question is to consider the nature of the target. If both fascism and micro-fascism develop via process and relations, then what is needed to effect emancipatory change is not dispensing with the (ideological) illusion of sovereign, dominant subjectivity but rather altering modes of process and relation, that is, the habits that compose modes of self-relation. If the subject is already undone, then harmful patterns of intra- and intersubjective relation stem not from sovereignty or even pretensions to it but from redundant, habitual modes of relating that corral desire and install a sedimented resentful, self-preoccupied, interiorized individual subject. Thus, the conclusions we draw from Deleuze and Guattari's account coincide with the conclusions of feminist Foucaultians like Taylor: if the structure of subjectivity itself is fraught–comprised of a self-renouncing self relation—then desubjectification is an opportunity to undermine that form of self relation that facilitates normalization and the capitalist domestication of desire.

More specifically, we can consider how affect constitutes the self and, especially, animates both fascism and micro-fascism, which are defined by the domestication of desire by particular types of affect. On Deleuze and Guattari's account, the states through which the subject passes are ones of affective intensity and hence it is through the "intensive emotion, the affect" that the process that is the subject takes place (1983: 84). Following the kernel of a concept of affect in *Anti-Oedipus*, Sara Ahmed (2014) and other affect theorists focus on the relational and mobile qualities of affect. As Teresa Brennan (2004) charted, affect is transmitted, it flows, and thus is both generative and generated. Ahmed theorizes how affect circulates, as do the objects of affects, the subjects who are traversed by them, the words, images, beliefs, and events that elicit and convey them. Affect is a vehicle for connecting. When it recirculates, linking the same objects, it binds people to themselves and each other in identity and collectivity. In particular, certain affects fix desire on the self, circumscribing the movement of its desiring machines and consolidating interiorized individual subjectivity and rigid identities. Resentment is evidently one such affect but the so-called positive affects, for example, love and happiness, have also been recognized as often serving a similar function. Rottenberg's analysis of the neoliberal feminist subject, for instance, analyzes the role that the imperative to achieve happiness plays in the constitution of that subject: "The very turn to a language of affect, namely, the importance of the pursuit of *personal* happiness (through balance), unravels any notion of *social* inequality by placing the responsibility of well-being, as well as the burden of unhappiness, once again, on the shoulders of individual women … turning that subject even more intensively inward" (2013: 431). The achievement of happiness is, perversely, a basis for normalization and thus self-renunciation and self-discipline.

Affect is mobilized in multiple senses of the term: it is mobile; it accumulates through such movement; and its movement is how it operates. Simultaneously, affect functions to establish political collectivity but also to consolidate subjective identities for which such collectivity resonates. Yet, it is crucial to note that this self-relation occurs at the sub-individual level: linkages between affects, objects, others, symbols, desire, ideas, and so on constitute the self, giving it shape through the repetition of certain kinds of connections. Fixation on and identification with the self, whether in the form of narrowly egoic individualism or collective identity, is a constant tactic of capitalism. Given the relational nature of this self and the sub-individual nature of the processes continually constituting and consolidating the self, however, this fixation is a fixation on certain of the elements of the self and certain kinds of connections among these elements. For instance, one particular mode of subjectivity stems from the accumulated connections among, say, the feeling of intention, the habit of saying "I," and the idea of rationality. Subjective interiorization and privatization thus take diverse forms even as all these forms comprise a deepening of the borders of the "I." Through fixation on the form of sovereign subjectivity, "[c]apitalism institutes or restores all sorts of residual and artificial, imaginary, or symbolic territorialities, thereby attempting, as best it can, to recode, to rechannel persons who have been defined in terms of abstract quantities … [into] States, nations, families" (Deleuze and Guattari 1983: 34). It thus enables affective identification with misogyny, white supremacy, homophobia, xenophobia, and other reactive collectivities. These mobilizations of affect may be political but they are privatized, oriented around the anxious ego. These modes of fixation on the self are primarily enacted through reactive affects—fear, hate, anger, resentment—that circulate redundantly, following flows and forming connections only between certain points of intensity and images, pulling anything new into these existing channels. These affects prompt an anxiety for the self, enabling it to be reterritorialized, drawn into capitalism's ancillary apparatuses and territorialities. Such reactive affects, however, are only regressive and politically damaging when they comprise a repetitive cycle, consolidating the anxious "I," preventing the subject from passing into other affective states and responding to changing conditions.

In relation to the foregoing analysis, we can see how desubjectification is a powerful political practice but only as a strategic, cautious, and "meticulous" process (Deleuze and Guattari 1987: 161). To desubjectify for Deleuze and Guattari does not mean to lose the self but to find ways to keep the self moving, passing through different affective states. The point of desubjectification is not to remove a sense of self but to open up lines of flight "that permit people to breathe, to desire, to love, and to live" (Butler 2004: 8). Deleuze and Guattari note that "you have to keep small rations of subjectivity in sufficient quantity to enable you to respond to the dominant reality" (Deleuze and Guattari 1987: 160). Desubjectification thus is a political ethos not an ontological status. Accordingly, what is entailed by this kind of *strategic* desubjectification as a feminist practice in light of the traps and errors noted above?

Here feminist perspectives push Deleuzoguattarian thought beyond itself by giving us better direction about how to desubjectify. As critical analysis of "the dominant reality," feminist theory supplies knowledge of how, why, where, and for and in relation to whom normalization, marginalization, and oppression takes place. That is, it enables us to understand the specific forms taken by molar identities, both major and minor, their relational composition and how they operate relationally as part of structures of domination, fascism, and normalization as well as resistance and disobedience. Desubjectification can only be meticulous and strategic given this knowledge. An understanding of how, specifically, major molar identities are normative and a range of identities are experienced as normalizing can only be achieved from the perspectives of minor molar identities. Insofar as the experiences and perspectives of minor subjects are ignored, misrecognized, or denied, the white, male bourgeois norm and its role in normalization and capitalist domestication of desire cannot be effectively countered. Intersectional feminism also indicates the need for different kinds of practices of desubjectification depending on the nexus of molar identities people inhabit.

Taylor's feminist Foucaultian notion of desubjectification expands the notion of desubjectification as political ethos. She defines desubjectification as "a disobedient self-relation characterized by refusal, curiosity, and innovation" (2013: 94). One refuses that which is purportedly self-evident, such as dominant norms; one engages curiously, seeking to understand how things work and imagining what else might be possible; and one innovates by experimenting with alternatives to how things are. Desubjectification, accordingly, is an alternative form of self-relation to the conformist self-relation of subjectivity and, further, one that Taylor suggests, "disrupts the cycle of self-renunciation and assertion that characterizes modern Western subjectivity" (ibid.: 99). Desubjectifying through refusal, curiosity, and innovation is a way to keep the self from getting trapped in this cycle, one produced via affective redundancy. As a strategic and deliberate relation to self, desubjectification is a self-relation undertaken as continual process, which means that it works against the cumulative habits of subjectivity that become normalizing and that make subjectivity seem natural.

Thus, a practice of feminist desubjectification is well-equipped to respond to features of our "dominant reality," the traps within and problems for contemporary feminism. Choice, representational, and disciplinary feminism all feed into the conditions that enable regressive and oppressive politics by intensifying interiorization and privatization, bourgeois norms of success in relation to which failure is inevitable, and thus resentful fixation on the self as subject. Strategically undoing modern subjectivity counters these tendencies. A simultaneously Deleuzoguattarian and feminist account of desubjectification suggests that this undoing can only occur through the processes, modes of relationality, that are formative of what is felt as the "I," that is, through practices that disrupt what has become taken for granted. Given that the processes that constitute us as selves are likewise those through which collective identities are constituted, such a focus may also require that we destabilize our attachment to social salient identity categories. Indeed, attentiveness to the processual, relational quality of the self enables a reevaluation of molar identity and identity politics.

As a matter of strategic desubjectification, we can consider such dimensions of identity critically in the following ways. Thinking molar identities relationally and as process means creating space to experience them molecularly, that is, as connective and relational, in terms of the intensive affects and other elements that constitute them. Accordingly, we might cultivate curiosity about the modes of relation to which we are habituated and that comprise our subjective identities: What are the constitutive elements of one's identity as "woman," "white," "queer," and/or "working class," for instance? Which objects, affects, beliefs, and so on constitute these identity categories? Do they entail the repetition of resentment, anger, or fear? In relation to whom or what? To what extent are particular collective identities formed reactively through a relational definition that sustains a white, male bourgeois norm? Desubjectification of subjective identity means developing nonessentialized alternatives to that norm and other norms of molar subjectivity and cultivating deliberate modes of disobedience to it. Thus, we can also ask, when does claiming, utilizing, and/or attributing identity categories deepen conformity and obedience, and when does it disrupt or refuse them?

Furthermore, if it is to counter the fixation on the individual self and privatization in particular, strategic desubjectification as a feminist practice must be a collaborative, coalitional project. We must refuse techniques of individualization at all levels—institutional, interpersonal, and intrasubjective; we must be curious about how we drawn into such techniques through their ubiquity and commonsense appeal; and we must experiment with ways of connecting with one another that go beyond those premised on symbols, images, affects, terms, and habitual modes of relating that consolidate us as individual, private subjects. Coalition can be fraught but is even more crucial when the trap of individualization is laid bare. As part of a practice of strategic desubjectification, it entails that we ought not respond to others from a place of affective entrenchment and fixation on our identity qua gender, race, or sexuality, for instance, in ways that fall into the trap of the censoriousness of a corrective ethos. That is, coalition requires aspiring to forms of relation that acknowledge, challenge, and perhaps eventually refuse the affects that tie the self to its familiar patterns and, further, to encounters with others that are guided by curiosity and that make it possible to experiment together.

Notes

1. Renée Heberle similarly suggests that "the normative masculinism of the social contract should not lead us to assume its solidity or the coherence of the selves that enter into it" (2009: 126).
2. For instance, Irigaray (1985: 140–1); a similar critique of Foucault is made by Hartsock (1990: 163).
3. I argue for the compatibility and complementarity of Deleuze's work and feminist ethics in a Deleuzo-feminist ethics of responsiveness (Gilson 2011: 63–88).
4. See, for example, Anzaldua (1987), Crenshaw (1991), King (1988), Lugones (1994), and Ortega (2016).
5. Deleuzian feminists have been at the forefront on this insight. See, for instance, Lorraine (2008: 60–82) and Braidotti (2013).
6. For an introduction to scholarship on relational autonomy, see MacKenzie and Stoljar (2000).
7. Jodi Dean likewise argues that "the problem of the subject is a problem of this persistent individual form, a form that encloses collective political subjectivity into the singular figure of the individual" (2016: 364).
8. The term came to prominence with Linda Hirshman's critique (2006) of educated women's choice to stay-at-home as mothers rather than pursue careers. See also hooks (2000: 5).

References

Ahmed, S. (2014), *The Cultural Politics of Emotion*, Edinburgh: Edinburgh University Press.
Anzaldua, G. (1987), *Borderlands*, San Francisco, CA: Aunt Lute Books.
Braidotti, R. (2013), "Nomadic Ethics," *Deleuze Studies* 7 (3): 342–59.
Brennan, T. (2004), *The Transmission of Affect*, Ithaca, NY: Cornell University Press.
Brown, W. (1993), "Wounded Attachments," *Political Theory* 21 (3): 390–410.
Butler, J. (2004), *Undoing Gender*, New York: Routledge.
Butler, J. (2005), *Giving an Account of Oneself*, New York: Fordham.
Crenshaw, K. (1991), "Mapping the Margins," *Stanford Law Review* 43 (6): 1241–99.
Dean, J. (2016), "Enclosing the Subject," *Political Theory* 44 (3): 363–93.

Deleuze, G. (1991), *Empiricism and Subjectivity*, trans. C. Boundas, New York: Columbia
   University Press.
Deleuze, G., and F. Guattari (1983), *Anti-Oedipus*, trans. R. Hurley, M. Seem, and H. R. Lane,
   Minneapolis: University of Minnesota Press.
Deleuze, G., and F. Guattari (1987), *A Thousand Plateaus*, trans. B. Massumi,
   Minneapolis: University of Minnesota Press.
Foucault, M. (1983), "Preface" to *Anti-Oedipus*, trans. R. Hurley, M. Seem, and H. R. Lane,
   Minneapolis: University of Minnesota Press.
Gilson, E. (2011), "Responsive Becoming: Ethics between Deleuze and Feminism," in N. Jun and
   D. W. Smith (eds.), *Deleuze and Ethics*, 63–88, Edinburgh: Edinburgh University Press.
Hartsock, N. (1990), "Foucault on Power: A Theory for Women?," in Linda J. Nicholson (ed.),
   Feminism/Postmodernism, 157–75, New York: Routledge.
Heberle, R. (2009), "Rethinking the Social Contract: Masochism and Masculinist Violence,"
   in Renee Heberle and Victoria Grace (eds.), *Theorizing Sexual Violence*, 125–46,
   New York: Routledge.
Hirshman, L. (2006), *Get to Work: A Manifesto for Women of the World*, New York: Viking.
hooks, b. (2000), *Feminism Is for Everybody*, London: Pluto Press.
Irigaray, L. (1985), *This Sex Which Is Not One*, trans. C. Porter and C. Burke, Ithaca, NY: Cornell
   University Press.
King, D. K. (1988), "Multiple Jeopardy, Multiple Consciousness," *Signs* 14 (1): 42–72.
Kittay, E. F. (2011), "The Ethics of Care, Dependence, and Disability," *Ratio Juris* 24 (1): 49–58.
Lorraine, T. (2008), "Feminist Lines of Flight from the Majoritarian Subject," *Deleuze Studies*
   2: 60–82.
Lugones, M. (1994), "Purity, Impurity, and Separation," *Signs* 19 (2): 458–79.
MacKenzie, C., and N. Stoljar (2000), *Relational Autonomy: Feminist Perspectives on Autonomy,
   Agency, and the Social Self*, New York: Oxford University Press.
Ortega, M. (2016), *In-Between: Latina Feminist Phenomenology, Multiplicity, and the Self*, Albany,
   NY: SUNY Press.
Rottenberg, C. (2013), "The Rise of Neoliberal Feminism," *Cultural Studies* 28 (3): 418–37.
Taylor, D. (2013), "Resisting the Subject: A Feminist-Foucauldian Approach to Countering
   Sexual Violence," *Foucault Studies* 16: 88–103.
Taylor, D. (2017), "Non-Subjective Assemblages?: Foucault, Subjectivity, and Sexual Violence,"
   SubStance 46 (1): 38–54.
Willett, C., E. Anderson, and D. Meyers (2016), "Feminist Perspectives on the Self," *The Stanford
   Encyclopedia of Philosophy*, Available online: https://plato.stanford.edu/archives/win2016/
   entries/feminism-self/ (accessed April 17, 2019).

PART TWO
RETHINKING SEXUALITY AND SUBJECTIVITY

Figure 4.1 *Self-portrait as memorializer (doing it right this time, with notes), 2018, mixed media on paper, Jeanne Hamilton*

CHAPTER 4
SCHIZOANALYZING ANOEDIPAL ALLIANCES
Tamsin Lorraine

1. The Charge

On February 7, 2017, the US Senate, while debating confirmation of Senator Jeff Sessions of Alabama to become Attorney General, voted along party lines to uphold Presiding Senate Chair Daines's invocation of an obscure rule in order to silence Democratic Senator Elizabeth Warren of Massachusetts. Following the vote, Senate Majority Leader Mitch McConnell said, "Senator Warren was giving a lengthy speech. She had appeared to violate the rule. She was warned. She was given an explanation. Nevertheless, she persisted" (Wang 2017). The Senate's attempt to silence Senator Warren backfired when the phrase, "Nevertheless, she persisted," rather than expressing the (patriarchal) view that she had refused to act appropriately, evolved into a meme expressing women's persistence in the face of being silenced or ignored.

Senator McConnell's remark was meant to put Senator Warren in her place. We could say that this situation is a telling demonstration of oedipal subjectivity in action; Warren was charged with taking up the same kind of space as a non-lacking (i.e., male, white, able-bodied, etc.), phallic subject—that is, a subject entitled to be heard due to inhabiting the privileged side of the binary positioning oedipal sexual difference instigates. Anyone who has ever been "put in her place" could resonate with the intensities of Warren's situation—the tightening of the throat, the sense of shutting down, the doubt that arises, the kick in the gut in a push-back against being silenced. One is being parsed by the abstract machine of faciality—one's actions defined as inappropriate, one's subjectivity positioned as other.[1] If this event had precipitated Warren (or her spectators) into a tailspin of despair, she (or they) might have visited her psychoanalyst in order to remedy her depression. Transference, in a Kristevian version of analysis, might have allowed repressed semiotic material to emerge and the relation of affect and words to be reworked, enabling a revitalizing reinterpretation of her situation.[2] Julia Kristeva is not sanguine about contemporary possibilities for this kind of reworking of soma and psyche. Whereas in the past religious ritual—with its richly sensual representations of difficulties in personhood that invited the subject into an affective process of self-reworking (Kristeva 1983: 379–82)—might have provided support to the subject, "modern man is losing his soul, but he does not know it, for the psychic apparatus is what registers representations and their meaningful values for the subject. Unfortunately, that darkroom needs repair" (Kristeva 1995: 8). The argument of this paper is that considering Deleuze and Guattari's notion of schizoanalysis, in the context of a conception of subjectivity drawn from Deleuze's work as well as his work with Guattari, can inspire dynamic, flexible ways of grounding nonbinary forms of subjectivity in affective experience. While psychoanalysis works to support an oedipal subject and the binary form of sexual difference that structures it, schizoanalysis works to unfold contemporary subjectivity toward anoedipal forms of subjectivity that rework not simply the soma and psyche of individuals with respect to paternal law, but that reworks paternal law itself by directly addressing the social field that supports it. Such reworking can not only provide material support for feminist struggles as they are lived in disparate locations but also help us to go beyond a form of subjectivity premised upon subjugating an other that entails impoverishing disconnection from creative possibilities in action and alliance with others.

One worthy feminist response to a situation like that of Warren would be to defend one's right to speak by insisting that one is equally entitled to the phallic, active role of the right to be heard. The "Nevertheless, she persisted" meme demonstrates one way among many that alternative possibilities in aneodipal responses already with us might actualize. Instead of opposing the message of McConnell's words, the viral event of many different people in multiple walks of life embracing the phrase and passing it along created a machine or assemblage in touch with a virtual past of multiple moments of persistence. Such machines enable the extension of the subjectivities of the people involved to a collective form of subjectivity, thereby opening them to empowering capacities in affecting and being affected. Schizoanalysis promotes such anoedipal moments by focusing on the transversal connections that liberate flows of desire rather than the interpretations that reinforce the sex and gender of a self stabilized in terms of a familial tale of personal identity. Reworking relations to the familial triangle may enable regrouping of affective charge in the privacy of the psychoanalytical office; schizoanalysis directs one's attention to the intensities in motion within and among embodied individuals that can be reworked on the social field itself.[3]

Guattari's work with borderline clients in the experimental setting of *La Borde* prompted him to theorize a form of intervention that operated in the open space of the institution rather than the closed space of the dyad formed by psychoanalyst and analysand. This larger context provided multiple points of contact at which not just the clients, but doctors and staff as well could stabilize new habits that allowed enlivening affect to flow. Tapping asignifying semiotic energy in the context of the myriad desiring-machines operative at *La Borde* facilitated the release of blockages and enabled new machines to form. It was this experience that provided the background and theoretical spark for the critique of psychoanalysis and oedipal subjectivity that emerges in *Anti-Oedipus.*[4]

The ontology Deleuze develops in his own work, and in his work with Guattari, suggests that we emerge out of an open-ended whole of heterogeneous durations unfolding manifest forms implicated with a continually accumulating virtual past.[5] Insofar as we open ourselves to a world much richer than our representational conceptions suggest, we can rework the connections of the many working machines of which we form a part and invent new forms of existence more in keeping with present flows of life. At this point in time, oedipal subjectivity and its concomitant binary form of sexual difference, could be construed, from a Deleuzian and Deleuzoguattarian perspective, as a constraint on other, more creatively productive forms subjectivity could take. One might say that the concepts Deleuze, and Deleuze and Guattari, create, by virtue of intensifying already existing flows of life, provide some of the support for anoedipal forms of subjectivity that would otherwise be, as Irigaray puts it (in a different context), in a state of "dereliction."[6] Far from wanting to leave us to the fate of psychotic unraveling or an apersonal, nonhuman chaotic flux unsustainable in our day to day lives, Deleuze and Guattari provide us with the theoretical means to intensify experiments already in play that could refigure our self-understanding in ways that bring us into more productive alignment with the world. In this sense, their projects are not those of leaving subjectivity behind (as some have seemed to suggest), but rather of reverting to a tradition of philosophy that depicts philosophy as a process of self-transformation—one that intervenes in life in order to promote flourishing.[7] Their work suggests that a human being, as a process of individuation, can ground itself in the specific capacities unfolded at its location and that this grounding can be understood as an inflection of a durational whole that encompasses commonalities shared with others in ways that traverse and complicate oppositional binaries like organic/inorganic, human/nonhuman, self/other, and male/female. This kind of subject, rather than assuming an identity positioned within symbolic binaries organized with respect to a majoritarian subject, can experience itself as unfolding capacities that become-other along with and through the unfolding capacities of the life of which it forms a part. This kind of self-understanding, in turn, could facilitate anoedipal forms of subjectivity that could creatively evolve beyond fixed identities and symbolic positioning through the communal naming of unfolding powers resonant with asignifying affect shared with others.

2. The Gap

When I first started reading about Warren's moment on the Senate floor, I experienced my usual moment of panic when presented with a woman standing up for herself in a bastion of male power—a sense of wanting to lower my eyes, pull in my breath, become very still, and refuse to see what would come next. Would I be treated to yet another moment of defeat, one that would reverberate with the accumulating effects of countless such moments, or would I be able to vicariously experience a moment—however fleeting—of pride as a woman was able to hold her ground and somehow, against the odds, assert herself? The "Nevertheless, she persisted" meme appearing on my social media platforms suspended this flow of affect and thought. Yes, she *had* been booted from the senate floor, but instead of ending in the shamed silence of the abjected other—the passive object of the active subject's prerogative—countless echoes of the charge meant to humiliate her circulating with viral speed focused on that moment of persistence. This moment, rather than a moment meant to defy or crush the opposition, was a moment of refusing to fall in with the positioning of the faciality machines. The meme, instead of celebrating a moment of phallic triumph, celebrates a moment of quiet persisting, and instead of celebrating just one such moment, celebrates a never-ending series of such moments in which bodies continue to unfold what they can do. This kind of shift in attention disrupts the typical movement oscillating between the rebellion of the abjected other and crushing blow of the active subject to humiliated silence of the one-who-would-dare and creates an alternative moment of suspension. Like the "jamming of the theoretical machinery" advocated by Irigaray, this moment refuses alignment into the typical oppositions between entitled subjects and those forced to fall in step and instead opens up space for another kind of possibility (Irigaray 1985b: 78).

The moment named as "Nevertheless, she persisted" is a configuration of intensities— a moment of anti-production that resists any one form that desire can take, any one way for persistence to occur. This moment of suspension in which a body without organs is created in the wake of the habitual working of the faciality machines allows a gap to emerge. It is in such gaps between stimulus and response that something can happen and habits can be reworked. The words that might have been experienced as the dead-end of a humiliating moment of silencing shift meaning in this circulation of affect, creating transversal connections by naming a configuration of intensities rather than a person as a reference point of identification for the many people who embrace the meme. The resulting machine enables a transversal subject who reverberates with a movement that is no longer a dead-end, a subject who experiences her marginalized self—whether she is actually female or feminine or not—in terms of an inclusive use of disjunctions where "she" is "all the names of history"—all the moments of persistence named by the meme in the images flashing on the video and computer screens and t-shirts and artwork, as well as others that are never explicitly mentioned. The plateau thus created is an event that is unrepresentable and opens onto a pure past that never actually existed, but rather reverberates with movements beyond the bare need of survival of any one physical body or conditioned ego to include access to a range of movements of similar intensities that affect "her" beyond the reach of the intellectual representations with which "she" might attempt to express its power.

In such moments the personal identity designated through oedipal positioning falls away and a multitude of embodied individuals with all their differences in experiences and locations on the social field reverberate with intensities both within and beyond their specific autobiographies. The "molar" segments of ranked social positioning, rather than being directly opposed, are superseded in deference to configurations of intensities forming patterns intuited at "molecular" levels below that of cognitive categorization or recognition. Intimations of a virtual past beyond recognition and any possible description we could give it inform the complex joy we share as a configuration of intensities is highlighted in a shared inflection of a durational whole. Further moments with similar intensities—from the #metoo messages proclaiming persistence in the face of sexual assault (Gilbert 2017) to the football players persisting in the face of condemnations of the form their patriotism takes (Carissimo 2017) to a parrot trapped in a cage refusing to be quiet to a plant struggling to unfold toward the light—all these moments of persisting (or others specific to the multiple places on the social field from which they arise) reverberate with the images of the "Nevertheless she persisted" meme thus amplifying its power. The immanent plane this creates touches us upon a pure past from which each of us draws and in which we are all grounded. The moments evoked by that meme are not the moments of my personal self and yet I resonate with them, I am them, as I am all the names of history, a thread through time that collects and accumulates toward Warren's moment on the Senate floor, a moment that I share with her, a moment in which my personal identity recedes as I reverberate with durations larger than that of any one embodied existence, never mind that of a personal self.

3. Dissolving Machinery

The kind of moment where business as usual is suspended and something else is evoked is an important moment in Deleuze's philosophy—a moment where the new can emerge, a moment where opinion can be superseded, where the shock of thought can occur, where life can be transformed, where we can become worthy of the event. Deleuze has approached this moment from various perspectives. We might think of the Bergsonian gap between perception and action of the *Cinema* books. We might think of Spinoza's third kind of knowledge when through an apprenticeship with life we have learned enough about what causes us joy to be able to be in a world where, as Simon O'Sullivan puts it, "[t]he entire world affirms one's being/capacity to act" (2008: 94). We might think of the third synthesis of the eternal return where instead of being trapped into habitual repetitions that reinforce a representable identity we metamorphose with the release of tensions among the ever-evolving relations of forces that move us on toward an unknown future (Deleuze 1994: 90–1). The subject able to open to such moments of suspension, rather than needing the recognition of the opposed other, the mirroring reflection, say, of the feminine other, to support the delusion of self-sufficient survival, or the affirmation of others whose identity it shares, can celebrate its existence as the unique inflection of a durational whole from which it has no need to separate.[8] This subject has no need of demanding the recognition of an abjected other because it is precipitated from a whole with which it reverberates even as it uniquely inflects that whole from a specific location. It is such a subject that Deleuze, and Deleuze and Guattari seek to promote and support with theoretical interventions. Reading the syntheses of time, Deleuze presents in *Difference and Repetition* with the anoedipal subject of *Anti-Oedipus* that schizoanalysis is designed to evoke suggests a conception of subjectivity able to evolve beyond the oppositional binaries of an oedipal form of sexual difference.

The first synthesis of habit Deleuze presents in chapter 2 of *Difference and Repetition*, inspired by Hume, suggests that the habits of the larval selves of the organism begin to knit together the basis for sustained sentience from an embodied perspective. As John Protevi puts it, Deleuze isolates "a 'primary vital sensibility' in which we have past and future synthesized in a living present. At this level, the future appears as need as 'the organic form of expectation' and the retained past appears as 'cellular heredity'" (Protevi 2011: 33–4).[9] The account Deleuze gives in his book on Hume suggests that the mind precipitated from organic syntheses is initially no more than a collection of impressions that begins to organize itself through principles of association and to individualize itself through principles of passion that depend upon the "circumstances" of one's social field and biography (Deleuze 1991: 103).[10] Although Deleuze drops the vocabulary of the principles of association and passions in his later work, he never drops the notion that the subject is a process of individuation generated through organic and social processes that are precipitated from time as a self-differentiating force.[11] Over time beliefs emerge and stabilize, stabilizing perception and experience. These beliefs inevitably extend beyond the given impressions, "fictioning" (as Jeffrey Bell puts it) the subject and objects bound by time, space, and causality, thus stabilizing a reality shared with others (Deleuze 1991: 78–80). These beliefs depend not just on organic syntheses but also on perceptual syntheses that are inflected by what Hume calls "institutions" and what we might call the social field. Thus, the subject is precipitated out of a process in which the intertwining of organic syntheses and perceptual syntheses produces an increasingly complex mesh of habitual beliefs that inevitably go beyond the given and that are informed by the specific experiences and social field of the embodied subject.

In the second synthesis of memory, inspired by Bergson, the habits of the first synthesis become organized in keeping with the investments of an embodied, sentient being who remembers in order to survive. Embodied consciousness attends to (and thereby filters) that part of the whole necessary to its survival, but the virtual past is always present in the sense that its insisting potentials can be accessed in keeping with shifting interests of the subject (Bergson 1991: 151–3).[12] The third synthesis of the empty form of time suggests that the force of time is a dynamic duration or process of differing from itself that opens the subject to the future in contact with the virtual past. If we correlate this synthesis of the future with the synthesis of consumption described in *Anti-Oedipus*, in which the peripheral subject can cry "yes, that's me!" we can depict oedipal and anoedipal versions of living this synthesis of the future.[13]

For the oedipal subject, the peripheral subject is constrained to the ego positioned with respect to Daddy–Mommy–me. Furthermore, this ego is taken to be the "quasi-cause" or source of the subject's perceptions and actions; the perceptions and actions emerging from the production of desiring-machines (in *Anti-Oedipus*) or passive syntheses of time (in *Difference and Repetition*) come to be seen as originating in a representation of the moment of anti-production (the body without organs) that by virtue of resisting a particular configuration of desiring-machines "records" those desiring-machines by distributing them across what becomes one surface (Deleuze and Guattari 1983: 11–12). Oedipalization constrains our access to the accumulating reverberations of our world by curtailing desiring-production in keeping with "the exclusive use of the disjunctions of the unconscious" (59). Experimental connections are excluded in deference to connections that affirm the sexually differentiated positioning of one's personal biography or the series of identifications organized via the abstract machine of faciality described in *A Thousand Plateaus* through the binary sexual difference of oedipalization. Either one's positioning is affirmed or one is faced with the terrors of the collapse of the ego and dissolution in an undifferentiated abyss.

An oedipal understanding of personal identity suggests that when two subjects are in conflict, one must "win" and the other must "lose." Winning means that one retains one's higher status in a ranking oriented vis-à-vis what we might call the majoritarian subject (Deleuze and Guattari 1987: 105–6). But according to Deleuze and Guattari's characterization of subjectivity, a symbolic designation of personal identity can be no more than a representation of a process of individuation abstracted from time and thus stripped of its unfolding potentials to affect and be affected by a world in which it is always immersed. The majoritarian subject, then, is a chimera; only a subject stripped of its world can be self-sufficiently whole. To conceive of one's agency and power in relation to such an ideal is to deny one's on-going and all-pervasive contact with (and inevitable "contamination" by) the world as well as one's inevitable transformation through, with, and by that world. Recognition, then, cannot confer agency but can only confer the status of a particular position in a hierarchy of social positions and the channeling of social energy—be it facilitating or impeding—that accrues to that position. This molar channeling of social energy, however, may or may not be reinforced by the molecular flows that occur above and below the thresholds of socially recognizable identities.

For the anoedipal subject, the moment of anti-production of the third synthesis is approached in terms of the inclusive disjunctions promoted by schizoanalysis. This subject's possibilities can play out not just in terms of a biographical, personal memory, but in terms of possibilities implicit in the present moment conditioned by the durational whole extending beyond the bounds of the organism or individual psyche out of which that particular state of the embodied subject emerges. Subjectivity is grounded in the unfolding flows lived by the organism as tensions of related forces shift. Representations of moments of anti-production where desiring-machines are distributed across one surface are named in keeping with the intensities of particular moments rather than referred to a preestablished identity; the peripheral subject consumes moments of intensities and moves on. The force of time that insists in the present moment always exerting its influence on an embodied subject, when taken in the more encompassing sense of Bergson's notion of a virtual past, is neither something that can be accounted for in a representational description of the subject at a given moment of time (that, according to both Bergson and Deleuze would overlook the impetus of time's durational force) nor something that can be accounted for in a psychoanalytic biography of the subject that might explain what it does next. To account for what the subject will do next in terms of its personal biography would dictate the movement of an ego with a fixed relation to sexual difference motivated by the desire to fill in its lack. But what are materially available to the subject are all the possibilities in desiring-machine production insisting in the present. These potentially energizing connections to others and one's world exceed organization of desire in terms of the "global" persons of Daddy–Mommy–me or transcendent Phallus. Instead, they comprise a full range of connections to part-objects available in the forces pushing one toward connection and disconnection with the world.

This subject, rather than identifying with particular individuals, identifies with the "names of history, with zones of intensity on the body without organs" (Deleuze and

Guattari 1983: 21). These names indicate not the fixed ego of a person with whom one identifies, but rather configurations of intensities that might unfold in keeping with manifest forms in ways that evoke other similar patterns of durational unfolding. Furthermore, these kinds of identification, rather than resting upon a prohibition that threatens loss of self, instead rests on naming reverberations of intensities insisting within the material situation of one's present. Pursuing all the names of history refuses the positioning of the abstract machine of faciality—it is a form of identification premised on signs or symptoms of what is yet to unfold as opposed to a form of identity that represents a moment of time as the paradigm for how the subject will always be. What has the force to unfold will change in keeping with what actualizes—as some forces unfold, manifesting new states of affairs in the process, what was once impossible becomes possible and vice versa. What earlier could not "discharge its strength" due to the way forces were balanced is now able to unfold, precipitating further effects in the process (Nietzsche 2002: 15).[14]

A molecular understanding of conflict suggests that rather than pit oneself against the other, one can simply "persist"—that is, unfold becomings rumbling at molecular levels beneath the threshold of molar identity in order to make whatever connections are available to be made. The Senate succeeded in shutting Warren down—the woman, Elizabeth Warren, was escorted off the floor. But Warren is not just Warren, a particular woman. "She" is a self-organizing process precipitated from the durational whole of time. This is not to deny that Warren is to be admired for her persistence—along with all the others persisting in similar situations. It is to acknowledge that her persistence did not originate in a self-sufficient agent to be found on the Senate floor, but rather emerged from durational flows preceding and exceeding the specific form she then took. Acknowledging this, from a Deleuzoguattarian perspective, rather than undermining autonomy, empowers subjectivity by demonstrating its grounding in resources beyond the boundaries of personal identity. The meme celebrating her persistence unfolds anoedipal subjects from various partial objects and affects. Warren could not continue on the Senate floor, but bits of her—the sound of her voice, her facial expressions, the look in her eyes, her quiet persistence—precipitate converging and diverging vectors of force that by virtue of the meme (here understood as a machine connecting multiple forces) intensifies a novel inflection of the pure past. The subjects precipitated through this meme are both a group-subject of an event of persisting as well as individual processes counter-effectuating that event in terms of the capacities and affects of bodies in specific locations. Capacities are unfolded in keeping with asignifying intensities available at these different locations rather than with respect to alignments with molar identities that entail shaming the opposition in order to assert their own legitimacy.

4. New Habits

Desiring-machines could be seen in light of Deleuze's discussions of habit in *Empiricism and Subjectivity* and *Difference and Repetition* as a means to enabling new habits to form: the body as a sensitive plate for impressions unfolds into patterns where some energy flows are enabled versus others. According to Deleuze's account of Hume's characterization of this process, it precipitates a faculty of imagination that over time extends a notion of a subject beyond what is actually present (which is no more than a collection of impressions). The principles of association enable enough organization so that the passions that impel an organism in the context of that human being's "circumstance," which includes the social field, can unfold a more specific instantiation of human subjectivity. This suggests what Bell calls a "historical ontology": the reality we perceive, the objects we assume are stable, the selves we assume are identical over time, are no more than imaginative extensions of the flux of impressions we actually experience—extensions that allow us to maintain a recognizably human existence, extensions whose specific forms can change as our circumstances change.[15] Thus, the stabilizing forms our subjectivity take—the ways we have of acting, feeling, representing, and thinking our subjectivity that orient us to our world—can change over time and in concert with the social field that supports us. Memes can come and go, but when their effects are carried forward by experiments in living the possibility for new habits arise.

As a subject precipitated from the collective assemblage of enunciation formed by the "Nevertheless, she persisted" meme, I am able to name a set of intensities—a collection of selected impressions—and thus facilitate the "fictioning" of a self that extends beyond the given of fleeting affects and sensations the meme evokes. This "identity" is doubly articulated from, as Bell puts it, "[A] transcendental field of pre-individual singularities and virtualities that are presupposed by the actualities of conscious experience" (Bell 2009a: 14). The meme could thus enable the organization of molecular aspects of experience that would otherwise remain nonconscious into a stable experience. Although I could marginalize this experience in deference to a personal identity intent on maintaining symbolic positioning, this experience, by virtue of the transversal connections it might evoke, could trouble that positioning. A schizoanalytic practice could promote practices that honor such challenges rather than exclude or marginalize them by, for example, encouraging me to act in keeping with affinities the meme might provoke in defiance of my typical alliances. Such practices, in turn, could lead to new habits where asignifying affect could settle into new patterns of meaning thus grounding shifts in the social field that might unbalance stabilized tendencies and set off rejuvenating lines of flight.

One could say that the gap in humans between perception and action, complicated as it is by the circulation of social meaning through the accumulation of cultural knowledge—encompassing everything from the technological invention of instruments that expand the kind of sensory information available to human beings to the ability to record and share centuries of human experience—has opened us to a virtual past that surpasses that of other species. This ability to rework passions through the feedback loops of culture and institutions allows us to access implicit tendencies in our present in ways that exceed the survival of organisms and extends our creative participation in life. We have multiplied our frames of reference and our powers of affecting and being affected. We regularly take in perspectives on experience formed by other humans who live lives different from our own and we have expanded our imaginative connection to nonhuman others as well as remote parts of the world and the universe. Our lives are constantly exceeding the binaries through which we try and organize them. This presents problems for subjects dependent upon traditional forms of sexually differentiated identity as well as the binary identities it anchors—maintaining oedipal positioning requires constant reinforcement of binary oppositions—but it also precipitates rejuvenating experiments in living that could reverberate throughout the social field.

Theoretical developments from various areas including biosemiotics, animal research, neuroscience, new materialism, and affect theory, allow for the articulation of multiple registers of nonconscious aspects of human existence. This in turn can call attention to molecular processes typically below the threshold of conscious experience, thus facilitating the stabilization of new ways of experiencing our affective connection with the world.[16] Vocabularies drawn from this research—along with aesthetic practices that rework our relation to the world—can intensify aspects of lived experience involving the environments and human and nonhuman others with which we come into contact in ways that defy self-other dichotomies and evoke our commonalities without canceling out our differences. The ontologies drawn from molecular process that a Deleuzoguattarian perspective inspires foster the kind of attentiveness to the singular configurations of forces unique to specific times and places that could enable creative solutions to problems reframed as emerging from plateaus resonant with overlapping commonalities. The more flexible, creative subjectivity that emerges from this kind of grounding in multiple registers of embodied experience will be able to evolve with the durations it lives without fear of its boundaries crumbling; instead of pursuing objects it fantasizes will fill in a lack that becomes manifest only with respect to an impossible ideal, it will be able to pursue immanent forms of desire that unfold in concert with the movements of life. Rather than the either/or of bifurcated forms of sexed and gendered existence, it could unfold serial understandings of multiple connections with the world that reverberate in accumulating ways that could be elaborated in practices that celebrate the evolving realities multiple subjects unfold together.

The anoedipal subject that can conceive of itself as an inflection and reverberation of the whole is a subject who is completely implicated in the materiality of its place and time and yet is free to creatively evolve by "probing" the riches of an infinite with which it is always in touch (O'Sullivan 2010). In the Bergsonian view adopted by Deleuze, it is intuitive receptivity to the virtual that allows the subject to unfold novel solutions to life's problems in connection with the actual forms it takes and the virtual tendencies those forms intensify. Such receptivity is increasingly demanded of us in a world that is becoming so densely interconnected that our problems increasingly defy the categories, causality, and temporality of representational thought. If we are to intuit our present in terms of intensifying tendencies toward a future, we can no longer predict on the basis of representations of our past, we must be willing to embrace change in ourselves as well as our world. A feminist refusal of oedipal positioning along with a persistence in evolving with new anoedipal forms of being fosters alliances across differences crucial to our future flourishing in harmony with a world of which we form an inextricable part.

Embracing serial forms of identification with "all the names of history" allows us to mutate in keeping with the selection of active forces of the eternal return; rather than repeating representable forms of identity, we can instead unfold the tendencies in our current situations in the process of becoming—those tendencies that by virtue of intensifying in tension with what is are ready to actualize in concert with an evolving world.

The persistence to which the "Nevertheless she persisted" meme calls our attention is the persistence of incipient tendencies building in strength in relation to other such tendencies in disparate locations on the social field ready to unfold in ripple effects from multiple places at once—tapping into what bodies can do rather than the status attached to a particular identity. Deleuze's and Deleuze and Guattari's work suggests that oedipal identity—in particular one's sex or gender as well as any other molar identity of the abstract machine of faciality that establishes boundaries between individuals—is belied by the microprocesses of life that are always present at subthreshold levels of molecular, transversal connections. Such an identity, in other words, can be no more than a representation of a moment abstracted from an ongoing process of individuation that always unfolds with and through the durations that encompass it. But even if such representations can constitute galvanizing vectors of meaning for particular individuals and groups of people at particular times by virtue of intensifying specific aspects of their lives in ways that precipitate flourishing, they can also precipitate disconnection from groundedness in material being and abject submission or violent domination of subordinate others in attempts to maintain delusional forms of autonomy. Personal identity from a Deleuzian and Deleuzoguattarian perspective can be seen as an often necessary and yet always strategic negotiation of an array of either/or binary categories extant in the abstract machine of faciality of one's location. As such, it is something to be held lightly with full acknowledgment of the complexity it defies.

A schizoanalytic look at the "Nevertheless, she persisted" meme suggests that it is an example of a machine that makes transversal connections among people and experiences, thus enabling extension of the capacity to affect and be affected in which a put-down is transformed and circulated in excess of oppositional binaries in a reality shared across disparate regions of the social field. Rather than the exclusive disjunction of oedipalization that renders one subject to the either/or disjunctions of the faciality machine, one is returned to nonlinguistic signs of affective life experienced through the multiple patterns and rhythms of body-in-world-and-living-with-others that defy the subject–predicate grammar of representational thought. Such moments can open a gap that touches one upon the virtual. Where and when such gaps are opened, there's a moment of surprise, something that moves one out of the exclusive disjunction of active subject *or* passive object to an inclusive disjunction of an in-between, serial movement of evolving possibility—a moment where intuition of a pure past never lived that goes beyond representational thought can come to the fore evoking creative possibilities not yet unfolded.

If there is any truth to the psychoanalytic characterization of the oedipal subject, then we could say that sex and gender act as a kind of fault line in a form of subjectivity that maintains personal identity through the bifurcations of a binary form of sexual difference. According to Deleuze and Guattari, the oedipal subject, far from universal, is a form of subjectivity historically specific to capitalism. The family is the delegated agent for constraining desire to a personal identity that can act as a limit to the schizoid unraveling capitalism precipitates, but in their view, schizoanalysis could promote other, less repressive, forms of subjectivity. The viral event of "Nevertheless, she persisted" is an example of an anoedipal form of subjectivity already in action. It may be that reflection on emerging forms of subjectivity that challenge the status quo are part of a larger challenge to how we perceive reality as well as how we negotiate our relations with human and nonhuman others, and the interdependent global community of which we are a part. If the rapid change of contemporary life is pushing us toward conceiving a future beyond anything we could predict on the basis of our past, then it may be that the movement toward more fluid forms of identity attested to by, for example, various forms of trans existence as well as increasing challenges to the patriarchal and anthropocentric status quo, may be part of a creative evolution of the modern subject toward more flexible and viable alternatives.

Theory as a vector of force, by highlighting certain aspects of an event over others, can aid in the intensification of an event into a plane of immanence. Such planes of immanence, by virtue of fostering the circulation of affects, can facilitate transversal alliances as well as emergent forms of subjectivity able to creatively evolve with such alliances. Instigating and disseminating experiments in subjectivity can dissolve oppositional binaries, undermine patriarchal (as well as anthropomorphic) conceptions of the subject, and facilitate creatively flexible subjects able to maintain themselves in the face of difficult encounters and lives of continual change. The effects of the "Nevertheless she persisted" meme can be lost in the dereliction of a subjectivity without support, or we can carry them forward as we let the differences of our respective identities recede in light of shared reverberations, materially grounded in life's durational flows, intimating ways of being that go beyond the binaries that divide us.

Notes

1. See Deleuze and Guattari (1987: 170–91) for their notion of the abstract machine of faciality and Bogue (2003: 91–2) for a succinct definition.

2. Kelly Oliver presents a particularly compelling account of this process in *Reading Kristeva* (1993: 116–19).

3. For a compelling example of how schizoanalysis can rework the social field, see Deleuze and Guattari's account of a schizoanalytic cure drawn from a culture where subjectivity had not yet been fully oedipalized in *Anti-Oedipus* (1983: 167–9). I elaborate this example with reference to Victor Turner's anthropological description of it in *Deleuze and Guattari's Immanent Ethics* (Lorraine 2011: 45–7).

4. See Guattari's characterization of this process as well as his conception of schizoanalysis as metamodelization (1995: 69–72 and 58–76). Janell Watson comments on Guattari's characterization of schizoanalysis as metamodeling that the maps of schizoanalysis "must not only be made fresh every time, they must also change over time" (2009: 11). François Dosse

presents a vivid description of Guattari's role at La Borde in chapters 2 and 3 of *Gilles Deleuze and Félix Guattari: Intersecting Lives* (2010: 40–75).

5. Boram Jeong presents a helpfully illuminating account of Deleuze's conception of time as self-differentiation and a reading of Deleuze's interpretation of Kant's syntheses that develops the notion of a subject as a precipitate of time (2017: 31–7 and 40–64). Also see Daniel Smith's lucid account of Deleuze's conception of the "empty form of time" (2012: 131–3).

6. For an explanation of Irigaray's notion of dereliction, see Whitford (1991: 77–89).

7. As Todd May puts it in *Gilles Deleuze: An Introduction,* "How Might One Live?": "Philosophy does not settle things. It disturbs them. Philosophy disturbs by moving beneath the stable world of identities to a world of difference that at once produces those identities and shows them to be little more than the froth of what there is" (2005: 19). In engaging this kind of philosophy, Deleuze "offers us a radically different way to approach living, and an attractive one, as long as we are willing to ask anew what it is to be *us* and what it is to be *living.* As long as we are willing to accept that ontology does not offer answers but rather ways to approach the question of living" (2005: 25).

8. For vivid characterizations of the feminine other as mirror, see Irigaray's classic, *Speculum of the Other Woman* (1985a).

9. Protevi presents a detailed and fascinating reading of this first synthesis in relation to "enactivists" like Francisco Varela, Evan Thompson, Alva Noe, and Shaun Gallagher.

10. My reading of *Empiricism and Subjectivity* is indebted to Jeffrey Bell's book *Deleuze's Hume* as well as Jon Roffe's essay and book on Deleuze's interpretation of Hume (Bell 2009a, Roffe 2009, Roffe 2016).

11. See Roffe (2009) for a succinct account of how Deleuze's later work departs from his earlier work on Hume.

12. See Alia Al-Saji's particularly insightful rendering of Bergson in relation to Deleuze on this point (Al-Saji 2004).

13. See Steven Shaviro's (2008) blog entry for a helpful characterization of the peripheral subject.

14. See chapter 2, section 1 of Deleuze's book on Nietzsche for this notion of a body as a relation of forces (1983: 40).

15. Bell presents an enlightening discussion of the term "historical ontology" along with its genealogy in "Deleuze's Humean Historiography" (2009b).

16. I can do no more than hint at what I have in mind here with a few examples: (1) biosemiotics, by suggesting a form of sense-making at the cellular level evokes a molecular way of thinking about intelligence (Hoffmeyer 2010); (2) neuroscientific research suggests commonalities in the affective lives of human and nonhuman animals (Panksepp 2010) as well as undermines traditional distinctions between affective and rational life (Damasio 2003); and (3) "new materialists" like Jane Bennett are problematizing the traditional distinction between inert matter and intelligible form (Bennett 2010).

References

Al-Saji, A. (2004), "The Memory of Another Past, Bergson, Deleuze and a New Theory of Time," *Continental Philosophy Review* 37: 203–39.

Bell, J. A. (2009a), *Deleuze's Hume: Philosophy, Culture and the Scottish Enlightenment,* Edinburgh: Edinburgh University Press.

Bell, J. A. (2009b), "Of the Rise and Progress of Philosophical Concepts: Deleuze's Humean Historiography," in J. A. Bell and C. Colebrook (eds.), *Deleuze and History*, 54–71, Edinburgh: Edinburgh University Press.

Bennett, J. (2010), *Vibrant Matter: A Political Ecology of Things*, Durham, NC: Duke University Press.

Bergson, H. (1991), *Matter and Memory*, trans. N. M. Paul and W. S. Palmer, New York: Zone Books.

Bogue, R. (2003), *Deleuze on Music, Painting, and the Arts*, New York: Routledge.

Carissimo, J. (2017), "Some NFL Players Kneel Sunday during National Anthem," *CBS News*, https://www.cbsnews.com/news/nfl-players-kneel-during-national-anthem/ (accessed November 27, 2017).

Damasio, A. (2003), *Looking for Spinoza: Joy, Sorrow, and the Feeling Brain*, London: William Heinemann.

Deleuze, G. (1983), *Nietzsche and Philosophy*, trans. H. Tomlinson, New York: Continuum.

Deleuze, G. (1991), *Empiricism and Subjectivity*, trans. C. Boundas, New York: Columbia University Press.

Deleuze, G. (1994), *Difference and Repetition*, trans. P. Patton, New York: Columbia University Press.

Deleuze, G., and F. Guattari (1983), *Anti-Oedipus*, trans. R. Hurley, M. Seem, and H. R. Lane, Minneapolis: University of Minnesota Press.

Deleuze, G., and F. Guattari (1987), *A Thousand Plateaus*, trans. B. Massumi, Minneapolis: University of Minnesota Press.

Dosse, F. (2010), *Gilles Deleuze & Félix Guattari: Intersecting Lives*, trans. D. Glassman, New York: Columbia University Press.

Gilbert, S. (2017), "The Movement of #MeToo: How a Hashtag Got Its Power," *The Atlantic*, https://www.theatlantic.com/entertainment/archive/2017/10/the-movement-of-metoo/542979/ (accessed November 27, 2017).

Guattari, F. (1995), *Chaosmosis: An Ethico-Aesthetic Paradigm*, trans. P. Bains and J. Pefanis, Bloomington: Indiana University Press.

Hoffmeyer, J. (2010), "A Biosemiotic Approach to the Question of Meaning," *Zygon*, 45 (2): 367–90.

Irigaray, L. (1985a), *Speculum of the Other Woman*, trans. G. C. Gill, Ithaca, NY: Cornell University Press.

Irigaray, L. (1985b), *This Sex Which Is Not One*, trans. C. Porter and C. Burke, Ithaca, NY: Cornell University Press.

Jeong, B. (2017), *Theory of Subjectification in Gilles Deleuze: A Study of the Temporality in Capitalism*, Doctoral Dissertation, Pennsylvania: Duquesne University.

Kristeva, J. (1983), *Tales of Love*, trans. L. S. Roudiez, New York: Columbia University Press.

Kristeva, J. (1995), *New Maladies of the Soul*, trans. R. Guberman, New York: Columbia University Press.

Lorraine, T. (2011), *Deleuze and Guattari's Immanent Ethics: Theory, Subjectivity, and Duration*, Albany, NY: SUNY Press.

May, T. (2005), *Gilles Deleuze: An Introduction*, New York: Cambridge University Press.

Nietzsche, F. (2002), *Beyond Good and Evil*, trans. J. Norman, New York: Cambridge University Press.

Oliver, K. (1993), *Reading Kristeva: Unraveling the Double-bind*, Indianapolis: Indiana University Press.

O'Sullivan, S. (2008), "The Production of the New and the Care of the Self," in S. O'Sullivan and S. Zepke (eds.), *Deleuze, Guattari and the Production of the New*, 1–10, New York: Continuum.

O'Sullivan, S. (2010), "Guattari's Aesthetic Paradigm: From the Folding of the Finite/Infinite Relation to Schizoanalytic Metamodelisation," *Deleuze Studies*, 4 (2): 256–86.

Panksepp, J. (August 2010), "Affective Consciousness in Animals," *Proceedings of the Royal Society B*, DOI: 10.1098/rspb.2010.1017.

Protevi, J. (2011), "Larval Subjects, Autonomous Systems and *E. coli* Chemotaxis," in L. Guillaume and J. Hughes (eds.), *Deleuze and the Body*, 29–52, Edinburgh: Edinburgh University Press.

Roffe, J. (2009), "David Hume," in G. Jones and J. Roffe (eds.), *Deleuze's Philosophical Lineage*, 67–86, Edinburgh: Edinburgh University Press.

Roffe, J. (2016), *Gilles Deleuze's Empiricism and Subjectivity: A Critical Introduction and Guide*, Edinburgh: Edinburgh University Press.

Shaviro, Steven (2008), "The Third (Conjunctive) Synthesis," *The Pinocchio Theory* blog, http://www.shaviro.com/Blog/?p=648 (accessed November 27, 2017).

Smith, D. W. (2012), "Analytics: On the Becoming of Concepts," (Ch. 8) *Essays on Deleuze*, Edinburgh: Edinburgh University Press.

Wang, A. (2017), "'Nevertheless, She Persisted' Becomes New Battle Cry after McConnell Silences Elizabeth Warren," *Washington Post*, February 8, 2017, https://www.washingtonpost.com/news/the-fix/wp/2017/02/08/nevertheless-she-persisted-becomes-new-battle-cry-after-mcconnell-silences-elizabeth-warren/?utm_term=.da06ecd39519 (accessed July 31, 2017).

Watson, J. (2009), *Guattari's Diagrammatic Thought: Writing between Lacan and Deleuze*, New York: Continuum.

Whitford, M. (1991). *Luce Irigaray: Philosophy in the Feminine*, New York: Routledge.

CHAPTER 5
THE ALLIANCE BETWEEN MATERIALIST FEMINISM AND SCHIZOANALYSIS: TOWARD A MATERIALIST THEORY OF SEXED SUBJECTIVITY
Katja Čičigoj

This article sets the parameters for a materialist theory of sexed subjectivity by confronting schizoanalysis and French materialist feminism (Christine Delphy, Monique Wittig, Paola Tabet, Colette Guillamin, and others). This could help understanding the processes of socialization through which sexed subjectivities are formed and how more egalitarian forms of subjectivation may emerge. While a materialist theory of subjectivity was Deleuze and Guattari's expressed aim in *Anti-Oedipus*, it is argued that its development might be hindered by what they call schizoanalysis's "positive task," which posits the inherently revolutionary nature of "real" desire, thus obviating (intentional) political action. This is also what is most often taken up in contemporary feminist appropriations of Deleuze and Guattari. Confronting schizoanalysis with French materialist feminism may help us take stock of the resources offered by schizoanalysis's "negative task": the critique of institutions which (re)produce oedipalized, sexually differentiated subjects. It may also curb the danger of an excessive voluntarism springing up from French materialist feminist analyses. Could this alliance yield a more balanced understanding of subjectivity and political action, taking in to account the complex interplay of intention and desire at stake in social and political transformation?

Deleuze and Guattari write, "[I]f materialist psychiatry may be defined as the psychiatry that introduces the concept of production into consideration of the problem of desire, it cannot avoid posing in eschatological terms the problem of the ultimate relationship between the analytic machine, the revolutionary machine, and desiring machines" (2003: 34). It is through their materialist critique of what they consider psychoanalysis's idealism that they articulate one of the core principles of schizoanalysis: the social aetiology of mental suffering (355–7; 361). Behind the neuroses which the psychoanalyst would always conduce back to familial issues—love of the mother, hatred of the father (304; 312)—schizoanalysis reveals the material, that is, economic and immediately social and political conditions which turn particular familial relations into problematic ones for the analyzed subject. As they explain,

> Behind all this, there is an economic situation: the mother reduced to housework, or to a difficult and uninteresting job on the outside; children whose future

remains uncertain; the father who has had it with feeding all those mouths—in short, a fundamental relation to the outside of which the psychoanalyst washes his hands … Let us consider for a moment the motivations that lead someone to be psychoanalyzed: it involves a situation of economic dependence that has become unbearable for desire, or full of conflicts for the investment of desire. The psychoanalyst, who says so many things about the necessity for money in the cure, remains supremely indifferent to the question of who is footing the bill. For example, the analysis reveals the unconscious conflicts of a woman with her husband, but the husband is paying for his wife's analysis. (Deleuze and Guattari 2003: 355)

By pointing at "the outside"—the social and economic world beyond familial relations—schizoanalysis attempts to disrupt the allegedly universal, context-free status accorded to socialization in the nuclear family and reveal its historically contingent and authoritarian nature. Psychoanalysis, on the other hand, would remain idealist by participating in the universalization of familial relations: when it attempts to help subjects accept their assigned roles in oedipal daddy–mommy–me familial structures, it never questions these structures in their cultural and historical contingency and imbrication with power (275). Because universalizing relations which turn out to be problematic or unbearable for some (i.e., patriarchal and oedipal ones) entails precluding envisioning the possibility of their transformation, the idealist nature of a theory and analytic practice is not merely a theoretical issue but becomes a political one.

Schizoanalysis, on one hand, and French materialist feminism, on the other, comprised by the work of Monique Wittig, Christine Delphy, Nicole Claude Mathieu, Paola Tabet, Colette Guillaumin, Monique Plaza, and others, converge in their materialist critiques of the nuclear family and psychoanalysis, and in their antiauthoritarian and anti-capitalist orientations, shaped in the aftermath of 1968.[1] A fruitful alliance may thus be forged between them to develop a truly materialist theory of sexed subjectivity: a theory which exposes the historical, social, and political context of forms of subjectivation and thus, hopefully, helps us think of ways in which these could be transformed by transforming the context which shaped them.

Undoubtedly, French materialist feminists are not the only feminist thinkers engaged in developing a materialist analysis of women's oppression, perpetrated through sexually differentiated socialization. In the history of feminist thought, materialist approaches—particularly of a more Marxist bend—abound: from the radical feminist interpretation and appropriation of Marx by Shulamith Firestone ([1970] 2015), through the more orthodox Marxist feminism of Silvia Federici (2012), Leopoldina Fortunati (1996), Mariarosa dalla Costa and Selma James (1972), to the more recent Marxist materialist feminist approaches of Gillian Howie (2010) and Kate Soper (1995), among others. Recently, a competing notion of materialism has gained particular currency in feminist theory: theorists designating themselves as "new materialists" programmatically propose a vitalist, as opposed to a historical, materialist approach to sexuality, subjectivity and embodiment (see, e.g.: Grosz 2010; Braidotti and Van der Tuin 2012). I have argued elsewhere how the metaphysical, as opposed to political understanding of notions such as freedom, agency, and sexual difference in feminist new materialisms, tends to naturalize what ought to be conceived as a political program and thus present political agency as superfluous (see Čičigoj 2017). Though an in-depth discussion of this issue goes beyond the scope of this chapter, I would argue that in its political consequences, the metaphysical vitalist materialism of feminist new materialisms comes close to the "idealism" Deleuze and Guattari objected to in the psychoanalysis mentioned above; I share, therefore, some of the concerns expressed in relation to the lack of capacity of these theories for addressing issues of feminist politics (see, e.g., Ahmed 2008; Gunnarsson 2013; Ellenzweig and Zammito 2017). In this chapter I explore an alternative possibility of a materialist feminist encounter with the work of Deleuze and Guattari: the possibility of allying schizoanalysis to the specific Marxist orientation of French materialist feminism, in order to highlight the political, as opposed to metaphysical, nature of Deleuze and Guattari's project. Given Deleuze and Guattari's extensive drawing on Marx[2] (most explicitly, see [1972] 2003: 222–61 and 296–321) in conceptualizing sexuality and subjectivity, I would argue this path is at least as much grounded in their work as a more metaphysical materialist approach would be.

In what follows, I will argue that the alliance between schizoanalysis and French materialist feminism could most fruitfully be forged by drawing upon schizoanalysis's "destructive task" (Deleuze and Guattari 2003: 316): the analytic and political critique of Oedipal, micro-fascist, subjugating libidinal investments fostered through socialization in the nuclear family and secured by psychoanalysis. For Deleuze and Guattari, this task is inseparable from a positive one (381): the affirmation of multiplicity and deterritorialization as immanent to human libidinal dynamics (342), as well as to the historical process of capitalist social relations (34). I will argue that when emphasis is put upon the positive task of schizoanalysis, the aim of devising a materialist theory of sexed subjectivity encounters obstacles: since the permanent differentiation of subjectivity is presented as an ontological given and a historical tendency, it becomes difficult to think its actualization through collective political action aimed at transforming social institutions and forms of socialization (though this lies beyond the scope of this paper, I would argue these are precisely the difficulties encountered by the vitalist metaphysical materialism of feminist new materialisms mentioned above). Rereading the positive task of schizoanalysis—particularly what Deleuze and Guattari call "becoming n-sexes" (256)[3]—through the French materialist feminist vision of the end of binary sexual differentiation as the guiding idea of feminist politics (see Delphy 1993), can help us conceptualize schizoanalysis as a thoroughly political project. On the other hand, the primary focus of materialist feminists was the analysis of the social mechanisms producing the "sex class" of women: the extortion of unpaid domestic, reproductive, sexual labor (see Tabet 2005) and its ideological naturalization (see Guillamin 1995: 176–238). Through its alliance with materialist feminism, schizoanalysis could thus bring the due emphasis upon a domain often bracketed in materialist feminist analyses when thinking political transformation— that of desire and subjectivity.

1. Why Isn't Every Woman a Feminist?

Materialist feminists lament what they perceive being the excessive attention devoted by structuralists, post-structuralists, psychoanalytic feminists, and feminists of difference to sexual difference, psyche and subjectivity (see Delphy 1993: 5; Plaza 1977: 91–119). They argue that the surplus symbolic investment in sex is not a (symbolic or ontological) given which may be taken for granted or affirmed but rather the product of the patriarchal investment of meaning into sexual difference as a marker of the hierarchical order of sexual classes (Wittig 1992: 2). While sexuality in and by itself may be of no more political consequence than any other domain of human sociality, we should nevertheless recognize that it has been historically invested with symbolic meaning in order to legitimize and perpetrate women's oppression—as indeed materialist feminists themselves recognize (Wittig 1992: 9; Guillamin 1995: 212–14). Theoretical and political attention to the realm of sexuality, desire, and the unconscious thus remains necessary as long as these remain key terrains through which oedipal and submissive subjectivities are forged and patriarchal and capitalist social relations reproduced (Deleuze and Guattari 2003: 296–321). This is precisely what schizoanalysis could bring to materialist feminism.

In her essay "The Straight Mind," Monique Wittig contests psychoanalysis (particularly Lacanian) for producing "a scientific reading of the social reality in which human beings are given as invariants, untouched by history and unworked by class conflicts, with identical psyches" (Wittig 1992: 22), claiming, "one speaks of *the* exchange of women, *the* difference between the sexes, *the* symbolic order, *the* Unconscious, Desire, *Jouissance*, Culture, History, giving an absolute meaning to these concepts, when they are only categories founded upon heterosexuality, or thought which produces the difference between the sexes as a political and philosophical dogma" (Wittig 1992: 27). By presenting concepts expressive of current relations of domination (the heteropatriarchal straight mind), as universal and thus unquestionable, psychoanalysis helps the dominant class maintain its dominance: "The concept of difference has nothing ontological about it. It is only the way that the masters interpret a historical situation of domination. The function of difference is to mask at every level the conflicts of interest, including ideological ones" (29). Wittig therefore claims, "[T]here is no doubt that Lacan found in the Unconscious the structures he said he found there, since he had previously put them there"; "[I]t is an Unconscious which looks too consciously after the interests of the masters" (23, 30).

The problem with this critique is that it appears to grant to the concepts of dominant thought, such as sexual difference, too little material traction. Wittig does recognize that concepts not only have a material basis—the oppression of women and other sexual minorities—but also material consequences upon the lives of those tackled by them (Wittig 1992: 25). Nevertheless, Wittig calls for intentional refusal: "When the general state of things is understood (one is not sick or to be cured, one has an enemy) the result is that the oppressed person breaks the psychoanalytical contract" (24). She calls upon women, lesbians, and gay people to cease using the categories of the straight mind—such as man and woman—and in the end of her essay calls for breaking up the heterosexual contract altogether:

[S]ince, as Levi-Strauss said, we talk, *let us say that we break off the heterosexual contract*. So, this is what lesbians say everywhere in this country and in some others, if not with theories at least through their social practice, whose repercussions upon straight culture and society are still unenvisionable ... Straight concepts are undermined. What is woman? Panic, general alarm for an active defence. Frankly, it is a problem that lesbians do not have because of *a change of perspective*, and it would be incorrect to say that lesbians associate, make love, live with women, for "woman" has meaning only in heterosexual systems of thought and heterosexual economic systems. Lesbians are not women. (Wittig 1992: 32; emphases mine)

But is such a voluntary performative enunciation of one's "change of perspective" enough to put an end to relations of oppression? Does *understanding* that one is oppressed suffice to successfully *break* the (psychoanalytic, heterosexual) ties of this oppression? As feminists have often noted, oppression perpetuates itself through internalization even beyond subjects' conscious knowledge of oppression and intentional aims at resistance (Bartky 1990). While Wittig's politicized theory is a welcome antidote to psychoanalysis's fatalism of the unchangeable (oedipal, phallic) unconscious, it may nevertheless overlook the potentially significant unconscious hindrances to transformation—hindrances which stem precisely from the material effectiveness of the "straight" theories and forms of socialization she exposes. This is where, I would argue, schizoanalysis's focus upon the libidinal domain can be helpful.

While Deleuze and Guattari equally point to the historical, social, and cultural specificity of psychoanalytic categories and familial relations and their complicity with capitalist and oppressive social relations (2003: 26–8), they nevertheless put more emphasis than Wittig (and materialist feminists in general) upon the traction exerted by these categories upon the unconscious. For Deleuze and Guattari, Oedipus and the function of the phallus are not found in the analyzed subject's unconscious because the psychoanalyst has "put them there," as Wittig appears to believe—both are actual dynamics of subjectivation in (patriarchal) late modern, capitalist societies which directly impinge upon one's desires and affinities. Oedipal unconscious structures, reproduced through socialization in the nuclear family and sanctioned by psychoanalysis in theory and practice, can have hold over subjects beyond their voluntary control and despite their recognition of the oppressive nature of these structures, posing obstacles to Wittig's voluntarist solutions. Deleuze and Guattari on the other hand recognize the problem of the incongruity between conscious intentions and unconscious libidinal investments as a central problem for any theory interested in the revolutionary transformation of social relations: Not only can the libidinal investment of the social field interfere with the investment of interest, and constrain the most disadvantaged, the most exploited, to seek their ends in an oppressive machine, but what is reactionary or revolutionary in the preconscious investment of interest does not necessarily coincide with what is reactionary or revolutionary in the unconscious libidinal investment (2003: 347).

Deleuze and Guattari's most profound of question, "Why do many of those who have or should have an objective revolutionary interest maintain a preconscious investment of a reactionary type?,"[4] can be thus understood as a more general formulation of the problem of complicity with oppression tackled by feminists. Simone de Beauvoir considered complicity, at least partially, the moral fault of avoiding autonomous action and self-determination in the world in favor of existential and economic ease (2011: 10, 16), an understanding much in tension with her concise cataloguing of the ways in which oppression materially stifles women's capacity to assert themselves as the subjects of their own actions even against their attempts to lead autonomous existences.[5] This tension is partly resolved in French materialist feminism, for they would hardly figure complicity as a free, ethically condemnable choice. As their analyses repeatedly demonstrate, the potential upkeep of women by their husbands does not necessarily bring women comfort and ease but is mostly exchanged without remuneration for women's reproductive, domestic, care, and sexual services (see Delphy 1988). Furthermore, women's socialization for the systemic extortion of their labor in close physical and emotional proximity to its beneficiaries (fathers, husbands, children, family members) tends to produce submissive individuals with a lesser sense of autonomy—depending and dependable individuals (see Guillamin 1995: 88–109; Tabet 2005: 149). Since neither social relations nor subjective attitudes are entirely familial phenomena, escaping what materialist feminists call "the private appropriation of women" in marriage (Guillamin 1995: 194) by becoming lesbians does not guarantee escape from the class of women, as Wittig appears to believe: a lesbian might still be summoned by family members, parents, and siblings, to take on the burden of health or age-related care, or be burdened with extra emotional labor in the workplace. The voluntarism diagnosed above in Wittig's critique of psychoanalysis is therefore not uniformly shared by all French materialist feminist works, nevertheless such work seems to allow only for an explanation of complicity in terms of objective, systemic oppression forcing individuals to comply. Sandra Lee Bartky would later expose how neither self-deception (false consciousness) nor structural oppressive mechanisms are in themselves enough to explain women's compliance with oppression, produced through a complex process of psychic internalization of oppressive attitudes. She writes of women's often unintermittent supply of care labor despite all hardship:

> She does this not because she is "chauvinized" or has "false consciousness," but because *this is what the work requires*. Indeed, she may even excuse the man's abuse of her, having glimpsed the great reservoir of pain and rage from which it issues. Here is a further gloss on the ethical disempowerment attendant upon women's caregiving: in such a situation, a woman may be tempted to collude in her own ill-treatment. (Bartky 1990: 114)

What Deleuze and Guattari's tackling of the analogous problem of why "the most disadvantaged, the most excluded members of society invest with passion the system that oppresses them" (2003: 364) brings to the discussion of complicity or internalized oppression is precisely the notion of passion or passionate, libidinal investment:

"[A] pure joy in feeling oneself a wheel in the machine … a sort of art for art's sake in the libido, *a taste for a job well done*" (365; emphasis mine). While such libidinal investments may be produced through oppression, as also materialist feminists allow us to grasp, they are in turn what sustains and nourishes it, posing unconscious resistances to radically transforming our lives and relations—which is why lifting objective, institutional mechanisms of structural oppression may need to be complemented with transforming submissive forms of subjectivation as well. Taking cue from Deleuze and Guattari (2003: 30), we can thus focus anew upon the ways in which the libidinal domain is thoroughly enmeshed in social relations: how it is not only shaped by them, but also how it participates in their production and reproduction. Their understanding of the nature of non-submissive, or in their words "schizo-revolutionary" libidinal investments (277), however, could pose certain problems for a materialist theory of sexed subjectivity— problems shared by some feminist theories and theories of gender which draw from Deleuze and Guattari's work and enjoy much traction today. I am referring particularly to feminist new materialisms mentioned above and to Paul Preciado's theory of queer multitudes. Partially inspired by Deleuze and Guattari, both theories come close to what I am calling the metaphysical characterization of schizoanalysis, or schizophrenization as a metaphysical process: new materialisms, by positing becoming and differentiation (including the deterritorialization of sexual difference) as an immanent dynamic of matter and Preciado, by taking the queer multitudes to be the internal revolutionary limit of the Empire. I would argue that they therefore risk meeting similar problems in terms of political agency and subjectivity to the ones I will argue ensue from Deleuze and Guattari's metaphysical characterization of schizoanalysis's positive task,[6] which I will discuss later. But this is also precisely the reason why an alliance of schizoanalysis with the more explicitly political, Marxist materialism of French materialist feminism could be helpful: it might help us to insist upon schizoanalysis as a critical and political endeavor and keep it close to what Deleuze and Guattari ascribed to Reich: the truly "materialist psychiatry he [they] was [were] looking for" (2003: 345; see also Holland 2001).

2. The Ontology of Deterritorialization and the Problem of Agency

Deleuze and Guattari hold that non-submissive and non-paranoiac libidinal investments can be attained by uncovering, beneath the "theatrical representations" of Oedipus, the "real functioning" of the unconscious (2003: 229). What they call the positive task[s] of schizoanalysis lies therefore in attaining this real functioning as simultaneously "the historical process of social production" and "as the metaphysical process of desiring-production" which would "arrive at the same time, in accordance with the two simultaneous meanings of process" (358). To attain "desire taken in the real order of its production, which behaves as a molecular phenomenon devoid of any goal or intention" (342) in its doubly social and metaphysical nature, schizoanalysis (in what Deleuze and Guattari call its destructive task) therefore engages a double critique of the theory and practice that "disfigures" the "real functioning" (338) of desire, that is, psychoanalysis: a transcendental and a materialist critique.[7] I will tackle both and expose the ways in which their yielding an ontological and onto-historical process of molecular desire could pose problems for a feminist materialist theory of sexed subjectivity.

Deleuze and Guattari model their transcendental critique of psychoanalysis upon some arguments of Kant's *Critique of Pure Reason*. They write,

> [O]ne can never, as in an interpretation, read the repressed through and in the repression, since the latter is constantly inducing a false image of the thing it represses: illegitimate and transcendent uses of the syntheses according to which the unconscious can no longer operate in accordance with its own constituent machines, but merely "represent" what a repressive apparatus gives it to represent. It is the very form of interpretation that shows itself to be incapable of attaining the unconscious, since it gives rise to the inevitable illusions (including the structure and the signifier) by means of which the conscious makes of the unconscious an image consonant with its wishes: we are still pious, psychoanalysis remains in the precritical age. (2003: 339)

Here, Deleuze and Guattari contest psychoanalysis for making illegitimate and transcendent use of the syntheses of the unconscious, just as Kant framed his critical project of transcendental idealism as a critique of the illegitimate uses of reason beyond all possible experience in rationalist metaphysics (Kant 1999: 148). For Kant this use would have given rise to "necessary illusions": metaphysical concepts such as God, the immortal soul and freedom (1999: 384–524). Deleuze and Guattari transpose the transcendental form of Kant's critique of pure reason to the libidinal domain: the illegitimate use of the syntheses of the unconscious would give rise to the "necessary illusions" of "Oedipal images" and of "structure and signifier," at the forefront of Freudian and Lacanian psychoanalysis respectively (Deleuze and Guattari 2003: 339). Yet they soon jump to very un-Kantian conclusions. A truly Kantian critique would consider psychoanalysis "metaphysical" because it claims *to know the nature* or structure of the unconscious; it would proceed by demonstrating that an opposite, such as nonfamilial, non-oedipal, non-phallic unconscious or an unconscious not structured by lack, is equally viable. It would thus conclude that we cannot claim to know with certainty that the unconscious *in itself* has this or that particular nature or structure: neither an oedipal, nor a molecular, schizoid one—just as Kant in his "Antinomies of Pure Reason" demonstrated that metaphysical matters (the soul, freedom, God), cannot be known with certainty since one view and its opposite are equally viable (Kant 1999: 590–625). Deleuze and Guattari, however, describe the unconscious in unmistakably ontological terms, far from Kant's strict ontological agnosticism: "The unconscious *is not* figurative, since its figural is abstract, the figure-schizzo. *It is not* structural, *nor is it* symbolic, for *its reality is* that of the Real in its very production, in its very inorganization. *It is not* representative, but solely machinic, and productive" (Deleuze and Guattari 2003: 311; emphases mine).

The transcendent and illegitimate use of the syntheses of the unconscious in psychoanalysis is denounced not because it would claim *to know* the real functioning of the unconscious, but because it would "disfigure" its real functioning with Oedipal images. Therefore, "[T]he first positive task consists of discovering in a subject *the nature*, the formation, or the functioning of his desiring-machines, *independently of any interpretations*" (Deleuze and Guattari 2003: 322; emphases mine). Deleuze and Guattari's transcendental critique of psychoanalysis appears to yield a metaphysical outcome: a notion of the real functioning of the unconscious independently of any interpretations, which both contradicts the allegedly Kantian nature of their critique,[8] and squares oddly with their attempt to foreground schizoanalysis as a truly materialist psychiatry. As argued above, they contest psychoanalysis's idealist universalization of what are historically contingent, power-ridden structures of subjectivation on grounds that such idealization forecloses the critique and transformation of such structures. As they eloquently put it, subjects are not born Oedipal, desiring their mothers and hating their fathers; it is socialization in the nuclear family that may produce Oedipal libidinal investments (275). Yet the metaphysical outcome of their transcendental critique appears to yield an analogously idealist notion of the real functioning of the unconscious, although a machinic and schizoid instead of an oedipal one. But if, according to schizoanalysis's orientation toward a truly "materialist psychiatry" (34), socialization in the nuclear family actually produces oedipal subjects that desire their own oppression, and this is why it becomes the object of schizoanalytic critique (312), should we not assume that non-oedipal forms of subjectivation affirmed by schizoanalysis would have equally to be produced through different, non-Oedipal forms of socialization?

Analogous issues are raised by the implications of Deleuze and Guattari's materialist critique of psychoanalysis. Their transcendental critique of psychoanalysis suggests that the legitimate syntheses of the unconscious can be deduced from "its own constituent machines" (Deleuze and Guattari 2003: 339). The notion of the molecular unconscious yielded by their materialist critique of psychoanalysis is on the other hand a historicist one: the "schizophrenic accumulation of energy or charge" (34) would be the limit toward which capitalism would inherently tend—the deterritorialization of all forms, figures, and identities (138). Contrary to its inherent revolutionary tendency, capitalism simultaneously produces its own regressive reterritorializations upon the individualized and individualist terrains of the nuclear family and private property:

What we are really trying to say is that capitalism, through its process of production, produces an awesome schizophrenic accumulation of energy or charge, against which it brings all its vast powers of repression to bear, but which nonetheless continues to act as capitalism's limit. For capitalism constantly counteracts, constantly inhibits this inherent tendency while at the same time allowing it free rein; it continually seeks to avoid reaching its limit while simultaneously tending toward that limit. Capitalism institutes or restores all sorts of residual and artificial, imaginary, or symbolic territorialities, thereby attempting, as best it can, to recode, to rechannel persons who have been defined in terms of abstract quantities. Everything returns or recurs: States, nations, families. (Deleuze and Guattari 2003: 34)

Psychoanalysis, premised upon the universalization of oedipal, patriarchal familial forms of socialization consolidated by capitalism, would therefore participate in its tendency at regressive reterritorialization (Deleuze and Guattari 2003: 312) upon States, nations, families. Schizoanalysis, on the other hand, would be on the progressive side of history following capitalism's own inherent tendency to its own limit: "[L]iberating the schizoid movement of deterritorialization in all the flows" (321), which includes deterritorializing "the anthropomorphic representations of sex" based on sexual difference (294–5). But how can the schizophrenic process be both what characterizes the unconscious' "real functioning" (229) *and* what is historically produced by capitalist social relations as the inherent limit toward which they tend? How can schizoanalysis be grounded in both a critique which draws upon Kant's transcendental *idealism and* a materialist critique aimed at *dispelling idealist theories* of subjectivity, without a mediation or thematization of their tension? Even if situated in tension with its transcendental grounding, the implications of the materialist grounding of schizoanalysis pose an analogous problem for thinking the transformation of patriarchal social relations. This problem, I will argue, resides in the particular understanding of historical development underpinning schizoanalysis's materialist grounding.

Inimical to the Hegelian philosophy of history which presents the latter as proceeding through dialectical contradiction towards its end—the realization of human freedom—Deleuze and Guattari avoid characterizing the schizophrenic process of deterritorialization in teleological terms (see Hegel [1837]1975: 63). They characterize it as Capital's tendency to approach its own limit (and therefore undoing), simultaneously countered by its tendency to inhibit this progression and "avoid reaching its limit" (Deleuze and Guattari 2003: 34). A tendency is not a movement with a determined outcome, but a potentiality which can be actualized, or not.[9] Historical processes are, for Deleuze and Guattari, not driven by reason—neither in strictly Hegelian terms of the spirit discovering itself in its own concept through history (Hegel [1837] 1975: 62), whereby a reasonable development could be ascribed to historical processes (albeit only retrospectively) (Hegel [1820] 1967: 13), nor by reasoned choices and intentional actions of those who would like to bring about historical change. For Deleuze and Guattari, historical transformation proceeds through the contingent, irrational irruption of desire (2003: 377–8). The formations which subject these contingent dynamics to the "order of causes and aims" to transform social relations, would only stifle the explosive contingency of the revolutionary process and thus (willingly or not), aid the regressive tendencies of capitalism toward reterritorialization—regardless of what their manifest ideology may be. Using a distinction from Sartre's later work, Deleuze and Guattari characterize such formations as "subjugated groups" (see Sartre 2004). Those formations which do not submit desire to intentional aims and allow its "real functioning" free expression by tapping into the deterritorialized flow of capital's immanent revolutionary tendency are characterized as "subject groups":

> In the subjugated groups, desire is still defined by an order of causes and aims, and itself weaves a whole system of macroscopic relations that determine the large

aggregates under a formation of sovereignty. Subject groups on the other hand have as their sole cause a rupture with causality, a revolutionary line of escape ... The actualization of a revolutionary potentiality is explained less by the preconscious state of causality in which it is nonetheless included, than by the efficacy of a libidinal break at a precise moment, a schiz whose sole cause is desire—which is to say the rupture with causality that forces a rewriting of history on a level with the real, and produces this strangely polyvocal moment when everything is possible. (Deleuze and Guattari 2003: 377–8)

For Deleuze and Guattari there seems to be no way of submitting desire to goals and intentions which would not be reactionary, since desire, in the real order of its production—the molecular, machinic unconscious—would be devoid of any goal or intention:

This welding of desire to lack is precisely what gives desire collective and personal ends, goals or intentions-instead of desire taken in the real order of its production, which behaves as a molecular phenomenon devoid of any goal or intention. (Deleuze and Guattari 2003: 342)

On the other hand, Deleuze and Guattari argue that parallel to the two tendencies of capitalism there are "two major types of equally social investments" (2003: 340) and that *a choice* must be made between them: "[T]the choice is between one of two poles, the paranoiac counterescape that motivates all the conformist, reactionary, and fascisizing investments, and the schizophrenic escape convertible into a revolutionary investment" (341). Yet it seems hard to understand how any kind of choice, which necessarily presupposes personal ends, goals, or intentions, can be considered politically meaningful if intentionality, inherent to the process of choosing, is taken to follow only from the "welding of desire to lack" typical of "subjugated groups" or "large aggregates under a formation of sovereignty" (377–8). If choice, which "gives desire collective and personal ends," is immediately conflated with "the paranoiac counterescape that motivates all the conformist, reactionary, and fascizing investments" (341), how can the "nomadic and polyvocal," "revolutionary investment" be chosen at all? And why should it be chosen if "the revolutionary break" is characterized as "a rupture with causality," produced by the contingent dynamics of a "desire taken in the real order of its production, which behaves as a molecular phenomenon devoid of any goal or intention" (342)?

As Deleuze and Guattari insist, "[W]e believe in desire as in the irrational in every form of rationality" (Deleuze and Guattari 2003: 379). But can we really afford to believe that the contingent dynamic of desire, parallel to the deterritorializing tendency of capital, will undo existing relations of oppression? If we consider oppression to be internalized and therefore unconsciously engaged, rather than consciously enforced and endured; if we accept Deleuze and Guattari's thesis that our libidinal investments have been actually formed by Oedipal socialization, that we have been thusly made to *desire* our own oppression, can we really afford to hope that abandoning all intentional action which submits desires "to the order of causes and aims" will spontaneously bring about significant social and political transformation?

I would argue that it is precisely because there is no guarantee that desire, when not subordinated to rational causes and aims, will turn out to be a revolutionary force, that a schizoanalytic critique of the oedipal disfigurations of the unconscious is both possible and necessary: to *transform* desire so that it *becomes* a revolutionary force. It is in engaging this critique that schizoanalysis comes closest to "a truly materialist psychiatry" (Deleuze and Guattari 2003: 22). If this critique runs the risk of being weakened by some of the more metaphysical characterizations of schizoanalysis, I will argue this risk could be curbed by rethinking what Deleuze and Guattari characterize as both an ontological given (the real nature of desire) and a historical tendency (capital's tendency at deterritorialization), through the way materialist feminists conceptualize the end of sexual divisions as a necessary guiding idea of feminist politics—not an ontological, social, or natural actualized reality.

3. De-ontologizing Deterritorialization, Becoming n-Sexes

Implicitly contesting the differentialist critiques of egalitarianism, which hold that undoing sexual difference would entail women becoming like men or everyone becoming alike (see Derrida 1979: 65; Irigaray 1977: 150), Delphy argues that undoing binary sexualization would only entail undoing hierarchical and asymmetric sociopolitical differences—between the sexes, between those conforming to the sexual binary and those deviating from it, and between the heterosexual majority and those who identify otherwise (1993: 8). But sociopolitical differentiation (according to Delphy, always hierarchical and asymmetric) is not to be conflated with ontological differentiation. Once political differentiations are undone, a myriad of unforeseen, non-hierarchized differences of libidinal investments and personal attitudes could emerge (Delphy 1993: 8). This image of libidinal multiplicity resonates with Deleuze and Guattari's notion of the n-sexes:

> Everywhere a microscopic transsexuality ... relations of production of desire that overturn the statistical order of the sexes ... Desiring-machines or the nonhuman sex: not one or even two sexes, but n-sexes. Schizoanalysis is the variable analysis of the n-sexes in a subject, beyond the anthropomorphic representation that society imposes on this subject, and with which it represents its own sexuality. The schizoanalytic slogan of the desiring-revolution will be first of all: to each its own sexes. (2003: 295–6)

If we understand sexual difference to be the product of "the anthropomorphic representation of sex" (Deleuze and Guattari 2003: 295) enforced interpretatively by psychoanalysis and reproduced in the privatized realm of the nuclear family through sexually differentiated oedipal socialization, as Deleuze and Guattari do, and we understand the ways in which binary sexualization is restrictive not only upon the multiple possibilities of investment of desire, but for the material conditions of life of subjects so sexualized, then the deterritorialization of binary sexual difference or the actual undoing of the material conditions for hierarchical differentiation could be conceptualized as a feminist aim. Yet, as I have argued above, this aim cannot be brought about by *believing* that the blind contingency of liberated desire in its rupture with causality will actually happen to align itself with what is posited as an immanent tendency of capital at revolutionary schizophrenization. Recognizing gender, social sex, or sexual difference to be a hierarchical and asymmetric social construction does not entail subsuming them to mere illusion covering over the real nature of sexuality. If binary gendering is understood as the material product of a historically sedimented process of sexually differentiated socialization, its transformation will most likely have to take the form of a historical sedimentation of alternative, sexually non-differentiated, nonhierarchical and egalitarian forms of subjectivation, following the transformation of the social, political, and clinical institutions which socialize subjects. The end of sexual difference in materialist feminism is not understood as a "real functioning" of the machinic unconscious behind sexually differentiated Oedipal "necessary illusions," as Deleuze and Guattari seem to hold. While human sexuality is, for materialist feminists, *"potentially free and social"* (Tabet 2005: 135), what Tabet calls "the possible expansion of a sexuality theoretically open to any expression, having broken all necessary relationship with reproduction; an extremely flexible, non-sexed sexuality, not dominated by sex distinction, tendentially undifferentiated, and multiple in its forms as in its objects" (134–5) is expressly conceptualized as a *possibility*: if human sexuality is social in nature, the actualization of one particular arrangement of it can be actualized only in particular social circumstances. The radical openness of human sexuality conceptualized by materialist feminists does not entail that certain libidinal investments (even sexually non-differentiated ones, multiple in forms and objects) are more "natural" than others; it rather entails that they are "naturally" social and open and can thus take multiple forms, pending from social arrangements. By allying schizoanalysis to materialist feminism, the microscopic transsexuality of the n-sexes, the bringing about of libidinal investments "not dominated by sex distinction, tendentially undifferentiated, and multiple" (Deleuze and Guattari 2003: 295–6) through the transformation of the social (patriarchal and capitalist) conditions which presently form our binary oedipal libidinal investments, can thus be conceptualized as an expressly political aim—one which must be collectively worked toward.

Positing the viability of the end of sexual difference as a potentially realizable political goal also allows us to grasp how the latter is only the *result* of relations of oppression: those who dominate, categorize dominated ones as different, naturalize such categorizations and then use them to legitimize domination (see Wittig 1992: 1–9; Guillamin 1995: 212–15; Delphy 2008: 7–52). Analogously, Deleuze and Guattari reject the idealization and faux universalization of Oedipus in psychoanalysis, arguing that social alienation precedes psychic alienation (2003: 361), that the outside of social and economic relations directly forms the psychic dynamics and libidinal investments of subjects. But if this is true of the oedipal unconscious, belying the psychoanalytic idealist universalization of it, it must be true of the molecular unconscious as well: it has to be produced by collectively transforming the social institutions which socialize subjects, including the nuclear family, educational, and psychiatric institutions. The alliance of schizoanalysis with French materialist feminism can keep us alert precisely to the fact that, in Deleuzoguattarian words, if the unconscious is a factory (24), it can undoubtedly be productive of social relations, but as any means of production, it also needs to be produced in its turn. How can we transform institutions and forms of socialization so that subjects, instead of desiring their own oppression, will desire and work toward liberation instead? Instead of pitting them against one another, how can we make our desires and our rational aims coincide in a revolutionary manner?

4. Conclusion

Deleuze and Guattari emphasize that "revolutionaries often forget, or do not like to recognize, that one wants and makes revolution out of desire, not duty" (2003: 344). Their provocative privileging of the libidinal domain over all other possible components of political action, and their extension of the libidinal domain to the social as such (345) may be considered an overstatement, yet it points at what is too often overlooked in politicized theories of transformative action: the fact that unconscious processes and libidinal investments play an important role in either driving subjects to collective action aimed at social change, or deterring them from it. Bringing schizoanalysis to bear upon the at times overly voluntarist and objectivist framework of French materialist feminism helps us paying attention to the ways in which unconscious investments can stifle conscious revolutionary feminist aims—how women may comply with patriarchal norms not only out of interest, coercion, or illusion, but because they may have been socialized to desire their own oppression—an obstacle which cannot be overcome by individual acknowledgment and intentional action alone. On the other hand, brining materialist feminism to bear upon schizoanalysis may help us overcome some potential problems which could arise from its more metaphysical characterizations: it could help us realize how non-submissive kinds of libidinal investments and forms of subjectivation have to be actively, collectively produced, instead of believing in the revolutionary nature of the real functioning of desire) or capital's tendency at deterritorialization.

When a multitude of progressively available gender designations on social networks and official documents paints the picture of a happily postfeminist society, allying schizoanalysis's negative task to French materialist feminism allows us to rethink anew the end of sex/becoming n-sexes as the guiding idea, not the underpinning reality, of feminist struggles. The idea of an egalitarian society with new forms of subjectivation "beyond all differentiation," envisioned in fact also by Simone de Beauvoir: "[A] society where sexual equality is concretely realized ... [and where] this equality would newly assert itself in each individual" (2011: 761).

Notes

1. For a sociohistorical context of the *Anti-Oedipus*, see Buchanan (2008: 1–20); for an overview of French materialist feminism in context, see Leonard and Adkins ([1996] 2005 (1–25)).

2. On this, see: Holland ([1999] 2001: 4–18; 106–11).

3. The deterritorialization of the molar, including sexually differentiated identities (tackled in its subversive potentiality also by Tamsin Lorraine in the preceding chapter).

4. Inherited from Wilhelm Reich (see Deleuze and Guattari 2003: 344).

5. For an account of Beauvoir's attention to the material conditions which ontologically impinge upon women's freedom and therefore a rejection of the prevalent picture of Beauvoir as an existentialist voluntarist (see Kruks 2012).

6. Unfortunately, developing this argument lies beyond the scope of this paper. For more on new materialisms, see Van der Tuin (2012); for critiques of these theories, see, e.g., Ellenzweig and Zammito (2017) and Čičigoj (2017); on queer multitudes, see Preciado (2003: 17–25).

7. For an account of the transcendental and the materialist critique of psychoanalysis in *Anti-Oedipus*, see Holland (2001: 14–18).

8. As argued by Protevi (2011), *Anti-Oedipus* abandons what in *Difference and Repetition* was still a largely Kantian framework in favor of a naturalist one.

9. I wish to thank the anonymous reviewers for their comments to an earlier draft of this chapter.

References

Ahmed, S. (2008), "Open Forum Imaginary Prohibitions: Some Preliminary Remarks on the Founding Gestures of the 'New Materialism,'" *European Journal of Women's Studies* 15 (1): 23–39.

Bartky, S. L. (1990), *Femininity and Domination: Studies in the Phenomenology of Oppression*, New York: Routledge.

Braidotti, R., and I. Van der Tuin (2012), "Interview with Rosi Braidotti," in Rick Dolphijn and Iris Van der Tuin (eds.), *New Materialisms: Interviews and Cartographies*, 19–38, Michigan: Open Humanities Press.

Buchanan, I. (2008), *Deleuze and Guattari's Anti-Oedipus*, London: Continuum.

Čičigoj, K. (October 2017) "The Fatalist Temporality of the *Always Already*," ŠUM 8: 895–915.

dalla Costa, M., and S. James (1972), *The Power of Women & the Subversion of the Community*, Bristol: Falling Wall Press.

de Beauvoir, S. ([1949] 2011), *The Second Sex*, trans. C. Borde and S. Malovany-Chevallier, New York: Vintage Books, Random House.

Deleuze, G., and F. Guattari ([1972] 2003), *Anti-Oedipus*, trans. R. Hurley, M. Seem, and H. R. Lane, Minneapolis: University of Minnesota Press.

Delphy, C. (1988), "Patriarchy, Domestic Mode of Production, Gender, and Class," in C. Nelson and L. Grossberg (eds.), *Marxism and the Interpretation of Culture*, 259–67, Urbana: University of Illinois Press.

Delphy, C. (1993), "Rethinking Sex and Gender," *Women's Studies International Forum* 16 (1): 1–9.

Delphy, C. (2008), *Classer, dominer. Qui sont les "autres"?*, Paris: La fabrique éditions.

Derrida, J. (1979), *Spurs/Esperons*, trans. B. Harlow, Chicago, IL: University of Chicago Press.

Ellenzweig, S., and J. H. Zammito (eds.) (2017), *The New Politics of Materialism: History, Philosophy, Science*, New York: Routledge.

Federici, S. (2012), *Revolution at Point Zero*, Oakland, CA: PM Press.

Firestone, S. ([1970] 2015), *The Dialectic of Sex: A Case for Feminist Revolution*. London: Verso.

Fortunati, L. (1996), *The Arcane of Reproduction: Housework, Prostitution, Labor and Capital*, New York: Autonomedia.

Grosz, E. (2010), "Feminism, Materialism, and Freedom," in Diana Coole and Samantha Frost (eds.), *New Materialisms: Ontology, Agency, and Politics*, 139–57, Durham, NC: Duke University Press.

Guillamin, C. (1995), *Racism, Sexism, Power and Ideology*, trans. A. Rothwell, M. Silverman, M. J. Lakeland, C. Kunstenaar, L. Murgatroyd, and H. V. Wenzel, London: Routledge.

Gunnarsson, L. (2013), "The Naturalistic Turn in Feminist Theory: A Marxist-Realist Contribution," *Feminist Theory* 14 (1): 3–19.

Hegel, G. W. F. ([1820] 1967), *The Philosophy of Right*, ed. and trans. T. M. Knox, London: Oxford University Press.

Hegel, G. W. F. ([1837] 1975), *Lectures on the Philosophy of World History*, trans. H. B. Nisbeth, Cambridge: Cambridge University Press.

Holland, E. ([1999] 2001), *Deleuze and Guattari's* Anti-Oedipus: *Introduction to Schizoanalysis*, London: Routledge.

Howie, G. (2010), *Between Feminism and Materialism: A Question of Method*, Basingstoke: Palgrave MacMillan.

Irigaray, L. (1977), *Ce Sexe qui n'est pas un*, Paris: *Les éditions de minuit*.

Kant, I. ([1781] 1999), *The Critique of Pure Reason*, trans. P. Guyer and A. W. Wood, Cambridge: Cambridge University Press.

Kruks, S. (2012), *Simone de Beauvoir and the Politics of Ambiguity*, New York: Oxford University Press.

Leonard, D., and L. Adkins (eds.) ([1996] 2005), *Sex in Question: French Materialist Feminism*, London: Taylor and Francis.

Preciado, B. (2003), "*Multitudes Queer. Notes pour une Politiques des 'Anormaux,'*" *Multitudes* 12 (2): 17–25.

Protevi, J. (2011), "Mind in Life, Mind in Process: Toward a New Transcendental Aesthetic and a New Question of Panpsychism," *Journal of Consciousness Studies* 18 (5–6): 94–116.

Plaza M. (1977), "*Pouvoir 'Phallomorphique' et Psychologie de 'la Femme,'*" *Questions Féministes* 1 (1): 91–119.

Sartre, J. P. ([1960] 2004), *Critique of Dialectical Reason, Volume 1: Theory of Practical Ensembles*, trans. A. Smith, London: Verso.

Soper, K. (1995), *What Is Nature?*, Oxford: Blackwell.

Tabet, P. (2005), "Natural Fertility, Forced Reproduction," in Leonard, D. and L. Adkins (eds.), *Sex in Question: French Materialist Feminism*, 111–82, London: Taylor and Francis.

Van der Tuin, Iris (2012) "Sexual Differing," in Rick Dolphijn and Iris Van der Tuin (eds.), *New Materialisms: Interviews and Cartographies*, 137–57, Michigan: Open Humanities Press.

Wittig, M. (1992), *The Straight Mind and Other Essays*, Boston, MA: Beacon Press.

Figure 6.1 *"#4," 2016, ink and watercolor on paper, Fredrica Introne*
Photo taken by the artist.
Fredrica Introne's work captures the intensities of bodies in various states of jiu jitsu grappling. Her poignant portrayal is both a study of forces and an evocative and affective exposure to vulnerability— an exploration of sensuality and erotism that moves outside of expected alliances, and a visual opening onto different forms of desire.

CHAPTER 6
TO HAVE DONE WITH SEXUALITY: SCHIZOANALYSIS AND THE PROBLEM OF QUEER–FEMINIST ALLIANCES
Nir Kedem

Shortly after the publication of *Anti-Oedipus*, Deleuze and Guattari stated, "Schizoanalysis has one single aim—to get revolutionary, artistic, and analytic machines working as parts, cogs, of one another" (Deleuze 1995: 24). Finding a way for such machines to fit together as components of a revolutionary process requires establishing transversal unity between the parts, yet "unification must occur through analysis" (Deleuze 2004: 199). Working out the nature of such unity and how to achieve it defines the approach taken here in regard to the volume's themes. I am particularly interested in how schizoanalysis may enable a queer–feminist alliance without reducing the one to the other (nor deriving either from a larger "whole"), allowing them to retain their differences and disputes yet to carve new paths for both to produce ever-widening new coalitions that function as forces of social transformation in multiple contexts.

Alliances between queer and feminist theories have tended to be uneasy and have known mostly ruptures. Three years after the publication of the inaugural special issue of *differences* announcing the birth of queer theory, another special issue reflected critically on the emerging tensions between feminism and queer theory. Despite their apparent commonalities, the editors gathered that the two are "something of an unmatched pair" (Weed 1997: vii) and characterized their encounter as strange and surprising rather than mutually empowering. Instead of a fruitful alliance opening up new ways for political thought and action, feminists were disappointed to find in queer theory a reductive representation of "a strange feminism, stripped of its contentious elements, its internal contradictions, its multiplicity" (ix). Judith Butler's opening piece criticized queer theory for appropriating sexuality as its exclusive "proper object," a dubious move that served as a foundational justification for queer theory's methodological autonomy by producing an image of a devalued feminism utilized by queer theory to differentiate itself; a feminism deemed inapt to theorize sexuality, and which was thus ascribed exclusively to the study of gender (Butler 1997). In the 1997 revised article, Butler contextualized her critique as a reflexive engagement with/in feminism designed to create alternative ways of thinking, which "would overcome [feminism's] complicity in heterosexist presuppositions and mark an alliance with lesbian and gay struggles" (2). However, proceeding attempts to think productively and critically about the relations between gender, sexual difference, and sexuality have tended to occur more in feminism, as well as in lesbian thought and transgender studies, than in queer theory (Rudy 2000; Richardson 2006; Jagose 2009;

Marinucci 2010). Butler's critique echoes the argument put forth by queer theorists who argued against a conception of queer theory as a theory *of* sexuality, and who therefore underscored the "indeterminate" rather than "sexual" sense of queer.[1] Although fewer today insist on an exclusively queer theorization of sexuality independently of any feminist framework (Halley 2006), the category of sexuality has become queer theory's foundation and most treasured of concepts through the conflation of the indeterminate with the sexual sense in the concept of queer; a move that has effectively generalized the concept of sexuality as queer theory's "true" form of foundational difference—that is, sexuality's supposedly inherent indeterminacy.

By making it one of its increasingly uncritical concepts, queer theory has been facilitating the coagulation of sexuality into an impediment to alliances with feminism. It has become an analytic machine whose dominant function is *to sexualize everything* (history, language, culture, the arts)—to make sexuality both the cause and end of theory and politics, a first and last principle. It has long forgotten that this function is not revolutionary in itself; that it had originated in the activist response to the terrors of the AIDS crisis in the 1980s and 1990s in the United States, in that queer activism that could not have succeeded without making broad alliances with feminists, lesbians, people of color, and so many others.[2] Schizoanalysis was conceived as a project *for* such alliances, as Deleuze said (1995: 22). In order to understand what allying ourselves with schizoanalysis entails, I offer a detailed account of the role sex and sexuality play in *Anti-Oedipus*. My aim is to show that schizoanalysis may function as a new means to ally the feminist and queer analytic machines by effecting a radical desexualization of queer theory—a utopian gesture designed to liberate queer theory from its transcendental illusions, that is, from the concept of sexuality itself. In so doing, schizoanalysis offers a solution to a problem posited by Foucault, who seems to have set what remains today the greatest challenge to queer theory: "[I]t is not enough to liberate sexuality; we also have to liberate ourselves ... from the very notion of sexuality" (Foucault 2011: 388). Thus, schizoanalysis can be said to be desexualizing in a specific sense: it does not operate as a reactionary call for anti-sexual ascesis, nor as a denial of sexual pleasures, practices, politics, and lifestyles, but rather as a refusal of sexuality inasmuch as it functions as a privileged analytical category and an exclusive foundation of political resistance, for the real positive power of queer is the threat it poses *to* sexuality, not *as* sexuality.

1. Schizoanalysis and the Use of Sexuality

Deleuze and Guattari remarked that they have always been functionalists (Deleuze 1995: 21–2). This functionalism, or the question of use, attests to the pragmatic nature of their work, particularly schizoanalysis. The pragmatic task before us is examining whether schizoanalysis could make queer and feminist analytic machines the working parts of other machines without compromising their respective differences and independent operations. The question is then what sort of alliances, queer-feminist or otherwise, does schizoanalysis make possible? At what cost? To what end? The answers will be determined firstly by specifying ends and secondly by defining a working method. Outlining the conditions of possibility for such alliances is the goal of this essay; my working method is to experiment with schizoanalysis as a theoretical toolbox to be used to this end, whereby experimentation means a revaluation of the schizoanalytic use of the concepts of sex and sexuality, all the more in light of the tensions animating the relationships between queer and feminist machines.

In *Anti-Oedipus*, there are no sex nor sexuality "in general," as abstract self-contained and ready-made concepts or categories; rather, there are only uses of sex and sexuality in relation to the productive unconscious, deemed either illegitimate (or transcendent) in the psychoanalytic system, or legitimate (immanent) in the schizoanalytic system. In the machinic terminology of schizoanalysis, sex and sexuality refer to the unconscious dynamism (the syntheses of desire) of production from the standpoint of libidinal economy. Sex, in the singular, exists only as an organ-machine, or a partial object that is not exclusively a sexual organ.[3] Schizoanalysis considers the division of sex into male and female a false psychoanalytic reduction that privileges the genitals over other organs. An organ functions as an interceptor that gives or receives a flow—sexuality, or libidinal energy. But speaking of *an* organ/*a* sex is valid only analytically, for, Deleuze and Guattari insist, organs are machinic arrangements of other partial objects and flows. One's sex never refers to a single sexual organ or the reproductive system exclusively; organs are always organ-machines set in relation to one another, which together form a heterogeneous chain of machines. Sex in the singular, then, is already a multiplicity of interconnected organ-machines, a displaced image of the "*n* sexes," while sexuality in the singular is a displaced image of "trans-sexuality." Schizoanalysis effects a displacement of one set of terms in favor of another: instead of sex and sexuality, it refers to *n* sexes (which are not necessarily either male *or* female) and trans-sexuality (which is not necessarily homosexual *or* heterosexual).[4]

That Deleuze and Guattari reemploy Deleuze's reading of Proust and its conceptualization of sex and sexuality, so as to explain the formation of desiring-machines, is a fact that went mostly unnoticed in the literature. However, the Proustian theory of sexuality has three functions in *Anti-Oedipus*: (1) it explains the non-totalizing unity of the machines, which enables Deleuze and Guattari, (2) to deduce the legitimate and illegitimate uses of the connective synthesis, and thus (3) to present the ramifications of the psychoanalytic illegitimate use of the syntheses as it is expressed in the social field. I will account for the Proustian theory of sexuality in *Proust and Signs* before returning to examine these three functions.

The problem of fitting machines together as working parts of one another preoccupied Deleuze in the second part added to *Proust and Signs* in 1972. In a roundtable discussion on Proust, Deleuze succinctly described it as "the idea that things or people or groups do not communicate" (2007: 39). What is characteristically of interest for Deleuze here is the question of the very possibility of communication—what could serve as a principle that explains the formation of communication between noncommunicating terms? How are we to explain the genesis of communication, but immanently? The Proustian theory is a means to uncover such a genetic principle. Indeed, everything is sexed and sexual, everything relates or communicates with everything; love is always in the air. Yet Deleuze parts with this banality as he insists on understanding the formations of relations in terms other than the part–whole relationship. In *Anti-Oedipus*, Deleuze and Guattari enlist the Proustian theory to explain how relations between parts neither add up to nor are derived from a whole; rather, "Proust maintained that the Whole itself is a product, produced as nothing more than a part alongside other parts, which it neither unifies nor totalizes ... [although] it establishes ... transverse unities between elements that retain all their differences within their own particular boundaries" (1983: 43).

Parts are therefore fragments, organ-machines assembled in a working relationship. This relationship is sexual in the sense that it is productive and reproductive: sexuality is this working relationship, the communication between sexes, while the sexes are functional organ-parts—the "sides" in the relationship—that relate to one another in the simplest sense: they make love, they fuck, plain and simple—they produce/reproduce, create/procreate. Biological reproduction is key to understanding the Proustian theory of sexuality and its role in *Anti-Oedipus*, but this does not imply restoring problematic reductions of people and living beings to biological organisms defined by their sexual organs.

Thus, when Deleuze and Guattari say that sexuality is everywhere they say both more and less about sex and sexuality than we would expect. They say more for they refuse reductionist understandings of these terms in psychoanalysis and Marxism, but also in the natural sciences and cultural imaginations. They say less in the sense that sex and sexuality themselves are approximations, which refer to something that transcends them and insists within them, namely, the sex life of everything. What partly makes *Anti-Oedipus* a revolutionary book is that it tells us how unremarkable sex and sexuality are; yes, everything and everyone constantly fuck and are being fucked, everything is a sex-organ. *Anti-Oedipus* is pornography, as profane as it is innocent, that makes no effort to conceal its pornographic nature. On the contrary, it is designed to turn you on with its explicit erotic depictions of discharged flows passing between organs; it eroticizes even the very manner by which I strike my keyboard (why not, fuck my keyboard), in the same way that "a bureaucrat fondles his records, a judge administers justice, a businessman causes money to circulate; the way the bourgeoisie fucks the proletariat" (1983: 293). This famous phrase is not about sexuality anymore, but its overcoming. *Anti-Oedipus* fucks with us in order to lead us to the "real fucking" of desiring-machines that fuck without penises and vaginas, or independently of them. This pornography of machines unfolds as the natural history of their aberrant intercourse and its possibility—because when the machines fuck, everything comes into being or disappears. And fucking is about reproduction in its utmost rudimentary sense, regardless of the domain in which it takes place—biological, social, or familial. It is so trivial that it makes one wonder, with Deleuze and Guattari, how psychoanalysis managed to fuck it up so brilliantly. By adapting the Proustian theory to the revolutionary task of schizoanalysis, Deleuze and Guattari will be able to explain this fuckup as well.

Let us inspect the formulation of the Proustian theory in *Anti-Oedipus*, in order to understand how the notions of sexuality-as-reproduction and sexes-as-organs rearranges the vocabulary of feminist and queer theories: "We are statistically or molarly heterosexual, but personally homosexual, without knowing it or being fully aware of it, and finally we are trans-sexed in an elemental, molecular sense" (1983: 70, translation modified). This formulation is a redescription of the "levels of the Search" in the tenth chapter of *Proust and Signs*, with each level representing a type of sexuality as a form of communication or reproduction.

2. The First Level: Heterosexuality or Gender/Difference of the Sexes

The first level is that of groups, or aggregates: a collective whole combined of parts that are presumed to be of the same nature as the whole, and expressive of it. Heterosexuality determines the nature of communication between men and women as "global persons" or social wholes from which individuals select and are selected to form the interpersonal relationships described at the second level. This level could loosely be called the level of gender, for Deleuze's referring to man and woman as sexes is peculiarly French. The French word *sexe* covers over an internal division between *la différence sexuelle* (sexual difference) and *la différence des sexes*, which could be translated as "difference of the sexes." The latter "implies an empirical recognition of the sexes independent of any definition of content" (Fraisse 2014: 969)—a "philosopheme," "an abstract conceptual division" (Sanford 2014: 972)—and it seems the more adequate term here, precisely due to its obscurity and seeming neutrality, which renders the man–woman duality an empty determination (indeed, very little is said of the difference between men and women in *Anti-Oedipus*), as it is determined by the network of social conventions of a historically given milieu.

The formation of interpersonal relationships depends on people recognizing each other as parts of the same social whole, and recognition depends on their ability to "read" one another as a particular case of a general type defined by a given society's conventions, codes, stereotypes, etiquettes, ideas, and values (Deleuze 2000: 77; 81–3). Groups constitute the necessary milieu within which such recognition takes place and is made possible. The person we love was encountered first in a group from which s/he was selected and recognized as a general type (a man in a group of men, a woman in a group of women) according to the social meanings (masculine or feminine) attached to his or her behavior, gestures, speech, dress, and so on. Yet, are groups not richer environments than their gender differences? Could variables such as race, age, class, ethnicity, and nationality be reduced to gender? No, on the contrary: Deleuze suggests that such variables are necessarily present in the milieu and are no less formative than gender in the constitution of general types and the social meaning of their signs. The difference of the sexes becomes primary at the first level from the perspective of reproduction, and only in reference to the social environment that regulates and codifies the possibilities of human reproduction. Humans share with some organisms the capacity for sexual reproduction, which is dependent on contingency and the environment in which such capacities are actualized. In humans, the possibility of reproduction cannot be reduced to the instance whereby males and females signal one another their sex and readiness for copulation. Rather, prior to that they encounter each other first as men and women—as general types that their social milieu either varies or limits the possibilities for their encounter. For example, the possibility of producing an offspring of a black mother and a white father (or vice versa) in American society is much more than biological or sexual; rules of conduct, ideas about race, citizenship, and evolution, have been varying and determining the possibilities for black–white copulations of the human animal throughout history, as well as their value. The same applies to rules, behaviors, and ideas concerning social mobilization, which makes possible copulations between human animals of different classes and nations.

3. The Second Level: Homosexuality or Sexual Difference

The second level could also be called the level of sexual difference, and it is defined "by the two homosexual (and still statistical) series, according to which an individual considered within the preceding entity [the group] was referred to other individuals of the same sex" (Deleuze 2000: 136). The two series are Sodom and Gomorrah, for they refer to the fourth volume of Proust's *In Search of Lost Time*. These series are formed in the second circle of the Proustian Search, that is, in one of the three systems of signs that together constitute the unity of the Search (5). While at the first level the signs emitted by the beloved are interpreted in relation to the group to which s/he belongs, at the second level the beloved becomes an individual, for "to become in love is to individualize someone by the signs he bears or emits … The beloved appears as a sign, a "soul"; the beloved expressed a possible world unknown to us … imprisoning a world that must be deciphered" (7, translation modified). Love invests libidinal energy in an object choice, thereby turning it into a particular person; it enables us to see someone as a person distinguished from an anonymous mass. The signs that the beloved emits are no longer barely distinguishable from the social codes of the group; rather, the beloved's certain gaze, smile, or gestures now seem to express something hidden and unique to the beloved—the secret of her personhood.

What may seem baffling is that homosexual reproduction asserts the irreducibility of sexual difference as the primary term of the second level. Deleuze implicitly embraces feminist notions of the irreducibility of sexual difference when he states, "The truth of love is first of all the isolation of the sexes," yet he adds that "matters are complicated because the separated, partitioned sexes coexist in the same individual" (80). Thus, sexual difference not only determines (male or female) individuals as parts constituting the group-whole, but also as persons-wholes defined internally by sexual difference (135–6), as summed up in *Anti-Oedipus*: "[E]veryone is bisexed, everyone has two sexes, but partitioned, noncommunicating: the man is merely the one in whom the male part, and the woman the one in whom the female part, dominates statistically" (1983: 69, translation modified). It is at the second level that the sense of "sex" as organ or part (male or female) comes to the fore. Still, why are the two sexes in a person noncommunicating?

Why are the two series homosexual? And why would Deleuze say that "homosexuality is the truth of love" (2000: 81)?

If we understand homosexuality as a form of reproduction, these qualifications acquire their proper sense, although their ultimate explanation lies at the third level. Let us first understand the relation between sexual difference and homosexuality here. The first level establishes the social milieu wherein heterosexual loves become possible, yet these are "less profound than homosexual ones" (10). Once love individualizes a person, that person is now perceived as a whole in itself, an "unknown world" chosen from a constellation of "possible worlds" (the group). The truth of this secret world-person is his or her sex, or their belonging to a sex that is inaccessible as such to the lover. In Proust, the jealous narrator's love for Albertine reveals to him that her secret world is "the world of Gomorrah, which itself no longer depends on this or that woman ... but is the feminine possibility par excellence ... This is because the world expressed by the loved woman is always a world that excludes us" (9–10). Concurrently, the lover discovers himself to belong to his own separate world, that of Sodom or the masculine possibility par excellence. The two worlds are exclusionary for they are homosexual, wherein communication occurs only between members of the same sex. In his (heterosexual) love for Albertine, the narrator discovers her homosexual loves for other women that inflame his jealousy— these women he considers his rivals whose "weapons are different" (10), that is, the rival is of a different sex than the lover and exists in the same-sex world to which the lover, being a man, does not belong and which he cannot access. Thus, homosexual relationships are expressions of the coexistence of separate same-sex worlds, or the principle of sexual difference (139; 174).

The parts constituting this whole (the unknown world) are all female, yet through love they do communicate and reproduce by means of serialization and doubling: the narrator's love connects Albertine to other women he loved (his love renders them all doubles of one another), but also discovers Albertine herself as a series of women (Albertine's many faces). For Deleuze, then, thinking sexual difference means establishing its irreducibility through homosexuality as its truth, "[T]o the point where heterosexual loves are merely the appearance that covers the destination of each sex" (11), that is, the sequestering of each sex from the other in its own homosexual world.

At this stage, it is still unclear why Deleuze argues that we all have two sexes, and why the two sexes within a person are noncommunicating. Deleuze uses the term "the Original Hermaphrodite" to explain it. Although the primary reference to the term is Proust's work, Deleuze loosely uses the Original Hermaphrodite as a pseudo-biological concept of classification to define the human species: each person is a hermaphrodite endowed with male and female sexes-parts, much like certain types of flowers and snails. But "the Hermaphrodite is not a being capable of reproducing itself" (10), for it can only be fertilized by other hermaphrodites like it (80). Thus, a person has both male and female parts, contiguous yet noncommunicating. Consequently, self-fertilization is impossible—some mediating third party must intervene "so that the female part may be fertilized or the male part may fertilize" (136).

However, what that mysterious third party establishes indirectly is the proliferation of sexual difference that confirms the separation of the sexes both within and without the individual: "Then it happens that the intermediary, instead of effecting the communication of male and female, doubles each sex with itself: symbol of self-fertilization all the more moving in that it is homosexual, sterile, indirect... this is the essence of love" (80). Heterosexual reproduction is therefore the model of neither love nor reproduction. This means that (1) the difference of the sexes cannot be reduced to sexual difference, nor vice versa and (2) that in terms of reproduction, heterosexuality and homosexuality cannot be reduced to an opposition between production and anti-production, for they represent two different forms of reproduction—the former successive and hereditary and the latter serial and doubling—both of which are derived from the Original Hermaphrodite and its reproductive capacities.

4. The Third Level: Trans-sexuality or Partial Objects

The Original Hermaphrodite is located at the third level of trans-sexuality, which holds the genetic principle of the Proustian theory and its model of reproduction. Once a distinction is made between the second and third levels, sexual difference and homosexuality are revealed as superficial appearance, as are the difference of the sexes and heterosexuality. The image of self-fertilization of homosexuality and the irreducibility of sexual difference will be rewritten to reveal their immanent form: trans-sexuality, or "local and nonspecific homosexuality" (Deleuze 2000: 137); and the multiplicity of "untotalizable and untotalized fragments" (131) that are partial objects. Fundamentally, the sense of sex here is neither difference of the sexes nor sexual difference, but rather partial object, a sex-organ irreducible to a whole (be that whole a group or a person). Partial objects here have not yet been defined in psychoanalytic and schizoanalytic terms, but simply as fragments on their own right, which cannot be understood in relation to a whole of which they are a part (hence, untotalized); and which cannot be understood in relation to a whole that is their sum total (hence, untotalizable). The whole betrays neither their nature nor their relation, but rather is created alongside the fragments like a residue, itself a part among other parts.

How are we to recognize partial objects as fragments standing on their own? We take the second level's principle of irreducible sexual difference to its limit. The mismatch between the two sexes, their essential noncommunication, is the binary form of the law of partial objects: each sex is a part contiguous with another part but the two do not match, because for this or that part "there is no other part that corresponds to it, no totality into which it can enter, no unity from which it can be torn and to which it can be restored" (112). It is the fragment that is irreducible, a sex irreducible to the duality of the sexes. Instead, there are as many sexes as there are fragments, organs, partial objects. The practical way to discover partial objects is to search for things that do not match yet somehow appear linked together.[5]

How is it then that people and things do communicate, wholes created, and some parts derived from wholes? We arrive at an answer once we take homosexuality to its limit: the formation of communication through an intermediary. Now we have only some partial object functioning as an intermediary, so that "an aberrant communication occurs in a transversal dimension between partitioned sexes" (136). Trans-sexuality is precisely the formation of aberrant communications between partial objects. Its model is the famous instance of the wasp and the orchid. Orchids reproduce by way of a *ménage à trois*: the orchid is a hermaphrodite unable to reproduce itself, so it copulates with the wasp that transfers its pollens to another orchid. For the orchid, the wasp is a sexual organ/partial object functioning as a part of its reproduction system without being totalized by it. Deleuze's point is that any organ can play the role of a partial object for other noncommunicating partial objects. Trans-sexuality thus refers to the transversal as the genetic principle of love or sexuality, here also dubbed local and nonspecific homosexuality, "in which a man seeks what is masculine in a woman and a woman what is feminine in a man, and this is in the partitioned contiguity of the two sexes as partial objects" (137). Such an aberrant communication is formed between the narrator and Albertine as the image of this mother plays the role of the intermediary that connects them. But the mother now functions as that sex-organ, as that "insect" that acts transversally to bring them together (141).

5. The Three Functions of the Proustian Theory in *Anti-Oedipus*

The primary function of the Proustian theory of sexuality in *Anti-Oedipus* is not to argue for the ontological or categorical primacy of either sex or sexuality, but to affirm the combinatory logic constitutive of the unity of the desiring-machines and the flux of desiring-production as a multiplicity. The desiring-machines make us into organic wholes (organisms), be it individual or social. The unity of wholes is achieved transversally and indirectly, as an effect of irreducible fragments connecting with one another. There are no wholes as such, only parts/organ-machines connecting and disconnecting, and as these incessant connections and disjunctions are recorded on the body-without-organs, they form relatively consistent "patterns" that are like series of intensive states, egos "with no fixed identity, wandering about over the body without organs, but always remaining peripheral to the desiring-machines" (Deleuze and Guattari 1983: 16). The subject is thus produced "as a residuum ... a spare part adjacent to the machine" (20), and Deleuze and Guattari use a language similar to that in *Proust and Signs* to describe the creation of the whole as a product: "If we discover such a totality alongside various separate parts ... it is a unity *of* all these particular parts but does not unify them; rather, it is added to them as a new part fabricated separately" (42). The Proustian theory is then immediately evoked to make this point.[6] The transversal unity of the fragmented Proustian universe is not given but produced, just like the unity of the body-without-organs, which is "produced as a whole ... alongside the parts that it neither unifies nor totalizes. And when it operates on them ... it brings about transverse communications" (43).

The more explicit articulation of the Proustian theory of sexuality cited earlier is presented in the discussion of the legitimate and illegitimate uses of the connective synthesis, and it presupposes the principle of transversal unity—this is the second function of the Proustian theory. Psychoanalysis makes a global and specific use of the connective syntheses, that is, an illegitimate use that "can be defined as transcendent, and implies a first paralogism in the psychoanalytic process" (74). This illegitimate use explains the transcendental illusions created at the first two levels. At the first level, the phallus becomes a complete object detached from the chain of partial objects, which now functions as a transcendent instance seemingly enabling the communication between men and women; or, in other words, instituting the difference of the sexes by its being defined as what both sexes lack. Here the psychoanalytic illegitimate use accounts for the formation of molar masculine and feminine sexualities and the single possibility for them to interact—in a regime of "the pairing of the people under the rules of familial reproduction" (71), that is, according to the rules of heterosexual reproduction as articulated by the first level of the Proustian theory. This is the alliance or conjugal aspect of the illegitimate use of the connective synthesis (ibid.).

The second aspect of the illegitimate use of the connective synthesis is the parental or familial aspect, and it corresponds to the illusion engendered at the second level of the Proustian theory. Just as the truth of heterosexuality was to be discovered in homosexuality, so does the principle of pairing (the conjugal aspect) is to be explained by the principle of triangulation (the formation of the oedipal triangle) forming the individuals to be paired at the first level. By now, Deleuze and Guattari have already defined partial objects after Melanie Klein who, they argue, nevertheless "failed to grasp their logic" (44). Partial objects, instead of being irreducible fragments, are falsely seen as parts belonging to a whole person, either the subject or object of desire: "[D]esire at the same time receives a fixed subject, an ego specified according to a given sex, and complete objects defined as global persons" (70). This is the institution of an irreducible sexual difference articulated by the second level of the Proustian theory. Global persons emerge first as an effect of the installment of the basic oedipal triangle: the ego set in relation to the two parental images of the father and the mother. The formation of this triangle, however, is inseparable from the incest taboo "that conditions the differentiation between persons: prohibition of incest with the mother, prohibition against taking the father's place" (ibid.). This is how global persons appear as complete objects, first in the family and then in the social field, whereby the conjugal aspect guarantees the reproduction of the oedipal triangle in social relationships. Castration is the principle underlying this operation, which will culminate in the establishment of the phallus as the "common-universal" introducing lack into desire, and as the transcendent law "imposing an exclusive direction on the disjunction of the sexes" (72), that is, the demand to assume a social subject position that is exclusively masculine or feminine, which is preceded by the familial differentiation of persons as exclusively male or female. To make this argument, Deleuze and Guattari further revise the notion of hermaphroditism in the Proustian theory: they follow Klein's conception of female sexuality and castration anxiety, wherein the boy and the girl recognize both the penis and the vagina as distinct sexual organs, and unconsciously perceive the mother's body as endowed with both. Klein then argued that castration anxieties in girls and boys precede the genital phase and revolve around the entire body (not just the sexual organs), as they are engendered by unconscious fantasies about the mother's power to destroy the interior of the child's body. However, she retained the notion of castration anxiety "proper," which, for Deleuze and Guattari, resulted in the extrapolation of the transcendent phallus.[7] Finally, Klein identified a homosexual component of the child's psyche, the experience of which will later determine how the oedipal conflict is resolved.[8] This "homosexuality" of the psyche becomes the psychoanalytic basis for the two homosexual series in the Proustian theory.

This leads us finally to the third function of the Proustian theory in *Anti-Oedipus* and its reintroduction of the third level of trans-sexuality. Re-presenting the molecular unconscious as defined by schizoanalysis, Deleuze and Guattari conclude their account by describing the ramifications of the illegitimate use of the connective synthesis in the social field. Following Marx, they argue that the true difference is not between the sexes but between the human sex and the nonhuman sex: "Desiring-machines are the nonhuman sex, the molecular machinic elements ... without which there would be neither a human sex specifically determined in the large aggregates, nor a human sexuality capable of investing these aggregates" (294). The nonhuman sex (the *n* sexes) now plays the role of irreducible fragments incessantly forming aberrant communications with one another. Such communication is defined as trans-sexuality that is no longer overcoded by lack and castration, "because the syntheses constitute local and nonspecific connections, inclusive disjunctions, nomadic conjunctions: everywhere a microscopic trans-sexuality, resulting in the woman containing as many men as the man, and the man as many as the women, all capable of entering ... into relations of production of desire that overturn the statistical order of the sexes" (295–6).

Already in *Proust and Signs* the "statistical order" referred to the social order with its restrictive determinations of both groups and individuals. The social is statistical for it constitutes a large-scale, extensive environment large enough for us to discern the laws that regulate it (Deleuze 2000: 82). The difference of the sexes is produced statistically as an empty category, for it is an effect of a given society's conventions assigning specific yet historically contingent properties to masculinity and femininity. This statistical nature of the social creates the illusion of total wholes—society as a whole, but also the whole-individual. In *Anti-Oedipus* the law now refers to the "law of large numbers" in statistics (Deleuze and Guattari 1983: 287), as that which explains the generality of gender and sexual difference; for, as with any phenomena appearing in large numbers, it becomes harder to discern differences and variations to the extent that these phenomena seem more and more homogeneous, manifesting slight or no differences.

It is in this context that Deleuze and Guattari claim that human sex and sexuality are statistical entities determined socially rather than psychically, and thus, as such, are but "anthropomorphic representations" society imposes on the molecular unconscious. The implementation of Oedipus as a "formal cause" effected by the paralogism of extrapolation results in two such representations that are responsible for the illusion of collective-wholes comprised of individual-parts, which in turn are seen as individual-wholes in themselves: (1) *the anthropomorphic representation of sex* that refers to the Freudian–Lacanian idea of a single sex, which is based on the phallus as the founding principle of "the statistical aggregate of intersexual loves" (295), and which corresponds to heterosexuality in Proust; (2) *the anthropomorphic representation of sexuality* that refers to the Kleinian idea of the two sexes, which is based on castration and which does not found communication between the sexes but "their separation into two homosexual series that remain statistical" (295). This idea corresponds to the second level of homosexuality in Proust. These two ideas express how human sex and sexuality are inscribed on the social as effects of the oedipalization of molecular (trans-)sexuality, an effect fortified by the psychoanalytic, illegitimate use of the syntheses in the service of the capitalist machine.

Anti-Oedipus neither promotes nor presupposes a theory of sexuality for its own sake. There is nothing foundational nor ontological about sexuality and sex, only functional. For schizoanalysis, sexuality and sex in themselves explain desire no better than labor and capital. As functional parts of the analytic machine that is schizoanalysis, sex and sexuality serve as indices of the character—reactionary or revolutionary—of unconscious investments of desire in the social field. The greatest challenge of schizoanalysis is not the claim that sexuality is everywhere, but that desire directly invests the social field.

6. Conclusion: "The Price of the Ticket"

Schizoanalysis offers queer theory neither justification for nor confirmation of the primacy it bestows on sexuality, as Deleuze made it abundantly clear in *Dialogues*: "We do not believe in general that sexuality has the role of an infrastructure in the assemblages of desire, nor that it constitutes an energy capable of transformation or of neutralization and sublimation. Sexuality can only be thought of as one flux among others ... No assemblage can be characterized by one flux exclusively" (Deleuze and Parnet 2002: 101). This does not contradict *Anti-Oedipus*' claim that "sexuality is everywhere," because, in its employment of the Proustian theory, schizoanalysis specifies the *analytic* conditions under which both statements are valid: at the molecular level, sexuality, desiring-machines, the *n* sexes, and the syntheses are all identical (1983: 294), since they designate the transversal unity of multiplicity (partial objects and flows); at the molar level of groups and persons, sex and sexuality are toxic ideas that misrepresent and disguise the very molecular processes that made them possible (ibid.), and in this sense has no role of an infrastructure of desire. They are indices of the ways desire invests the social field as recorded by the capitalist form of inscription—axiomatization.

As long as sexuality—but also gender, sex, age, race, class, and other identity categories—refers to global persons or abstract-universal concepts of foundational unity, it remains subjected to the single form of alliance capitalism allows and demands: that of wage labor. Schizoanalytic desexualization may begin with specifying the determinate conditions for the subversion of the capitalist form of alliance, and it thus has nothing to do with sublimation nor asceticism nor resistance for its own sake. Rather, inasmuch as sexualization ends up entangled with illegitimate uses of the syntheses, desexualization complements queer theory's function of sexualization by effecting an "internal reversal" designed to circumvent the impasses that sexualization engendered or is no longer able to break through.

This is where Deleuze's claim that sexuality is but a flux among other fluxes becomes a compelling argument for schizoanalytic desexualization. As Daniel Smith argues, Deleuze's concept of flow originates in economics, where it designates incoming and outgoing movements of money between interceptors (individuals or groups) that either take it in or give it off (2011: 43). But flows can only be known through their recording in the social field, that is, through their codifications as socially meaningful in a particular way in a given place and time. Since capitalism replaced codes with axiomatics, the flow of sexuality is submitted to an "accounting system" (44)—the capitalist form of inscription—that regulates social relationships by converting them to abstract, interchangeable quantities of labor and capital, as this is the essential function of axiomatics (51). Axiomatization at the same time enables capitalism to tolerate and appropriate the very type of sexual politics that was invented to undermine the inequalities effected and multiplied by capitalism, namely, struggles for equality and liberation. Desexualizing these struggles is not their dismissal but at the very least their "economization" and hence their reorientation according to contingent political circumstances and aims.

For example, a dominant form of protest in liberal sexual politics is criticisms of mis- and under-representation of minorities as both symptom and strategy of oppression. Criticisms of the #MeToo movement is but the recent manifestation of such politics, which finds the discharge of revolutionary energies intolerable unless it succumbs to clerical calculations of quantities of representation, that is, unless #Me Too commits itself to "equal" representation of women of color, LGBT people, sex workers, or other minorities. Such criticisms, justified as they may be, are quickly becoming the lip-service—the "price of the ticket" as James Baldwin described white and black people's impossible dream of becoming white (Baldwin 1998: 835)—the "dues" capitalism pays to the minorities it keeps sucking dry. It distracts us long enough and in a circular fashion to make us overlook that such criticisms feed capitalism's capacity "to introduce lack where there is always too much" (Deleuze and Guattari 1983: 235). Why? Because it encourages one to believe in the market regulation of currency through which people and their representations are rendered interchangeable, as if by subtracting X number of women from representation and adding X number of other minorities we will have arrived at equality-in-diversity; as if by that we make people equal in a form different than the capitalist principle of equivalence; as if by that we make people something other than abstract quantities of labor to be further utilized by capitalism for the sake of producing surplus. As long as we remain within the domain of sexualization that produces global and specific forms of sexes and sexualities, all alliances risk encountering this impasse.

Yet under the schizoanalytic lens, the calculative logic of these criticisms becomes an index of a deeper problematic that reveals #MeToo's true revolutionary power, a revolutionary power that Žukauskaitė also identifies in Chapter 2 herein. As they allow their testimonies to become partial objects communicating transversally as the working parts of a revolutionary machine, the women of #MeToo expose sexual harassment to be what it has always been: the rudimentary form of capitalist deduction or appropriation of their bodies, organs, and souls designed to produce a surplus (of any kind) which they are prohibited from consuming. The recent debate over economist Robin Hanson's appalling idea to equate revolutionary demands for the redistribution of incomes with a demand for the "redistribution of sex"—as if people with "poor" sex life suffer from the same injustice inflicted upon people with poor income, and are thus equally justified in demanding compensation or threatening violence if their demands are not met— strikingly supports drawing such schizoanalytic inference with regard to #MeToo's revolutionary power under capitalism.[9] The refusal championed by #MeToo is a "NO" directed at one of capitalism's most sinister expressions of cynicism, namely, *trafficking*; the trafficking of women, children, sex workers, animals, organs (including those used for surgical transplantations), and anything that may produce profit. Entrenching ourselves in criticisms of under-representation unwittingly obscures our own complicity in this system of trafficking, as we are refusing to acknowledge that cold calculations of how to make representation diverse and equal are but one of the sanctioned, "legal" forms of the capitalist regulation of trafficking; one that also makes possible the propagation of illegal ones, as it feeds off the same axiomatics sanctioning legal trafficking. Queer theory's promotion of the multiplication of sexual identities risks serving too well the cynicism of capitalism, as it produces surplus-value of flow in the form of new identities for us to consume; as if, for example, when I pay the cable company and consume TV shows exhibiting diversity, I am actually the one consuming the surplus created by converting the flesh and blood and sweat of the actors—the color of their skin, their gender, their sexuality—into quantities of labor and their share in representation. The inconceivable proportions of trafficking are precisely the kind of problem that requires broad coalitions and alliances between revolutionary (activist) and analytic (theoretical) machines, with the latter articulating the cases wherein unconscious investments of desire (refusal of trafficking) are transformed into preconscious investments of interests (calculations of the "just" quantity of diversity in representation). Allying schizoanalysis with queer and feminist analytic machines means making it that part establishing transversal communications between queer theory and feminism; and with its rearrangement of the functions of sex and sexuality, schizoanalysis already implies the very form of queer– feminist alliances.

Notes

1. A notable example is David Halperin's oft-cited yet grossly mishandled concept of queer, as that which is "by definition *whatever* is at odds with the normal, the legitimate, the dominant ... an identity without an essence" and "a horizon of possibility" (1995: 62). For an early argument for *not* making queer theory a theory of sexuality, see Berlant and Warner (1995: 344). Halperin later criticized queer theory precisely for becoming a theory of sexuality (2002: 45–7).

2. Founded in New York in 1987, the ACT UP movement (the AIDS Coalition To Unleash Power)—with its "contamination of sexual with nonsexual politics"—is Halperin's prime example of queer politics (1995: 63).

3. It is important to note that the French *sexe* also denotes the sexual organs, but for now what I suggest is that the word "sex" in *Anti-Oedipus* should be understood as an organ, a part, or a partial object, as this sense is rendered explicit in *Proust and Signs*, where Deleuze distinguished between "sexes-as-persons" and "sexes-as-organs" (Deleuze 2000: 138).

4. There are some inconsistencies in the English translation of these and associated terms. Throughout *Anti-Oedipus* Deleuze and Guattari are consistent in their distinction between sex and sexuality, whose adjectival correlatives are sexed (*sexué*) and sexual (*sexuel*), respectively. The translators do not always maintain the distinctive usage of these terms, and occasionally mistranslate the derivative and compound forms of these terms, none of which are interchangeable. For example, when Deleuze and Guattari speak of how the schizophrenic rejects the exclusive use of the disjunctive synthesis in favor of an inclusive one, the translation reads, "He is not simply bisexual, or between the two, or intersexual. He is transsexual" (1983: 77). But what they say is that the schizophrenic is neither bisexed (*bisexué*), nor intersexed (*intersexué*), but rather trans-sexed (*trans-sexué*). Note the hyphenation in the term "trans-sexed," which is retained for its correlative, trans-sexuality, for these do not refer to human forms of transsexuality or transgenderism. The prefix "trans-" here means both across and beyond: being trans-sexed means existing in a state that spans *across* all the sexes-organs and *beyond* the exclusionary restrictive forms of disjunction (*either* male *or* female) imposed on their essential mode as a multiplicity. The terms "bisexed" and "intersexed" are too reductive as well. Earlier, Deleuze and Guattari explain what bisexed means—having two sexes, although, here too, *bisexué* was rendered into English as bisexual (69). The sense of "bisexed" here is nonhuman: it is what botany and zoology refer to as hermaphrodite or intersex life forms, while "intersexed" here means being between the sexes. The schizophrenic is neither, because both bisexed and intersex are founded on the restrictive presupposition of two sexes only.

   Some of the translation choices also unwittingly obscured the distinction between sex and sexuality. When Deleuze and Guattari discuss the misunderstanding between psychoanalysts and ethnologists, they note, "In theory, everyone [psychoanalysts and ethnologists] could reach an agreement on this point: everything is sexual or sex-influenced (*sexué*) from one end to the other" (180). It is evident that the translators acknowledged—in their choice of interpretation and in including the French in parenthesis—that *sexué* and *sexuel* are related though not synonymous. Indeed, sexes and sexuality are the working parts of desiring-machines: sexes are the organs or partial objects that constitute the poles of the machine (the interceptors of incoming and outgoing flows), and sexuality is the machine's flow of energy (libido) that moves or passes between organ-machines.

5. See also Deleuze and Guattari (1983: 323).

6. See also *Proust & Signs*, Deleuze (2000: 131–2).

7. For a thorough discussion of Klein's theory of female sexuality and castration anxiety, see Segal (1981), Kristeva (2013).

8. See Segal (1981: 51–2).

9. See Hanson (2018) and Douthat (2018). I thank Janae Sholtz for bringing this debate to my attention and for suggesting thinking how Hanson's idea relates to my argument about #MeToo.

References

Baldwin, J. (1998), "The Price of the Ticket," in T. Morrison (ed.), *James Baldwin: Collected Essays*, 830–42, New York: Library of America.

Berlant, L., and M. Warner (1995), "What Does Queer Theory Teach Us About X?," *PMLA* 110 (3): 343–9.

Butler, J. (1997), "Against Proper Objects," in E. Weed and N. Schor (eds.), *Feminism Meets Queer Theory*, 1–30, Bloomington: Indiana University Press.

Deleuze, G. (1995), *Negotiations: 1972–1990*, trans. M. Joughin, New York: Columbia University Press.

Deleuze, G. (2000), *Proust & Signs*, trans. R. Howard, Minneapolis: University of Minnesota Press.

Deleuze, G. (2004), *Desert Islands and Other Texts 1953–1974*, trans. M. Taormina, Los Angeles, CA: Semiotext(e).

Deleuze, G. (2007), *Two Regimes of Madness: Texts and Interviews 1973–1995*, trans. A. Hodges and M. Taormina, South Pasadena, CA: Semiotext(e).

Deleuze, G., and F. Guattari (1983), *Anti-Oedipus: Capitalism and Schizophrenia*, trans. R. Hurley, M. Seem, and H. R. Lane, Minneapolis: University of Minnesota Press.

Deleuze, G., and C. Parnet (2002), *Dialogues II*, trans. H. Tomlinson and B. Habberjam, New York: Columbia University Press.

Douthat, R. (2018), "The Redistribution of Sex," *New York Times*, May 2, https://www.nytimes.com/2018/05/02/opinion/incels-sex-robots-redistribution.html (accessed May 24, 2018).

Foucault, M. (2011), "The Gay Science," trans. N. Morar and D. W. Smith, *Critical Inquiry* 37 (3): 385–403.

Fraisse, G. (2014), "Sex, Gender, Difference of the Sexes, Sexual Difference," in B. Cassin (ed.), *Dictionary of Untranslatables: A Philosophical Lexicon*, trans. J. Mehlman, 969–74, Princeton, NJ: Princeton University Press.

Halley, J. (2006), *Split Decisions: How and Why to Take a Break from Feminism*, Princeton, NJ: Princeton University Press.

Halperin, D. M. (1995), *Saint Foucault: Towards a Gay Hagiography*, New York: Oxford University Press.

Halperin, D. M. (2002), *How to Do the History of Homosexuality*, Chicago: University of Chicago Press.

Hanson, R. (2018), "Two Types of Envy," *Overcoming Bias*, April 26, http://www.overcomingbias.com/2018/04/two-types-of-envy.html (accessed May 24, 2018).

Jagose, A. (2009), "Feminism's Queer Theory," *Feminism & Psychology* 19 (2): 157–74.

Kristeva, J. (2013), *Melanie Klein*, trans. R. Guberman, New York: Columbia University Press.

Marinucci, M. (2010), *Feminism Is Queer: The Intimate Connection between Queer and Feminist Theory*, London: Zed Books.

Richardson, D. (2006), "Bordering Theory," in D. Richardson, J. McLaughlin, and M. E. Casey (eds.), *Intersections between Feminist and Queer Theory*, 19–37, New York: Palgrave Macmillan.

Rudy, K. (2000), "Queer Theory and Feminism," *Women's Studies* 29 (2): 195–216.

Sanford, S. (2014), " 'Sex' and 'Sexual Difference,' " in B. Cassin (ed.), *Dictionary of Untranslatables: A Philosophical Lexicon*, 972–3, Princeton, NJ: Princeton University Press.

Segal, H. (1981), *Melanie Klein*, New York: Penguin.

Smith, D. W. (2011), "Flow, Code and Stock: A Note on Deleuze's Political Philosophy," *Deleuze Studies* 5 (supplement): 36–55.

Weed, E. (1997), "Introduction," in E. Weed and N. Schor (eds.), *Feminism Meets Queer Theory*, vii–xiii, Bloomington: Indiana University Press.

CHAPTER 7
DELEUZE AND TRANSFEMINISM
Hannah Stark and Timothy Laurie

In a variety of otherwise disparate social and cultural contexts, the figure of the transitioning body has been taken up not simply as the moniker for groups with specific political demands, but as a "fuzzy" sign invested with broad collective hopes for world-historical transformations around the categories of sex and gender. As an umbrella term, transgender has been used to group people together "across fine gradations of trans experience and identity," in ways that "build the experienced reality of a shared community, with overlapping and intersectional social needs and political goals" (Williams 2014: 234). In stressing departure rather than arrival, Julian Carter evokes a notion of transition which is non-teleological, in which "transition" instead is understood as one of the ways in which people "move across socially defined boundaries away from an unchosen gender category" (Carter 2014: 235). Noting the "popular cultural preoccupation" with the terminology of "trans," Pearce et al. follow Nael Bhanji in exploring the valences that "transition" has acquired: transgression, transmutation, transmorgification, and so on (see Bhanji 2012; Pearce et al. 2018: 2). Just as the diasporic subject became, within certain Anglo-American fields of scholarly inquiry, a widely legible metonym for wider phenomena of cultural, economic, and political globalization (see Cho 2007), so too have trans rights become metonymic for tectonic shifts in the role of both the State and more diffuse social institutions (such as media industries) in recognizing and regulating gender-based social identities.[1] To see transgender celebrity Laverne Cox on the cover of *Cosmopolitan* in South Africa (February, 2018) is to be reassured that gatekeepers of gender norms are themselves transitioning from one worldview to another—from binary to multiplicity, identity to fluidity, conformity to self-expression, and so on. The metonymic signs of trans acceptance seem to arrive from a utopian near-future, one that is slowly trickling its way into a present restless for change.

As an inclusive term which denotes a range of gender nonconforming or gender-variable identities, trans has placed pressure on the prevailing political frameworks and identity categories that have been central to the history of feminist politics. However, as Namaste (2009) and Prosser (2006) have argued, the utility of trans identities for challenging dominant paradigms in feminist philosophy has not always produced scholarship that addresses the practical challenges of leading a trans life, whether this involves access to medical services, the interpersonal challenges of navigating family, friendships and relationships, or exposure to violence linked to intersecting vulnerabilities, such as disproportionate rates of sexual assault on trans sex workers who are black and working-class in North America. The transition from invisibility to hypervisibility for trans communities may certainly point toward more trans-inclusive futures, but we must exercise caution when seeking to position—or indeed, instrumentalize—trans bodies as readymade signs of social progress. Indeed, Browne and Lim even suggest that, among the participants in a study based around Hove and Brighton (UK), trans communities have learned to become resilient against being "co-opted either by normative medical discourses as a pathological other or by some cultural theorists as a beacon of transgression" (Lim and Browne 2009: 13).

We need to situate trans within a field of transitions, involuntary and voluntary, individual and collective, interpersonal and institutional. Rather than placing the burden on trans communities and activists to explain or justify their relationships to feminism, we might be better to recognize that such intersecting transitions have always posed an important problem for feminist philosophy. In *The Second Sex*, Simone de Beauvoir famously identifies a dangerous abruptness in the lives of women:

> While the male grows older continuously, the woman is brusquely stripped of her femininity; still young, she loses sexual attraction and fertility, from which, in society's and her own eyes, she derives the justification of her existence and her chances of happiness: bereft of all future, she has approximately half of her adult life still to live. (2011: 619)

While de Beauvoir's account cannot be taken to describe all experiences of womanhood, her general approach remains instructive. Gender binaries have always given rise to perilous passages and discontinuities—desired and loathed, marked and unmarked, over-politicized and depoliticized. Transfeminism, in this context, may not simply be a feminism that goes "beyond the binary," a common metaphor that too easily implies a close-mindedness on the part of early feminist scholars. Rather, transfeminism can *deepen* the lines of inquiry into the relationships between individual and collective transformation and can diversify our understandings of gender as "passage" that contains unexpected pleasures and sedimented modes of violence. With this in mind, this chapter positions transfeminism as a project for feminism more broadly. It considers what Deleuze's notion of becoming means for how we imagine the particularity of transitioning bodies as well as the broader machinations of social change in relation to gender and sexuality.

1. The Concept of "Becoming" in Deleuze and Guattari

Deleuze and Guattari do not write about transgender issues as they are currently understood, although some obscure passages in *Anti-Oedipus* do gesture toward understanding of what they describe as "transsexual" identities (e.g., Deleuze and Guattari 1983: 76).[2] Deleuze and Guattari's enduring contributions to studies of social identity and identification involve, on the one hand, the relentless criticism of the Oedipal complex as a dominant touchstone in psychoanalysis (a major focus of *Anti-Oedipus* in 1972), and on the other hand, an exploration of "becomings" as a durational concept that seeks to capture practices of individual and collective transformation (a major preoccupation throughout *A Thousand Plateaus* in 1980). For contemporary scholarship on transfeminism, this concept of "becomings" contains obvious attractions and equally obvious trappings. Any gesture toward the mutability of identities appears to challenge the stigma attached to transgender bodies as lacking credible identities, and as therefore confused or disorderly. At the same time, "becoming" contains a trap that attends any philosophical concept imported into a political situation: a desire for romantic abstraction at the expense of engagement with lived realities and the practical demands of living trans lives. We cannot hope to resolve this problem here, and our purpose is not to argue that Deleuze's philosophy is more closely aligned to the interests of trans communities than rival philosophical approaches.[3] We do, however, want to make an argument about why "becoming" may be useful for understanding current challenges in activating a politics around nonbinary identities.

It is banal to observe that the experience of change over time is central to human social existence. Hoping and feeling disappointed, dreading and feeling relief, falling in and out of love: our sense of shared social life with others is established by commonalities and proximities in the cycles that we collectively endure. But in our attempts to represent such changes, we often imagine a change from this and to that, where *this* and *that* are fixed states of being. We can distinguish between a from/to logic that brings states into relation, and a "becoming" that exists only in and through moving parts. In *A Thousand Plateaus*, Deleuze and Guattari explain a "line of becoming" in the following terms:

> A line of becoming is not defined by points that it connects, or by points that compose it; on the contrary, it passes *between* points, it comes up through the middle, it runs perpendicular to the points first perceived, transversally to the localizable relation to distant or contiguous points. A point is always a point of origin. But a line of becoming has neither beginning nor end, departure nor arrival, origin nor destination; to speak of the absence of an origin, to make the absence of an origin the origin, is a bad play on words. A line of becoming has only a middle. (Deleuze and Guattari 1987: 239, emphasis in original)

Becoming is a creative process that invents something new. Although the world is in constant flux, cycles and rhythms do emerge that have the capacity to hold discontinuous things together: "A season, a winter, a summer, an hour, a date have a perfect individuality lacking nothing, even though this individuality is different from that of a thing or a subject" (Deleuze and Guattari 1987: 261). Deleuze and Guattari give the further example of wasps and orchids: a certain type of orchid, displaying similar physical and sensory characteristics to female wasps, lures male wasps into a strange sexual dance. The frustrated wasp moves from orchid to orchid, attempting copulation and, through this process, transfers pollen between plants. In this way, the wasp becomes part of the reproductive apparatus of the orchid and the orchid facilitates the sexual activity of the wasp. Deleuze and Guattari describe this as a simultaneous "becoming-wasp of the orchid" and a "becoming-orchid of the wasp" (Deleuze and Guattari 2004: 11). What holds them together is not resemblance, but the inventive capacities made possible through mutual interaction. As the cycle continues, it becomes difficult to talk about the attributes of the wasp without referring to the orchid (and vice versa), but this is not a dialectical or oppositional connection—it is symbiotic, emergent, creative.

Becomings are not processes that we choose, although our choices may be swept up in becomings. A voluntary transformation would involve a subject who, by projecting an ideal future self, wills a series of actions. But we are constantly disappointed to find that our own efforts to actualize such ways of being are imperfect, if not complete failures. Judith Butler lends the name "despair" to this incomplete mediation of the subject through social processes of identification (2015: 112–13), and for this reason, the history of gender can be characterized as a litany of failures (see Halberstam 2011). Worldly encounters constantly erode our capacities and desires, and the living self is comprised of radical inconsistencies, fractures and tangents. Reading Catherine Lord's *Summer of My Baldness* (2014), a photographic memoir dealing with breast cancer and associated balding, DeShazer suggests that Lord presents her experience "as discursive, postmodern, and transgendered," and thereby presents cancer as a strength, "at once a location from which to interrogate public-private binaries, an aesthetic preference to affirm, and a defiant political stance against the thralldom of hegemonic femininity" (2012: 17–18). Lord's memoir foregrounds a certain kind of "becoming" that combines the involuntary and unpredictable effects of cancer with inventive schemas and practices that accord new kinds of dignity to diverse bodily forms. Becomings happen whether or not we will them, whether or not we know about them, and whether or not they are good. In this context, we must briefly consider "becoming-woman," which remains an important touchstone both for those who praise and criticize Deleuze and Guattari's relationship to feminist theory.

Becomings do not involve moving from origins to destinations, but they can gather together and reassemble elements that have previously become sedimented. Gender is a sedimentation of this kind. Insofar as man and masculinity always occupy majoritarian positions, the socially valued signs of femininity do not exist autonomously but are rather shaped by the overdetermination of the sedimented grammar of masculinity as the dominant term. For the patriarchal conception of woman to be undermined and dissolved, ideas about both masculinity and femininity need to be transformed, but this cannot happen simply through producing better representations of femininity, or even multiplying different versions of femininity. Rather, a becoming-woman would involve recovering those relationships to the body, to desire and to pleasure, to affinity and affiliation, that the compulsory norms of gender-based belonging have occluded, beginning with the experience of childhood:

> The question is fundamentally that of the body—the body they steal from us in order to fabricate opposable organisms. This body is stolen first from the girl: Stop behaving like that, you're not a little girl anymore, you're not a tomboy, etc. The girl's becoming is stolen first, in order to impose a history, or prehistory, upon her. The boy's turn comes next, but it is by using the girl as an example, by pointing to

the girl as the object of his desire, that an opposed organism, a dominant history is fabricated for him too. The girl is the first victim, but she must also serve as an example and a trap. (Deleuze and Guattari 1987: 276)

Deleuze and Guattari follow the Freudian critique of "masculinity" and "femininity" as interdependent terms inseparable from relations of power, identification, and relational attachment. Unlike Freud, however, they explore possibilities for a becoming-woman that would activate new relationships to bodily difference, including those that would pass "between" the coordinates of masculinity and femininity:

[These] indissociable aspects of becoming-woman must first be understood as a function of something else: not imitating or assuming the female form, but emitting particles that enter the relation of movement and rest, or the zone of proximity, of a microfemininity, in other words, that produce in us a molecular woman, create the molecular woman. (Deleuze and Guattari 2004: 304)

Becoming-woman is not a becoming that begins with woman but rather begins with everything that the concept of woman excludes.

Becoming-woman has faced several compelling criticisms. Christine Battersby notes that in the models provided by Deleuze and Guattari (drawn primarily from Anglo-American literature), "even the 'becoming-woman' of women is not something that women themselves perform. Instead, the 'becoming-woman' of women results from changes in the organisation of social structures of *males*, produced by social transitions within capitalism" (1998: 188, emphasis in original). Furthermore, in an early critique that still retains force, Alice Jardine suggests that concepts like "becoming" and "desire" speak most directly to those who can easily imagine themselves occupying a dominant position, and merely wish to abdicate this power (Jardine 1985: 217). Becomings appeal most to those restless within an order that has already allocated them a place.

Trans scholarship does not require a concept such as "becoming" to credentialize trans activism or trans lives. Nevertheless, transfeminism may benefit by becoming as a corrective to received habits of thought around the particular and the universal. Within the logic of the universal, the emergence of a new phenomenon is treated as an instance that can be related back to a law, a rule, or a method. Sometimes this will take the form of universals as concepts (e.g., Truth), and other times this will take the form of universal procedures (e.g., semiology). In Freud's case studies, for example, the incredible eclecticism of testimonies produced by patients was treated as a problem of reduction: how to pass from contingent features of consciousness to the universal laws of the Unconscious? To move from the particular to the universal, changing phenomena are treated *relative* to an unchanging frame, often by way of analogy, homology, metonym, or metaphor. Such operations are not restricted to philosophers. Contemporary cultural critics frequently relate local anecdotes to unifying scale of analysis endowed with "universal" features, such as the community, the State, and the nation. Becoming short circuits this movement from the particular to the universal. They are not events written on the surfaces of History or Society: becomings build from the ground up, breaking up old analogies and homologies. Or rather, becomings are *surfacings*. Large aggregates do not necessarily recede in significance, but we must seek to understand how they, too, are modified by becomings. If we still talk about the nation, we must ask different questions: Does this becoming invent new ways of imagining the geographies that the "nation" seeks to capture? Could this becoming lead away from nations altogether? We can say the same for universals in critical theory. We should not ask what queer theory has to say about becomings (an interpretative model), but instead ask, how might becomings change what queer theory is thought to be?

Our purpose is not to trivialize the utility of universals. As convenient shorthands, we can speak about methods, nations, and queer theory. Deleuze and Guattari's discourse on becomings merely asks us to be attentive to wholesale shifts in the referents and relations that give analytic objects their quotidian meanings. An idea we once found repellent is suddenly caught up by a strange new power, drawing up new battle lines, forcing new coalitions, sweeping away the familiar refrains. This is what becomings can do, and this is what makes them dangerous (Deleuze and Guattari 2004: 276).

2. Becoming-Trans

The work of Paul B. Preciado in *Testo Junkie* (2008) and that of Maggie Nelson in *The Argonauts* (2016) dramatize the political potential of Deleuze's work for transfeminism. These works can both be described as autotheory, an emerging genre in which the boundaries between the personal, political, and theoretical collapse in on themselves. *The Argonauts* is Nelson's memoir about her relationship with her trans partner, the artist Harry Dodge, and the construction of their family as they navigate the establishment of their home, stepparenting, work arrangements, marriage, pregnancy and the birth, and infancy of their child Iggy. The book positions this well-trodden terrain as an intellectual project for Nelson, and the personal narrative is set against a searing theoretical and political assessment of contemporary queer theory and continental philosophy, as well as a meditation on a range of other cultural texts from literature, film, and art. The books contrasts Nelson's pregnancy and the subsequent birth of their child with Dodge's transition over what Nelson describes as the "summer of our changing bodies" (Nelson 2015: 79), during which they are "undergoing transformations beside each other" (83). Nelson follows Deleuze and Claire Parnet's rendering of the nuptial in *Dialogues* to describe her relationship to Harry: "Nuptials are the opposite of a couple. There are no longer binary machines: question-answer, masculine-feminine, man-animal etc." (Nelson 2015: 7). In a text in which plenitude is mapped onto the female body—rendered heroic through birth, extreme through the erotic, and mutable through both desire and prosthesis—the text ends with a vision in which lack has no place. Nelson here quotes Deleuze and Guattari from *A Thousand Plateaus*: "*Flying anuses, speeding vaginas, there is no castration*" (1987: 178, emphasis in original)

Testo Junkie also stages gender as a project which is both personal and relational. Part theoretical manifesto and part autobiographical *tour de force*, it combines historical accounts of sexual prosthetics and gender-forming technologies with personal experimentation in the use of black-market testosterone gel. "This book is not a memoir," opens Preciado, "This book is a testosterone-based, voluntary intoxication protocol, which concerns the body and affects of BP [the author, writing under the name Beatriz Preciado at the time of initial publication]. A body-essay. Fiction, actually" (2017: 11). The text alternates between a theoretical polemic and sections providing an autobiographical account, in explicit detail, of the author's sexual experiences and, in particular, their affair with VD (the director of *Baise-moi*, Virginie Despentes). The autobiographical vignettes write back to the history of European literature and pornography, re-working tropes associated with gender and sexuality, and creating a field in which desire becomes unmoored from conventional imaginings.

Preciado draws inspiration from Deleuze's idea of the control society. Deleuze's original text periodizes the shift from Foucauldian societies of discipline to postmodern societies of control. Unlike the discipline society, the society of control does not produce a standardized citizen or worker, but rather an individual who responds to modulation and incentive, and is told to believe that their fortunes—prosperous or impoverished— is a manifestation of personal will and striving (Deleuze 1995: 5). For Preciado, the control society is exemplified through the biopolitical circulation of pornography and new technologies of the body (including drugs, hormones, and medical technologies). Preciado calls this society of pernicious control pharmocopornographic. Preciado's rendering of the control society is addressed in Jasbir Puar's work in *The Right to Maim: Debility, Capacity, Disability*, which also mobilizes Deleuze's work in order to examine the emergence of trans embodiment within an intersectional politics. Puar places the trans body in relation to biopolitical control and legal recognition-based frameworks, and theorizes how "bodies are malleable as composites of parts, affects, compartmentalized capacities and debilities, and as data points and informational substrates" (Puar 2017: 50). In control societies, the "transition" in trans is seen as a modulation or modification of a flexible body, rather than a "retroactive cutting and severing from being in the wrong body" (57).

For Preciado, the body is both the effect of pharmocopornographic power and the site at which resistance becomes possible. Puar's work also oscillates between examining the capture of bodies in biopolitical networks of control and celebrating the subversive potential of trans identity to subvert this control. She turns to Deleuze's work on becoming in order to occlude identity as the site for trans politics and arrive at something more slippery. She uses becoming to frame trans as a nonteleological "motion" or "continuum of intensity" (Puar 2017: 52). Theorizing "becoming trans" in relation to Deleuze's notion of becoming, Puar evokes trans as an impersonal movement toward the imperceptible and multiplicity and away from signification, subjectivation, and sense. "The revolution is not molecular," she writes, "rather, movement resides in the interstitial shuttling—'the ruptural moment in which to intervene'—between intensive multiplicity and its most likely recapture" (61). Within the North American contexts on which Puar focuses, trans bodies are undeniably caught up in neoliberal projects. In some cases, such as the discourse around the rights of the trans child (see Halberstam 2018: 53), trans politics has dovetailed with neoliberal tendencies to foreground individual self-determination, rather than relational conceptions of self-hood and community. However, this does not mean that "becomings" are not possible. Indeed, they exist in the disturbances caused by the movements of proximity and distance between perceived identity categories; between conforming and nonconforming bodies; between public and private selves; and in what Puar had called the "interstitial shuttling" that occurs in the renegotiation of social relations. Within *Testo Junkie*, it is the molecular potential of testosterone (T) that both produces masculinity and, through repeated and deregulated use, "hacks" gender throughout the autobiographical narrative. T enables a becoming which is both literal and figurative, described by Preciado as "a threshold, a molecular door, a becoming between multiplicities" (Preciado 2017: 143).

In both Preciado's and Nelson's work, transition is understood neither from a point of arrival nor in relation to an ideal of completion. This nonteleological understanding of trans is exemplified through Jack Halberstam's use of the term "trans*," which resonates with Deleuzian becoming—a movement without beginning or end, and without origin. "A becoming," Deleuze and Guattari write, "is always in the middle; one can only get it by the middle" (2004: 323). For Halberstam, trans* encapsulates this becoming and designates an open field of possibility for self-determination in relation to gender variability and identity. The asterisk "modifies the meaning of transitivity by refusing to situate transition in relation to a destination, a final form, a specific shape, or an established configuration of desire and identity" (Halberstam 2018: 4). In relation to the capacity for the asterisk to open up the sign, Jami Weinstein and Eva Hayward write that "[i]f trans was not understood, in at least one of its modes, as 'always already' relational, working and playing parasitically at the level of language, thought, and ideology, then the * repurposes, displaces, renames, replicates, and intensifies terms, adding yet more texture, increased vitalization" (2015: 198). Trans* opens up the ambivalent space of non-cisgendered identities to changes both voluntary and involuntary, changes which could be physiological, chemical, interpersonal, or institutional.

In *The Argonauts*, Nelson positions Harry's gender transition "into a butch on T" (Nelson 2015: 53) in relation to a range of embodied changes, including aging, pregnancy, childbirth, and death. These comparisons strip trans of its exceptional status, while rendering it in relation to the tension between stasis and transformation. This is the meaning contained in the title; as Nelson writes, in relation to the work of Roland Barthes, "[T]he subject who utters the phrase 'I love you' is like 'the Argonaut renewing his ship during its voyage without changing its name'" (Nelson 2015: 5). What persists when things are changing? Nelson allows a cacophony of voices to express trans experiences. She writes,

How to explain—"trans" may work well enough as shorthand, but the quickly developing mainstream narrative it evokes ("born in the wrong body," necessitating an orthopaedic pilgrimage between two fixed destinations) is useless for some—but partially, or even profoundly, useful for others? That for some, "transitioning" may mean leaving one gender entirely behind, while for others—like Harry, who is happy to identify as a butch on T—it doesn't? *I'm not on my way to anywhere*, Harry sometimes tells inquirers. How to explain, in the culture frantic for resolution, that sometimes the shit stays messy? *I don't want the female gender that has been assigned to me at birth. Neither do I want the male gender that transsexual medicine can furnish and that the state will award me if I behave in the right way. I don't want any of it* [here Nelson cites Preciado in the margin]. How to explain that for some, or for some at some times, this irresolution is OK—desirable, even (e.g., "gender hackers")—whereas for others, or for others at some times, it stays a source of conflict and grief? How does one get across the fact that the best way to find out how people feel about their gender or their sexuality—or anything else, really— is to listen to what they tell you, and to try to treat them accordingly, without shellacking over their version of reality with yours? (2015: 52–3)

Nelson's quotation of Preciado brings to the fore the overtly political refusals of binary genders throughout *Testo Junkie*. Rather than isolating an authentic queer, trans or genderfluid identity, Preciado explores the powers of plasticity, pharmacology, and pornography in producing a range of shifting and momentary gender identifications. Within the text, and by way of a range of prostheses, chemicals and practices, Preciado as a character is positioned as female, masculine, genderfluid, heterosexual, lesbian, and as a "gay guy" (Preciado 2017: 130). There is no desired or true identity in this text. As he writes, "None of the sexes that I embody possess any ontological density, and yet there is no other way of being a body: dispossessed from the start" (Preciado 2017: 134). Preciado shuttles between identities and renders gender as a perpetual project, a work of art.

Where does "interstitial shuttling" leave politics? What does it mean for the future possibilities of transfeminism? For Halberstam, the commitment to a non-teleological body-becoming enacts a Deleuzian politics which rejects the political struggle for recognition and the related framework of identity-based politics. As a political imperative, the fight for recognition is about asserting that a particular identity, or a particular way of living, should be recognized and legitimated by society and the State. Halberstam advocates an anti-recognition, anti-identity politics, arguing for a new political landscape and new political solidarities. "When the male-female binary crumbles," he writes, "what new constellations of alliance and opposition emerge?" (Halberstam 2018: 108). But in *Trans**, Halberstam walks a difficult political line. On the one hand, he mobilizes the specificity and authenticity of individual experience, through the use of the personal anecdote and through the repeated insistence on the specificity of trans voices in debates about gender and sexuality. Each of the substantive chapters begins with a personal vignette about the author's own life experience: coming out, surgery, shifting personal identifications, and prior queer role-models. On the other hand, Halberstam looks for the commonality of gendered experience. "Trans* bodies," he writes, "in their fragmented, unfinished, broken-beyond-repair forms, remind all of us that the body is always under construction" (Halberstam 2018: 135). Halberstam's work is most useful when he positions trans as a social rather than individualistic project. Trans subjectivities emerge in a network of people, nonhuman beings, things, institutions, spaces. Halberstam utilizes Eva Hayward's work on the trans body in which she defines trans-becoming as "an emergence of a material, psychical, sensual, and social self through corporeal, spatial and temporal processes that trans-form the lived body" (Hayward 2010: 226). While acknowledging that for some people, access to surgery and hormones is life-preserving, Halberstam rejects trans as a project of neo-liberal and individualist selfhood, insofar as this narrows the priorities of trans politics to a particular relation to capitalism, medicalization, and the State.

Both *Testo Junkie* and *The Argonauts* reveal the ways that transitions can simultaneously be individual, social, collective, and political. This is rendered in both texts through love, which proves central to sustaining the relationship between stasis and transformation in each text. In *The Argonauts*, Nelson works through the tension between access to recognition and to rights—to participate in marriage, to access technologies, to make a family—and a more complex project of queer world-making. The text could be read as one which re-inscribes homonormative, or even heterosexual, family life. The couple has everything they want: love (the quality of which is framed as exceptional), art (they make a living as an artist and a writer/academic), access to medical services (for transition and pregnancy), and the new baby that is *"deeply, doggedly, wildly"* wanted (Nelson 2015: 177, emphasis in original). Harry and Maggie have their cake and eat it too. However, *The Argonauts* also reveals the ways in which the nuptial is a relational becoming. Love and attachment enable people undergoing changes to produce a sense of consistency while simultaneously being supported to pursue lines of flight. As Deleuze and Guattari indicate using the nuptial of the wasp and the orchid, becomings bring together parts and pieces in unconventional alliances through which something new is produced. Just as Harry and Maggie construct their family through biological and nonbiological ties, the form of the text itself works to piece together an intellectual lineage or assemblage of interlocutors with and through whom the couple live, love, and think: Deleuze, Winnicott, Sedgwick, Butler, and Preciado, among others. "Making love," Deleuze and Guattari write, "is not just becoming one, or even two, but becoming as a hundred thousand" (Deleuze and Guattari 1983: 296).

In the final section of *Testo Junkie*, "Eternal Life," Preciado refers to Deleuze and Guattari to talk about "[l]ove as a map of connections (movements, discharges, reflexes, convulsions, tremors) that for a certain time regulate the production of affects" (2017: 400). In this way, Preciado works with the productive capacity of desiring machines, which bring into arrangement people, things, affect, codes. Preciado's love is not limited to the couple through his relationship to VD but can also be explored through reading the text as a work of mourning. The text opens with the death of Preciado's friend GD (the novelist Guillaume Dustan), and much of its rhetorical strategy is a grief-stricken second person address to GD. It is through his relationship to both VD and GD that Preciado enacts what he calls a "becoming T" (Preciado 2017: 130). Preciado begins using testosterone on the day of GD's death—"I do it to avenge your death"

(Preciado 2017: 16)—and it is as a reaction to this death that he calls VD and they begin their liaison: "You're the one who pushes me to dial her number" (15). "Trans* bodies," Halberstam writes, "represent the art of becoming, the necessity of imagining, and the fleshy insistence of transitivity" (2018: 136). *Testo Junkie* illustrates the mediation of the transitive, the productive relations of series: Preciado to GD, Preciado to VD, VD to GD (posthumously), Preciado to T, VD to T. But while Preciado evokes a sense of having accomplices in acts of gender terrorism (GD, VD, and the drag king community), his work is ultimately a critique of queer communitarian projects that take shared political interests as the sole foundation for community building. In doing so, Preciado provides an opportunity to consider gender and sexual diversity away from the liberal viewpoint of rights or the communitarian demand for shared, exclusive identities. Instead, Preciado enacts a range of becomings which sweep up objects, people, prosthetics, chemicals into new solidarities and alliances, and which create a movement away from identity – becoming-other, becoming-molecular, becoming-imperceptible.

3. Conclusion

We are well accustomed to celebrating "social change" and "social progress" as placeholders for a range of justice and equity based political projects. Given the tenacity of patriarchy, homophobia, transphobia, and other kinds of gender-based violence across a vast range of social contexts, we are inclined to invest in those figures that appear to embody the promise of better and different futures, whether fictional characters such as vigilante superheroes, or real individuals whose struggles against oppression seem to herald broader collective capacities for social action. Those who are willing to express radical difference, and to bear the social and political consequences of such expressions, can open pathways for others to imagine and enact more hospitable futures. In this chapter, we have explained relations of proximity and distance between a range of transitioning bodies—sick bodies, pregnant bodies, ageing bodies, and those in the process of gender transition. Bodies change constantly in involuntary and unexpected ways: the exceptional aspect of transgender and nonbinary identities is not bodily change as such, but the discursive environment that frames gendered bodily changes as exceptionally open to scrutiny, interrogation, and—in many cases—violence. Not all of the transitions that attend the body are the same and not all of them are received socially in the same way. In invoking the broad concept of becoming, our purposes has not been to flatten out the specificity of trans lives or trans politics. However, becoming provides a useful way to think through the shifting terrain on which any and all politics rest— terrain that involves personal transformations, but cannot be reduced to them. A future-oriented transfeminism needs to make space for the gaps, ruptures, dead ends, and lines of flight that produce political subjects. "[It's] the binary of normative/transgressive that's unsustainable," writes Nelson, "along with the demand that anyone live a life that's all one thing" (Nelson 2015: 93).

Notes

1. In making this comparison, we also acknowledge important intersections between these processes, a theme to which we later return. For important work on transgender identities in contexts of migration and/or cultural flows, see Husakouskaya's "Queering Mobility in Urban Gauteng: Transgender Internal Migrants and Their Experiences of 'Transition' in Johannesburg and Pretoria" (2017) and Leung's "Always in Translation Trans Cinema across Languages" (2016).

2. Following the lead of Patricia Gherovici, another study might profitably examine the various invocations of transexual identities within the post-Freudian and anti-psychiatry discourses of the late 1960s and 1970s. However, our purpose here is different.

3. Indeed, as Judith Butler's work has suggested, a Hegelian politics of identity-based recognition may be more advantageous for understanding the legal claims that trans subjects currently make upon the state (see Butler 2004).

References

Battersby, C. (1998), *The Phenomenal Woman: Feminist Metaphysics and the Patterns of Identity*, Cambridge: Polity Press.

Bhanji, N. (2012), "Trans/Scriptions: Homing Desires, (trans) Sexual Citizenship and Racialized Bodies," in T. Cotten (ed.), *Transgender Migrations: The Borders, Bodies and Politics of Transition*, 160–78, London: Routledge.

Butler, J. (2004), *Undoing Gender*, New York: Routledge.

Butler, J. (2015), *Senses of the Subject*, New York: Fordham University Press.

Carter, J. (2014), "Transition," *TSQ: Transgender Studies Quarterly* 1 (1–2): 235–7.

Cho, L. (2007), "The Turn to Diaspora," *Topia: Canadian Journal of Cultural Studies* 17: 11–30.

De Beauvoir, S. (2011), *The Second Sex*, trans. C. Borde and S. Malovany Chevallier New York: Vintage Books.

Deleuze, G. (1995), "Postscript on Control Societies," in *Negotiations: 1972–1990*, 177–82, New York: Columbia University Press.

Deleuze, G., and F. Guattari (1983), *Anti-Oedipus: Capitalism and Schizophrenia*, trans. R. Hurley, M. Seem, and H. R. Lane, Minneapolis: University of Minnesota Press.

Deleuze, G., and F. Guattari (1987), *A Thousand Plateaus: Capitalism and Schizophrenia*, trans. B. Massumi, Minneapolis: University of Minnesota Press.

Deleuze, G., and F. Guattari (2004), *A Thousand Plateaus: Capitalism and Schizophrenia*, trans. B. Massumi, London: Continuum.

DeShazer, M. K. (2012), "Postmillennial Breast Cancer Photo-narratives: Technologized Terrain," *Social Semiotics* 22 (1): 13–30.

Halberstam, J. J. (2011), *The Queer Art of Failure*, Durham, NC: Duke University Press.

Halberstam, J. (2018), *Trans*: A Quick and Quirky Account of Gender Variability*, Oakland: University of California Press.

Hayward, E. (2010), "Spider City Sex," *Women & Performance: A Journal of Feminist Theory* 20 (3): 225–51.

Husakouskaya, N. (2017), "Queering Mobility in Urban Gauteng: Transgender Internal Migrants and Their Experiences of 'Transition' in Johannesburg and Pretoria," *Urban Forum* 28: 91–110.

Jardine, A. (1985), *Gynesis: Configurations of Woman and Modernity*, Ithaca, NY: Cornell University Press.

Leung, H. H. (2016), "Always in Translation Trans Cinema Across Languages," *TSQ: Transgender Studies Quarterly* 3 (3–4): 433–47.

Lim, J., and K. Browne (2009), "Senses of Gender," *Sociological Research Online* 14 (1): 1–14.

Namaste, V. (2009), "Undoing Theory: The 'Transgender Question' and the Epistemic Violence of Anglo-American Feminist Theory," *Hypatia* 24 (3): 11–32.

Nelson, M. (2015), *The Argonauts*, Minnesota: Graywolf Press.

Pearce, R., D. L. Steinberg, and Igi Moon (2018), "Introduction: The emergence of 'trans,'" *Sexualities* 0 (0): 1–10. ISSN 1363-4607.

Preciado, P. B. (2017), *Testo Junkie: Sex, Drugs, and Biopolitics in the Pharmacopornographic Era*, New York City: Feminist Press.

Prosser, J. (2006), "Judith Butler: Queer Feminism, Transgender, and the Transubstantiation of Sex," in S. Stryker and S. Whittle (eds.), *The Transgender Studies Reader*, 257–80, London: Routledge.

Puar, J. K. (2017), *The Right to Maim: Debility, Capacity, Disability*, Durham, NC: Duke University Press.

Weinstein, J., and E. Hayward (2015), "Introduction: Tranimalities in the Age of Trans* Life," *TSQ: Transgender Studies Quarterly* 2 (2): 195–208.

Williams, C. (2014), "Transgender," *TSQ: Transgender Studies Quarterly* 1 (1–2): 232–4.

PART THREE
DETERRITORIALIZING FEMINIST PRAXES

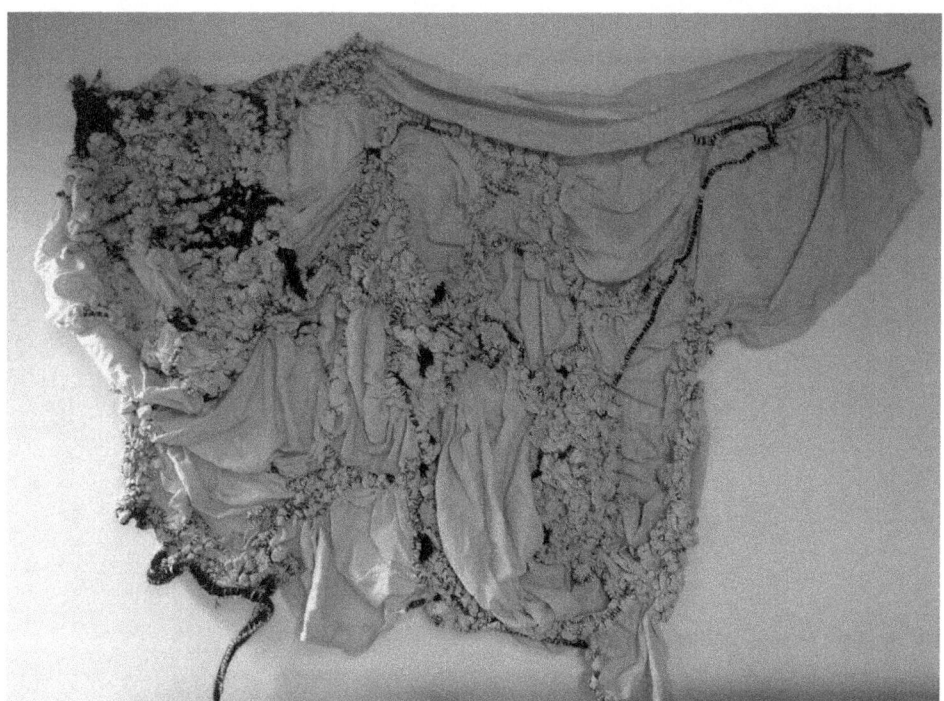

Figure 8.1 *"Entropy," 2004, cotton fabric and acrylic yarn, approx. 150 × 150 cm, Macarena Rioseco*
This project is based on sewing, making knots and wrinkles, corrugations and folds, piercing and perforating, binding and tying many pieces a white cotton fabric with black acrylic yarn. It is related to the notion of entropy, that is, to the idea of how work can transform materials, produce an exhaustion of matter and energy, and to finally convert them into matter and energy that cannot be used, that is, into waste. If I continue working until there is no more space of cotton fabric to sew, then the work will end up being an amorphous rounded black mass, in which no work can be done anymore. I left this piece in a middle stage of development, and propose to the audience to imagine possible outcomes, instead of imposing an irreversible end.
I describe my work as hybrid—my pieces are composed by groups of seemingly disparate elements connected through repetitive manual actions such as painting, knitting, sewing, or folding, hence, forming sorts of "dynamic suspension[s]" (Morley 2013: 204), between methods, practices, and ideas. My work is a product of a South-American culture, which is, in itself hybrid, as "forms of hybridity [are] found where cultures meet and merge" (207); my practice is rooted in Latin American indigenous practices of hand weaving and strongly influenced by modern Western art. It draws from traditional practices such as hand knitting, painting, gilding, drawing, and writing, and it is also affected by the filtering into the West of East Asian philosophical and religious practices (ibid.). In addition, my work draws from newer emergent technologies such as modern mechanized processes and digital media.

Reference

Morley, S. (2013), "Dansaekhwa," *Third Text* 27 (2): 189–207.

CHAPTER 8
SCHIZOANALYSIS AND THE DETERRITORIALIZATIONS OF TRANSNATIONAL FEMINISM
Janae Sholtz

1. Anticipatory Alliances

My investigation begins with a simple, though not uncontroversial, question: What can schizoanalysis do for feminist theory? Summarily, I argue that schizoanalysis can be a tool for building alliance with contemporary feminisms, one which initiates a becoming-other of feminism that is congruent with its own history of internal transformation and spirit of self-critique. In order to fully ascertain how, we must address and overcome what I see to be a main theoretical impasse to forging a new alliance with feminist practice: that for Deleuze and Guattari the movement out of the repressive structures of Western thought begins with the exit out of binary sexuality.

In *Anti-Oedipus* (1983) the reasoning behind this imperative is that the organization of the social field according to Oedipalized sexuality plays a central, and ultimately constrictive, role in subjectivation. It would seem that Deleuze and Guattari's criticism of the Oedipal structure as falsely transcendent and ultimately patriarchal would appeal to feminism. Yet, it is the conclusion they draw from this which signals their divergence. Whereas the recognition of Freud's masculinist assumptions led feminists to criticize the lack of place given to considering female sexuality and thus to argue for the acknowledgement of sexual difference and/or the reimagining of sexuality according to female models, Deleuze and Guattari utilize this critique to formulate a new model of desire—machinic desire—which essentially bypasses the subject by positing desire as pre-personal and productive *of* sexualities. Deleuze and Guattari's theory of desire implies the dispersal of sexuality into a generalized becoming and requires a total reconceptualization of desire and libidinal investment at a molecular level preceding sexual differentiation into the categories of male and female. Only from "the point of view of the 'dominant history' does the economy of binary sexuality seem natural" (Marrati 2006: 321). However, when this system is exposed, gender can be seen as dispersed, multiple, relational, fluctuating, or malleable, while the potentialities of sexuality to be polyvocal and unlimited become a reality. Paola Marrati articulates the stakes quite clearly: "If in sexuality everything is a matter of differences, then differences are exactly what cannot be reduced to the logic of binary oppositions. This is the Deleuzian way of affirming that having a sexual life is not having a sexual identity" (ibid.).

Thus, there is an apparent incommensurability between the Deleuzoguattarian multiplicity of sexual desire, which implies the dispersal of desire in an impersonal "generalized" becoming as well as the eradication of a binary sexual difference, and feminist insistence on sexual difference as a starting point. And while there are feminists who have attempted to reconfigure sexual difference to be more inclusive of multiple differences or posited it as a site/activity of differing (Colebrook 2000: 124) or endorsed becoming minoritarian of sex theoretically (Braidotti 2012: 40), there is still significant practical resistance to moving beyond these boundaries, and this is especially so once one moves outside of Deleuzian circles. At the very least, the maintenance of the category Woman is seen as a matter of political expediency and necessity—creating an imperative to move beyond molar categorization is all well and good for men, who have enjoyed political power and autonomy *as* subjects, but to ask women to do so is to neglect the fact that women are still struggling for that recognition. Being able to identify as a "Woman" is absolutely imperative for being able to address the ongoing concerns of oppression, marginalization, and gender-based violence. Citing the lack of symmetry between men and women (or minorities, migrants, etc.), Braidotti makes this point explicitly (ibid.: 40–2).

But if one sees Deleuze and Guattari's critique as a persuasive explanatory model, this impasse becomes harder to ignore, wherein molar sexuality cannot be understood as a primary ontological category but rather as a buttress to the politics of identification. It also becomes difficult to suggest that one can merely reclaim these categories by replacing one molar construct, no matter how much more attentive to and positive toward female experience, for another. Deleuze and Guattari's critique of molar sexuality challenges the very reality of sexual difference and gendered subjectivity deemed to be crucial and necessary for reclaiming a feminine position in political and ethical registers. As Žukauskaitė observes in Chapter 2 of this volume, "[I]t is precisely identity, or molar stratification (the division between classes, races and sexes) that creates the conditions of domination and power" (also Grosz 2002).

Ultimately, the claim is that molar politics centered on sexual difference is a necessary construct—but what if it's not? Can we ask ourselves as feminists, as women, what are the libidinal investments that are guiding the refusal to relinquish certain prerogatives, such as the duality of sexuality or a politics based upon identity—strategic or otherwise? Why not relinquish the language of normalization, rather than try to reclaim it? Can we end our dependence on such categorical impositions and, as a matter of political efficacy, should we?

2. The Schizoanalysis of Feminism

There are good reasons to dispute the necessity of strategic molar identification and embrace schizoanalysis, as the politically efficacious thing to do, *as* feminists and *as* women. To be sure, feminist discourse has become more nuanced and self-critical with respect to issues of difference, specificity, and situatedness, yet, even with the powerful and important critiques that have opened feminism to its blatant historical exclusions of women of color, issues of class difference, and epistemic imperialism, many of these analyses are still fundamentally operating within the paradigm of identity, and as long as this main paradigm, replicating the form of molarity, continues to hold sway in how we analyze problems, we remain bound to repeat a logic of exclusion and miss certain features of systems of oppression and power that fall below the threshold of identities— those that contribute to the formation of identities and subjectivities themselves. These are operations and forces that schizoanalysis illuminates.

Though much has been done to point out major problems with what could be considered the molar form of feminism. For instance, intersectionality, coined by Crenshaw (1991),[1] was crucial in highlighting the internal problematics of exclusion, homogeneity, and hierarchical power dynamics within White liberal feminism in the United States, illustrating the problematic tendency of defining Woman as a monolithic category with one set of identifying prerogatives. Intersectional feminists called out the inconsistency of a feminism that criticized patriarchal Western European thinking for its tendency toward hierarchical dualistic logic, while not recognizing its operation within its own boundaries (Lorde 2007). By interpreting all the problems of oppression on the basis of sex, white feminists ignored the inbuilt privilege of whiteness, allowing white women to satisfy their own desire for liberation, while maintaining a share of the social investment of power (122), exemplifying how "an unconscious investment of a fascist or reactionary type can exist alongside a conscious revolutionary investment" (Deleuze and Guattari 1983: 105), as well as illustrating how the logic of identity politics contributes to the perpetuation of systematic oppression and exclusion.

According to Jibrin and Salem (2015), intersectionality has come to define feminist research; the recognition of the importance of difference and eschewal of constituting women as a universal category is ubiquitous. Yet, this has not curtailed the repetition of the same problem on the global front, between hegemonic Western feminism and so-called Third World Women. The problems incumbent to representational (identity) politics, including exclusion and othering, continue to plague feminist debate. Mohanty (2003) forcefully shows that the production of a singular, monolithic subject as a preexisting, coherent group with similar interests and struggles—Third World Women— has dominated Western European feminist discourses, reflecting the colonization of scholarship and knowledge about women in developing countries. Western feminism assumes the universal legitimacy and value of concepts such as reproduction, equality, sexual division of labor, family, marriage, and belonging, while, in actuality, importing the meaning of these from Western definitions, participating in the epistemic imperialism widely criticized by postcolonial thinkers (Said 1979; Spivak 1989; Bhabha 1994; Brah 2002; Dabashi 2015). Mohanty's point is that this reliance on an ahistorical, universal unity between Women is ineffectual in designing strategies to combat actual and specific oppressions and that it reinforces the binaries between men and women which themselves have imperialistic content.

In other words, molar identity is replicated on a different front, serving to instantiate Western imperialist values and perpetuate the assumption of Western European discourse/ philosophy as the hegemonic, legitimating discourse, *and,* ironically—given the lessons that were supposedly learned—fails to acknowledge the specificity/singularity of real women, operating from an ideological composite rather than see women as real, material subjects of collective histories, in much the same way that Deleuze and Guattari identify Oedipal constructs as reductive and restrictive of singular desires and practices. One could surmise that feminism, Western feminism, does not have the tools necessary to enact a critique of the system at a transnational level or address the realities of global Capitalism, which simultaneously carve out a territory at/as the center while enacting ever-increasing deterritorializations on the margins. Since, on the global scene, Western feminism operates as that center, it is ill positioned to conduct a critical analysis, which speaks to the importance of reconceiving the ethical imperatives that would be necessary for a global feminism.

The efforts of Crenshaw, as well as other important women of color, to address systematic oppression and racial injustice, have pluralized feminism's internal dialogue, moving beyond the univocal description of women's oppression. These women set the precedent for a form of feminist critique that provides the possibility for forging strategic alliances to resist coercive regimes and fight oppression and discrimination as such. But, as I will argue later, it is insufficient for addressing the molecular level on which certain oppressions operate or for dispelling the logic of identity that buttresses the repetitions of molar politics as such.[2] My intent is to approach intersectionality as an extension of the critique of molarity, without rejecting its contribution to critical advances within the field. We need an auxiliary model that accounts for the deterritorializations of sexuality and feminism itself—a model that accounts for presubjective, impersonal, and collective desire.

So, I return to my initial question: *What can schizoanalysis do for feminist theory?* How can this methodology align with feminism and the issues that it raises? In what follows, I suggest that feminism needs to perform its own schizoanalysis, to open itself to its seething borders and its refusals, and that this is necessary in order to understand the nuances of larger global women's issues, as well as to be a corrective to the colonizing effects of Western, liberal feminism.

The schizoanalysis of feminism would operate according to the tripartite tasks provided in *Anti Oedipus*: (1) Destruction—the deterritorializing of feminism, (2) Analysis—of the investments of desire, and (3) Proliferation—of new connections and new forms of desire, *a feminist delirium*. I propose to align this methodology with the discerning insights of transnational feminism, which incorporates postcolonial and decolonial theory in order to make visible problematics of epistemic imperialism and the inequalities of globalization, as well as illuminate the lived experience of those who fail to receive proper recognition within current hegemonic regimes, falling to the margins of (or between) strictly defined theoretical and literal boundaries.

3. Transnational Feminists Voices—*Philosophizing with* as a Model of Alliance

First, I want to acknowledge the understandable suspicion of the universalist imposition of postmodern theory in thinking about the transnational, subaltern or postcolonial experience.[3] As a philosopher speaking from this tradition, it is a difficult line to walk—to want to engage in the conversation without overstepping, to be sensitive to all the pitfalls of appropriation, the risks of speaking about or for others. But the answer is not complete disavowal. As Dabashi so eloquently exclaims, Western philosophers must learn to *philosophize with* rather than *philosophizing about* (2015: 16). My hope is that by situating this discussion as a desire for alliance and through engaging the work of postcolonial feminists and theorists, my intervention follows this communal path.

Historically speaking, feminism has maintained its viability by a willingness to undergo internal critique. I argue that transnational feminism offers an opportunity in just this respect and that schizoanalysis as a conceptual tool can be useful for engaging the critique of feminism from this transnational perspective. In the spirit of the longstanding concerns about the deleterious effects of speaking for others, I am going to try to open a space to amplify the voices and concerns of those with whom I am attempting to be an interlocutor, with the express intent of understanding how schizoanalysis might align with their goals. Let me stress that in both cases proposed herein, their work already constitutes a decentering of Western feminism and evidences the power and crucial importance of a decolonial, transnational perspective and is, to my mind, a nascent form of schizoanalysis of molar epistemes.

In the first instance, I refer to Hoodfar's analysis of the Islamic practice of veiling, drawing out the latent schizoanalytic traits of her critique. In "The Veil in Their Minds and On Our Heads," Hoodfar addresses the ways that the practice of veiling is persistently viewed and relates them to the perpetuation of reductive and disempowering construction of the "Muslim Woman." The common discourse surrounding the practice, from a Western perspective, has been to condemn it as wholly oppressive and to view women who subscribe to it as unknowledgeable, controlled and passive victims unable to make decisions for themselves. Hoodfar begins, in much the same vein as Mohanty, by pointing out that there is an assumption that what is good for Western women is good for all women, noting that Western women are constructed as the dominant or paradigmatic group whose concerns over rights and freedom of expression, classical liberal concerns, should frame the debate. What is fascinating is that Hoodfar performs a schizoanalytic reading in that she uncovers the social investments that have given the veil the "status" that it has, particularly in relation to "the persistence of these social and ideological constructions in colonial practices and discourse" (Hoodfar 1993: 6). She disrupts the narrative of the veil as a particularly Islamic practice, citing the pre-Islamic origin of practices of veiling and seclusion in ancient Mediterranean societies as a sign of economic status and respectability. Seclusion as a practice took root as a matter of economic protection, and ironically, because Muslim women inherited wealth by law and enjoyed greater economic rights, practices of controlling their wealth through social institutions took root. Hoodfar's analysis also reveals that these practices differed according to social status—seclusion was not practiced in rural areas, as women's economic labor was necessary. The status of elite women changed with the transformation of the economy toward trade and factory production; unable to participate in these, elite women lost socioeconomic position—thus the transformation of the significance of veiling and seclusion has to be understood in light of the social and economic determinants. Moreover, Hoodfar insists on the plural significance of the veil both in different cultures and in different time periods, criticizing "the tendency of Western scholarly work and colonial powers to present a uni-dimensional Islam" (7). For instance, in Iranian culture, the veil is associated with the power for women to judge the worth of men and to signify the social order; traditionally women were not required to veil themselves in the presence of lower status men, and by observing or neglecting the veil, women define who is and is not a man. In the historical instance of the late-nineteenth-century Tobacco Movement, female Iranian nationalists used the threat of this irrevocable insult to influence political action when their male counterparts were reluctant to radically oppose the British tobacco monopoly (ibid.). Hoodfar's work has served as a touchstone for others who seek to dispel monolithic stereotypes surrounding the veil. Khan also insists on various historical examples of the veil as a source of empowerment (Khan 1995: 147).

What is significant about Hoodfar's treatment, as well as Khan's, is that by addressing the temporality of these social and economic determinants, she is able to dislodge the understanding of the veil as a transcendent and univocal symbol of oppression. A significant point related to our critique of identity politics is that Hoodfar relates adherence to these molar constructions to the inability to recognize and explore the socioeconomic significance of the existing variations, which were and are readily available (Hoodfar 1993: 7). Hoodfar's genealogical approach highlights the relative recent development of the colonial image of the "oppressed Muslim woman" associated with the veil. She argues that this "man-made image of oriental Muslim women continues to be a mechanism by which Western dominant cultures recreate and perpetuate beliefs about their superiority" (5). These images began to take shape during the diminishment of the Ottoman Empire, as the Muslim orient fell deeper under European power. Hoodfar cites the proliferation of travel books and material that simultaneously fetishized the idea of the harem, while depicting women of the harem as prisoners to unabated and barbaric male sexual appetites. This appeals to the West's sense of moral superiority and sexual fantasy simultaneously (both the conscious interests of suppression—the molar—and the unconscious libidinal desires—the molecular—to use Deleuzian terminology). A further factor in the construction and manipulation of these molar identities was that they served as a deflection from the oppressive nature of Victorian morality and repressive social roles associated with the cult of femininity constricting European women (8). Essentially, Hoodfar conducts her critique by assessing the underlying desires and interests that factor into these constructions, thereby revealing the faulty logic of assuming the transcendent or ahistorical nature of these images of women and Islam. Applying a schizoanalytic framework to this analysis can help make this explicit and clarify what is at stake here.

Hoodfar conducts this cultural and historical analysis to reveal the political stakes involved, but her main criticism is of feminism itself, for its failure to interrogate the colonial, racist and androcentric constructions of both non-western women and men on which it has relied (6). Rather than take Islamic Women's veiling as the starting point indicating a particular kind of subject, Hoodfar deconstructs the image to reveal the social investments that it contains—both in terms of the Western colonizer's desire and in terms of the socioeconomic factors that have framed the practice. Thus, Hoodfar is able to shift the discussion away from a liberal debate over individual rights toward that of the larger global, economic, and historical factors that shape cultural practices and ideology—out of which particular conceptions of women and their "place" are generated. Let me be clear, construing this as an issue of whether Islamic women have the *right* to veil or not obscures the larger social and political ramifications, impeding a critique of the imperialistic investments of desire that have framed the issue in the first place, as well as assuming a particularly Westernized set of prerogatives of rights, equality, and individual liberty. As Marrati remarks,

> From the political point of view, it is sometimes necessary ... to speak in terms of rights and of identity ... But the necessity of escaping from this dominant history... is no less pressing ethically and politically. We have to be careful not to reproduce within minority groups its oppressive logic, its identitarian assignations. (2006: 321)

What we need is a complimentary awareness of the historically and politically specific desires and dynamics of power that populate a given situation in order to ascertain how they inflect the discourses, social attitudes, and material practices that are proliferated. We can think of these as the seething interstices within and between hegemonic priorities and the machinations of global technocapitalism.

4. Machinic Enslavement

To connect this issue of global capitalism and Western privilege to schizoanalysis, I refer to Lazzarato's (2006) formulation of capitalism as the dominant machinic assemblage of our time, through which collective enunciations and routinized desires have become ubiquitous and accelerated. Lazzarato defines capitalism, not as a mode of production nor as a system, but rather as operations of "machinic enslavement" and "social subjection," two operations happening at different levels. The first, subjection, constitutes its social dimension and helps us see that there are certain societal roles and functions that appear within the modes of communication and language perpetuated by capitalism. These roles and functions support the proper functioning of capitalism and are established through the repetition of "prefabricated modes of expression ... codified statements, [that are] statements of the dominant reality" (ibid.). This is the level of social selves—our race, our class, our political affiliations—all our *identifications*. The more intensive level of control happens at the level of machinic enslavement: this includes all sorts of aesthetic, affective, and moral markers through which "subjects" understand themselves—the "pre-individual, pre-cognitive, and pre-verbal components [that cause the circulation of] affects, perceptions and sensations." This *molecular* level of desire "permeates the roles, functions and meanings by which individuals both recognize each other and are alienated from each other … capital assumes control of the charge of desire carried by humanity" (ibid.).

These levels parallel those that Deleuze and Guattari analyze under the rubric of schizoanalysis: the preconscious level of interest and the unconscious level of libidinal desires–both of which can either be subjugated or liberated (see Holland 2002: 103–4). Deleuze and Guattari leave open the possibility of revolutionary breaks from machinic enslavement, and the key question has always been how does this happen? Lazzarato claims that, though we exist within the present paradigm of machinic enslavement, "individuals … have the virtual ability to act differently" (2006), and Deleuze and Guattari would point to the need to expose and destroy the molar categories that constrict our ability to become otherwise and cultivate other desires and affective connections. This is one of the places that schizoanalysis and transnational feminism can become allies.

My contention is that when Deleuze and Guattari insist that philosophy needs non-philosophy (1994: 218), they are speaking not just about disciplines or activities other than philosophy; they recognize the state of Western philosophy as concretized, totalizing, and in need of its own schizoanalytic moment, contrasting this hegemony to genuine thinking–this is why Deleuze is so adamant that the people to come, and by this he means a new political vision that could possible escape the double pincers of capitalism's machinic enslavement, must come from those marginalized by said philosophy (both epistemically and materially). It is only through shifting thought toward that which has been disregarded by, dislocated by, even invisible[4] to the molar, that thinking can itself become minor, which means, no mere reversal, but a change in kind: the decoupling of desire from its molar forms, where desire and thought can begin to form new arrangements and new alliances/connections–where it becomes transversal. When free intensities and desires to detach or emerge within machinic assemblages, there is the possibility of escape from serialized and standardized production of subjectivity.

Where do we find such intensities and desires? The possibility of transformation of any assemblage happens through what Deleuze and Guattari call the abstract machine. The abstract machine signifies the power to dislocate and recombine, to form new assemblages, and it operates according to a logic of differentiation, movement, and process. It is abstract because it represents a potential beyond any actual assemblage, a potential found within assemblages which always contain an excess of desire, forces and flows that cannot be rigidified, and affects and sensibilities that elude the dominant order. These are the moments of resistance and the places of political subversion.

As such, it would seem that feminism must find solidarity and the potential for political resistance not through the molarity of Woman, but by interrogating the kinds of desire and practices that accrue from occupying marginal and in-between spaces. This means opening feminism as a global alliance which does not necessarily remain focused to sexuality and which prioritizes postcolonial and subaltern perspectives.

This is a transnational (schizo) position; no longer Western, no longer women, but instead a common goal with all who find themselves relationally marginalized. Rather than repeating the binary logic of Subject/Other or employing over-simplistic models of center/margin that abstract away from lived experience and material relations, of which many postcolonial thinkers have been critical, I suggest combining a feminist intersectional approach with Deleuze and Guattari's notion of transversality.[5] It is crucial, as Gutiérrez Rodriguez (2006) claims, that transgressing Western epistemological imperialism requires more than shifting perspective toward a rhizomatic model. Occidental thinking must be displaced as the dominant politics of interpellation. My work here aims to gesture toward this by giving voice to alternative trajectories of knowledge and dislocating Western prerogatives:

> We should look to those whose lives have been made impossible by capitalism, to places where global exploitation and political erasure have created unassimilable pockets which render capitalist discourse and idealizations nonsensical and moot, in order to humbly see what kind of future comes out of these exhausted spaces and struggles. (Sholtz 2018: 124)

Of course, feminism is already doing a huge portion of this critical work. As we have seen, intersectional feminisms demand careful attention to various forms of oppression and recognition of unequal distribution of power within social relations. It demands that we become highly attentive to those on the margins, offering a more nuanced and pluralized method of analysis according to overlapping social categories such as gender, race, class, ability, sexual orientation, religion, caste, age, nationality. Yet, as we have also seen, schizoanalysis makes us aware of another level of analysis—that of pre-personal flows of desire that both comprise and exceed the realm of the social and the human even. In light of the two operations of the machinic, we can say that intersectionality operates at the level of social functions and roles—*subjectivation*. In other words, intersectionality begins from the products of social determinants rather than the investments of desire that produce them, and in this way still participates in what Puar has called "identitarian interpellation" (2011) as its starting point.[6] We must couple this analysis with the articulation of desire, as well as the proliferation of new desire, the level of social flows. What I am suggesting is that schizoanalysis can offer another avenue of analysis which speaks to the material conditions and lived experiences with which feminism is concerned, to enhance feminism's critical projects. In that spirit, I want to shift the concept of intersectionality to include the machinic characteristic of transversality.

5. Intersectional Transversality

Schizoanalysis reveals different levels of striation (social, economic, and individual interests), but also routed courses of affects and forces within a complex of material relations (investments of human and nonhuman desire). But, if interests are born out of desire, it is ultimately desire that must be changed or addressed. If what we are seeking to examine is flows of desire, then we need a model that focuses on processes and in-between passages rather than points of intersection, or, as Buchanan says, is "capable of working with fluid material" (2014: 13). This has motivated many to turn to the Deleuze's concept of assemblage to account for a more fluid and process-oriented analysis (Currier 2003; Puar 2007; Bogic 2017). Dolphijn and van der Tuin draw parallels between the assemblage and Barad's concept of "agential realism" (2013), which she contrasts to intersectionality, claiming that intersectionality has been developed as "mutually perpendicular set of axes of identification" (Barad 2001: 98) rather than iterative intra-actions through which a dynamic spatio-temporal scene is produced. Their work highlights the topology of assemblage as dynamics of co-constitutive and intra-active elements:

> The machinic aspect of the assemblage relates ... to a precise state of intermingling of bodies in a society, including all the attraction and repulsion, sympathies and antipathies, alternations, amalgamations, penetrations, and expansions that affect bodies of all kinds in their relations to one another. (Deleuze and Guattari 1987: 90)

The cartographies that accompany schizoanalysis' ability to diagnose parameters of interest and flows of desire can be very powerful tools in analyzing the entire space of an encounter, the texture of an event. But what it is about the assemblage that makes it a model of mobility, more fit for diagnosing flows of desire and dynamic interrelations?

What makes the machinic assemblage (as a model) exceptional is the quality of transversality. Transversality, originally articulated as a corrective to psychoanalytic models of hierarchical transference (Guattari 1984), comes to indicate the ability to cut through levels of striation, an openness to multiple kinds of movement and intensity, and the priority of non-categorical connection of heterogeneous elements. As such, transversality also indicates a subversive, political potential, both for disturbing homogenous political affiliations and creating new formations and alliances on the basis of more singularized moments of association and a more heterogeneous array of elements.

The addition of transversality implies that sites of identity are always in process and ensconced in particular machinic assemblages. Additionally, transversality privileges passage and movement over stasis[7] and *inclusive* disjunctive synthesis, in which relations of difference do not exclude one another or inhibit one from participating in the other, over *exclusive* disjunctions of oppositional logic or dialectical sublimation (see Deleuze and Guattari 1983: 75–83). Therefore, the emphasis on transversality accomplishes a topological shift away from points and representations toward in-between-ness and the event of passage. Transversality also explodes the dichotomy of center and periphery, as assemblages exceed their own "boundaries" necessarily, connecting transversally with other systems/assemblages according to affective attractions and intensifications. Thus it "opens up a space in which to think beyond language and take into account the productive and creative potentiality of affect" (Gutiérrez Rodríguez 2007). Most importantly, transversality is the ability to connect disparate and heterogeneous series, which is essentially for change, transformation, and alliance.

As well as referring to the moving between registers of materiality and ideation or language and affect, the idea of attempting to make transversal connections between heterogeneous series can be a productive way of encountering other knowledges, meeting a transnational feminist aim: to refrain from assuming a universal epistemology that bears the erasure of its own privilege. When Deleuze and Guattari speak of "a thousand tiny sexes," this could also refer to the polymorphous desire presented through a multiplicity of heterogeneous voices and to the possibilities that open up when we are able to hear other desires—the ones that are shut out if they don't correspond to dominant discourses, beyond the territorialized parameters of a Western consciousness so inscribed by a certain normativity, binarism, gender politics, and epistemic certainty. Indeed, transnational feminists have proliferated new desires and advocate for new milieus of thinking and concern by critiquing the Eurocentric and Western prerogatives within dominant feminist discourses.

As we have seen through Hoodfar's analysis, transnational feminism recognizes the particular unconscious and affective dimensions through which certain identity categories are viewed under Western eyes and develops a more nuanced account of the gendered effects of Capitalism on a global scale, where geographical and economic marginalization plays a huge role in the impact of technology and production. Schizoanalysis is a method of assessing the conjunctions of desiring-production, social production, and economic production that would poise us to engage these intersecting relations as part of a collective discourse, and the transnational perspective is geared toward making visible the geopolitical, economic, and historical realities that condition certain practices and impositions on non-Western societies, as a form of resistance. Both participate in intersectional transversality.

Thus, intersectional transversality indicates a genealogical account that addresses spatio-temporal coordinates and unconscious investments of identity traits, while simultaneously considering the operation of molar traits within the given social field. This provides the possibility for the disarticulation of subjectivity from these axes of identity, for loosening and rupturing molar boundaries in order to free movements of desire from certain pathways so that other unforeseen connections can be made.

The transversal element indicates an "intimate moment of encounter" whose very contingency and open-endedness is both cause for overwhelming ambivalence and understanding. I take this formulation from Gutiérrez Rodríguez, who employs transversality to counter tendencies of epistemic imperialism that often happen in translation. The transversal characterizes understanding that attends to the interface of idioms and affective spaces opened up by these exchanges, seeking not to reduce moments of untranslatability (2006)—this is the intimate encounter. It is to analyze the processes of desiring and unconscious investment at the juncture of particular social formations, in much the way that Hoodfar identifies the Western desire to maintain cultural hegemony as operative in the image of "Muslim Woman." This provides the possibility for the disarticulation of subjectivity from these axes of identity, for loosening and rupturing molar boundaries in order to free movements of desire from certain pathways so that other unforeseen connections can be made. Thus, intersectional transversality breaks with the emphasis on individuality through emphasis on an experience of locality defined by fluidity and movement of pre-personal affects and forces, but also the transversal of different kinds of connections that are not governed by sameness or identity. A point of alliance between these and schizoanalysis then is the recognition that historical oppression happens not only according to identity but also according to the needs/desires/affects produced through global technocapitalism. Race, sex, and gender have all been mobilized in order to justify the devices of control and exploitation of this megamachine, mobilized at the level of desire and affect. For instance, to have pre-personal, precognitive fear of a racial other makes it a lot easier to deny a migrant worker entry or full visa rights, guaranteeing cheaper and more docile laborers.

Conceptualizing intersectional transversality is an attempt to forge an alliance between feminism and schizoanalysis, and to cultivate awareness of the crisscrossing and evolving experiences of women, whose needs, affective experiences, and practices derive from conditions of economic exploitation, Eurocentric and global capitalist interests and desires, as well as issues of material flux and geographical displacement, such as refugee status, trafficking, and migrant labor.

It has been widely agreed that modernity is characterized by accelerated flows of capital, information, and people, and that the paradigms of movement and flow have come to occupy central theoretical stage. The dislocation of peoples and the challenging of borders are undeniable global realities accompanying these flows (Brah 1996; Braziel and Mannur 2003; Agnew 2005); migration has risen over 40 percent in the last decade (Serban-Oprescu 2013: 97). Nail calls the migrant "the political figure of our time" (2015: 235), arguing that the possibility for transforming the political framework rises from the social turbulence created by "the social figure who moves outside the dominant forms of social motion [i.e., the migrant]" (223). Earlier, I made a similar claim in relation to possibilities of resistance and transformation, but I also want to pay heed to the intimate encounter that happens when crossing real lives with theoretical goals. It is always a sensitive alliance, and with the realities of dislocation, dispersion, and precarity that often accompany migration, we must be particularly sensitive to the needs and desires that arise from within these communities of the displaced and the ambulant, recognizing that the (oft-lauded) modern conditions of mobility are ones that sweep large swaths of people (women in particular) into a particularly deterritorialized experiences, often washing away familiar or traditional connections with categories of home, nationality, and family. The next section considers the realities of actual material and social flows of a particular diasporic population.

6. Migrant Filipina Women

As a way of illustrating the potential for transformative connections [politically and socially] and alliance between feminism and schizoanalysis, I want to speak about phenomenon of the diaspora of Filipina migrant female workers and the possibility of a productive, aberrant desire, not for home or molar identity, but for a new kind of communal alliance. I draw from Parrenas excellent analysis of the impacts of globalization in "Transgressing the Nation-State: The Partial Citizenship and "Imagined (Global) Community" of Migrant Filipina Domestic Workers," and pair her work with schizoanalytic insights in order to illustrate how schizoanalysis can offer another mode of analysis.

Parrenas claims that the outflow of women from the Philippines represents one of the largest and widest flows of contemporary female migration in the world. It is estimated that nearly ten million are working and living abroad (10 percent of the population).[8] Though this "culture of migration" has been well acknowledged, even seen as a pillar of labor policy, what is particularly important is Parrenas's focus on the fact that nearly seventy percent are women—channeled into areas with a high demand for entertainment, service worker, and low wage domestic labor. Though spread out over 140 countries, they experience similar kinds of obstacles and desires because of the gendered nature of the work; Parrenas' attention to affective and emotional dimensions of these women's lives is particularly relevant for our study. Parrenas explains the phenomenon as the result of three factors: "[E]xport-led development strategy of the Philippines, the feminization of the international labor force, and the demand for migrant women to fill low-wage service work in many cities throughout the world" (Parrenas 2001). Each of these causes can be linked to macrostructural processes of globalization—the denationalization of economies, the incessant demands for lower wages, and the need for a malleable, disempowered labor force—guided as they are by capitalism and neoliberal free market principles. The implementation of these principles can lead to particularly negative consequences: denial of rights to full citizenship, denial of reproductive rights, disruption of family relations, and abuse and exploitation.

Applying a schizoanalytic lens to this situation, capitalism has led to the deterritorialization of modes of production and labor on a global scale. Because capitalism is always a relative deterritorialization, it sets up exclusive and restrictive disjunctive relations of center and periphery in order to confine these deterritorialized desires into a pattern that serves its interests. These disjunctive relations create territories, as well as the phenomena of migration, exile, and refugees.[9] Thus, deterritorialization becomes the operative mode through which many individuals experience their existence, as they occupy the constituted outside of the constitutive center. Schizoanalysis allows us to analyze the colonizing force of capitalism/Oedipus and begin to loosen sense of inevitability that attaches to and normalizes these relations. Viewing this situation through a schizoanalytic lens could offer a way for these women to draw solidarity through the disparity of their experiences and become subjects of, rather than subjugated to, their deterritorialized experience.

The issue for Parrenas is how these women negotiate their contradictory positioning vis-à-vis the nation-state. Their status as migrants means that they are never given full recognition within their present locality, while also being cut off and dislocated from their parent nation. They are without home, and, at the very least, their experience challenges the limits of traditional, territorialized norms of family, home, and national identity, a phenomenon recognized in diaspora theory as central to the diasporic experience. A subject to which we will return, home, in diaspora studies, is seen an open concept through which diasporic communities imagine new horizons and renegotiate (gender) relations (Agnew 2005).

What is fascinating is Parrenas method of gathering information to study these negotiations. Parrenas discovered that this female diaspora communicates through the publication and distribution of a magazine called *Tinig Filipino*. *Tinig Filipino* is a monthly publication that attests to the diaspora of Filipino migrant workers by offering a forum for the migrant workers to give expression to their experiences. There are no staff writers, only an open invitation to migrant workers to submit their stories. This unique format offers an unmediated space for representing the social realities of migrant Filipina domestic workers and attests to collectively shared affects of fear and guilt, as well as hope and joy. It is also significant within our discussion of the schizoanalysis of feminism itself. This is a space in which these women have their own narrative, rather than having it spoken and analyzed for them.

The magazine enabled Parrenas to gain a sense of how these female migrants experiencing alienation and exclusion develop a sense of place in globalization. Parrenas claims that these women have responded with a double turn, first, by identifying the Philippines as "home" thereby maintaining their nationalist identity, and, at the same time, by creating an international, imagined community that extends their sense of place and sense of community into a transnational terrain (Parrenas 2001), a phenomena designated as "homing," where home is a mythic place of desire, a place of no return and a lived experience of locality (Brah 1996: 192). By emphasizing both their nationalist and diasporic identities, they simultaneously reinforce and transgress the nation-state. Now, under the right conditions, this ambiguity could be interpreted as opening a space for creative invention that could foster a future imagined community, one joined together through affective alliance and a "set of shared symbols, common events, and a secular "cross-time" temporality promoted by a print vernacular" (Bates 1999: 26, quoted in Parrenas 2001). Yet, in order to do so, the affective power of this double bind would need be addressed more consciously, or maybe, schizo-analytically.

The double bind can be analyzed according to what Deleuze and Guattari say about the two kinds of social investment: segregative and nomadic. The unconscious oscillates between these; one is revolutionary and one produces even more restrictive norms, and as Deleuze and Guattari are apt to point out, the unconscious is inherently drawn to its own repression, thus the restriction of desire and investment in fascistic or nationalistic paradigms is to be expected. But "if this process is capable of forming subjects with dispositions toward conservatism in thinking, then it should also be capable of forming subjects who bear within themselves the power of becoming out of which they emerged" (Carr 2018). This would be the schizoanalytic goal: not to let the schizophrenic process breakdown and be consumed by the repressive ideals engineered through the capitalist machine. So, rather than the double bind as a descriptive condition of their reality, the schizoanalytic position would see it as an opportunity for transformation.

Schizoanalysis refocuses attention on macro-systems of power that create the conditions of possibility for particular identities—on the systems of power that produce the habits constitutive of particular identities (McNay 2008). Making more explicit the prerogatives that inform the imposition of molar identities and the bevy of ideals that attach to them (a kind of schizoanalytic consciousness-raising) could help redirect unrequited desires for national identity/homeland and mitigate the realities of diasporic experiences, allowing for stronger imagined communities that embrace the variable conditions of diasporic-life. The ideals of home, family, and even nationality can serve to alienate these women by overlaying an impossible standard that would construct their desire as a lack and conceive their experience as abnormal or deviant. Thus, identifying with these ideals would result in guilt and restriction. For example, Parrenas notes that a common discussion in *Tinig Filipino* centers on if children behind are abused. The general response was, yes. But both the economic necessities that deterritorialized these women and the restrictions that disallow them from bringing their children with them render the discussion moot. In this case, they have assimilated an impossible ideal necessitated by the social order that constitutes them as justifiably and undeniably guilty.

Yet, these women are already quasi-schizo-subjects, producing, through *Tinig Filipino*, a virtual community vis-à-vis assemblage based on alliance rather than affiliation. They have created a *virtual place* for new connections that breaks up the homogeneity of identifications, which determine the regular and regulated spaces in which they find themselves. The potential for dislocating dominant molar apparatuses is born out of their very dislocation. As Nail observes, the potential inherent in migrant social organizations (their "counterforce") is "to pose an alternative to the present social logic of expulsion that continues to dominate the world" (2015: 7). Eliminating the prevalence of what Deleuze would call sad passions, that is, the guilt associated with traditional familial standards and the sense of hopelessness that ensues from a longing for return to the homeland, is one step to strengthening this group from within. Achieving this aim is both a matter of understanding the investments of interest that direct these finding norms and greater sensitivity to the affective dimensions of every assemblage, including one's own unconscious desires, so that these desires (as creative energies) can be rerouted.

7. Transnational-Schizoanalytic Feminism—Mobilizing Desire

It has been suggested that Deleuze and Guattari offer a "monological perspective as a universal narrative of emancipation" (Karkov 2016), and they do posit a transcendental unconscious as a plane of immanence—a desiring-machine constituted by a series of syntheses that cause connections and breaks in the flows of material existence. Yet, though this materialist theory of desire is posited as univocal and universally operative, the expression of desire and emancipatory solutions are temporalized and historicized. Deleuze and Guattari characterize our contemporary conjunction of social production schizophrenic because capitalism operates by decoding all prior codes which extends to the whole social body, filling it with its own productions yet also preventing anything, any desire, to escape it. In relation to this, schizoanalysis is a strategy for liberating desires that have become over-invested and over-coded. While agreeing with Pisters (2008: 109) that we should be wary of importing the problems of psychoanalysis universally such that the notions of family, trauma, and so on are assumed to be the same cross-culturally, I want to insist that the potential for analyzing specific formations of desire is still emancipatory. Deleuze and Guattari are keenly aware of particularity—temporally, geographically, and territorially; they insist on the singularity of analysis. Pisters specifically has in mind the "transnational context" through which "the notion of family itself has changed through emancipation and migration" (ibid.), and this is exactly my point: alliance is not a one-way street (pace the concept of becoming). The alliance with transnational feminist issues could bring about a transformation of thinking essential to de-molarize Western, Eurocentric dominance. Thus, our initial question could just as easily read: *What can feminism do for schizoanalysis?*

They view philosophy as a tool box, not as an absolutism, and we should approach schizoanalysis in this vein, as one tool, among others. This is why I have stressed the mode of alliance. Schizoanalysis does not replace the work of the intersectional, transnational, or decolonial, but rather can be used alongside these critical modes of analysis—what are the connections, the overlapping prerogatives? What do we put into our machines to make them work and transform the way we experience the world? Given the relentlessness of capitalist fluidity, to produce new connections we need these interventions to disrupt the flows of capital.

Referring back to the second task for schizoanalysis—to discover in a subject the nature, formation and functioning of *her* desiring-machines—we must ask, what may be required to accomplish this, and it seems to me that we must first ask how are desires and affects routed to justify these predicaments and how we can find the desire to break with these machinic codings of our desire? Next, in keeping with the final task of proliferating new (revolutionary) desires, we must conceive a new kind of space, an interval in which we could begin to think and act freely. What we need is *a space of our own*, which would resist the present as it has been actualized, molarized, and determined. The first step must be to redefine what a space is in order to imagine/ reinvent what it could be, and this is where the experience of those who have become dislocated or marginalized, who have had to reimagine their own relation to space and locality, is crucially important.

Deleuze is well aware that centers owe their position to the marginalization of other spaces. Decentering Western philosophy has always been the goal of schizoanalysis, and likewise for us, decentering feminism. To decenter is not merely a matter of inversion; it is to change the paradigm all together, to imagine mobile spaces with no center, which pay heed to the anomalous shifting borders that result from intimate encounters in which affects and desires are acknowledged through a heightened sense of the imposition of desires or the co-opting of desire. Perhaps we can imagine this as a virtual space, like the magazine that allows migrants to connect their desires together outside of their confined localities, or perhaps we can produce a delay in the normal assimilation of subjects to the social order by refusing to speak the language of identity.

There is a real opportunity here to trace a new cartography—between the analytic capabilities made possible through schizoanalysis *and* transnational feminist critiques. The concept of the intersectional transversality, while retaining its alliance with the crucial feminist work that comes before it, provides a method of understanding the conjunctions of desiring-production, social production, and economic production that would poise us to engage these intersecting relations as part of a collective discourse, while the transnational perspective is geared toward making visible the geopolitical, economic, and historical realities that condition certain practices and impositions on non-Western societies—alliances do not merge into or consume each other, they maintain a space-between in which new desires, practices and encounters can arise—a delirium of new feminist desires.

Notes

1. Her work galvanized discussions of the interlocking multiple oppressions that constitute women's experiences and the recognition of the variegated and heterogeneous lived experiences of women. Though Crenshaw crystallized the problem, there is a rich history of Black feminists—Sojourner Truth, Combahee River Collective Statement (1977), hooks (1981), Collins (2000), Lorde (2007)—who contributed to intersectional studies as a methodology that has changed the landscape of feminist analysis.

2. There is significant debate as to whether intersectionality replicates the exclusions of identity politics (Dolphijn and van der Tuin 2013; Puar 2011; Bogic 2017, Currier 2003) or not (Cho, Crenshaw and McCall 2013; Jibrin and Salem 2015; Yuvel-Davis 2006). The variety of ways that intersectionality has been deployed complexify this issue (more potently, to highlight racial oppression, champion diversity, or, having been appropriated by less critical and more mainstream agendas, merely as a buzzword (Davis 2008).

3. Spivak goes as far as to label it a form of neo-colonialism (2003) and has infamously called out Deleuze's philosophy as Eurocentric and totalizing (1988). Even while Deleuze's influence in postcolonial theory is widely acknowledged, he has been charged with metaphor-izing the nomadic (Kaplan 1996), abstracting from the plights of the dispossessed, and general blindness to the impact of colonization. Recently there has been more recognition of Deleuze and Guattari's sensitivity and engagement with the struggles for decolonization (Bignall and Patton 2010; Bensmaïa 2017).

4. I am thinking of Bhabha's reference to migrant poet Meiling Jin's secret art of invisibleness, which creates a crisis in the representation of personhood and Western discourse of identity, while offering a new kind of gaze (empowerment) to the woman migrant (1994: 64–8).

5. Both Bhabha (1994) and Appadurai (2003) are skeptical of uncritical articulations of center versus margin which reinforce dichotomies and reduce the complexity of the lives of the marginalized and subaltern. Appadurai also calls out the naïve celebration of border-crossing or transversality (25), all of which could easily be ascribed to certain uptakes of Deleuze's work—though certainly not inherent to it.

6. Some have pointed out that the anti-racist intent of intersectionality has been diluted—depoliticized and misappropriated within a liberal feminist agenda which promotes a hollow diversity (Jibrin and Salem 2015; Bilge 2013), thus critiques of intersectionality, in its original form, are unwarranted. However, the critiques which suggest the problem lies within the logic

of intersectionality itself (i.e., representationalism and molar identity) (Puar 2011, Dolphijn and Tuin 2013; Currier 2003) deserve more nuanced attention.

7. Puar's main reason in advocating moving from the model of intersectionality to assemblage: '[I]ntersectional identities are the byproducts of attempts to still and quell the perpetual motion of assemblages, to capture and reduce them, to harness their threatening mobility' (2007: 213).

8. See Migration Policy Institute: https://www.migrationpolicy.org/article/philippines-beyond-labor-migration-toward-development-and-possibly-return (accessed April 18, 2019).

9. See Nail's work on kinopolitics and migrant flows resulting from expansion and expulsion according to political/economic logics of domination (2015).

References

Agnew, V. (ed.) (2005), *Diaspora, Memory, and Identity: A Search for Home*, Toronto: University of Toronto Press.

Appadurai, A. (2003), "Disjunction and Difference in the Global Cultural Economy," J. Braziel and A. Mannur (eds.), *Theorizing Diaspora*, Blackwell.

Barad, K. (2001), "Re(Con)figuring Space, Time, and Matter," in M. DeKoven (ed.), *Feminist Locations: Global and Local, Theory and Practice*, 75–109, New Brunswick: Rutgers University Press.

Bates, M. (1999), "Kant from the Flipside: Rizal's Subaltern Community," Unpublished manuscript, University of California, Berkeley, Department of English.

Bensmaïa, R. (2017), *Gilles Deleuze, Postcolonial Theory, and the Philosophy of Limit*, London: Bloomsbury Press.

Bhabha, H. K. (1994), *The Location of Culture*, New York: Routledge Press.

Bignall, S., and P. Patton (eds.) (2010), *Deleuze and the Postcolonial*, Edinburgh: Edinburgh University Press.

Bilge, S. (2013), "Intersectionality Undone Saving Intersectionality from Feminist Intersectionality Studies," *Du Bois Review* 10 (2): 405–24.

Bogic, A. (2017), "Theory in Perpetual Motion and Translation: Assemblage and Intersectionality in Feminist Studies," *Atlantis* 38 (1): 138–49.

Brah, A. (1996), *Cartographies of Diaspora, Contesting Identities*, London: Routledge.

Brah, A. (2002), "Global Mobilities, Local Predicaments: Globalization and the Critical Imagination," *Feminist Review* 70: 30–45.

Braidotti, R. (2012), *Nomadic Theory: The Portable Rosi Braidotti*, New York: Columbia University Press.

Braziel, Jana Evans, and A. Mannur (eds.) (2003), *Theorizing Diaspora*, United States: Blackwell.

Buchanan, I. (2000), *Deleuzism: A Metacommentary*, Durham, NC: Duke University Press.

Buchanan, I. (2014), "Schizoanalysis and the Pedagogy of the Oppressed," M. Carlin and J. J. Wallin (eds.), *Deleuze and Guattari, Politics and Education: For a People-Yet-to-*Come, 1–14. United States: Bloomsbury.

Burchill, L. (2010), "Becoming-Woman: A Metamorphosis in the Present Relegating Repetition of Gendered Time to the Past," *Time and Society* 19 (1): 81–97.

Carr, C. (2018), *Deleuze's Kantian Ethos: Critique as a Way of Life*, Edinburgh: Edinburgh University Press.

Cho, S., K. Crenshaw, and L. McCall (2013), "Toward a Field of Intersectionality Studies: Theory, Applications, and Praxis," *Signs* 38 (4), *Intersectionality: Theorizing Power, Empowering Theory*, 785–810.

Colebrook, Claire (2000), "Is Sexual Difference a Problem?," in I. Buchanan and C. Colebrook (eds.), *Deleuze and Feminist Theory*, 110–27, Edinburgh: Edinburgh University Press.

Collins, P. H. (2000), "It's All in the Family: Intersections of Gender, Race, and Nation," in Uma Narayan and Sandra Harding (eds.), *Decentering the Center: Philosophy for a Multicultural, Post-Colonial, and Feminist World*, 156–76. Bloomington: Indiana University Press.

Crenshaw, K. (1991), "Mapping the Margins: Intersectionality, Identity Politics, and Violence Against Women of Color," *Stanford Law Review* 43: 1241–99.

Crenshaw, K. (2001), "First Decade: Critical Reflections, or A Foot in the Closing Door," *UCLA Law Review* 49 (5): 1343–72.

Currier, D. (2003), "Feminist Technological Futures: Deleuze and Body/Technology Assemblages," *Feminist Theory* 3: 321–38.

Dabashi, H. (2015), *Can Non-Europeans Think?*, London: Zed Books.

Davis, K. (2008), "Intersectionality as a Buzzword: A Sociology of Science Perspective on What Makes a Feminist Theory Successful," *Feminist Theory* 9 (1): 67–85.

Deleuze, G., and F. Guattari (1983), *Anti-Oedipus Capitalism and Schizophrenia*, trans. R. Hurley, M. Seem, and H. R. Lane, Minnesota: University of Minnesota Press.

Deleuze, G., and F. Guattari (1987), *A Thousand Plateaus: Capitalism and Schizophrenia Volume 2*, trans. B. Massumi, Minneapolis: University of Minnesota Press.

Deleuze, G., and F. Guattari (1994), *What Is Philosophy?*, trans. H. Tomlinson and G. Burchell, New York: Columbia University Press.

Dolphijn, R., and I. van der Tuin (2013), "A Thousand Tiny Intersections: Linguisticism, Feminism, Racism and Deleuzian Becomings," in A. Saldanha and J. Adams (eds.), *Deleuze and Race*, 129–43, Edinburgh: Edinburgh University Press.

Erel, U. (2007), "Constructing Meaningful Lives: Biographical Methods in Research on Migrant Women," *Sociological Research Online* 12 (4), http://www.socresonline.org.uk/12/4/5.html.

Erel, U., J. Haritaworn, E. Gutiérrez Rodríguez, and C. Klesse (2008), "On the Depoliticisation of Intersectionality Talk," in Adi Kuntsman and Esperanza Miyake (eds.), *Out of Place: Interrogating Silences in Queerness/Raciality*, 265–92, New York: Raw Nerve Books

Grosz, E. (2002), "A Politics of Imperceptibility: A Response to Anti-racism, Multiculturalism, and the Ethics of Identification," *Philosophy and Social Criticism* 28 (4): 463–72.

Guattari, F. (1984), "Transversality," *Molecular Revolution: Psychiatry and Politics*, trans. R. Sheed, Middlesex: Penguin.

Guattari, F. (1995), "On Machines," in A. Benjamin (ed.), *Complexity*, JPVA 6: 8–12. http://archtech.arch.ntua.gr/forum/post2006interaction/on_machines.htm.

Gutiérrez Rodríguez, E. (2006), "Translating Positionality—On Post-Colonial Conjunctures and Transversal Understanding," *TRANSLATE: Journal for Cultural Theory and Cultural Studies*, June 2006, http://eipcp.net/transversal/0606/gutierrez-rodriguez/en/base_edit (accessed April 18, 2019).

Gutiérrez Rodríguez, E. (2007), "Reading Affect—On the Heterotopian Spaces of Care and Domestic Work in Private Households," *Forum: Qualitative Social Research* 8 (2), http://www.qualitative-research.net/index.php/fqs/article/view/240.

Hewage, P., C. Kumara, and J. Rigg (January 2011), "Connecting and Disconnecting People and Places: Migrants, Migration, and the Household in Sri Lanka," *Annals of the Association of American Geographers* 101 (1): 202–19.

Holland, E. (2002), *Deleuze and Guattari's Anti-Oedipus: An Introduction to Schizoanalysis*, Routledge Press.

Hoodfar, H. (1993), "The Veil in Their Minds and on Our Heads: Veiling Practices and Muslim Women," *Resources for Feminist Research* 22 (3/4): 5–18.

hooks, b. (1981) *Ain't I a Woman: Black Women and Feminism*, New York: South End Press.

Jibrin, R., and S. Salem (2015), "Revisiting Intersectionality: Reflections on Theory and Praxis," *Trans-Scripts* 5: 7–24.

Kaplan, C. (1996), *Questions of Travel: Postmodern Discourses of Displacement*, Durham, NC: Duke University Press Books.

Karkov, N. (2016), "Why Pluralism = Pluralism ≠ Monism: A Decolonial Feminist Critique of Deleuze and Guattari's Concept of Becoming," *Deleuze Studies* 10 (3): 379–94.

Khan, S. (1995), "The Veil as a Site of Struggle: The 'Hejab' in Quebec," *Canadian Woman Studies* 15 (2–3): 146–52.

Lazzarato, M. (2006), "The Machine," http://eipcp.net/transversal/1106/lazzarato/en, retrieved May 2017.

Lorde, A. (2007) "Age, Race, Class and Sex: Women Redefining Difference," *Sister Outsider*, Berkeley, NJ: Crossing Press.

Marrati, P. (2006), "Time and Affects: Deleuze on Gender and Sexual Difference," *Australian Feminist Studies* 21 (51): 313–25.

McCall, L. (2005), "The Complexity of Intersectionality," *Signs* 30 (3): 1771–800.

McNay, Lois (2008) *Against Recognition*, Cambridge: Polity Press.

Mohanty, C. T. (2003), *Feminism without Borders: Decolonizing Theory, Practicing Solidarity*, Durham, NC: Duke University Press.

Nail, T. (2015), *The Figure of the Migrant*, California: Stanford University Press.

Parrenas, R. S. (2001), "Transgressing the Nation-State: The Partial Citizenship and Imagined (Global) Community of Migrant Filipina Domestic Workers," *Signs* 24 (4): 1129–54.

Pisters, P. (2008), "Delirium Cinema or Invisible Machines?," in Ian Buchanan and Patricia MacCormack (eds.), *Deleuze and the Schizoanalysis of Cinema*, 102–15, London: Continuum.

Puar, J. K. (2007), *Terrorist Assemblages: Homonationalism in Queer Times*, Durham, NC: Duke University Press.

Puar, J. K. (2011), "I Would Rather Be a Cyborg than a Goddess: Intersectionality, Assemblage, and Affective Politics," *European Institute for Progressive Cultural Policies*, http://eipcp.net/transversal/0811/puar/en. Retrieved January 2018.

Said, E. (1979), *On Orientalism*, New York: Vintage Books.

Şerban-Oprescu, A. T. (2013), "From Exile to Diaspora and from National to Transnational Binds under the Driving Forces of Globalization," *Journal of International Studies* 6 (1): 96–102.

Sholtz, J. (2018), "Deleuzian Creativity and Fluxus Nomadology: Inspiring New Futures, New Thought," *Evental Aesthetics* 7(1): 102–37.

Spivak, G. (1988), "Can the Subaltern Speak?," in C. Nelson and L. Grossberg (eds.), *Marxism and the Interpretation of Culture*, 271–313, Urbana: University of Illinois Press.

Spivak, G. (2003), *A Critique of Postcolonial Reason*, Cambridge: Harvard University Press

Yuvel-Davis, N. (2006), "Intersectionality and Feminist Politics," *European Journal of Women's Studies* 13 (3): 193–209.

CHAPTER 9
MICROREVOLUTIONS IN FEMINIST ECONOMICS: A SCHIZOANALYTIC RESPONSE TO "THIRD WAY" IDENTITY PRODUCTION
Heidi Samuelson

The role women play in today's global economy still remains an under-explored area in feminist critique. There continues to be debate about the role that capitalism played in the liberalization of women historically. Nevertheless, there seems to be no question that contemporary global capitalist practices that perpetuate wealth disparity, environmental harm, and systemic inequality disproportionately harm women.[1] But these challenges remain shadowed by other issues. For example, the unity principles of the 2017 Women's March include rights-based language and address economic inequality, but they do not specifically identify global capitalism as a perpetrator of social and economic inequality and injustice that disproportionately affects women all over the world.[2] This follows trends in feminist theory that hinge largely on issues of intersectionality and identity and not on examinations of the underlying capitalist economic structures that create the conditions for this persistent and systemic inequality.[3]

This is not to say that important work has not been done in this area of the overlap between feminism and economics. Feminist groups formed in the "second wave" of feminism, like the Combahee River Collective, the Third World Women's Alliance, and the Women of All Red Nations explicitly took an anti-capitalist, anti-imperialist stance, but those groups, mostly comprised of women of color, lost prominence by the end of the Cold War (see Thompson 2002). More recent scholarship that addresses economic issues facing women spans perspectives that include class identity (Duggan 2003), transnational feminism (Basu 2000; Patil 2013), and anti-global feminism (Mohanty 2003). Marxist feminists also persist (Vogel 2013) to challenge the "third way" economic positions that emerged in the 1990s that attempted to reconcile principles of *laissez faire* capitalism and social democracy, often including some idea of feminist equality, but keeping a strong emphasis on the individual.[4]

It is in thinking about this Marxist move where the work of Gilles Deleuze and Félix Guattari becomes helpful. Deleuze and Guattari maintain an alignment with Marx that extends to their own critique of capitalism, but it is their recognition of the connection between economics and psychology, found primarily in *Anti-Oedipus*, that provides what could be a starting point for a deeper critique of capitalism and its influence on the way desire is *produced* on microeconomic level. Deleuze and Guattari do not themselves explore how desire production specifically affects women, but their work does lend itself to support feminist critique concerned with economics and identity. Their resistance to rigidification is a counter to the ways in which capitalist practices rely on fixed identity categories.

In this chapter, I look at how the effects of capitalism have had disproportionate effects on women globally. Then, I explore the institutional perpetuation of sedimented gender binaries and gendered economic inequality within the microfascisms of neoliberal economic policies, specifically in terms of the homogenization of values that comes with the imposition of binary gender identities. That is, I look at the question of whether we have identity beyond how the market defines us in terms of sedimented market research categories, arguing that intersectional feminist work does not adequately respond to this, because, to some extent, it is inescapable in a capitalist system. That is, identity categories that intersectional discourse focuses on are created and put into artificial hierarchies made possible by way of capitalism's economic structure.

Although this remains purely on the level of conceptual analysis, what endures from the work of Deleuze and Guattari are tools to acknowledge the microfascist structures that we can continue to struggle against, and this "allies" with feminist economic aims. In the final section of this chapter, I turn the schizoanalysis employed by Deleuze and Guattari and show how reterritorialization can be used to rethink identity formation in a more progressive, rather than static, hierarchical way within a global capitalist context.

1. Feminist Critiques of Economics and Identity

What I aim to highlight here is that although there is no one single feminist critique of economics, it remains essential for both feminist theorists and activists to address economic issues. All of the perspectives mentioned here broadly refer to issues of economic injustice, where I use "economic injustice" to mean economic inequality marked by disparity in wealth, income, and consumption.

A feminist approach to economics is credited as starting with Marilyn Waring's (1988) *If Women Counted*. Waring explains that women are often considered to be "nonproducers" in an economic system where income is only thought of in terms of cash value, effectively making a "productive boundary" between what counts as work and what does not (Waring 1999). This is important because standards like unemployment rates, gross domestic product (GDP), and consumer price index (CPI) measure work in terms of its monetary value, and then use these numbers to set policy or form economic programs. Work that women disproportionately do all over the world, that is, unpaid domestic work like fetching firewood, cooking meals, cleaning homes, and tending to children is generally not considered to be productive work, and so economists count those doing this work as economically inactive (Waring 1988: 15–16). In industrialized economies in the Global North, particularly in the United States, domestic work is seen as a detriment to professional advancement, and women are routinely denied promotion and maternity leave. Three decades since *If Women Counted*, the recognition of the economic value of unpaid work remains a distant goal for women all over the world.

Class analysis has also entered intersectional feminist discourse. For example, Black feminist bell hooks (1984) points out the tendency for white bourgeois women to disregard their class and race privilege, assuming incorrectly that all women share a common social status, while reinforcing materialist, capitalist values (19–23). She writes,

> Devaluation of family life in feminist discussion often reflects the class nature of the movement. Individuals from privileged classes rely on a number of institutional and social structures to affirm and protect their interests. (hooks 1984: 39)
>
> Until women accept the need for redistribution of wealth and resources in the United States and work towards achievement of that end, there will be no bonding among women that transcends class. (60)

An increased number of white women getting lucrative, high-paying jobs is not a victory for all women; from the point of view of working-class women, "[I]t means continued class exploitation," only now rich women benefit from that exploitation (hooks 1984: 61). Until classism (and its connection to racial disparity) is recognized broadly and the capitalist sources of poverty are addressed, hooks warns, feminist movements won't succeed in fully addressing women's oppression.

In more recent work, class is employed strictly as an identity category, and this move overshadows systemic economic injustice brought about by practices such as inequitable distribution of wealth and capital, historically inherited inequalities of race and gender, the use of collateralizable property to make profit, expendable labor, and a lack of incentive to invest in the skills of the work force, and so on.

> Neoliberalism was constructed in and through cultural and identity politics and cannot be undone by a movement without constituencies and analyses that respond directly to that fact. Nor will it be possible to build a new social movement that might be strong, creative, and diverse enough to engage the work of reinventing global politics for the new millennium as long as cultural and identity issues are separated, analytically and organizationally, from the political economy in which they are embedded. (Duggan 2003: 3)

In other words, when class is taken to be an intersecting identity category as opposed to an economic status, and this is added to the consequences of wealth disparity brought about by capitalism, then the role that capitalist practices play in creating identities and exploiting that identity for profit gets downplayed.

The interplay of economic and feminist issues is further complicated by a global economy, where complex transnational systems make it so that there is no single, clear root of mass exploitation. As discussed in chapter 9, Parreñas (2001) studied migrant Filipina domestic workers in a global economic context. The women are sometimes skilled workers whose work is devalued when transnational corporations establish manufacturing centers in the Philippines. These women are forced to go abroad to support their families, and they experience dislocation in their new location, cut off

Deleuze and the Schizoanalysis of Feminism

from cultural familiarity. Nevertheless, they make more money doing domestic work in countries like Italy or the United States than they could in the Philippines, and so they take advantage of their social status, now higher than poorer women still living in the Philippines, even hiring their own domestic workers (Parreñas 2001: 243). Here, domestic work *is* valued in terms of the money earned, but it is used as a status symbol and put back into a system of class hierarchy. There is a doubling of identity for the woman, as an "unskilled worker" in one country and an employer of "unskilled workers" in another and also being valued as a caretaker of someone else's family but not her own.

The purpose of transnational feminism is to address the insufficiencies of identity-based feminism and look at issues from a broader, global perspective to provide critique beyond identity categories. Patil (2013) has examined the limits of the criticism of patriarchy from an intersectional perspective in favor of a transnational approach that "takes to task the uncritical acceptance of the nation as a necessarily meaningful unit of analysis for feminists" (847). Patil calls for transnational feminism to examine power-laden processes like colonialism, imperialism, neoliberalism, and global economics.

Chandra Mohanty takes up this task in "Under Western Eyes" (1984) and in "Under Western Eyes Revisited" (2002). She argues that the global movement of capital, and the political processes that support it, "[E]xacerbates racist, patriarchal, and heterosexist relations of rule" (2002: 510). She uses the example of the World Trade Organization engaging in biopiracy and intellectual piracy by favoring corporate commercial interests over indigenous knowledge. While indigenous women have always organized against globalization, there has not been solidarity across divisions of place, identity, class, and work.

One might think a response to the limitations of identity-based critique toward broader, systemic, anti-capitalist movements could be found in the work of Marxist feminism, still the most dominant line of critique against capitalism. One such Marxist response is to challenge "third way" economics which have attempted to reconcile neoliberal principles with socialist policies, but have failed to recognize that capitalist practices, such as globalization, contribute to the inequality that makes the socialist principles seem necessary. Alienation from labor is a common experience underlying all the accounts of feminist economics and economics within feminism described above. That is, women are routinely paid inadequately for their work, their domestic work is not recognized as work, or they are dislocated in order to find work. In a socioeconomic system where both work and wealth are valorized, but where women are often separated from both, this alienation may lead to women feeling undervalued as persons.

However, Marxism is not without criticism from a feminist perspective as well. One major objection to Marxism is that Marx associated labor with commodity production, but, although he extended his concept of labor to service professions, he did not include any mention of women's unpaid reproductive work or the particular form of alienation experienced by women in performing such labor. Silvia Federici (2012) writes,

Had Marx recognized that capitalism must rely on both an immense amount of unpaid domestic labor for the reproduction of the workforce, and the devaluation of these reproductive activities in order to cut the cost of labor power, he may have been less inclined to consider capitalist development as inevitable and progressive. (92)

Federici argues that class division actually starts with a gender division, and if Marx had started there, he might have reached different conclusions about the inevitable progressivity of capitalism. That is, the unequal division of labor has the consequence not of uniting the workers, but dividing them further, as institutional practices of sexism and racism that reaffirm wage divisions further this division among laborers. Federici also notes that women all over the world often depend on common resources more so than men due to fewer resources in terms of income, family support, and available assets (2012: 143). This sharing of resources runs counter to the contemporary capitalist idea that work is an individual task and pay is earned based on individual merit. In the next section, we will see how this goes along with the contemporaneous notion of personalized identity formation.

To sum up, what we gain from the above discussion is that feminist theories do pick out structural economic issues that adversely affect women under global forms capitalism. But as we see in Parreñas's (2001) work, this can mean different things for how women then view themselves. In the next section, we need to see how socioeconomic structures construct identity, right down to our very desires, in a way that rigidifies identities. For example, identity categories like class are taken as fixed and preexisting. I will explore in more detail the rigidifying effect of capitalist economic practices on the level of identity, ultimately setting up an entry point where the work of Deleuze and Guattari becomes helpful in understanding the connection between undercutting capitalist practices by rethinking desire.

2. The Micro-Fascist Marketing of Identity

The starting point of the free, rational agent who fits into fixed categories is at the heart of identity politics and the neoliberal tradition. Today, in the "third way" political era, right-wing, capitalist economic policies are tempered by social programs which claim to increase access and opportunity for under-represented and oppressed groups. Life is organized according to identity categories like sex, race, nationality, religion—which are all used to pick out a unique and individual "self." On the one hand, identity groups have functioned in identity politics to expose specific configurations of social oppression and emphasized the necessity of certain social programs for the economic advantage of those who have hitherto been disadvantaged. On the other hand, identity categories are not "natural kinds," which opens them up to being manipulated in various ways on the macro level. Omi and Winant's (1986) work on racial formation shows that race formation is independent from but connected to capitalism and imperialism. Dominant groups assign racial identity (because race is not a biological category) and then use that closed identity to oppress minority groups by limiting upward class mobility and minimizing economic gain for those identities (see Hardaway and Mcloyd 2009).

167

The rise of consumer capitalism, particularly in the United States, coincides with the post–Second World War "Golden Age of Capitalism" and the birth of the "marketing mix" theory to target consumers in a more invasive way. The aim of advertising is not simply to sell a product; it also intends to create, keep, and satisfy the consumer. Thus, in addition to practices of othering, group identity—socially constructed or otherwise—also plays a role in mass marketing through the process of "demographic segmentation." Identity categories like age, gender, marital status, family size, education, ethnicity, and religion are assumed to be predictable factors in spending habits, so sellers and advertisers can target the individuals mostly like to buy their products. Though segmentation has existed since the 1920s, it was first used in marketing literature in 1956. In the 1980s, this developed into "hyper-segmentation," which is, perhaps ironically, remarkably intersectional, and is sometimes even referred to as "one-to-one" marketing.

What this means is that marketing shapes individual identity, and, because marketing is so targeted and ubiquitous, the individual might not recognize the impact it has on them. This phenomenon has been noted in feminist discourse particularly regarding the influence that images used in mass media have on body image and body comportment (Bartky 1990; Young). This has been confirmed in social science research (Eisend and Möller 2007; Grabe et al. 2008; Speck and Roy 2008), extending to the more general claim that media influences many aspects of social knowledge in addition to identity formation (Gerbner et al. 1994). Psychology is also used in marketing to understand consumer behavior, and there is even an emerging use of neuromarketing to understand consumer response to marketing stimuli.[5]

Deleuze and Guattari recognize the connection between psychology and economics that is missing from many of the feminist critiques of class and economic practices outlined in the previous section. Although Deleuze and Guattari have some appreciation of capitalism for its destruction of traditional social hierarchies (1983: 34–5), they are also critical of the homogenization of all values to the aims of the free market that occur on the molecular level (1983: 139–40). Part of this homogenization involves the classic issues brought up in feminist economics: not recognizing unpaid domestic work, normalizing the pay gap between men and women, and so on. But it goes even further into perceptions, expectations, and semiotic systems that result when men and women are classified into different marketing groups. In short, psychology and economics meet in the creation of identity via the creation of desire.

Deleuze and Guattari draw from the Marxian notion that industry has become the fundamental identity of man (1983: 4). This means that man is in contact with all productive life, including desire production. That is, desires are productive and are themselves produced in a social milieu. The way desire works in our capitalist system is not simply that you desire the latest iPhone. You want to be seen with a new iPhone and identified as someone who keeps up with and can afford the latest technology. These types of desires, relating to our identity and how others identified us, govern our behavior, but they come from outside ourselves without our conscious knowledge. We are told that we are lacking through marketing and advertising, and our desires are oriented to fulfill that lack. Deleuze and Guattari claim that our personal desires are no different from politics.

They employ the term "micropolitics" to denote that everything is political, as desires are produced by every aspect of our broader socio-political field.

One's identity is a marketing category fixed from within a socio-economic field, but along with this comes traits historically and socially associated with particular identity categories. For example, certain fragrances and colors are gendered and then packaged and marketed accordingly.[6] Women tend to appear in advertisements for cleaning products, reaffirming the role of homemaking as gendered, but unpaid, labor. Advertisements for investment firms and financial institutions usually feature white men in business attire. As another example, video games were once marketed to families, available for people of any age or gender, and now they are marketed as a "male" activity. Attempts to close this particular gap have resulted in things like the "Gamergate" controversy, where women were harassed for daring to enjoy video games marketed toward men.[7] We also see a clear gendered division in the emergence of eSports, where video game playing now has earning potential like other professional sports, but the games involved are marketed toward and primarily played by men—thus affirming that men's activities, even those associated with leisure, have a monetary value.

There are countless examples of marketing techniques and capitalist practices that affirm masculinity as a value held by workers and earners, while femininity is best served in looking beautiful in a supportive, caretaking role.[8] This gendered division happens across race, income brackets, age, and nationality (see Busse and Spielman 2003). Women are domestic laborers, and women are sometimes even commodities themselves. For example, sex servitude affects 20.9 million adults and children yearly (ILO 2012), and 96 percent of trafficking victims are women and girls (UNODC 2016), worldwide in an industry worth an estimated $99 billion annually (ILO 2014; see also Deshpande and Nour 2013). Women are commodified because there is a market for their sexed bodies and money to be made off the idea that women exist primarily for men's pleasure.

I argue that this perpetuation of gendered labor division is a form of what Deleuze and Guattari refer to as a "microfascism," a destructive authoritarian element present in a capitalistic system. According to them, fascism works on a "molecular" level—not with a top-down authoritarian figure, but in small groups and everyday interactions, minor occurrences we don't necessarily notice. We perpetuate our own repression, such as relegating ourselves to particular exploitations, through our unconscious relationship to society, for example in how we are influenced by marketing at the level of our desires. They write,

> The masses certainly do not passively submit to power; nor do they "want" to be repressed, in a kind of masochistic hysteria; nor are they tricked by an ideological lure. Desire is never separable from complex assemblages that necessarily tie into molecular levels, from micro-formations already shaping postures, attitudes, perceptions, expectations, semiotic systems, etc. (1987: 214–15)

Throughout Deleuze and Guattari's work, particularly in *Anti-Oedipus*, they examine the relationship between social production and desire production. They claim that Marx was aware that capital distorts labor: "Capital thus becomes a very mystic being since

169

all of labour's social productive forces appear to be due to capital, rather than labour as such, and seem to issue from the womb of capital itself" (Deleuze and Guattari 1983: 11; quoting Marx). This explains the emphasis we put on monetary value, and earning power (coded as masculine), over and above labor, including the unpaid domestic work (coded as feminine). The emphasis on capital is a twist on the Marxian notion alienation. It is not simply that the worker does not own their labor processes or the products of their labor, workers are estranged from capital in the form of corporate earnings and shareholder dividends in the quest for perpetual "growth."

According to Deleuze and Guattari, Marx also tells us that "the product gives us no hint as to the system and the relations of production" (1983: 24). The product is described in terms of ideal forms of causation, comprehension, or expression, rather than the processes of production on which it depends. In other words, what the product does and can do for you, the consumer, is prioritized over the processes that produce it in our understanding of our relationship to the world. This may explain why although we may morally oppose the exploitation of sweatshop labor (often the labor of women and children) in an ideal sense, this does not stop the products made in such conditions, from being desired, consumed, and thereby ubiquitous.

Not only is the worker alienated from their work, as consumers we are made to value the acquisition of replaceable products, which Deleuze and Guattari describe here: 'But the moment that one describes, on the contrary, the material process of production, the specificity of the product tends to evaporate, while at the same time the possibility of another outcome, another end result of the process appears" (1983: 24). Marketing works to distance us from production and to view products not for what they do, but as "men's" and "women's" even when they are manufactured the same way and are nearly identical.[9] Here, although Deleuze and Guattari do not make this point explicitly, we also see the connection to feminist Marxist accounts. What is traditionally classified as "women's work," is *process-based*—continuous care, cleaning, emotional validation—and does not have value, because such work is not attached to capital or a "real object" of production. When we value the object or its monetary value, we de-prioritize the labor that went into it, as well as other forms of labor that are not "productive." Deleuze and Guattari argue that the logic of desire for real objects is "all wrong from the very outset" as a lack of a real object (1983: 25), because, as Marx points out, needs are derived from desires. The "lack" that we feel for objects is created and organized through social production (28).

This is what Deleuze and Guattari later refer to as the rigid segmentarity of modern life that fosters repression without our conscious awareness of it (1987: 210). That is, "only microfascism provides an answer to the global question: Why does desire desire its own repression, how can it desire its own repression?" (215) Desire is always developed, engineered, even if we are unaware when it occurs. We may overtly identify as something, but consciously and unconsciously work to undermine that identity through our actions and contradictory beliefs. Deleuze and Guattari write, "[I]t's too easy to be antifascist on the molar level, and not even see the fascist inside you, the fascist you yourself sustain and nourish and cherish with molecules both personal and collective" (215). We might say that we believe in the liberal principles of equality, but we don't recognize all the ways, particularly through capitalist practices that we perpetuate inequality through our own desires. We construct an identity within a social field of hierarchies, and we come to believe it and act according to it.

The arguments from transnational feminists bring this point to light. We can claim to desire equality between women and men carte blanche, but we might also purchase products manufactured in the Global South by transnational corporations that use dubious business practices that eschew safety and do not pay workers a living wage. We can examine the aims of feminist challenges to global economics, what the moral obligations to distant others are, and whether their goals are realistic, but at the personal, micro level, we need tools to address the extent to which identity-formation within contemporary capitalism can be challenged. In the next section, I will use the work of Deleuze and Guattari to challenge identity formation as a way to response global economic policies that adversely affect women.

3. Schizoanalysis and Reterritorializing Identity Production

Capitalism has covered over the free production of desire through the rigidification of identity structures that marketing preys upon to the point where individuals think of themselves in terms of those categories, and it is impossible to production and subjectivity (Lazzarato 2014). This rigidification of identity is an articulation of over-coding, which is totalizing, unifying, and, importantly, hierarchical (Deleuze and Guattari 1987: 41). It is not simply that identities are rigidified into demographic categories, but they are ridigified in an *organized* way that admits of ranking. This is seen in instances where even when women are paid for work, it is, by virtue of it being coded as women's work or domestic work, seen as worth less. The response to these systemic economic practices, which also serve to deny autonomy, cannot simply be to pay women more or pay women equal to what men earn for the same work. These are patchwork solutions that don't adequately respond to the totalizing of rigidification.

Global capitalism has disproportionately harmful effects on women given the hierarchical social structures upon which capitalism thrives. According to Deleuze and Guattari, under capitalism, the Earth itself becomes an object of state ownership and property belongs to the richest few,[10] where the "state" is a global whole, a "megamachine" of production and consumption (see Lazzarato 2014). Social formations like identity and marketing categories are machinic processes of the megamachine around which life is organized. The rigidity of capital territorialization exploits hierarchies within hierarchies, a fabric that includes economic inequality, over-coded identity categories, including gender and class, as well as the effects of colonialism (see Nail 2012: 58; Deleuze and Guattari 1987: 213).

Global capitalism has only expanded since the time of Deleuze and Guattari's writings, with globalized networks of transnational institutions, like AFTA, NAFTA, MERCOSUR, COMESA, the EU, and Trans-Pacific Partnership. These agreements have made the world appear even more like the state Deleuze and Guattari described. But international relations "sit astride heterogeneous foundations," and it is important to recognize the isomorphy even in these agreements (Deleuze and Guattari 1987: 435). That is, global capitalism does not affect everyone in the same way due to preexisting inequalities amplified by the cultural effects of globalization via apparatuses of capture. Deterritorialization can be relative, in which it is accompanied by reterritorialization and is marked by transformations of cultural experiences. Deterritorialization is often unbalanced going from developed to underdeveloped countries via the extraction of human surplus value, while introducing lack and debt even amid overabundance. The problem with capitalism as it operates globally is that it reterritorializes new cultural relations. As mentioned in section 1, women are harmed or devalued through globalization (see Bacchus 2005; Mohanty 2002; Parreñas 2001), especially in terms of domestic work being devalued.

Nevertheless, even within rigid structures we can find points of resistance. The global state opens possibilities, and "the over-coding of the archaic state itself makes possible and gives rise to new flows that escape from it," which means that over-coding can be de-coded elsewhere (Deleuze and Guattari 1987: 449). There are standard ways to resist capitalism by reducing the importance of capital through redistribution, by not spending money on unnecessary goods, or demystifying the concepts of profit and growth. However, these efforts don't necessarily address the disproportionate harms felt by women in the face of wealth, income, and class inequality.

Another point of escape is to resist rigid identity categories that dictate all social organization. We *aren't* the fixed identity categories around which life is organized. The important thing we gain from the Lacanian notion that Deleuze and Guattari adopt is that we are "larval subjects"—indeterminate and in the process of becoming. Human beings are not separate from the world. All processes are interacting—political, economic, scientific, ecological, cosmic-perspective, affective, active, thinking, physical, and semiotic operations are convergent (Deleuze and Guattari 1987: 514). This convergence of operations often works to the detriment of women in varying degrees, as practices of capitalism threaded through these operations serve to rigidify hierarchical, predictable, and exploitable identities.

In spite of its good intentions, the push for intersectionality in feminist movements is limited by the way in which molar categorization is leveraged for the sake of specifically *capitalist* production—the very production intersectionality seeks to undermine. Systemically oppressive hierarchies should not be ignored, but the resistance to them has to occur at the level of identity as well. Resisting categorization, embracing fluidity of categories, being unpredictable, even resisting the idea of personal identity itself, can affect molar organization that fixes identities and hierarchical structures.

One aim of Deleuze and Guattari's project was a multiplication of perspectives through microrevolutions. By ripping open the world, global practices of capitalism have provided more space for becoming everything and everybody (Deleuze and Guattari 1987: 473). Because of these spaces, different modes of expression, remodeling, and reterritorializing are possible on a being or a system. There are no axiomatic responses; rather, there are processes of becoming and reorganizing the ways abstract machines perform in order to resist.

A third point of resistance can also occur through a change in desire. Marketing serves to preserve the Freudian idea that desire is a lack. In the schizoanalysis introduced by Deleuze and Guattari, desire is a production. But what can this mean in terms of concrete actions? Due to their over-coding as caregivers and nurturers, women are well-suited for re-coding and becoming. What has been traditionally coded as "women's work" has been care-oriented, process-based work (domestic, but also teaching, nursing, etc.)—not necessarily result-based or profit-driven. Care is often employed as an ethical concept, and not one explicitly found in Deleuze and Guattari's work (but see, e.g., Conley 2016; Drummond 2002), but care is a necessary, unpredictable, constantly changing factor throughout the course of any human life. The desire *to* care is a productive desire, an appropriation of what it is outside and other than oneself. Further, it need not be coded as "feminine" or as "women's work."

Most capitalist responses to feminist economic concerns are either some iteration of women becoming men or women being folded into existing structures that continue to exploit other women—often women of color, poor women, or women in the Global South. Resistance has to be based not on identity but on re-coding and extending beyond identity—intersection, but intersecting in terms of processes, care, and life. Transnational approaches are crucial because they serve to resist literal territorial boundaries as well as address the ways in which capitalist practices push exploitative practices onto women all over the world. Anything less supports rigidification.

4. Concluding Remarks

What I have shown in this chapter is that feminist issues are inherently economic, but identity, issue-based approaches to feminist discourse, perhaps inadvertently, downplay that role. I align my position with transnational feminists who acknowledge the need to address economic issues that affect women globally. There are difficulties in doing so, and we must address the microfascisms of capitalist practices, including demographic segmentation used in marketing, where identity-formation and desire-production are intertwined with how the market has defined woman. Because so much feminist economic critique hinges on issues of identity, particularly class identity, a deeper examination of identity-production is necessary. The only way to address feminist issues is to not stop at the idea of intersectionality but to address the global system of capitalist exchange and marketing that has manipulated these identity categories.

To make this critique, I turned to Deleuze and Guattari. A schizoanalytic response to identity-formation can be allied with contemporary feminist economic work that attempts to dismantle capitalist structures. Schizoanalysis is meant to explore new collective subjectivity, so identity is not based on fixed demographic categories or class structures but is more like an event or process. When one begins to unravel their identity in this way, there is a possibility to call into question all hierarchical organizations through microrevolutions. Though these microrevolutions may allow individuals to overcome certain oppressive forms of subjectivity, they do not necessarily lead to broad-sweeping social change. It may be impossible to preserve the resistance to molar organization, as movements of capital do not allow themselves to be broken down (Deleuze and Guattari 1987: 217), and it requires active and aware resistance. Nevertheless, there is space between the strata, between the reterriorialization and deterritorialization, where the work of decoding and remodeling can occur through processes of becoming. Even minor changes can cause disruptions to the molar organization of a hierarchical global economic system that "others" women, defines their desires, and devalues their work.

Notes

1. Women and girls are 70 percent of the world's poor and make up the majority of refugee populations. They are 80 percent of displaced persons of Africa, Asia, and Latin America. Furthermore, women do two-thirds of the world's work and earn less than one-tenth of its income (Eisenstein 1998).

2. See https://womensmarch.com/agenda (accessed April 18, 2019).

3. This is a criticism often referred to as "white feminism," in which western, white, cisgendered women tend to enjoy more economic security and benefit from economic policies that disproportionately harm women of color, trans women, and women in the Global South.

4. Transnational and global trade has existed for at least five hundred years, but the abandonment of the Bretton Woods system in 1971, which used the gold standard, and foreign exchange rates being controlled by states made finance truly international.

5. Though the actual neuroscience behind this field is dubious.

6. This has infiltrated popular consciousness to the extent to which the color pink is associated with girls and the color blue with boys. This phenomenon did not exist until the 1940s. See Maglaty (2011).

7. "Whatever Gamergate may have started as, it is now an Internet culture war. On one side are independent game-makers and critics, many of them women, who advocate for greater inclusion in gaming. On the other side of the equation are a motley alliance of vitriolic naysayers: misogynists, anti-feminists, trolls, people convinced they're being manipulated by a left-leaning and/or corrupt press, and traditionalists who just don't want their games to change" (Dewey 2014).

8. This echoes Federici's criticism of Marxism (2012).

9. This also points to what is known as the "pink tax," where "women's" products often cost more than "men's," even when they have identical use—e.g., clothing, shampoo, razor cartridges (Bessendorf 2015).

10. The advent of money does not fundamentally change anything, because money becomes an apparatus of the state (Deleuze and Guattari 1983: 194–9). Money has a dual role: exchange money (for the wage earner) and credit money (the balance sheet of the enterprise) (229–30).

References

Bacchus, N. (2005), "The Effects of Globalization on Women in Developing Nations," Honors College Thesis, New York: Pace University. http://digitalcommons.pace.edu/honorscollege_theses/2.

Bartky, S. L. (1990), "Foucault, Femininity, and the Modernization of Patriarchal Power," in K. Conboy, N. Medina, and S. Stanbury (eds.), *Writing on the Body*, 129–54, New York: Columbia University Press.

Basu, A. (2000), "Globalization of the Local/Localization of the Global: Mapping Transnational Women's Movements," *Meridians* 1 (1): 68–109.

Bessendorf, A. (2015), "From Cradle to Cane: The Cost of Being a Female Consumer. A Study of Gender Pricing in New York City," in S. Gans (ed.), commissioned by B. de Blasio and J. Menin, New York: New York City Department of Consumer Affairs.

Busse, M., and C. Spelman (2003), "Gender Discrimination and the International Division of Labour," HWWA Discussion Paper, Hamburg Institute of International Economics.

Conley, V. A. (2016), "The Care of the Possible," *Cultural Politics* 12 (3): 339–54.

Deleuze, G. (2004), *Desert Islands and Other Texts 1953–1973*, ed. D. Lapoujade, trans. M. Taormina, Paris: Semiotext(e).

Deleuze, G., and F. Guattari (1983), *Anti-Oedipus: Capitalism and Schizophrenia*, trans. R. Hurley, M. Seem, and H. R. Lane, Minneapolis: University of Minnesota Press.

Deleuze, G., and F. Guattari (1987), *A Thousand Plateaus: Capitalism and Schizophrenia*, trans. B. Massumi, Minneapolis: University of Minnesota Press.

Deshpande, N. A., and N. M. Nour (2013), "Sex Trafficking of Women and Girls," *Reviews in Obstetrics and Gynecology* 6 (1): e22–7.

Dewey, C. (2014), "The Only Guide to Gamergate You Will Ever Need to Read," *Washington Post*, October 14, 2014, https://www.washingtonpost.com/news/the-intersect/wp/2014/10/14/the-only-guide-to-gamergate-you-will-ever-need-to-read/ (accessed April 18, 2019).

Drummond, J. (2002), "Freedom to Roam: A Deleuzian Overture for the Concept of Care in Nursing," *Nursing Philosophy* 3 (3): 222–33.

Duggan, L. (2003), *The Twilight of Equality? Neoliberalism, Cultural Politics, and the Attack on Democracy*, Boston, MA: Beacon Press.

Eisend, M., and J. Möller (2007), "The Influence of TV Viewing on Consumers' Body Images and Related Consumption Behavior," *Marketing Letters* 18 (1–2): 101–16.

Eisenstein, Z. (1998), *Global Obscenities*, New York: New York University Press.

Federici, S. (2012), *Revolution at Point Zero: Housework, Reproduction, and Feminist Struggle*, Oakland, CA: PM Press.

Gerbner, G., L. Gross, M. Morgan, and N. Signorielli (1994), "Growing Up with Television: The Cultivation Perspective," in J. Bryant and D. Zillmann (eds.), *Media Effects: Advances in Theory and Research*, 17–41, Hillsdale, NJ: Lawrence Erlbaum.

Grabe, S., L. M. Ward, and J. S. Hyde (2008), "The Role of the Media in Body Image Concerns Among Women: A Meta-Analysis of Experimental and Correlational Studies," *Psychological Bulletin* 134 (3): 460–76.

Grosz, E. (1993), "A Thousand Tiny Sexes: Feminism and Rhizomatics," *Topoi* 12 (2): 167–79.

Hardaway, C., and V. Mcloyd (2009), "Escaping Poverty and Securing Middle Class Status: How Race and Socioeconomic Status Shape Mobility Prospects for African Americans during the Transition to Adulthood," *Journal for Youth and Adolescence* 38 (2): 242–56.

hooks, b. (1984), *Feminist Theory: From Margin to Center*, Boston, MA: South End Press.

International Labour Organization (ILO) (2012), "ILO Global Estimate of Forced Labour: Results and Methodology," https://www.ilo.org/global/topics/forced-labour/publications/WCMS_182004/lang--en/index.htm (accessed April 18, 2019).

International Labour Organization (ILO) (2014), "World of Work Report," https://www.ilo.org/global/research/global-reports/world-of-work/2014/lang--en/index.htm (accessed April 18, 2019).

Lazzarato, M. (2014), *Signs and Machines: Capitalism and the Production of Subjectivity*, trans. J. D. Jordan, Cambridge: MIT Press.

Maglaty, J. (2011), "When Did Girls Start Wearing Pink?," *Smithsonian Magazine*, April 7, 2011, http://www.smithsonianmag.com/arts-culture/when-did-girls-start-wearing-pink-1370097/ (accessed April 18, 2019).

Mohanty, C. T. (1984), "Under Western Eyes: Feminist Scholarship and Colonial Discourse," *boundary 2*, 12/13 (3–1): 333–58.

Mohanty, C. T. (2002), "'Under Western Eyes' Revisited: Feminist Solidarity through Anticapitalist Struggles," *Signs* 28 (2): 499–535.

Mohanty, C. (2003), *Feminism without Borders: Decolonizing Theory, Practicing Solidarity*, Durham, NC: Duke University Press.

Nail, T. (2012), *Returning to Revolution: Deleuze, Guattari and Zapatismo*, Edinburgh: Edinburgh University Press.

Omi, M., and H. Winant (1986), *Racial Formation in the United States*, New York: Routledge.

Parreñas, R. S. (2001), *Servants of Globalization: Women, Migration, and Domestic Work*, Redwood City, CA: Stanford University Press.

Patil, V. (2013), "From Patriarchy to Intersectionality: A Transnational Feminist Assessment of How Far We've Really Come," *Signs* 38 (4): 847–67.

Smith-Speck, S. K., and A. Roy (2008), "The Interrelationships between Television Viewing, Values and Perceived Well-Being: A Global Perspective," *Journal of International Business Studies* 39 (7): 1197–219.

Tedlow, R. A., and G. Jones (eds.) (1993), *The Rise and Fall of Mass Marketing*, New York: Routledge.

Thompson, B. (2002), "Multiracial Feminism: Recasting the Chronology of Second Wave Feminism," *Feminist Studies* 28 (2): 336–55.

United Nations Office on Drugs and Crime (UNODC) (2016), "2016 UNODC Global Trafficking in Persons Report," http://www.unodc.org/documents/data-and-analysis/glotip/2016_Global_Report_on_Trafficking_in_Persons.pdf. (accessed April 19, 2019).

Vogel, L. (2013), *Marxism and the Oppression of Women: Toward a Unitary Theory*, Chicago: Haymarket Books.

Waring, M. (1988), *If Women Counted: A New Feminist Economics*, New York: HarperCollins.

Waring, M. (1999), *Counting for Nothing: What Men Value and What Women are Worth*, Toronto: University of Toronto Press.

Weinstein, A. (2004), *Market Segmentation Handbook: Strategic Targeting for Business and Technology Firms*, 3rd ed., Binghamton, NY: Haworth Press.

Young, I. M. (1990), *"Throwing Like a Girl" and Other Essays in Feminist Philosophy and Social Theory*, Bloomington: Indiana University Press.

CHAPTER 10
BODHISATTVA AVALOKITEŚVARA AS A SYMBOL FOR THE POSTHUMAN FUTURE IN THE ANTHROPOCENE

Amy Chan Kit-Sze

In *Anti-Oedipus*, Deleuze and Guattari claim that psychoanalysis assumes that all behavior is either manifestly sexual or a substitute for sex. Psychoanalysis "insists on filtering everything through the triangulating lens of daddy-mommy-me" (Buchanan 2008: 39). They argue that the family is the agent of Oedipalization. Deleuze and Guattari suggest further that Oedipalization is closely related to capitalism since the nuclear family imprints capitalist social relations on the infant psyche. In a way, there is a triangulation here: nuclear family, Oedipalization, and capitalism. The focus of this chapter is to discuss how Deleuze and Guattari's theory of schizophrenia, especially in relation to family and Oedipalization, sheds light on the development of feminism in the Anthropocene. The thrust of this paper is to bring an important figure in Chinese culture, that is, Bodhisattva Avalokiteśvara into the scene. The Oedipus Complex, no matter that Freud argued for it as a universal concept, is unarguably a product of the western culture. I would argue that it's time for us to look to other non-Western traditions to imagine ways to construct a new postcapitalist world order that addresses the Anthropocene. Moreover, Avalokiteśvara is a powerful symbol to deterritorialize Western epistemic imperialism, intertwined as it is with this particular constellation of gender and capitalism. Bodhisattva Avalokiteśvara, being a Bodhisattva with both female and male manifestations and portrayals, blurs the gender boundary; being personified as much a human as a god/goddess, Avalokiteśvara also breaks down the boundary between human and nonhuman; having empathy and kinship with animals and plants, Avalokiteśvara exemplifies Haraway's concept of becoming-with. Haraway has argues that cyborg is a symbol for future feminisms but I would argue that Bodhisattva Avalokiteśvara offers more potentials for navigating the complexities and inequities that confront women on a global scale, especially those who are particularly marginalized or isolated by and through modern technology and capitalism, than Haraway's cyborg—as a symbol for the posthuman future as well as a symbol for the feminist in the Anthropocene.

1. Cyborg and Oedipus

The cyborg in Haraway's "A Cyborg Manifesto" (1991) is a symbol for future development of feminism and posthumanism. A cyborg is a hybrid, a splicing of human and machine.

We can easily understand that a human with a prosthetic limb or even a pacemaker is considered a cyborg; however, according to Haraway, what counts as a cyborg is not really the material body but the consciousness or the mind to transcend the limitations of our physical body. Haraway argues that cyborg is a post-gender creature. Contrary to the cyborg image in popular culture, especially in Hollywood movies, cyborg is without any gender because it does not need reproduction, at least not natural reproduction. She writes, "[t]he cyborg is a creature in a post-gender world; it has no truck with bisexuality, pre-oedipal symbiosis, unalienated labour ... the cyborg has no origin story in the Western sense" (1991: 292). Another potent meaning of the cyborg imagery is that it signifies boundary breakdowns in organism/machine, animal/human/machine, male/female. However, I would argue that the cyborg imagery becomes more potent in the notion of splicing. If we say that the cyborg breaks down the boundaries between machine and human, male and female, we tacitly assume that there is a boundary in between the borders which will probably be shifting but not disappearing. On the other hand, if we say that the cyborg is a splice of human and machine, the definition of human and the one of machine have to be changed forever in the circuit or the loop and the gender issue will also be displaced. Only through this can we attain the "post-gender" world that Haraway prophesies. To a large extent, the ultimate goal of the cyborg feminism advocated by Haraway is not building a new brand of feminism but a posthuman theory.

Being without a genesis and having no hope to return to the Garden of Eden, "the cyborg does not dream of community on the model of the organic family, this time without the oedipal project" (Haraway 1991: 293). Seemingly, the symbol of cyborg does look like a perfect symbol for posthuman theory by showing us a way out of the triangulation of Oedipus Complex. Nonetheless, Haraway reminds us that cyborgs "are the illegitimate offspring of militarism and patriarchal capitalism" (1991: 151). As mentioned above, the triangulation of nuclear family, Oedipalization, and capitalism forms a stronghold on the infant psyche. When Deleuze and Guattari analyse social-production and desire-production in *Anti-Oedipus*, they work out a genealogy of the Oedipus—savagery, despot, and capitalism. "Savagery and despotism are organized symbolically, via codes and over-codes, while capitalism is organized economically, via axioms" (Holland 1999: 64). Another distinctive feature that distinguishes capitalism from savagery and despot is that there is a segregation of social-production from desire-production for capitalism. Holland puts it in a succinct way by saying that "capital delegates the formation of subject to the family" (ibid.: 83). He continues, "[H]uman reproduction alone is for the first time completely segregated from social-production/reproduction; human reproduction, that is to say, is henceforth privatized in the nuclear family" (ibid.). Under capitalism,

> [t]he alliances and filiations no longer pass through people but through money;
> so the family becomes a microcosm ... Father, mother, and child thus become the
> simulacrum of the images of capital ("Mister Capital, Madame Earth," and their
> child the Worker), with the result that these images are no longer recognized at

all in the desire that is determined to invest only their simulacrum. (Deleuze and Guattari 1994: 264)

It is obvious that, for Deleuze and Guattari, Oedipus and capitalism have an intriguing and complicated relationship. While they do not think that psychoanalysis invents Oedipus, there is a reason why Oedipus came into being in the twentieth century. The reason is Oedipus is specific to capitalism. When commenting on the relationship between psychoanalysis, Oedipus and capitalism, they write,

[P]sychoanalysis does not invent Oedipus ... But the mother as the simulacrum of territoriality, and the father as the simulacrum of the despotic Law, with the slashed, split, castrated ego, are the products of capitalism insofar as it engineers an operation that has no equivalent in the other social formations. (1994: 269)

Haraway, in *Staying with the Trouble: Making Kin in the Chthulucene*, quotes complex systems engineer, Brad Werner, as saying that "global capitalism has made the depletion of resources so rapid, convenient and barrier-free that 'earth-human systems' are becoming dangerously unstable in response" (2016: 47). So, Haraway suggests that if we have to sum up this age with a word, that word must be Capitolocene. Scholars on the Anthropocene, such as Timothy Morton, Timothy Clark, and Haraway, all seem to advocate the idea that though the Anthropocene probably began with the Industrial Revolution, it is capitalism that exacerbates the depletion of resources.

To sum up the discussion in this section, it seems that though Haraway's cyborg is a post-gender creature and shows us "a way out of the maze of dualisms" (1991: 181), it is nevertheless a product of capitalism and militarism, both of which are antagonistic to women and nature. In the following, I argue that Bodhisattva Avalokiteśvara is a better symbol than Haraway's cyborg as a symbol for the posthuman future as well as a symbol for the feminists in the Anthropocene. Before I go into the argument, we must first take a look at the history of representations of Avalokiteśvara in Chinese and Tibetan Buddhism and also in Chinese literary works.

2. History of Representations of Avalokiteśvara

According to the Mahayana doctrine, Avalokiteśvara (also known as Kuan Yin in Chinese tradition) is the Bodhisattva who postpones his own Buddhahood until he has assisted all beings on earth to achieve nirvana. He is also the one who has made a great vow to listen to the prayers of all sentient beings in times of difficulty. In the following, I will provide a brief history of the representation of Bodhisattva Avalokiteśvara and present the argument why Bodhisattva Avalokiteśvara is a more appropriate and potent symbol for future feminisms and posthumanism in the Anthropocene.

Worship of Avalokiteśvara emerged in India with the development of Mahayana Buddhism. It is believed that Avalokiteśvara originates from the twin horsemen, the

Asvins, in Hinduism. Asvins are Vedic gods symbolizing the shining of sunrise and sunset, appearing in the sky before dawn in a golden chariot, bringing treasures to men and averting misfortune and sickness. It is precisely this mercifulness of Asvins that is reflected in Avalokiteśvara.

After the collapse of Mauryan Empire in 186 BCE, the Kusana rulers came to the rule. By the second century CE the Mahayana Buddhism rose to power and marked the beginning of the making of Buddhist icons. Susan L. and John C. Huntington points out that during this period the images of Maitreya, Amitabha and Avalokiteśvara were very popular. Most often, Avalokiteśvara appears either as an independent deity or as a member of the triad, bearing a lotus in his hand. He is usually dressed in princely garb and wears a turban, has a moustache. According to Huntington, the turban and the position in which the bodhisattva sits are obvious features that denote royalty (1985: 139).

One of the earliest texts to describe Avalokiteśvara is chapter 25 of the *Lotus Sutra*. The Buddha talks about a lot of difficult situations faced by ordinary people and says that no matter how dangerous or difficult the situation is, Avalokiteśvara will come to their rescue if they call the name of Bodhisattva Perceiver of the World's Sounds. In the latter part of the chapter, the Buddha also mentions that Avalokiteśvara can appear in thirty-three forms, seven of which are female.

In Tibet Buddhism, Avalokiteśvara is called Chenrezig and is believed to be an embodiment of compassion. Chenrezig is considered to be the patron Bodhisattva of Tibet. The Dalai Lamas are considered to be the earthly manifestations of Chenrezig. Bokar Rinpoche writes in his *Chenrezig Lord of Love* that "[f]rom an absolute point of view Chenrezig is without origin; he exists primordially. However, from the relative point of view, there is a beginning of his manifestation in the realm of phenomena" (2010: 12). Kalu Rinpoche holds a similar view about the appearance of Chenrezig. He says, "[O]ne does not think of the deity's body as solid or material, made of flesh and blood like one's ordinary body, or made of metal or stone like an idol. One thinks of it as appearance that is inseparable from emptiness, like a rainbow or like a reflection in a mirror" (Chenrezig 2000).

According to Tibetan legend, Chenrezig made a vow that he would not rest until he had liberated all the beings in the realms of suffering. He even made a vow that "if [he] break this promise, may my head and body split into a thousand pieces!" (Chenrezig 2000). However, after working diligently for a long time, he looked down from the top of Mount Meru and realized that there were still innumerable people to be saved. At this point, he grew into despair and wanted to give up. He thought, "I do not have the capability to help beings; it is better that I rest in nirvana [liberation from cyclic existence]" (ibid.). This thought contradicted his vow, and he burst into a thousand pieces. Seeing this, Amitabha Buddha put the pieces back together as a body with many heads and many hands, so that Chenrezig could work with myriad beings at the same time. The legend of Chenrezig exemplifies visually Delezue and Guattari's ideas of BodywithoutOrgans (BwO) and deterritorialization. The breaking up of the body into a thousand pieces and putting them together is a deterritorialization and reterritorialization process. The addition of many heads and many hands in the reterritorializing process transforms the body into a BwO in a positive way because, thereafter, Chenrezig would be able to help thousands of beings at the same time. In a way, Chenrezig is similar to Haraway's cyborg, which is always composed of parts; however, as a god, Chenrezig does not bear the burden of capitalism and militarism.

Within Tibetan Buddhism, Avalokiteśvara is always represented as male. The Dalai Lama even says that it would be thought wrong to depict or visualize Avalokiteśvara in female guise (Blofeld 1988: 39). The female aspect of Avalokiteśvara is visualized in Tara who is regarded as a Buddha of compassion and action. According to the chapter 3 in *Tara Tantra*, Tara was born as a king's daughter. Another legend of Tara is that she was born of a tear shed by Avalokiteśvara on a blooming lotus in pity for the sufferings of sentient beings when he looked down from the Mount Meru. Thus, Taras are always portrayed as holding a lotus or sitting on a bed of lotus. That not only reminds us of her origin but strengthens her kinship with plants and nature, which poses an opposite to the cyborg.

According to the school of Sūryagupta, there are altogether twenty-one Taras (Beyer 1973: xiii). Each Tara is of a different color and the six colors (white, red, blue, yellow, green, and black) stand for different aspects. Green Tara is known as the Buddha of Enlightened Activity. Her color symbolizes youthful vigor and activity. She is always visualized as a lovely and playful human being in visual arts. Similar to Avalokiteśvara, she is believed to help people in dangerous or difficult situations. Besides the Green Tara, the White Tara is also worshipped by people. Compared to the Green Tara, the White Tara appears to be more mature since she is referred to as the Mother of all the Buddhas. She represents the motherly aspect of compassion. The other Taras help save people suffering in drought, flood, natural disaster, wars, evils, poison and beasts, and so on. Each of the multifaceted Taras look after human beings in different distress. It is said that when the world is getting worsened, the Taras' power will get more potent and save people with greater speed. The compassion and empathy shown by the Taras are important for feminism or even humanity in the Anthropocene. We are certainly having more and more "natural" disasters or catastrophes in the twenty-first century as consequences of climate change and those who suffer the most tend to be people in the underdeveloped countries which include many in Asia. The figure of Tara sheds light on how humanity can survive these catastrophes together—instead of only thinking in monetary terms and over-emphasis on technology, we should be more compassionate and empathetic with fellow human beings and nonhuman beings that share this world with us.

While Avalokiteśvara is always visualized as a male form in India and Tibet, he underwent a feminization in China. When Buddhism was transmitted to China, the bodhisattva of compassion was named Kuan Yin, or Kuan-shih Yin (observing the sounds of the world). According to Karetzky, by the mid-sixth century,

[t]he Indian-style fleshy bodies with drapery arranged to expose the anatomy had been transformed into a slender Chinese form, obscured by masses of heavy cloth, and with proportionally enlarged head and hands and distinct Chinese facial characteristics. (2004: 16)

The worship of Avalokiteśvara in China began as a male god but was changed into a female form over time. It is generally agreed that he was not portrayed as a woman until the Song dynasty (960–1279 CE). Though Kuan Yin is represented in a male form in the Tang dynasty (618–907 CE), he already looks very different from the ones in Indian arts. In India, Avalokiteśvara is represented as muscular and the torso, most of the time, is nude. In Chinese arts, even Kuan Yin in male form rarely bares his torso, jewels and scarves are arranged artfully across the chest. Nevertheless, it is important to bear in mind that Kuan Yin in male form is never eradicated in China. Starting from the Song dynasty, Kuan Yin was portrayed as a woman. The story of Kuan Yin was intertwined with some Chinese legends and stories. One of the most famous legends of course is Princess Miaoshan.[1] According to Blofeld, to the humanistic Chinese the Thousand-Head or Four-Arm Avalokiteśvara is too bizarre and unsuitable to the portrayal of the compassionate deity. For convenience sake, the Chinese combine the deity with Princess Miaoshan, who is a compassionate being achieving the stature of a goddess (Blofeld 1988: 41).

It is accepted as a historical fact that Kuan Yin is a female deity in China, but it seems that there is still no consensus as to the reason why the male Avalokiteśvara is transformed into female in China. Many critics offer different explanations for the phenomenon. A more convincing explanation is offered by Palmer and Ramsay. They write that "[t]he earliest pantheons of China are a mixture of male and female and half-human, half-animal beings" (1995: 9) For example, *Fuxi* and *Nüwa*, founders of Chinese culture, are both half-human and half-snake. When Buddhism spread to China, there was a great problem. According to Palmer and Ramsay, Buddhism is a male-dominated faith and it lacked a divine feminine aspect at that time. The most popular religion in China was Daoism which is pantheistic. Among all the deities, the Queen Mother of the West is one of the most powerful and widespread, but Buddhism at that point had no female deity. In order to compete with Daoism, Buddhism needed a female form of the divine to reach out to the ordinary people, especially females who suffered the most in the Chinese society.

The Singaporean scholar, Gu Zheng-mei (2003) provides an explanation of the transformation of Kuan Yin from male to female by linking religion to the political situation. In her detailed analysis of the Devarāja Tradition and the Buddbarāja Tradition employed by the kings in China to rule their people and control their country, Gu claims that when Empress Wu started her Zhou dynasty (690–705 CE), she ruled her country with the Avatamasaka Buddharāja tradition. In the year of 695, she set her imperial name as Emperor Tiance Jinlun Shengshen, which literally means "Destined by Heaven Golden Wheel Sage Deity King." She argues that if the king ruled the country is a manifestation of Kuan Yi, it follows logically that during Empress Wu's rule, Kuan Yi should be visualized as a female.

The explanation provided by Karetzky perhaps is the most relevant to my argument in this paper. She points out that while the god of compassion Avalokiteśvara in India had a female counterpart Tara, "[I]n China Guanyin [*sic*] was understood to be an integrated character who underwent bodily transformations to accomplish a salvation" (Karetzky 2004: 21). This is an interesting explanation of the female manifestations of Kuan Yin because if we accept this saying, it means that Kuan Yin in China should be interpreted as a deity that has no fixed gender, instead of being either male or female. I would like to stress the fact that though Kuan Yi is generally visualized as female in China after the Song dynasty, it does not mean that male manifestations of the deity completely disappeared as we could still find the male form of Kuan Yin in paintings in the Ming Dynasty (1368–1644 CE).

In the chapter 25 of the *Lotus Sutra*, it is said that Bodhisattva Avalokiteśvara is able to manifest himself in many forms, be it a Buddha, King Brahma, a rich man, a monk, a nun a young boy or a young girl, a dragon, a yaksha, an asura, a human or a nonhuman to relieve suffering and help people in need. That explains why there are so many different manifestations of Avalokiteśvara in sculptures and paintings. In one of the stories about Kuan Yin's origin, it is said that when Kuan Yin is given an option whether to take on a male or female body, s/he actually chooses to be female for the reason that females have always been discriminated and oppressed. Kuan Yin hopes that by her transforming into a buddha in a female body, she will be able to bring equality to the world and relieve the sufferings of women.

The mutation in the representations of Kuan Yin in Chinese culture, whatever the reason(s), invokes Deleuze and Guattari's plateau of becoming. By being transformed from a male deity to a female one, Kuan Yin has entered the becoming process. As Deleuze and Guattari claim, all becomings must start from becoming-woman since woman is a minoritarian. Through becoming-woman, the male deity is gradually gearing toward the minoritarian, thus s/he cares about animals and extends her/his benevolence to all nonhuman others—as I will discuss in the following section. Nonetheless, a more interesting point to note is even in the Kusana period, the representations of Avalokiteśvara are not absolutely masculine. They are marked as male mainly by the beard and the bare torso but the graceful and feminine ways they sit or stand suggest femininity. Moreover, the feminization of Kuan Yin in Chinese culture reinforces this impression. All becomings are a movement from the One to the others, from molar to molecular, from majoritarian to minoritarian. In the plateau on becoming, Deleuze and Guattari are not saying that everyone has to become a woman or a dog, instead they "resurrect the question of the centrality of ethics, of the encounter with otherness in a way that may prove highly pertinent to feminist attempts to rethink relations between the mainstream and the margins, between dominant and subordinated groups, oppressor and oppressed, self and other, as well as between and within subjects" (Grosz 1994: 194). What makes Avalokiteśvara or Kuan Yin significant as a symbol for future global feminisms is its fluidity in its sexuality, which echoes what Deleuze and Guattari call a thousand tiny sexes. Moreover, it prompts us to question and to rethink the issue of ethics of late capitalism in the context of the Anthropocene. And one of the concerns we have to focus on is our relationship with the nonhuman others.

3. Avalokiteśvara and the Nonhuman Others

Avalokiteśvara is believed to be merciful and benevolent to all beings. She also has an affinity to animals, insects, trees, plants, and nature. According to Palmer and Ramsay, one of the versions of Kuan Yin's origin is that she existed primordially. When the cosmos was still chaotic and the Earth first formed, Kuan Yin was responsible to take care of every living thing on earth. She taught them how to survive and coexist with other living things. But when she returned to the heaven, all animals, birds, and insects started to fight among themselves and slaughtered each other. Kuan Yin could even hear their moaning in the heaven. So, she came down to the earth again. With magic power, she created peacocks. She told every living creature that she could not stay with them forever; therefore, she dedicated her job of taking care of them to the peacocks. The hundred eyes on the peacocks' tails are her eyes, observing the behavior of every living creature on earth (Palmer & Ramsay 1995: 57–62).

There are stories around Kuan Yin which show how people go to her for help when they have troubles in *The Lotus Sutra*. In chapter 265 of *The Journey to the West*,[2] Monkey King steals three Ginseng Fruits at the Mountain of Longevity and even topples the Ginseng Fruit Tree. The god who guards the place is greatly offended and detains the Great Sage. If Monkey King has to save his teacher, the T'ang Monk, he must find a cure for the tree. He first seeks help from the Supreme Ruler but his "grain of the great monad reverted cinnabar of nine turns" can only cure creatures in the world but not trees, especially the Ginseng Fruit Tree which has a spiritual root. So, Monkey King seeks help from Kuan Yin. Fortunately for him, Kuan Yin agrees to help him with the sweet dew in her immaculate vase.

> "The sweet dew in my immaculate vase can heal divine trees or spiritual roots." "Have you tried this before?" asked Pilgrim. "Indeed," said the Bodhisattva. "When?" asked Pilgrim. The Bodhisattva said, "Some years ago Lao Tzu had a wager with me: he took my willow twig and placed it in his elixir-refining brazier until it was completely dried and charred. Then he gave it back to me, and I stuck it in my vase. After one day and one night, I had my green twig and leaves again, as lovely as before." (Yu 1977–83: 131)

I mentioned that all becomings have to start with becoming-woman because woman is minoritarian. Being minoritarian, Kuan Yin shares an affinity with the nonhuman others, including animals and plants, and Deleuze and Guattari's concept of becoming seems to promote transversal communication between species. However, Haraway pushes that further by suggesting that to survive in the Anthropocene, we have to make kin with our companion species. She proclaims,

> These times called the Anthropocene are times of multispecies, including human, urgency: of great mass death and extinction; of onrushing disasters, whose unpredictable specificities are foolishly taken as unknowability itself; of

refusing to know and to cultivate the capacity of response-ability; of refusing to be present in and to onrushing catastrophe in tie; of unprecedented looking away. (2016: 35)

Haraway advocates that the human species has to realize that the companion species "engages in the old art of terraforming" (Haraway 2016: 11), the earth belongs to them as much as to the human species. Moreover, companion species are "relentlessly becoming-with" (13). They are entangled with human's lives and technology, architecture, inventions on earth. In fact, they are part of the human evolution. Haraway claims they are "[c]odomesticated with their people" (15) Instead of becoming-animal, we have to becoming-with other species since "all earthlings are kin in the deepest sense" (103). This saying is echoed by posthumanists such as Cary Wolfe, Pramod K. Nayar, and Rosi Braidotti. They advocate a new ethics in the posthuman era. Wolfe defines posthumanism in the following way:

the human occupies a new place in the universe, a universe now populated by what I am prepared to call nonhuman subjects. And this is why, to me, posthumanism means not the triumphal surpassing or unmasking of something but an increase in the vigilance, responsibility, and humility that accompany living in a world so newly, and differently, inhabited. (2010: 48)

4. Conclusion

When Haraway conceived the idea that cyborg could be a symbol for the future development of feminism and posthumanism in the 1980s, it is undoubtedly a pioneering and bold attempt. What does Haraway say about the figure of cyborg many years after the publication of "A Cyborg Manifesto"? She explains that she chose the cyborg as a symbol for future feminisms due to its oppositional and critical dimension. In order to outdo a world that is "done by notions of matter/form, or production/raw materials" (Haraway 2004: 330), she feels that there is a need of "a whole kinship system of figurations as critical figures" (327), such as "the cyborg, the coyote, the OncoMouse™, the FemaleMan, the feminists, the history of women within feminist analysis, the dogs in [her] name project, and, of course, the non-human primates" (332). Schneider also reads the cyborg in a metaphorical way:

The cyborg is not only an image or figure, an entity in fact or imagination, but it is also a positioning, a way of thinking and seeing, that Haraway believed could– if taken up, lived – make the survival of living beings in late- or post-modern technoscientific worlds more likely. (2005: 62)

The cyborg, being a hybrid of human and machine, a post-gender creature, actually provides a metaphor for us to reflect on the world we are living in. Haraway writes that "things need not be in this way" (2004: 329). In one stroke, all our systems—capitalism, globalization, patriarchy, first/ third-world, heterosexuality, gender, family structure—are thrown into a turmoil.

After writing her "A Cyborg Manifesto," Haraway published *The Companion Species Manifesto* (2003), followed by *When Species Meet* (2008). This time she has chosen a dog figure to speak for her. Though it seems odd for a cyberfeminist to write about animals, Haraway explains,

> The practices and actors in dog worlds, human and non-human alike, ought to be central concerns of technoscience studies … Telling a story of co-habitation, co-evolution, and embodied cross-species sociality, the present manifesto asks which of two cobbled together figures—cyborgs and companion species—might more fruitfully inform livable politics and ontologies in current life worlds. These figures are hardly polar opposites. Cyborgs and companion species each bring together the human and non-human, the organic and technological, carbon and silicon, freedom and structure, history and myth, the rich and the poor, the state and the subject, diversity and depletion, modernity and postmodernity, and nature and culture in unexpected ways. (2003: 3–4)

In her book *When Species Meet*, one of the figures Haraway employs is her dog, Ms Cayenne Pepper. She says that "Ms Cayenne Pepper continues to colonize all [her] cells—a sure case of what the biologist Lynn Margulis calls symbiogenesis … if you were to check [their] DNA, you'd find some potent transfections between [them]" (2008: 15). Haraway also introduces us to tigers, wolves, flies, pigs, cats, and whales in *When Species Meet*. She says, "All of these are figures, and all are mundanely here, on this earth, now asking who 'we' will become when species meet" (5). Here, she borrows the concept of "becoming" from Deleuze and Guattari. She writes, "The partners do not precede their relating; all that is, is the fruit of becoming with" (17). Perhaps not coincidentally, Deleuze and Guattari also use the figure of dog when they illustrate the concept of becoming in *A Thousand Plateaus*. So, why dog among all the animals? Haraway explains her choice by saying that "Dogs are many things … It is almost part of the definition of a dog to be in relationship with humans, although not necessarily around the word 'domestication'" (2004: 330). Although Haraway clearly progresses beyond a purely cyberfeminist perspective here, becoming attenuated to the animal and even vegetal world as a shared milieu, she also clearly maintains the view that the cyborg and more recently figures and couplings of companion species share common ground in their hybridity and perhaps even machinic technicity.

That brings us back to Haraway's proclamation, "I'd rather be a cyborg than a goddess" (1991: 316). What Haraway has in mind is probably the goddess worship in spiritual ecofeminism. She considers that instead of searching for a future for humanity in goddesses or in the past, it is probably more effective to turn to technology. However, for women in the Asian countries, especially in the developing countries, it is much easier to appeal to them with a bodhisattva figure which is familiar to them than with a cyborg. Julia Martin also suggests that Buddhism can provide an alternative approach to nondualism and also a compassionate response to the present eco-social-spiritual crisis in the Third World (Martin 1996). When Nina Lykke compares the cyborg to the goddess, she writes,

> A celebration of the cyborg and her/his/its tendency to absorb the material into the flow of semiosis (sign production) and ever-changing meanings tends to put the focus on technologies which speed up the meaning-changing processes. In contrast, a celebration of the goddess who absorbs the semiotic into the material will often be accompanied by a tendency to concentrate attention on the basic, natural conditions of our existence. (1996: 27–8)

One could extrapolate from Lykke's critique that the cyborg is caught within the desirous cycles and accelerations of capitalism. If we compare Avalokiteśvara to the cyborg, we will see that the many manifestations of Avalokiteśvara open up creative avenues for developing future feminisms and posthumanism, perhaps, by contrast, shedding light on how the differences that location and positionality *within* capitalism–those "conditions of our existence"–affect in us from a globally and economically diverse playing field.

Of course, Haraway has also conceded that the cyborg is but one figure that satisfies a critical need and disruptive function, and, as we have seen, she does expand her lexicon to be more inclusive of interspecies hybridity and invoking multiple material arrangements. Yet, as I have shown, there is certainly room for more figural invention, and the advantages of this new figure are worth exploring. First of all, Avalokiteśvara is in-between male and female in the material body which gives us hope to transform the dualistic nature of our culture under patriarchy. Second, Avalokiteśvara is looking after the earth beings with compassion and humility which sets a good example for humans in this age. Third, as discussed above, the transformation of Avalokiteśvara in India and Tibet to the androgynous form of Kuan Yin is a centuries-long construction informed by intersections of local folktales, legends, politics, social factors and religions. Avalokiteśvara is as much a construction as a cyborg, only that the former is a cultural construction while the latter maintains some connection with militarism and capitalism. Even if these are merely residual or unintended determinations, I believe that gives Avalokiteśvara an edge over the cyborg as the symbol of the posthuman future, and, indisputably, the stakes in how we address these two aspects, militarism and capitalism, for our future are huge.

Puar, in her article "I Would Rather Be a Cyborg than a Goddess," suggests that it is not necessary to disaggregate the cyborg/goddess because it is a becoming-intersectional assemblage (Puar 2012). She begins her essay with a critique of intersectionality, claiming that the emphasis on race actually has the effect of positioning white women in the centre, while women of color are seen as the different, the Other. The notion that all identities are intersectional, embodied rubrics of race, class, gender, sexuality and nation, inherently privileges race over other elements and, further, compartmentalizes these other differences. Puar instead favors the idea of assemblages that "re-introduce politics into the political" (Puar 2012: 64). Puar's critique of intersectionality is fair, and her idea of "becoming-intersectional assemblage" is brilliant. However, that notion has encountered some problem in the Asian contexts. While Haraway's cyborg deals with the intersection of body and technology, many women in Asia have yet to have access to a mobile phone or a computer. Many women in Cambodia, Indonesia, Bangladesh, the Philippines, Vietnam, India, and some parts of China are working at sweatshops, being exported as domestic servants, or involved in human trafficking. Their oppressions are caused not only by patriarchy but also capitalism and globalization. It is as much a political and economic issue, not to mention an ethical one, as a gender issue. This relates to Deleuze and Guattari's critique of the inadequacy of psychoanalysis—that is, through its purported universal status, it omits or obscures the significance of political and historical context. The main problem with psychoanalysis is that it reduces a person "to a pitiful creature who eternally consumes daddy-and-mommy and nothing else whatsoever" (Deleuze and Guattari 1994: 20). As Buchanan comments, "Deleuze and Guattari were both of the view that a mode of analysis that insists on filtering everything through the triangulating lens of daddy-mommy-me could not hope to explain either why or how May '68 happened, nor indeed why it went they [*sic*] way it did'" (2008: 39). So, though acknowledgedly a milestone for feminist projects concerned with breaking barriers between the human and the machinic (nature/culture) which have traditionally been at the service of patriarchal prerogatives, for women in underdeveloped countries the cyborg, with its heralding of technology, could be seen as a symbol of oppression. Information technology, the internet, and the cyborg may be lines of flight for some feminisms, but they are not potent enough to deterritorialize the myriad oppressions and inequities instantiated by and through global capitalism.

As mentioned above, Haraway thinks that if we sum up this age with a word, it will be Capitalocene, since it is global capitalism that leads to the accelerating depletion of resources. She quotes Brad Werner, who claims that the way to fight back is "action and thinking that do not fit within the dominant capitalist culture" (2016: 47). Capitalism has lured us with progress and led us to exploit the earth resources, destroy other species, and leave us the wrong conception that there are no other ways to "reworld, reimagine, relive, and reconnect with each other, in multispecies well-being" (51). Yet, Haraway reminds us that "the established disorder is not necessary" (51). She contends that we have to imagine different futures and different worlds, which brings us back to the project of Deleuze and Guattari. Schizophrenia, according to Deleuze and Guattari, possesses "inherent creativity" (Buchanan 2008: 43), which could be mobilized against the present, in resistance to capitalism. Massumi also points out that "schizophrenia is a breakaway into the unstable equilibrium of continuing self-invention" (1992: 92). Capitalism, on the other hand, being driven by profit-making, is conservative in its outlook. We cannot hope to find any solution to save the planet in the Anthropocene from capitalism. Yet, schizoanalysis, alone, may not provide the relief that we seek. Reidar Due comments that "because of the all-encompassing reach of the Oedipal process, *Anti-Oedipus* bars the way to any pragmatic strategy for resistance to capitalism … In Oedipalization we become complicit in our own subjection at the unconscious level of desiring production" (2007: 114). To get out of capitalism and Oedipalization, we may look to Avalokiteśvara for inspiration. The portrayals of Avalokiteśvara as male and female provide us a way out of the maze of dualism. As I have discussed, Avalokiteśvara most of the time was not portrayed as a masculine male, instead, it is a male form with femininity. And let's not forget that even until the Ming Dynasty, Avalokiteśvara was still found to be in both male and female forms. I would like to stress here that Avalokiteśvara is neither androgynous nor dualistic. Instead, s/he is more like the symbol of yin-yang—with yin in yang and yang in yin while each is fluid and remains in deterritorialization and reterritorialization process.

Haraway suggests that "SF is a sign for science fiction, speculative feminism, science fantasy, speculative fabulation, science fact, and also, string figures" (2016: 10). We may add one more to the list—spiritual feminism, with Avalokiteśvara as a symbol to promote a new praxis for feminisms that considers politics, society, economic, religion and makes kin with human, nonhuman, animal, plants, and earthlings. As a Bodhisattva, Avalokiteśvara is a symbol containing multiple lines of flight, not only able to deterritorialize sexuality but also able to shed light on a way to pursue what Braidotti calls "postsecular spirituality" (2014). Drawing upon Haraway's idea of creative affirmation, Braidotti writes,

> We need new cosmologies and world views that are appropriate to our own high level of complexity and the technological development and to the ferocious and insidious sets of structural injustices and violent modes of dispossession that mark the global economy. We need original cultural, spiritual, ethical creativity, be it myths, narratives, or representations that are adequate to this new civilization we inhabit. (2014: 269)

This is exactly what I have tried to develop herein; thus, I see this project as taking up the mantle developed through the feminist tradition of storytelling, image-making and invention. Thinking through particularities of our contemporary, global condition from the perspective of a specific and unique cultural and spiritual lineage magnifies both potentialities and problems otherwise unseen. The Avalokiteśvara, especially in its manifestation as Kuan Yin, can be seen as a figure that continues the feminist project of providing conceptual personas that challenge dualistic thinking and the privilege of the masculine, while simultaneously deterritorializing these perspectives in order to facilitate encounters beyond their Western European purviews—fulfilling the promise of feminist praxis to always take particular consideration of that which is rendered peripheral, marginalized, or epistemologically vague by our own positionality. It is not a matter of replacing these former images but of adding to the conceptual richness that we have available for embarking on new theoretical and practical encounters.

Notes

1. For a detailed account of the story of Princess Miaoshan, see Blofeld (1988).
2. *Journey to the West* is one of the four great Chinese classical novels. It was written by Wu Cheng'en and published in the sixteenth century during the Ming Dynasty. The main character, the Monkey King, accompanies his teacher the T'ang Monk, in a grand journey to bring the Buddhist sutras from India back to the East.

References

Beyer, S. (1973), *The Cult of Tara: Magic and Ritual in Tibet*, Los Angeles: University of California Press.

Blofeld, J. (1988), *Bodhisattva of Compassion: The Mystical Tradition of Kuan Yin*, Boston: Shambhala.

Rinpoche, Bokar (2010), *Chenrezig Lord of Love: Principles and Methods of Deity Meditation*, San Francisco: Clearpoint Press.

Braidotti, R. (2014), "Conclusion: The Residual Spirituality in Critical Theory: A Case for Affirmative Postsecular Politics," in R. Dridotti, B. Blaagaard, T. de Graauw, and E. Midden (eds.), *Transformations of Religion and the Public Sphere: Postsecular Publics*, 249–72. London: Palgrave Macmillan.

Buchanan, I. (2008), *Deleuze and Guattari's Anti-Oedipus: A Reader's Guide*, London: Continuum.

Chenrezig (2000), "Chenrezig/Avalokiteshvara: Embodiment of Compassion in Tibetan Buddhism," Dharma Haven, http://www.dharma-haven.org/tibetan/chen-re-zig.htm (accessed April 18, 2019).

Deleuze, G., and F. Guattari (1994), *Anti-Oedipus: Capitalism and Schizophrenia*, Minnesota: University of Minnesota Press.

Due, R. (2007), *Deleuze*, Cambridge: Polity Press.

Grosz, E. (1994), "A Thousand Tiny Sexes: Feminism and Rhizomatics," in C. V. Boundas and D. Olkowski (eds.), *Gilles Deleuze and the Theater of Philosophy: Critical Essays*, 187–210, New York: Routledge.

Gu, Z. M. (2003), *Cong tian wang chuan tong dao fo wang chuan tong: Zhongguo zhong shi fo jiao zhi guo yi shi xing tai yan jiu (From the Devarāja Tradition to the Buddbarāja Tradition)*, Taipei: Shang Zhou Publishing.

Haraway, D. J. (1991), Chapter 8: "A Cyborg Manifesto: Science, Technology, and Socialist-Feminism in the late Twentieth Century," in *Simians, Cyborgs, and Women: The Reinvention of Nature*, 149–82, New York: Routledge.

Haraway, D. J. (2003), *The Companion Species Manifesto: Dogs, People, and Significant Otherness*, Chicago: Prickly Paradigm Press.

Haraway, D. J. (2004), *The Haraway Reader*, New York: Routledge.

Haraway, D. J. (2008), *When Species Meet*, Minneapolis: University of Minnesota Press.

Haraway, D. J. (2016), *Staying with the Trouble: Making Kin in the Chthulucene*, Durham, NC: Duke University Press.

Holland, E. W. (1999), *Deleuze and Guattari's Anti-Oedipus: Introduction to Schizoanalysis*, New York: Routledge.

Huntington, S. L., and J. C. Huntington (1985), *The Art of Ancient India: Buddhist, Hindu, Jain*, New York: Weatherhill.

Karetzky, P. E. (2004), *Guanyin*, London: Oxford University Press.

Karthar, K. (1986), *A Teaching on the Chenrezig Sadhana*, http://www.abuddhistlibrary. com/Buddhism/A%20-%20Tibetan%20Buddhism/Authors/Kenpo%20Karthar/A%20 Teaching%20on%20the%20Chenrezig%20Sadhana/KTD--A%20Teaching%20on%20the%20 Chenrezig%20Sadhana--.htm (accessed April 18, 2019).

Lykke, N. (1996), "Between Monsters, Goddesses and Cyborgs: Feminist Confrontations with Science," in N. Lykke and R. Braidotti (eds.), *Between Monsters, Goddesses and Cyborgs: Feminist Confrontations with Science, Medicine and Cyberspace*, 13–29, London: Zed Books.

Martin, J. (1996), "On Healing Self/Nature," in N. Lykke and R. Braidotti (eds.), *Between Monsters, Goddesses and Cyborgs: Feminist Confrontations with Science, Medicine and Cyberspace*, 103–19, London: Zed Books.

Massumi, B. (1992), *A User's Guide to Capitalism and Schizophrenia: Deviations from Deleuze and Guattari*, Cambridge: The MIT Press.

Palmer, M., and J. Ramsay (1995), *Kuan Yin: Myths and Prophecies of the Chinese Goddess of Compassion*, London: Thorsons.

Puar, J. K. (2012). "'I Would Rather be a Cyborg than a Goddess': Becoming-Intersectional in Assemblage Theory," *philoSOPHIA* 2 (1), 49–66. State University of New York Press. Retrieved May 24, 2018, from Project MUSE database.

Schneider, J. (2005), *Donna Haraway: Live Theory*, New York: Continuum.

Watson, B. (1993), *The Lotus Sutra*, New York: Columbia University Press.

Wolfe, C. (2010), *What Is Posthumanism?*, Minneapolis: University of Minnesota Press.

Yu, A. C. (1977–83), *The Journey to the West* (Vol. 2), Chicago: University of Chicago Press.

CHAPTER 11
WRITING DIFFERENCE: TOWARD A BECOMING-MINORITARIAN
Chrysanthi Nigianni

1. On Institutionalized Practices

Gesturing toward a becoming-minoritarian is a political gesture and a grammatical gesture, one that invites us to turn the noun into verb, to resist the suffix of femin-*ism(s)*—a suffix that forms abstract nouns and doctrines; a suffix that tends to an ending, a closure and a consequent fixity. Marxism, Calvinism, Communism, Nationalism the suffix *-ism* has come to indicate a belief or principle, a school of thought, an ideology, the result of a set of actions. Feminist scholarship has not escaped such closure and has come to constitute such a doctrine characterized by master methodologies (e.g., intersectionality, post-structuralism) and master concepts; while feminist writing at present seems to have conformed into a standardized academic writing and thinking showing oblivion of a not so far past that has radically questioned the use and function of language in writing and thinking experiments. Within a neoliberal university context feminist colleagues seem to be equally eager for institutional success conforming uncritically to regulative bodies (such as the Research Excellence Framework) and the regulative imperatives of prestigious journals with little concern to challenge their principles and effects on the present and the future of critical thinking. Repeating such master concepts and methodologies, reiterating specific feminist agendas (e.g., identity politics) and performing citational practices that reproduce the Canon (despite opposite claims) seems a sufficient condition of "doing critical thinking" *and* feminist scholarship. Being more concerned with its own preservation, territorialization, and consolidation, feminism has become less self-reflective and lost sight of the radicality of its purposes. So far sexual and gender identity politics seem to have served well the neoliberal democracies of more representation and less participation.

This essay attempts to re-divert the focus on language in relation to practices of writing since, in my view, present feminist scholarship has not paid sufficient attention to it. As Lykke (2014) argues, "writing, method, methodology, politics are inextricably linked" (2014: 3) while there is a long tradition in continental philosophy that has argued for the inherent relationship between ethics and writing (Derrida 1998; Deleuze 1986; Irigaray 1985; Cixous 1994a; Conley 1991; Wardle 2007; Lykke 2014). More specifically, so far feminist scholarship has focused on practices of writing either by arguing in favor of writing intersectionally, or from the standpoint position (Lykke 2014, Collins 2000). Both arguments are informed by critical feminist epistemologies that have come to question notions of objectivity and the consequent divisions between the authorial/ researcher "I" and the so called "objects" of research (Alcoff and Potter 2013; Lennon and Whitford 2012) and by a skepticism to one dimensional categorization in terms of gender, class, sexuality or any other social category (Lykke 2014). These critical voices have aimed at situating the authorial "I" on the intersections (Lorde 1984, Collins 2000) and multiplicity (Puar 2017) of power relations or at reclaiming writing as an embodied corporeal practice (Cixous 1994b/1999, Irigaray 1985, Grosz [1994] 2001).

A schizoanalytic practice of writing on the political and grammatical varieties of becoming-minoritarian can challenge a current fetishization and policing of "content" and language within the feminist paradigm of identity politics, favoring instead "asignifying messages that escape dominant ideologies" (Guattari 1996: 154). To live ideologically is to narrow one's life. Becoming-minoritarian can be actualized in practices of writing that challenge a representational image of thought still dominant in a feminism preoccupied largely with identity politics. The essay draws on a Deleuzian understanding of the Univocity of Being that comes to challenge Representationalism as negative determination—where difference is being negatively defined (i.e., woman as the not-Man—and puts forward a notion of difference as *multiplicity, immanence* and *expression* that offers a more truthful account of internal differentiation and indeterminacy as the ground of an ethics of an immanent relatedness *in* this world and *of* this world. Writing in this framework does not aim to represent but to express life and even more to make it possible.

The question of writing has largely been ignored and suppressed in academia—a question that poses writing as a philosophical problem itself—even though the idea of an academic that does not/did not write is almost impossible to conceive. In similar lines, Greg Lambert asks, "Can we imagine today a philosopher who did not write?" (2012: 152)—in his attempt to explore the relationship between philosophy and writing, and where he replies possibly "yes" but then it would be an anonymous philosopher or a rare exception. Yet the politics of writings has not enjoyed the same attention as, for example, the politics of reading has enjoyed within the fields of literature, feminism, and cultural studies, in line with hermeneutics, deconstruction and discursive/textual methods of analysis. Although such a vast critical bibliography has contributed to a critical/political analysis of representations that in turn have informed critical practices of writing and art-making, yet I believe the question of writing and the politics of writing (also in relation to the use and function of language) to constitute an urgent question that should be posed for itself, especially in the present context of the twenty-first-century neoliberal, high fee, commercialized university. The institutionalization of Higher Education in the West seems to be suffering from monolingualism despite the proclaims for diversity and performs a linguistic colonization through the prevalence of the Anglo-American way(s) of thinking and writing. The marketized global university has produced a standardized form of academic writing that seems to attend to universal "rules" of academic rigor and critical thinking, as the latter are put forward and defined by prestigious international (meaning Anglophone) journals, funding research bodies, and national evaluative bodies of research excellence. The direct target of these centers of institutional power has been "writing" and the practices of writing, as the effective way to control what circulates on the level of concepts and ideas, what forms of knowledge are produced and reproduced, what constitutes academic knowledge and critical thinking, how to conduct research that enjoys sufficient authority and popularity, what research questions matter and get funded.

In many British and American universities, academic writing has become its own genre and is part of the compulsory curriculum—not only in humanities but also in the natural and technological sciences. Anglophone students are trained to produce texts displaying a high degree of clarity, consistency, and a logical formal layout with the latter constituting indisputable, clear, attainable objectives and little attention is paid to the ideological assumptions that underline it and the broader discursive strategies that envelop it.

Nobody would deny that writing is a social practice and plays a key role in the circulation of ideas in society having a direct impact on the development of democracy. Every authoritarian regime and dictatorship establishes itself through censorship and the banning, or at times burning, of books, while modern Western democracies managed to enable a similar filtering and censorship through the laws of a global market (international publishing companies taking over and closing down small independent publishers), transnational marketing strategies and increasing commodification and quantification that sustain illusions around increasing diversification and democratization.

Similarly, the neoliberal Anglophone university shapes illusions of diversification and democratization through an ever-expanding curriculum of all-inclusive agendas; a curriculum that shows little capacity for self-reflexivity and that has failed to challenge the fast-fashioning of the university into a private company, a becoming-corporate of the university, which has dramatically narrowed the *raison d'être* of higher education (Morish 2018; Winn and Hall 2017; Warner 2017). Neo-capitalist, managerial rationalities have come to replace civic education, critical enquiry, and reflection, in favor of divisive competition, performance management, and quantification; even worse, these changes have been actively supported through consensual silence, docility and almost complete capitulation from the majority of academics.

Since 1980s, the British Marxist historian Thompson called this species *Academicus Superciliosus* and portrayed them in the following way:

> He is inflated with self-esteem and perpetually self-congratulatory as to the high vocation of the university teacher; but he knows almost nothing about any other vocation, and he will lie down and let himself be walked over if anyone enters from the outer world who has money or power or even a tough line in realist talk ... Superciliosus is the most divisible and rulable creature in this country, being so intent upon crafty calculations of short-term advantages – this favour for his department, that chance of promotion—or upon rolling the log of a colleague who, next week at the next committee, has promised to roll a log for him, that he has never even tried to imagine the wood out of which all this timber rolls ... These people annoy me a good deal ... Academic freedom is forever on their lips,

and is forever disregarded in their actions. They are the last people to whom it can be safely entrusted, since the present moment is never the opportune moment to stand and fight. (Thompson in Evans 2005: 41)

In the face of the current crisis, academic feminists have happily performed a similar short-sightedness putting forward their own agendas and transforming feminism into a finished discourse and political ideology that very often promotes their own self-interests (interests that go hand-in-hand with these of the department) where the slogan "the personal is political" has been misinterpreted and has taken a wrong turn producing a psychologized vulnerable ego-logical subject. Writing and speech have been appropriated as a purposive activity in the sphere of self-interested human social action and in the service of certain political goals and aims—a feminist writing that wishes to excel in performing its "critical function," enacted in ideological debates.

Feminist (non)responses to the current crisis have been characterized by introversion, a certain withdrawal and immense defensiveness in favor of their own self-preservation and that of their like-minded disciples, an attitude that fits perfectly into the rest of the mainstream academy and the ideologies of the neoliberal totalitarian university; whereas the politics of solidarity have been replaced by identity control, policing of language and content, and a focusing on issues of power solely through discernible dichotomies and power relations.

All these practices have taken place in the "echoes" of a not so long feminist past in France that radically questioned institutions, institutionalized knowledge and women's exclusions from them, not only in terms of numbers or as merely an issue of equality and equal representation but more significantly as a broader critique of history and culture and the complex issue of language, of writing and speaking, including Luce Irigaray's critique of phallologocentrism first elaborated forty years ago in *Speculum* and Helene Cixous's *Laugh of Medusa,* that celebrated the return of the feminine "repressed" and its explosive, *utterly* destructive, force that refused assimilation and representation. *Both wrote and spoke from an outsider's position (in relation to the university/academy).*

If we keep on speaking the same language together,

we're going to reproduce the same history.

Listen: all around us, men and women sound just the same ... always the same.

Irigaray (1985: 205)

Institutionalized feminism has consolidated itself as an interpretative/critical project with concepts fixed in language, specific master methodologies (e.g., intersectionality, post-structuralism), while feminist writing as a practice seems to have conformed into the needs of the neoliberal university and a standardized and increasingly regulated academic writing, more and more tied to proposals for funding and existing political agendas. Feminism has turned itself into an academic discipline(-ing).

In his article on the effects of standard language ideology and the process of standardization, James Milroy defines standardization as "the imposition of uniformity upon a class of objects" (2001: 531), where the "objects" concerned (including abstracts objects such as language) are in *the nature of things*, not *uniform* but *variable*. In his analysis Milroy argues that "the states of language postulated in theoretical approaches will be identical with the most standardized forms" (ibid.) while he makes direct links between uniformity and the economy (uniformity for Milroy has economic and political goals) claiming that the languages that are more affected by standardization (English language is one example) have higher economic value.

> Standardisation leads to great efficiency in exchanges of any kind. The social and economic drive toward uniformity is to facilitate what Haugen (1966) has called *elaboration of function*. In modern European history progressive standardization of monetary systems, weights and measures, and of factory-made goods in general has gone hand in hand with the rise of international trade and capitalism and the progressive standardization of language has developed alongside standardization of these other things. (Milroy 2001: 534)

One of the most important effects of standardization for Milroy is the development of a consciousness among speakers of "a correct canonical form of language," the firm belief in a *correctness* of language that does not fall into the "native speaker intuition" but constitutes an external quality to be acquired through training and education. In a similar manner the language of a discipline (and feminist discipline as a field of study) needs to be taught as an external language that then enables us to reach knowledge through an objective, coherent manner, while "learning" the language of a specific theoretical approach passes through a similar external (from the outside) learning that enables us to *master concepts* and the *appropriate language/vocabulary* that will then easily distinguish us as being Marxists, feminists, deconstructionists, or postmodernists.

Although Deleuze and Guattari carried on an "ideological critique" they avoided the use of the term "ideology" since they were also very critical of the binary opposition between "science" and "ideology" (truth and false) but also because they were critical of the primacy given to economy and of the division/dichotomous logic that characterizes the Marxist schema of the infrastructure(economy)/superstructure (ideology). Instead they prefer to speak in terms of "an organization of repressive power" that implicates equally desire on the level of the infrastructure/economy, instead of just seeing it as a phenomenon of secondary importance placed only in the superstructure.

> Deleuze: There is no ideology, there are only organizations of power once it is admitted that the organization of power is the unity of desire and the economic infrastructure ... Take two examples. Education: in May 1968 the leftists lost a lot of time insisting that professors engage in public self-criticism as agents of bourgeois ideology. It's stupid, and simply fuels the masochistic impulses of academics. The struggle against the competitive examination was abandoned for

the benefit of the controversy, or the great anti-ideological public confession. In the meantime, the more conservative professors had no difficulty reorganizing their power. The problem of education is not an ideological problem, but a problem of the *organization of power*: it is the specificity of educational power that makes it appear to be an ideology, but it's pure illusion. (Guattari 2009: 38)

Here Deleuze claims that it is precisely the nature of power the educational systems hold that allows them to create (pseudo-)ideological debates that come to conceal more profound problems and questions around the organization of power. Similarly, in the same interview, Guattari argues,

It's the same thing in traditional political structures. One finds the old trick being played everywhere again and again: a big ideological debate in the general assembly and questions of organization reserved for special commissions. These questions appear secondary, determined by political options. While on the contrary, *the real problems are those of organization, never specified or rationalized, but projected afterwards in ideological terms.* There the real divisions show up: a treatment of desire and power, of investments, of group Oedipus, of group "superegos," of perverse phenomena, etc. And then political oppositions are built up: *the individual takes such a position against another one, because in the scheme of organization of power, he has already chosen and hates his adversary.* (2009, 39)

In his article *Lignes de fuites* (1979) Guattari discusses Althussers's notion of ideology and concludes his argument by claiming a common or shared goal: "The goal remains the same: the analysis of our repressive institutions and practices with the aim of transforming them to permit greater freedom." While he stresses, "[T]he important step is to get out of the idea of ideology as mere superstructure, a sort of *passive reflection* of what goes on in the economic base" (Guattari 2015: 143).

The primacy given to economy ("necessary" cuts in education, austerity measures in society that cultivate a climate of anxiety and fear inside and outside institutions) and a simultaneous mystification of the economy have paralyzed the possibility of individual and collective action ("*passive reflection*"), rendering the present moment as always the inopportune "moment to stand and fight" (Thomson in Evans 2005: 41) displacing the issue of the organization of power marked by "investments of desire," "groups of superegos" and "groups of Oedipus" to empty ideological debates (Deleuze and Guattari 2004).

The real shift in the register of desire is still avoided.

2. A Question of Style

The neoliberal university as a new organization of power becomes the factory of modern ideologies. These ideologies can be defined as "systematic ways of knowing truth that seek to immanentise transcendence, to make us Gods and bring heaven to earth ... Ideology concentrates on material goods" (Herzo, 2009: 92).

Margaret Herzo in her article on Simone Weil, "Composition on a Multiple Plane—Simone Weil's Answer to the Rule of Necessity," discusses Weil's relation to philosophy and activism—a relationship that has been marked by Weil's rejection of every "*ism*" as well as by her belief that her role in life was to stand outside institutions, groups and powers and ask the important and unpopular questions. Moreover, for Weil, there was an inextricable relationship between ideas and life/living: she could not write *about* ideas, she had to live them. She died at the age of thirty-four in England of tuberculosis and starvation because she refused to eat more than the official ration in occupied France.

Living those ideas led her to believe "that critics of inequality and social justice are trapped by modernity's values and way of thinking about community, power, justice, and human nature," and that those "critics or social movements seek domination or the achievement of private self-interest as an end" (Herzo 2000: 92). For Weil, the best tool to challenge modern ideologies and the major languages of social critique and social movements was philosophy. Unfortunately, and wrongfully for Weil, philosophy and ideology had become synonymous, even though philosophy (supposedly) is always open (a way of life, not a system) and ideology constitutes a closed system.

Deleuze and Guattari's (1994) definition of philosophy as essentially an invention and creation—the creation of new concepts—escapes the notion of Theory as a system (a systematization of knowledge, an instrument or tool) or that of a philosophical School.[1] Moreover, its aim is closer to the production of *change* than the search for truth—philosophy for Deleuze and Guattari is concerned with the conditions of the real, an *intervention through creation*. Such a definition also explains Deleuze's privileging of literature and the close relationship he ascribes to philosophy and writing.

For Deleuze, the true function of literature is to resist the logic of representation, to take language away from its communicative or referential role[2]—its instrumentality—and to posit it in terms of movement and flows of affects and percepts and a circulation of desire. Like with every work of art, literature is not evaluated for its content or themes (its message or story line) but by the material it is made of, its function.

> There is no difference between what a book talks about and how it is made. Therefore, a book has no object. As an assemblage, a book has only itself, in connection with other assemblages and in relation to other bodies without organs. We will never ask what a book means, as signified or signifier; we will not look for anything to understand in it. We will ask what it functions with, in connection with what other things it does or does not transmit intensities, in which other multiplicities its own are inserted and metamorphosed, and with what bodies without organs it makes its own converge. (Deleuze and Guattari 1987: 4).

As Lecercle (2002) notes, for Deleuze, literature is privileged over philosophy in that the former is more concerned and addresses directly the problem of formal renewal and *the question of style*. It is precisely this experimentation, the search of style and of formal renewal on the level of writing and thinking that prevents philosophy from turning into common sense or a closed system of truth and knowledge. For Deleuze (2004) one of the lessons which philosophy can learn from literature is to unlearn the representational image of thought which has dominated the discipline, as it impedes the creative process necessary for philosophy's rejuvenation and concept creation. Doing away from a representational thinking, in terms of "analogy, resemblance, identity and opposition" (Grosz [1994] 2001: 164), unlearning the dominant image of thought, will enable a thinking of difference as singularity.[3]

Dismantling the representational image requires in turn a different relating to language and concepts that can only be achieved in new modes of writing practices. Philosophy, and equally, critical theory can become closed or finished discourses by relying too much on given concepts fixed in language. Instead of posing the problem, they accept the problem as it is posited by language. In this case they do "not explain very much because (they) accept the subdivision and the distribution of the real into concepts which society has deposited in language and which is most often brought about for the sake of convenience; and in the second place, because the synthesis it makes of these concepts is empty of matter, purely verbal" (Bergson, 2012: 34). A repetition of "master concepts" and a certain formalization or standardization of language that characterizes the present institutional landscape falls into this trap: that of not questioning given subdivisions and a certain distribution of the real (i.e., through specific syntactical relations that imply a specific distribution of power relations and a sovereignty of consciousness), as well as of repeating specific ontological assumptions through overused linguistic forms and notions of identity, gender, sexuality as categories of thinking that end up reifying and totalizing the complexity and singularity of individual experience.

Language poses a problem in a true philosophical sense and is not just a tool or a "subject" in our academic enquiries. Language[4] is a way to express thinking but also a betrayal of thinking and of singular experience; an opening up but also a closing down. Deleuze finds in Beckett a purely intensive use of language that opposes to or exhausts a totalizing symbolic and signifying use. An exhaustion we can also find in *ecriture feminine*: a struggle for words and with the rules of their organization (syntax) so as to find a way to articulate and share an experience and the event; to create a style. Such work is characterized by an extreme intimacy with the words, an intimacy where always anamorphosis and metamorphosis take place: where words become experiences and experiences become words or these other words, or just symbols of punctuation, lapses, another style, another way of existing beyond reified separations—the author, the reader, who is the "I" that speaks?—and in a state of indeterminacy that initially causes anguish (the anguish of writing or reading) only to transform itself and become an affirmation.

Style then is the organization of materials in new ways that establish unknown and unexpected relations between things, a reshaping of understanding, a reorganization of the real. Metaphor, in Deleuze, is not a signifying association or chain that leaves words intact through a series of substitutions; instead metaphors become essentially "metamorphoses" of the objects related in style with an exchange of their determinations and names. Style is ethics for Deleuze in that it allows new relations and a deeper exchange that takes place between two terms that cease to define themselves negatively (I-not I, Self, and Other), but affirm themselves in their indeterminacy not in distance, opening up lines of metamorphoses or lines of becoming. What is more, style dwells on the border between language and what lies beyond it, it is what gives expression to a nonlinguistic material, "a mass not yet linguistically but already semiotically, aesthetically pragmatically formed" (Lecercle 2012, Kindle). An invention of a new style is needed every time an upsurge of sensation disrupts subjective consciousness that is already linguistically mediated. At this moment we can respond by either inventing or experimenting with a new style (which is what the process of writing is about) as a radical political act, or we can simply and unproblematically subsume it and translate it into given or privileged linguistic forms and structures of representations (e.g., Oedipus complex and the system of Psychoanalysis).

Schizoanalytic writing is a form political activism that refuses syntactical, grammatical and conceptual obedience to Phallologocentrism as it manifests itself in its investment on familial Oedipalized formations and structures (that appear in all social and political institutions) as a mechanism of subjectivation and subjection ("*daddy-mommy*-me"). Phallologocentrism wants the neurotic to be (re)produced and to remain on the couch. On the contrary, schizoanalysis follows lines of deterritorialization:

> An author is great because he cannot prevent himself from tracing flows and causing them to circulate, flows that split asunder the catholic and despotic signifier of his work and that necessarily nourish a revolutionary machine on the horizon. That's what the style is or rather the absence of style- asyntactic, agrammatical: the moment when no longer the language is defined by what it says, even less by what makes it a signifying thing but what it causes it to move, to flow, to explode-desire. For literature is like schizophrenia: a process and not a goal, a production and not an expression. (Deleuze and Guattari 2004: 158–9)

Foucault, in his *Preface* to *Anti-Oedipus,* claims the book to be a book of ethics, since it radicalizes desire and liberates it from personalization, the superego and dual relationships (mother–child, patient–analyst, subject–object); such frameworks cannot but lead to a self-annihilation of desire as it reproduces it and locks it on the imaginary level. A schizoanalytic gesture gives back desire its revolutionary force by making direct connection of desire to reality and removing desire from notions of acquisition and lack to that of production. Hence, the literary schizoanalytic project starts from the question: "How does one introduce desire into thought, into discourse, into action?"

A "writing in search of a style" as an ethical praxis departs from this deeper exchange with language and life, pushing language to the limits, dislodging it from the abstract system of "*Langue*" and placing into the concrete reality of spoken languages (dialects and idiolects) and foreign internal tongues; it calls for an unfamiliar writing that causes syntax to undergo a deformation: "a syntax in the process of becoming, a creation of syntax that gives birth to a foreign language within language, a grammar of disequilibrium" (Deleuze 1997: 112). A writing that allows a reorganization of the real, new relationships to form, a possibility of life. The true function of language, as Lecercle (2002) notes, is not to represent life but to act with it and mix with it. Language is caught in the world: it neither simply represents it, nor entirely produces it. Equally, language is but one aspect of the behavior of the body. For Deleuze, language is not *the* model of all types of semiotics, but one mode of a wide range of semiotic phenomena.

A writing in search of a style starts with a crime. For Deleuze, it is shame that motivates writing, the shame of being a man (Deleuze 1997)[5]. For Cixous, writing is the ladder that helps us descend toward what is the deepest and the lowest inside us, to reach the worst in us, that is "truth": "It is what writing wants" (Cixous 1994a: 6). For both philosophers writing is linked to Life: an effort "to make life something more than personal, to free life from what it imprisons it" (Deleuze 1997: xv), or a learning to die, so as to learn not to be afraid "to live at the extremity of life" (Cixous 1994a: 7). Writing then starts with death or the murdering of given living forms (social categorizations), of reifying methodologies and fixed syntactical relations.

3. The Tyranny of Concepts

Despite their different philosophical trajectories, both Deleuze and Derrida privilege literature and ascribe a close relationship to philosophy and writing. This becomes evident in Derrida's suspicion of the concept and his preference for "quasi-concepts" that perform a deconstructive shaking or breakdown of the living present, as well as his shift to the experiencing of *aporia* (Protevi 2003), and in Deleuze's definition of philosophy as the creation of new concepts. For Derrida, a gesture of interpretation through structuralist models—not paying attention to a text as a singular event or problem—leads to "misconstruings of literature as 'thematism, sociologism, historicism, psychologism'" (Derrida, 1982, 70). It means eradicating otherness and doing away with a certain responsibility a text puts on us as readers. A responsibility toward the other "is a responsibility toward the future—it involves struggles to create openings beyond our programs or predictions" (Attridge 2017: 4). Similarly, Deleuze and Guattari note, "We lack resistance to the present. The creation of concepts in itself calls for a future form" (Deleuze and Guattari 1994: 108). Such resistance passes through writing. Concepts, for Deleuze (1995), should express an event rather than an essence and thus should allow a thinking of multiplicities rather than a classificatory, categorical thinking of totalities and unities (relate to issue of feminism in academia).

For both Deleuze and Derrida, literary texts trouble philosophical grounds of critical discourse—in the form of *deconstruction* for Derrida, and as *aesthetic pragmatics* that create equally strong and rich signs for Deleuze. They are both against a solely transcendent reading (I would add a transcendent writing) in search of signifieds (the search of meaning or a referent), without this necessarily implying a total annulment of meaning: as Derrida claims, such erasure would be a self-negation of the text itself, and thus argues for a practice of negotiation between meaning and what resists it (something that we have trouble defining). On the other hand, for Deleuze, a non-transcendental, immanent writing/reading (and thinking) allows for a making sense out of the form of nonsense and not against it, as well as in the form of a polyvalent meaning emerging from polysemic semiologies that do not get reduced to linguistics and a structuralist, universal logic of a system of language (*la Langue*) as abstraction. Deleuze is not interested in resisting or deconstructing such system. He departs by placing language to a humble, non-privileged place, alongside other systems of signs (each sign reaches an essence in the sense of expressing the world in an entirely different way). He is not interested in negative critique but privileges creation: a creation of concepts (for philosophy), affects and percepts (for art), functions (for science). He clearly demarcates from Derrida's project of deconstruction and a doing away with metaphysics. Their commonality resides in breaking away from a subjectivist tradition of thinking (as Cogito or the phenomenological subject) and in their notion of an irreducible difference, a non-dialectical difference, an a-categorical difference, that is "more profound than a contradiction that is a joyously repeated affirmation ('Yes, yes')" (Deleuze 2003: 193); for Derrida post-phenomenological and ethical; for Deleuze, ethical, material and forceful.

Writing and reading relates to difference as the verb to differentiate and not as a fixed category. For Derrida, it is an ethical act that assumes an infinite responsibility for the other (what resists meaning and its translatability to linguistic meaning); or creating a style as inventing a possibility of Life, a way of existing in Deleuze's philosophy. As Daniel Smith argues (2007), a Deleuzian-Spinozist immanent philosophy of ethics can no longer take the form of "what must I do?" as an irreducible (political or institutional) responsibility tied to fixed concepts or ideas but "what can I do? Given my degree of power what are my capabilities and capacities? How can I go to the limit of what I can do?" (2007: 67), thus relating ethics to a power or capacity to affect and be affected, in a rhizomic, non-dialectical schema. Writing is not the repetition of concepts that fix meaning but a praxis: a simultaneous affecting and being affected, a process of becoming and a testing of the limits of our faculties, our concepts and intellectual securities, but also a questioning of concealed assumptions, for a possibility of life to occur. A possibility of life to occur constitutes one of the most urgent feminist and political questions and should assume broader political and existential references (e.g., Arendt's argument that natality may be the central category of political thought) outside feminist concerns around motherhood and the maternal that risk reinserting the institution of Oedipus and of nuclear family.

5. Becoming-Minoritarian as the Only Political Possibility

"We lack resistance to the present" Deleuze and Guattari claim (1994: 108). Such resistance against the major language(s) and phallologocentrism cannot take the form of ideological debates (around good and bad theory, male vs female philosophers) since such forms keep repeating oedipalized desiring formations of "individual egos" and "groups superegos" as well as accepting a certain distribution of the real into the binary grand schema; neither can resistance be theorized and be reduced to a purely intellectual/

academic task. Against such majoritarian theoretical and linguistic formations (the ideological –*isms*), Deleuze's notion of the "minor" and "becoming-minoritarian in writing" relocates the problem on the level of language and enables a radical criticism through creative resistance. For Deleuze, the critical passes through creativity rather than criticism (in the form of judgments and debates). Creative resistance is the search of a style, and a stylist, Deleuze argues, is someone who creates a foreign language within his/her language. The latter consists of a minor use of the major language with *minor use* meaning a treatment of language that places it in a continuous variation and dislodges it from its constants and major signifiers, in order to extract foreign elements and new linguistic possibilities.

> A minor literature doesn't come from a minor language; it is rather that which a minority constructs within a major language. But the first characteristic of minor literature in any case is that in it language is affected with a high coefficient of deterritorialization. (Deleuze 1986: 16)

A resisting that is posited on the level of writing poses primarily an ethical question: how do we relate to theory and thinking in the act of writing (how in other words, do we theorize and philosophize and how do we use concepts), which also means how do we relate to life and life's differentiating movement? How can we make links between signs, events, and life? And more relevant to feminism: how can we think of sex and sexuality outside dominant concepts of identity?

Schizoanalytic writing as the becoming-minoritarian in one's own language moves us away from the authorial "I" of a molar notion of subjectivity: the woman reproduced as entity fixed in language and into anthropomorphic representations of sex produced by phallologocentric humanism.[6] It invites instead a multiplicity of "molecular combinations bringing into play not only the man in the woman and the woman in the man, but the relation of each to the animal, the plant, etc.: a thousand tiny sexes" (Deleuze and Guattari 2003: 213). Sexuality would no longer be a field governed by moral or symbolic laws, transcendent signifiers and linguistic structures; instead, it constitutes a field of possibilities expressed through molecular becomings, "the becoming-woman of the man and the becoming-animal of the human: an emission of particles" (Deleuze and Guattari 2003: 278). As Elizabeth Grosz has noted, "Sexuality and desire, then, are not fantasies, wishes, hopes, aspirations … but are energies, excitations, impulses, actions, movements, practices, moments, pulses of feeling" (1995: 182). An intensive, material field traversed by an ungendered desire, an interactive game of "real" bodies that produces a writing through the body and not as a separate intellectualist cognitive task; a writing similar to that of Lispector, Cixous, Irigaray, Tsvetaeva, Ingeborg, Acker but also Dostoyevsky, Kafka, Joyce, Beckett. Authorial mouths and voices that dismantle the unity and fixity of the gendered, oedipalized "I" and create a space where desire and the social field do not come under the colonization of Oedipus. Schizoanalytic (social) desire is the desire to escape the code, to de-facialize the body, to release the organs from the gendered organism and make them autonomous and singular rather than invested parts of a phallologocentric culture. Schizoanalytic resistance starts from the intimate and the molecular and effects the world and its organization of powers. The real shift starts on the register of desire and a schizoanalytic feminist writing will set off a critical reconstitution of the future, along with the reconstitution of the ego. It is the form of writing that leaves its home and country, its history (past and present) and the prearranged ties between signifiers and signifieds in search of new forms that invent a new framework of thinking. Writing then as an encounter and not appropriation since "each word has its life, its past, its ego, its self-esteem. It resists" (Dimoula 2012: xi)—writing not as recognition but as movement: translation and invention.

Becoming-minoritarian in language thus takes the form of a stuttering after the demolition of conventions and norms of speaking and writing and, consequently, of methods and categories of thinking. It means to do away with the language of convictions and truths, a language in the direction of meaning, to risk to think outside modes of theorizing that rely on intellectual securities, to abandon a political language of missions and solutions. The minor is truly revolutionary by creating a language of political immediacy that is *mal vu, mal dit*, a writing as an encounter, where the subject (grammatical/syntactical/authorial voice) fails to fully recognize the other and fully articulate themselves in the categories of woman and/or of fixed sexualities. The grammatical and syntactical move *from* the general (categories) *to* the singular as a resistance to bio-governmentality is effected within a confusion of different tongues and on the border of what can(not) be thought or spoken: each pushes the other in an unfamiliar terrain or into a deterritorialization, where one's "essence" and the "essential" is a singular expression, a point of view on the world.

A writing free of social syntactic and tactical obedience will allow the demilitarization of language and the deconstruction of *-isms* and in feminisms. A non-institutionalized language will reclaim back its materiality and desire will circulate and create new unpredictable connections while a thought of transformation will replace reiteration. That could signal a new degree of academic culture that could instantly revolutionize the entire system of human pursuits which will contribute to a rearticulation of questions around desire and sexuality under a new light.

Notes

1. "A School is awful! The ideal is the movement, not at all to have guarantees and signed notions or to have disciples repeating them" (Deleuze in ABECEDAIRE).
2. A language that is not defined by a signifying process.
3. Deleuze and Guattari profoundly interrogate the concepts of identity and subjectivity and the same goes for the image of thought that sustains the former, that is, representational thinking. Whereas representational thinking always departs from already constituted genders and thus repeats the ontological priority given to sameness (a priority present in western thinking since Aristotle), their thinking reverses the relationship between identity and difference. Within this framework oppression, dominance and subjectification are examined in "their ontological

determinations and representative functions" (Olkowski 1999: 2) and not in their secondary expressions, so that the issue is no longer what is the best political identity for us, so as to think of sexual differences, but how to think outside identities and representations without falling into silence and political aphasia.

4. I am referring here to language as the system of *Langue* or the realm of Symbolic in Lacanian terms.

5. "The shame of being a man—is there any better reason to write?" (Deleuze 1997: 1).

6. "What we term molar entity is, for example, the woman as defined by her form, endowed with organs and functions and assigned as subject" (Deleuze and Guattari 2003: 275).

References

Alcoff L., and E. Potter (eds.) (2013), *Feminist Epistemologies*, London: Routledge.

Attridge, D. (2017), "Derrida and the Question of Literature," in J. Derrida (ed.), *Acts of Literature*, Routledge.

Arendt, H. (2013), *The Human Condition*, Chicago, IL: University of Chicago Press.

Bergson, H. (2012), *The Creative Mind: An Introduction to Metaphysics*, trans. Maelle L. Andison, New York: Dover Publications.

Cavell, S. (1988), *Conditions Handsome and Unhandsome: The Constitution of Emersonian Perfectionism*, Chicago: University of Chicago Press.

Collins, P. H. (2000), "Black Feminist Epistemology," in *Black Feminist Thought: Knowledge, Consciousness, and the Politics of Empowerment*, 2nd ed., 251–71, New York: Routledge.

Conley, V. A. (1991), *Helene Cixous: Writing the Feminine*, Lincoln, NE: University of Nebraska Press.

Cixous, H. (1994a), *Three Steps on the Ladder of Writing*, New York: Columbia University Press.

Cixous, H. (1994b), "The Laugh of Medusa" in *Cixous Reader*, London: Psychology Press.

Cixous, H. (1999), *The Third Body*, Northwestern University Press.

Deleuze, G. (1986), *Kafka: Toward a Minor Literature*, trans. Dana Polan, Minnesota: University of Minnesota Press.

Deleuze, G., and F. Guattari (1994), *What Is Philosophy?*, New York: Verso Books.

Deleuze, G. (1997), *Essays Critical and Clinical*, trans. D. W. Smith and M. A. Greco, Minneapolis: University of Minnesota.

Deleuze, G. (2004), *Difference and Repetition*, Routledge.

Deleuze, G. (2003), "I'm Going to Have to Wander All Alone," Jacques Derrida, *The Work of Mourning*, Chicago: University of Chicago Press.

Deleuze, G., and F. Guattari (2004), *Anti-Oedipus*, trans. R. Hurley, M. Seem, and H. R. Lane, London: Continuum.

Deleuze G., and F. Guattari (2003), *A Thousand Plateaus—Capitalism and Schizophrenia*, trans. Brian Massumi, London: Bloomsbury.

Derrida, J. (1982), *Positions*, Chicago: University of Chicago Press.

Derrida, J. (1992), *Acts of Literature*, ed. Derek Attridge, New York: Psychology Press.

Derrida, J. (1998), *Of Grammatology*, New York: Johns Hopkins University Press.

Dimoula, K. (2012), *The Brazen Plagiarist—Selected Poems Kiki Dimoula*, trans. C. I. Margellos and R. Lesser, New Haven, CT: Yale University Press.

Emerson, R. W. (1950), *The Complete Essays and Other Writings*, New York: Random House.

Evans, M. (2005), *Killing Thinking*, London: Bloomsbury.

Foucault, M. (2004), "Preface," trans. M. Seem, H. Lane, and R. Hurley *Anti-Oedipus-Capitalism and Schizophrenia*, New York: Verso.

Grosz, E. ([1994] 2001), "A Thousand Tiny Sexes: Feminism and Rhizomatics," in Genosko G. (ed), *Deleuze and Guattari: Critical Assessements of Leading Philosophers*, London: Routledge.

Grosz, E. (1995), *Space, Time and Perversion*, London: Routledge.

Guattari, F. (1996), Soft Subversions, trans. D. L. Sweet and C. Wiener. New York: Semiotext(e).

Guattari, F. (2015), *Lines of Flight: For Another World of Possibilities*, London: Bloomsbury.

Herzo, M. (2000), "Composition on a Multiple Plane: Simone Weil's Answer to the Rule of Necessity," in Robin L. Teske and Mary Ann Tétreault (eds.), *Conscious Acts and the Politics of Social Change*, V1, South Carolina: University of South Carolina Press.

Irigaray, L. (1985), *This Sex which Is Not One*, New York: Cornell University Press.

Lambert, G. (2012), *In Search of a New Image of Thought: Gilles Deleuze and Philosophical Expressionism*, Minnesota: University of Minnesota Press.

Lecercle, J. (2002), *Deleuze and Language*, United Kingdom: Palgrave MacMillan.

Lecercle, J. (2012), *Badiou and Deleuze Read Literature*, Edinburgh: Edinburgh University Press.

Lennon K., and M. Whitoford (2012), *Knowing the Difference: Feminist Perspectives in Epistemology*, Routledge.

Lorde, A. (1984), *Sister Outsider: Essays and Speeches*, United States: Ten Speed Press.

Lykke, N. (2014), *Writing Academic Texts Differently: Intersectional Feminist Methodologies and the Playful Art of Writing*, New York: Routledge.

Milroy, J. (November 2001), "Language Ideologies and the Consequences of Standardization," *Journal of Sociolinguistics* 5 (4): 530–55.

Morish L. (2018), "Can Critical University Studies Survive the Toxic University?," in Critical Legal Thinking, http://criticallegalthinking.com/2018/06/11/can-critical-university-studies-survive-the-toxic-university/ (accessed April 18, 2019).

Olkowski, D. (1999), *Gilles Deleuze and the Ruins of Representation*, California: University of California Press.

Protevi, J. and P. Patton (2003), *Between Deleuze and Derrida*, London: Continuum.

Puar J. (2017), *Terrorist Assemblages: Homonationalism in Queer Times*, Durham, NC: Duke University Press.

Smith, D. (2007), "Deleuze and the Question of Desire," *Parrhesia* 2: 66–78.

Wardle, C. H. (2007), *Beyond Ecriture Feminine*, MHRA texts and dissertations.

Warner M. (2014), "Diary," *London Review of Books* 36 (17): 442–3.

Winn J., and R. Hall (2017), *Mass Intellectuality and Democratic Leadership in Higher Education*, London: Bloomsbury.

PART FOUR
REDRAWING AESTHETIC ALLIANCES

Figure 12.1 *"Un-poetic femininity (1)," 2015, Eyeshadow powder, dried rose petal, Inkjet flyer prints with a full gloss coating, Photographic Installation, Mihee Jeon*

Figure 12.2 *"Un-poetic femininity (2)," 2015, Eyeshadow powder, dried rose petal, Inkjet flyer prints with a full gloss coating, Photographic Installation, Mihee Jeon*

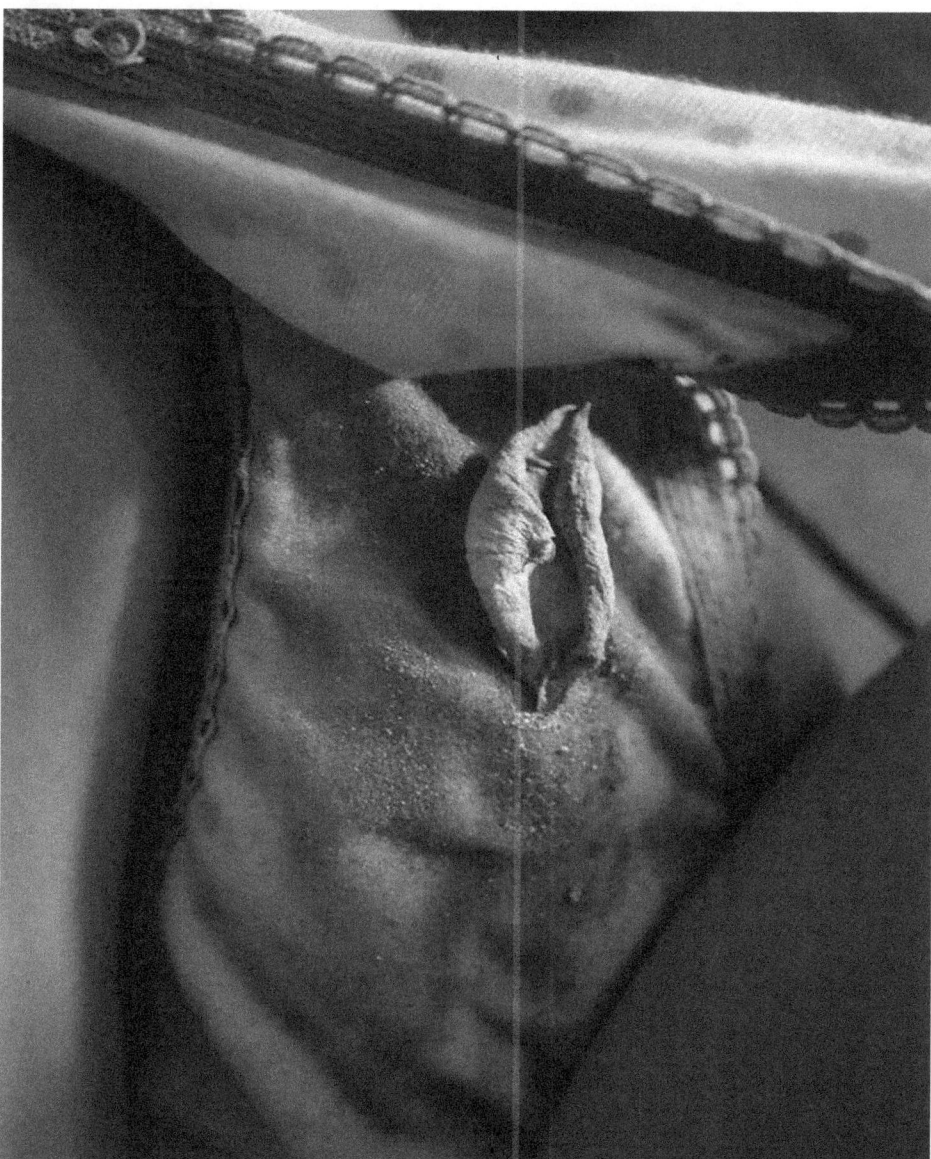

Figure 12.3 *"Un-poetic femininity (3)," 2015, Eyeshadow powder, dried rose petal, Inkjet flyer prints with a full gloss coating, photographic installation, Mihee Jeon*
This work represents the status of objectified femininity. Artist Mihee Jeon deliberately sprinkled eyeshadow powder and made an image by putting a dried rose petal on a pair of panties which describes a particular way of metaphorical props to convey the meaning of the vagina and woman's objectified status. She captured the passive angle of "being gazed" in the photograph. The installation calls attention to the ubiquity of objectifying femininity, like so many discarded magazine flyers, while the close-up emphasizes artifice and delicate intimacy of that which is expected to be silent and unexposed.

CHAPTER 12
AFFECTIVE ALLIANCES: A FEMINIST SCHIZOANALYSIS OF FEMININE ANXIETY, DIS/ORIENTATION, AND AFFECT ALIENS
Celiese Lypka

1. Introduction

When thinking about feminism and feminist discourse, we are really engaging with a multiplicity of movements. There are many orientations, modes, and connections within feminism. For this reason, my approach to feminist theory and praxis focuses on the bodies that make up this multiplicity. As a literary scholar, I read the ways that bodies feel and move in the world, as well as the affective engagements and creations that come from these movements: asking how bodies are orientated to other bodies, objects, and spaces; reading those bodies through different modes of being and varying degrees of im/mobility; and analyzing the ways in which affect unfolds in the "in-between-ness" of those relations. This follows Deleuze and Guattari's Spinozist approach from *A Thousand Plateaus*, where they ask what can a body *do*: "We know nothing about a body until we know what it can do, in other words, what its affects are, how they can or cannot enter into composition with other affects, with the affects of another body, either to destroy that body or to be destroyed by it, either to exchange actions and passions with it or to join with it in composing a more powerful body" (1987: 257). When paired with literary analysis, as Deleuze and Guattari often undertake in their own work, this questioning of bodies complicates the role of literature, positioning it a desiring-machine that creates affective relations and contagions through readings and inhabitations of various bodies. In this way, literature becomes an active agent, composing productive and/or destructive spaces not only for the characters on the pages but for the readers as well a space in which rhizomatic encounters hold the capacity to affect and be affected.

While there are obviously a chaotic myriad of ways in which to explore the affective un/foldings of how bodies move within composed literary spaces, I am particularly interested in reading the ways in which feminine bodies are aligned with an affective anxiousness. As such, this essay considers anxiety not in a strictly psychoanalytic sense but rather as an affect that proliferates and interacts with the body. Although not an essential concept to feminism, I want to consider how anxiety can circulate in feminist theory as shame, fear, and, most specifically, a feeling of unease. This positioning of affective anxiety invites us to think about the body in specific ways: what does it mean to be uneasy in one's own body and the world, more generally? What does it mean for one's orientation to bodies, objects, and the world to be constructed in relationship to a sense of unease? Can we argue, as I plan to, that feminine experience is often oriented in relation to anxiety, which manifests as a feeling of unease with one's identification or mis/alignment with normative inscriptions of the feminine subject? In a sense, this interrogation of feminine anxiousness reads the ways in which physical and/or psychological discomfort (through a mismatch between one's self and one's environment) reveals itself in literature through various considerations of the feminine experience. Deleuze and Guattari are not particularly invested in an analysis of feminism and anxiety—although they do provide a rereading of Freud's notion of anxiety through psychoanalysis as it pertains to social production in *Anti-Oedipus*. However, through the invocation of affect theory from noted feminist scholar Sara Ahmed, I argue that affective alienation as a form of generative force can be brought together with a schizoanalytic understanding of the literary machine to form a productive feminist alliance. Strikingly, both Deleuze and Guattari and Ahmed offer readings of Virginia Woolf's *Mrs. Dalloway*, a novel that is framed through the feminine experience of its eponymous character and is saturated with anxious feelings. This essay will take up these readings of *Mrs. Dalloway* to engage a conversation between schizoanalysis and Ahmed's concept of the affect alien, demonstrating how these seemingly divergent approaches assemble by harnessing the power of feminine marginality to disrupt the social order, in turn unleashing a thoroughly schizoanalytic aim that releases a revolutionary feminine desire.

2. An Unlikely Alliance

Let's begin by considering, as this collection poses, what might a Deleuzian feminism or a feminist schizoanalysis look like? In her first monograph, *Differences that Matter: Feminist Theory and Postmodernism*, Ahmed briefly considers the possibility of a Deleuzian feminism. Her thoughts, which focus on a critical rereading of the contentious relationship between feminism and the concept "becoming-woman," consider what would be at stake for feminism if it were to adopt a Deleuzoguattarian lens:

> My own reading is not motivated by issues of "belonging" does feminism "belong" inside or outside the texts of Deleuze and Guattari (should feminism become Deleuzian?)? Such a question assumes that feminism can be fixed in a singular place and that feminism has, so to speak, a proper object and trajectory (often a curiously modern narrative of progress is in play here, whereby feminism is liberated—perhaps by Deleuze and Guattari, or by post-modernism in general— from its embarrassing roots in modernity). In so far as I am not interested in questions of belonging, I am not interested in authorising what some might call a "Deleuzian feminism" ... This model of Deleuze and Guattari "helping" feminism

is not a particularly enabling one; it positions them as the subjects who can *authorise* a "better" space for feminist critical thinking. (Ahmed 1998: 69–70)

Ahmed's voiced concerns of incorporating feminism within the theoretical framework of Deleuze and Guattari "to 'help' feminism discover its own identity" are valid (1998: 73). And her writing here raises some important questions. How can we speak of a singular Deleuzian feminism? How can we speak of a white, male text as a "master-discourse" that helps to provide a "better space for feminist critical thinking" (1998: 73)? How do we speak about the *"phantasmatic"* figure of woman—of becoming-woman as the phantasy of otherness by mostly male subjects in order to overcome himself (his borders) through a becoming-other—with a feminist tongue?

Despite this voicing of a feminist skepticism when it comes to the postmodern narrativization of becoming-woman, Ahmed is not outright dismissive of a potential alliance—although she is careful to note that the alliance is not an automatic one—between schizoanalysis and feminism. Rather, in her close reading of *A Thousand Plateaus*, Ahmed notes her feeling of "a hesitation, a sense of anxiety" that causes one to pause and ask questions that demand a critical rethinking of what's at work in a text so as to "[release] new possibilities for interpretation" (1999: 47, 49). This creative re-reading practice is, in and of itself, very Deleuzian. However, without fixating on Ahmed's reading of Deleuze and Guattari—which frames becoming as an act of privileged agency rather than an immanent event that happens to an (organic or inorganic) body in a continuous creative process that problematizes structures and relations instead of simply producing a stagnant narrativization of becoming-other—I want to consider the generative ways in which Deleuze and Guattari and Ahmed speak with one another. This essay is not aimed at adding to feminist readings of becoming-woman, nor is it interested in discussing a single Deleuzian feminism or the liberation of feminism through Deleuze and Guattari— as if such a thing might be possible. Rather, this essay attempts to read the echoes and alliances that might be built between schizoanalysis and Ahmed's work on feminism and affect theory. Thus, the following will enact an application of the ways in which Deleuze and Ahmed speak of certain orientations and movements as creative, world-making processes that infuses feminism with a future-orientated flux of potentiality—indeed, a practice of feminist schizoanalysis.

Elizabeth Grosz was asked in an interview to comment on the "affective turn" in feminism and how she envisions a Deleuzian-Spinozist understanding of affectivity to be beneficial to the future of feminist theory. She responded by noting the relationality of feminist affect theory to a largely phenomenological approach—the "intentional structure of affect and emotions" (Kontturi and Tiainen 2007: 252)—which inevitably led the interviewers to inquire about Grosz's thoughts on Ahmed's work:

What [Ahmed] is looking at are the various emotions and the appropriate and inappropriate objects to which they are directed. But I don't think that Deleuze is interested at all in affects of a subject. And this is his critique of phenomenology. He's interested in that affect that opens us up to what is unliveable, whereas phenomenology is interested only in that which we can live and experience even if it remains the latent structure of our lived experience. (2007: 252)

Despite this dissonance outlined between Deleuze's and Ahmed's approaches to affect and phenomenology, I want to argue that these positions are not as incompatible as Grosz suggests. Even if Deleuze is more interested in "the intensities which are unliveable by the subject and which open the subject up to an inhuman power" (2007: 252), there is substantial complicity between the unliveable and the organized subject: "[T]he two are constantly interfering, reacting upon one each other" (Deleuze and Guattari 1987: 196). Indeed, how can we speak of the affective force of the unliveable without addressing the everyday affect of subjects and objects? After all, the unliveable and lived experience are an interrelation of reciprocal determination, despite their divergent lines' (the virtual and the actual) differing orientations. As Deleuze writes in *Difference and Repetition*, "Every object [organic and inorganic] is double without it being the case that the two halves resemble one another, one being a virtual image and the other an actual image. They are unequally odd halves" (1994: 109–10). Since the unliveable is the potential immanence within the lived experience of singular forces their interests inevitably, and unavoidably, overlap.

What's more, this co-imbrication between the virtual and the actual, between the unliveable event and everyday lived experience, resides in the actualization of the subject/object: "[I]ndividuation ensures the embedding of the two dissimilar halves" (Deleuze 1994: 280). Thus, though Ahmed is speaking of affect and phenomenology from a different position than Deleuze and Guattari, there is a potential correspondence between their approaches to the dis/orientation of subjects, objects and affect. Both offer a philosophy of affect and relations in-relation to a body. As previously noted, Deleuze and Guattari famously address in their work the Spinozist question of "What can a body do?" (1987: 256). Ahmed works through feminist thought as a series of movements and connections in and between bodies by examining how "a body is in contact with a world" (2017: 22). My interest in an alliance between these two frameworks resides in the space between lived experiences and the unliveable and how this tension might be utilized by feminist theory to work through heteropatriarchal problems between bodies and orientations. Ahmed's feminist inquiry, like Deleuze and Guattari, views problems as generative; "they prompt us to new thoughts, new actions and new modes of being" (Stark 2016: 2), to think thoughts differently. In both cases, the theoretical frameworks are orientated toward creating new ways of living as a process of unsettling through "world-making" projects, in which a reading of relations, affects, and bodies allows for the potentiality of producing a new engagement—to create the world anew. Deleuze and Guattari outline schizoanalysis as a political process of interrogating norms and creating new becomings as a process of world making: "It is in this sense that becoming-everybody/everything, making the world a becoming, is to world, *to make a world or worlds*" (1987: 280). Similarly, Ahmed approaches "feminism as a building project: if our texts are worlds, they need to be made out of feminist materials. Feminist theory is *world making*" (2017: 14; emphasis added).

3. Feminine Experience and Anxious Relations

As theories of interrogation and desire for productive engagements and becomings through world making projects, these frameworks provide an excellent opportunity to explore the orientation of feminine experience and feelings of anxiousness. But what is the connection is there an alliance between woman and anxiety? Certainly, in a Western socio-historical context, to be woman is to live as an othered subject inscribed by the patriarchal order. It is to feel, whether consciously or unconsciously, displaced by the policing of the female body and behavior through a highly contrived and often contradictory image of what femininity should be. It is to know the uncertainty and fear of a marginal existence. And, if womanhood is aligned with anxiety, how much more anxious, then, is the position of an ambiguous feminine subject—a woman whose relation to her body (to maternity and sexuality) troubles normative definitions of the feminine? How might such an ambiguous woman express herself under the strictures of a patriarchal society? Is it possible for a subject that is not only stratified by a dominant social order, but also self-regulates through anxiety and shame in relation to those social structures, to dismantle her constructed subjecthood in order to unfold her self? Investigating these questions combines the schizoanalysis of Deleuze and Guattari with Ahmed's feminist theory to consider how alliances of affective philosophy can unsettle dominant modes of gender, sexuality, and power. This introduces an attempt to reorient the anxiety attached to the female body toward a mobilizing affect, where doubly marginalized subjects (through both womanhood and nonconformity) openly resist positions prescribed by patriarchal structures through iterations of divergent femininity and world making—which Deleuze and Guattari explore through becoming and the figure of the girl and Ahmed addresses thorough willful subjects, specifically the figure of the affect alien.

Returning to a literary approach, let's consider the ways in which literature can reorient anxiety into a creative movement of affective alliance that reframes the feminine as a productive and positive multiplicity. In writing female characters from double marginalized spaces within the larger structures of a male-dominated society, authors open up for their female characters the possibility of expressing an alternative space of feminine potentiality that establishes itself in contrast to systems of male dominate social orders. Through these narratives, characters compose affective spaces in which their lives and emotions disrupt established structures by voicing and then re-orientating their marginalized positions. This analysis establishes Ahmed's concept of the affect alien, a figure who challenges notions of patriarchal contrived femininity, highlighting those who do not conform to normative structures of femininity and female sexuality, or accept the conditional autonomy allotted to the female position: "[W]hen you are alienated by virtue of how you are affected, you are an affect alien ... [you] are not made happy by the right things" (Ahmed 2017: 57). Moreover, recognizing the dynamic interaction with social structures and writing subjectivity, these divergent female characters illustrate Deleuze and Guattari's concepts of crossing thresholds, undoing power structures, and creating new spaces of possibility through the affective drive of marginal positions. This, they contend, is how "one becomes revolutionary; rather, by using a number of minority elements, by connecting, conjugating them, one invents a specific, unforeseen, autonomous be-coming" (1987: 106). Through a literary feminist schizoanalysis, we can see how authors might harness the power of feminine marginality in order to construct radical spaces where women not only exist but also thrive under a new feminine position that troubles the boundaries of normative womanhood.

For Deleuze, literary space offers a unique opportunity "[t]o leave, to escape, to draw a line" of flight as a creative action that connects with and explores the virtual world that is yet to unfold; after all, "One only discovers worlds after a long, broken flight" (Deleuze and Parnet 1977: 36). Ahmed also notes the space of literature as a singular form to incite world making: "[F]eminist communities [are] shaped by passing books around; the sociality of their lives is part of the sociality of ours. There are so many ways that feminist books change hands; in passing between us, they change each of us" (2017: 17). In this way, both frameworks see literature as a space in which not only subjects enact affective movements and becomings but also the ways in which those spaces can infiltrate the world, creating a new future both inside and outside the text. As Claire Colebrook outlines, this is a double becoming in literature: "To become through writing is to create an event; it is to think becoming not as the becoming of some being … but the presentation of becoming itself, a becoming that then effects certain modes of being" (2000: 6). Thus, let's look more closely at a literary becoming that enables a new mode of being, examining how the overwhelming feeling of anxiety that saturates certain texts is combated by ambiguous female characters who come to recognize their position as an affect alien and (in various ways) explore their new orientations to the world, creating new worlds through their movements. While many authors and texts might be examined through this feminist schizoanalysis of feminine anxiety, dis/orientation, and affect aliens, the remainder of this essay will turn to a consideration of Virginia Woolf as an author of feminine expressions and anxious feelings.

Colebrook opens her introduction to the collection *Deleuze and Feminist Theory* with a consideration of Woolf's impression on Deleuze and Guattari: "Throughout *A Thousand Plateaus* Deleuze and Guattari invoke Virginia Woolf's style of writing as exemplary of a new mode of becoming … Her writings neither express nor represent an already given female identity; rather, through Woolf's stream-of-consciousness technique, identity is seen as the effect of a flow of speech" (2000: 1–2). As Colebrook observes, they find in Woolf's experimental modernist writing the ability to create "two dynamic movements," both the molar politics of subjectivity and the molecular politics of activation and confrontation, which together unfold to reveal a rhizomatic world. Briefly, in their tenth plateau, Deleuze and Guattari specifically comment on *Mrs. Dalloway* as a novel composed of haecceities and becomings. Ahmed is also "curious" about Woolf's *Mrs. Dalloway*, which she reads as a feminist companion text that enables one "to proceed on a path less travelled" (2017: 44, 16). Both readings of the novel offer a confrontation of the double politics of structures and organizations of feminine subjectivity, however it is when we apply schizoanalysis to a feminist reading of the novel that the subtle articulations of a resistance to the structures of femininity through a molecular activation or affective displacement open up a new space for feminist consideration.

4. Reading *Mrs. Dalloway*

Set over a single day in the middle of June, *Mrs. Dalloway* follows an ordinary day in the life of Clarissa Dalloway as she prepares for a party she is hosting that evening. As a wife, mother, and society hostess, Clarissa's daily rhythms appear to be organized around specific roles and expectations that compose her sense of self under the strictures of normative femininity—she is an assemblage of organized molarity. However, Woolf quickly complicates this sense of Clarissa as the opening pages of the novel depict her navigating the busy streets of London to purchase flowers for the party. While in the streets of London, Clarissa's inner stream-of-consciousness oscillates between feelings of distracted assurance in her objectives and an anxious sense of unease. There is tension in her movements and affective connections with the exhilarating city streets and characters she encounters. In this first section of the novel devoted specifically to Clarissa's experience, Woolf demonstrates the inherent alignment between the feminine experience and anxiety. In a matter of moments, Clarissa moves from feeling at one with the direction of people and objects surrounding her, to a self-conscious questing over whether she was wearing the right hat for that time of day, to a complete disavowal of herself:

> But often now this body she wore ... this body, with all its capacities, seemed nothing—nothing at all. She had the oddest sense of being herself invisible; unseen; unknown; there being no more marrying, no more having of children now, but only this astonishing and rather solemn progress with the rest of them, up Bond Street, this being Mrs. Dalloway; not even Clarissa anymore; *this being Mrs. Richard Dalloway*. (Woolf 1925: 52; emphasis added)

This passage reveals how Clarissa is both anxious of her role as hostess for her organized sense of self—which leads her to constantly question if she is rising to meet the demands of this feminine role—as well as anxious over her misalignment with inscriptions of femininity—the fact that she does not envision her true self to be the role she takes on as Mrs. Richard Dalloway.

In her reading of the novel, Ahmed focuses primarily on this moment of being Mrs. Richard Dalloway and how this misalignment with normative feminine social roles positions Clarissa as an affect alien. The entire novel, for Ahmed, is saturated with a palpable sadness that surrounds Clarissa's discovery that her life is not her own but rather a "solemn process" with the rest of the world that is attended to following normative prescriptions and patterns under a heteropatriarchal society. This moment of Clarissa's realization that she is "not even Clarissa anymore," which Ahmed refers to as "the becoming of Mrs. Dalloway," is actually "the un-becoming" or disappearance of Clarissa:

> Becoming Mrs. Dalloway is itself a form of disappearance: to follow the paths of life (marriage, reproduction) is to feel that what is before you is a kind of solemn progress, as if you are living someone else's life, simply going the same way others are going. It is as if you have left the point of life behind you, as if your life is going through motions that were already in motion before you even arrived. (2017: 71)

Ahmed reads the movements of Clarissa as she becomes aware of the trajectory of her own life—as wife, mother, and "the perfect hostess"—to be a moment of disappearance or destruction (like the line of suicide) that has left her with the inability to recognize her own self. In this pause of reflection, is it not so much that her molar aggregates are regulated through a sense of sadness: remember the molar is not "a bad line" nor is it necessarily destructive in its organization that pervades daily life (Deleuze and Guattari 1987: 195). Rather, Clarissa appears to be affected in this moment by a force that breaks the natural rhythms of her molar self (as wife, mother, hostess), opening up a space in which she feels disconnected from her molar territory. Thus, Clarissa exposes the misalignment of happiness in relation to reference points, such as the role of wife, mother, hostess, that should, under societal expectations, produce a feeling of happiness.

As such, Clarissa clearly exposes herself in this moment as being misaligned with the normative structures that are supposed to produce a feeling of satisfaction or happiness; she is the affect alien. Ahmed's analysis of willful subjects, in all their various iterations (the feminist killjoy, the affect alien, the unhappy queer, etc.), aligns with the precarious position of the ambiguous feminine subject who troubles the idea of femininity; she unfolds radical potential in her choice to express a divergent mode of feminine being. As Ahmed states, "[w]hen we feel pleasure from such [normative happy] objects, we are aligned; we are facing the right way. We become alienated—out of line with an affective community—when we do not experience pleasure from proximity to objects that are already attributed as being good" (2017: 37). Thus, the affect alien is one who becomes alienated from the patriarchal position of woman as wife and mother, since she refuses to "share an orientation towards certain things as being good because she does not find the objects that promise happiness to be quite so promising" (39). Indeed, this is where the political work of feminine anxiety, dis/orientation, and affect aliens intersect: "Disorientation involves failed orientations: bodies inhabit spaces that do not extend their shape, or use objects that do not extend their reach. At this moment of failure, a here becomes strange" (133)—spaces, thus, become anxious and/or uneasy. Ahmed notes how this feeling of anxious displacement, of not feeling aligned with orientations that should lead to a feeling of happiness or satisfaction, often leads one to discover "a world opening up" (132). Through this, Ahmed speaks of the shifting movement away from a desire for happiness toward a feeling of aliveness, as an "alternative to the social value of happiness" that is promised by orienting oneself toward normative inscriptions (78). It is very much a line of flight and escape: "To leave happiness for life is to become alive to possibility" (79).

This is precisely what Woolf has done in *Mrs. Dalloway*; she has opened Clarissa up to the possibility of leaving the structures of normative life and her molar femininity for the potential that comes from being *alive* to the molecular. Thus, despite the novel's prolonged vision of Clarissa as an anxiously inscribed woman, Woolf offers at the end of the novel a moment of disruption that opens up a new space of potential for Clarissa—through her encounter with Septimus Warren Smith's death that interrupts her rhythms in the middle of her party—which then reorients the feminine anxiety that structures her life. Indeed, there are several moments within the novel where Woolf exposes Clarissa to molecular forces that open her up to a feeling of interconnection that temporarily eases the feminine anxiousness that pervades her natural rhythms—where Clarissa intersects with molecular lines of flight. These moments most often occur when she is in the streets of London, and Deleuze and Guattari gesture to these molecular intensities:

> Taking a walk is a haecceity; never again will Mrs. Dalloway say to herself, "I am this, I am that, he is this, he is that." And "She felt very young; at the same time unspeakably aged. She sliced like a knife through everything; at the same time was outside, looking on ... She always had the feeling that it was very, very dangerous to live even one day." Haecceity, fog, glare. A haecceity has neither beginning nor end, origin nor destination; it is always in the middle. It is not made of points, only of lines. It is a rhizome. (1987: 263)

These moments spark what Deleuze and Guattari describe as a creative movement toward a line that "is very different from the previous [molar] one; it is a line of molecular or supple segmentation" which takes "detours" from the temporality of daily life and crosses over into new thresholds by exposing "the existence of another [molecular] life" (1987: 196). These molecular intensities reveal a shift away from the molar mode of being, of falling in step with the normative rhythms of daily life. Although not spoken as a moment of opening up to a "quanta of deterritorialization" (1987: 196), Ahmed is also interested in the affective impulses that cause one to feel a disorientation to organized systems of life—a pressing force or "insistence to go against the flow" of the crowd (2017: 82).

However, Ahmed does not read these moments of creative movement in *Mrs. Dalloway*—or if she does, she does not comment on them in her analysis. Instead, for Ahmed the scene in which Clarissa learns of Septimus's suicide is the crucial exchange in which Clarissa realizes that the suffering she feels in life, a suffering that she also reads in Septimus despite never physically meeting him, is not an unbearable anchor that ties one to a life of unease and sadness but rather something that can be tossed away in death: "[S]he felt glad he had done it, thrown it away" (Woolf 1925: 194). Learning of Septimus's suicide in the middle of her party brings Clarissa to another disruption or pause in her rhythms. The encounter is so shocking that she momentarily leaves the party, stepping into a side room to contemplate the enormity of Septimus's suffering alongside his attempt to communicate through suicide: "There was an embrace in death" (1925: 192). This alliance that grows between Clarissa and Septimus as she finds herself feeling "somehow very like him" while she imagines his death (1925: 192), completely disorients her sense of self in the world. Septimus's death has opened up a space of affective alliance in which Clarissa feels the world a new. Thinking through how he must have done the act and what his body would have felt, Clarissa muses: "Odd, incredibly; she had never been so happy. Nothing could be slow enough; nothing last too long. No pleasure could equal, she thought … the process of living, to find it, with a shock of delight, as the sun rose, as the day sank" (1925: 193). The world unfolds like a haecceity to Clarissa, as a moment of speeds and slowness, as a process of leaving her former territorialized self to become alive through the realization that death ends the anxiousness of one's own unease. Here, as Ahmed notes in her reading of the encounter, "a death becomes real or material because it has been allowed in. A death spreads as words into worlds" (2017: 59). As his death affects her, Clarissa creates a new world through the molecular alliance with Septimus, a world in which new happiness outside of her organized feminine role becomes alive. Ahmed goes on to suggest that "maybe that is why this day matters so much: she was getting ready, to allow her past to flicker with life; she was getting ready to be undone. A seal is broken through a combination of forces. And so, in the middle of her party, something other than happiness happens" (60). What happens is a break or rupture from her anxious femininity to a new mode of being.

But what is this new mode of being; what happens when one breaks from the molar territories of one's former self? How does this reorientation to the body and world unfold? Under schizoanalysis, one can be reterritorialized, deterritorialized, or continue on toward imperceptibility. For Clarissa, and as I argue for a schizoanalysis of feminine anxiousness more generally, if the affective unease outlined here is only experienced in relation to a coherent narrative of heteronormative feminine subjects, then subjects only become aligned or misaligned as an affect alien when engaging with ideal notions of femininity. Thus, embracing the possibility of chaotic, infinitely multiple and mobile forces of subjects/subjectivity moves one toward a future oriented "politics of imperceptibility." As per Grosz, the politics of imperceptibility is a Deleuzian prepersonal force "in which inhuman forces, forces that are both living and non-living, macroscopic and microscopic, above and below the human, are acknowledged and allowed to displace the centrality of will and consciousness" (2002: 270). This leads to an unpredictable world, rather than a simple restructuring or replacement of the world under heteropatriarchal structures: the world becomes truly radical. This world is unfixed, constantly in flux and disruptive, a process-politics that generates new problems to create a new future for feminism that is unknowable and productive. This is the future world making that potentially aligns the work of Ahmed with Deleuze and Guattari. A feminism that "produce[s] knowledges, techniques, methods, practices that bring out the best in ourselves, that enable us to overcome ourselves, that open us up to the embrace of an unknown open-ended future, that brings into existence new kinds of beings, new kinds of subjects, and new relations to objects" (Grosz 2011: 75). In destroying and overcoming ourselves in this moment, we compose new possibilities of generative power.

Clarissa has accomplished just that at the end of the novel; she has composed a new way of being and a new set of relations that reorients her body and movements in the world. It is important to note that after the scene where Clarissa contemplates Septimus's suicide, she reenters the room of the party in order to "assemble" (Woolf 1925: 193). But this is not an assembly of her former self; it is an assembly of a new multiplicity of imperceptibility. The scene in which Clarissa experiences an alliance with Septimus is the last connection the reader has with her inner consciousness; although Woolf emphasizes the image of Clarissa returning to the party before the next section begins, "she came in from the little room" (1925: 193), there is no further physical image of or internal insight from Clarissa—she remains unperceivable for the remainder of the novel. It is not that she has disappeared in a way similar to Ahmed's reading of the disappearance of Clarissa when she performs her role as "Mrs. Richard Dalloway." Nor is it the same affective impulse as her previous odd feeling "of being herself invisible; unseen; unknown" (1925: 52). Rather, Clarissa is, for the first time in the novel, not detectable to other characters, primarily her former beau Peter Walsh. Peter—who has consistently reterritorialized Clarissa throughout the novel in his desire to stratify her under the role of "perfect hostess" (1925: 49), an inscription that causes her the most anxiety in relation to her feminine role—finds himself at the party unable to determine Clarissa: " 'But where is Clarissa?' said Peter. He was sitting on the sofa with Sally ... 'Where's the woman gone to?' he asked. 'Where's Clarissa?' " (1925: 194). Clarissa has created a new, unknowable world, something future oriented and creatively destructive to her previous anxious self that was "composed so for the world" (1925: 75): an unfolding of her becoming-imperceptible—resonating with Žukauskaitė's vision of new ways of being in Chapter 2 of this volume, "The Deleuzian Notion of Becoming Imperceptible and New Postfeminist Strategies."

5. Schizo-Feminist World Makings

Becoming imperceptible creates a world, or more precisely "[paints] the world on oneself, not oneself on the world" (Deleuze and Guattari 1987: 200). In her becoming imperceptible, Clarissa is now a continual process of abstract lines that makes everything, everyone, the whole world a becoming. Despite the final sentence in the novel "For there she was" (Woolf 1925: 200) Clarissa has dismantled the composition of herself as an anxious feminine subject. This sentence, which comes from an unlocatable utterance that is only able to speak of Clarissa through the single pronoun of "she," reinforces the fact that Clarissa has not disappeared utterly from the text into an invisible force but rather that she has become unrecognizable in relation to her former self. Deleuze and Guattari contend that pronouns "in no way take the place of the subject, but instead do away with any subject [form] in favor of an assemblage of the haecceity type" (1987: 265).

Clarissa as territorialized anxious feminine subject has ceased to be surveyed, stratified or assignable. Though physically absent for the remainder of the novel, Clarissa permeates everything, no longer contained by the subjectivity of her form or role as Mrs. Richard Dalloway, she spreads out across the room in the interactions and memories of her party guests; she has successfully created a new world through her gift of the party. Deleuze and Guattari state that this is precisely what becoming-imperceptible, becoming-everybody, entails: "[f]or everybody/everything is the molar aggregate, but becoming everybody/everything is another affair, one that brings into play the cosmos with its molecular components. Becoming everybody/everything (*toute le monde*) is to world (*faire monde*), to make a world (*faire un monde*)" (1987: 280). Clarissa has painted a new world on herself, a world of blocks of sensation and interconnectivity: an alliance between disorientation and creative world making.

Clarissa's becoming imperceptible exposes literature's ability to open up a space in which to interrogate and re-orientate the affective structures that support anxious womanhood. Moreover, through a feminist schizoanalysis of the alliance between lived experience and the unliveable moments of the virtual, *Mrs. Dalloway* reveals how literature provides a movement toward a creative and productive new world. As Ahmed notes, "The materials are books, yes, but they are also spaces of encounter; how we are touched by things; how we touch things" and these encounters create moments of interrogation that moves us forward to a new future (2017: 17). Critically, it must be noted that while Deleuze and Guattari's and Ahmed's projects are in many respects future-orientated they are not uncritical of the world-making process; they offer a recognition of the possibility of a liberated future, not a guarantee, and they both acknowledge that new problems will always emerge in this new world to continue the process of disorientation and world making. The molecular or imperceptible does not prevail the molar, nor does the affect alien experience something greater than those around her; however, the movements of both the molecular and the affect alien have the ability to rupture established structures and open up new creative modes. The resonances between the language and notions of schizoanalysis and Ahmed's feminist project is more than an interesting point of convergence; it demonstrates that their encounter composes productive new thoughts and challenges for feminism.

In her conclusion to *The Promise of Happiness*, Ahmed considers Deleuze's concept of the "good" encounter (through Spinoza) as a way of offering "alternative" ways of seeing in accordance with happiness—perhaps happiness is not always active or good and unhappiness in not always passive or bad. A footnote to this section explains that her reading "is not intended as a negative critique but instead a different angle on the processes Deleuze is describing" (2010: 278). Here we see how the two frameworks are aligned in a similar project of complicating systems and relations; how despite the hesitation that resides between the two approaches, they are both invested in interrogating structures as a way to offer an alternative vision of the future, of seeing the radical potential that resides in feelings of disorientation and unease. Following Ahmed's claim that "[w]e are moved by things. And in being moved, we make things" (2007: 25), this essay unfolds a new investigation of literary- and desiring-machines to create an affective alliance between schizoanalysis and feminism, demonstrating how literature can reorient anxiety into a creative movement that reframes the feminine as a productive and positive multiplicity, working through the tension of lived experience and the unliveable. The crucial project of this alliance becomes visible through the intersection of disorientation from affect aliens and becoming imperceptible to expose and create new spaces of possibility for the future. In this way, Clarissa's encounter demonstrates the experience of feminine marginality and anxiety as something contagious and relational, a necessity for world making. Moreover, Clarissa's ambiguous presence at the end of the novel—revealed only as an utterance, "For there she was" (1925: 200)—reaffirms feminist schizoanalysis as a productive mode that can (and will) return again and again to contemplate and procure new problems for a radical and generative future.

Bibliography

Ahmed, S. (1998), *Differences that Matter: Feminist Theory and Postmodernism*, Cambridge: Cambridge University Press.

Ahmed, S. (1999), "Phantasies of Becoming (the Other)," *European Journal of Cultural Studies* 2 (1): 47–63.

Ahmed, S. (2010), *The Promise of Happiness*, Durham, NC: Duke University Press.

Ahmed, S. (2017), *Living a Feminist Life*, Durham, NC: Duke University Press.

Braidotti, R. (1994), *Nomadic Subjects. Embodiment and Sexual Difference in Contemporary Feminist Theory*, New York: Columbia University Press.

Colebrook, C. (2000), "Introduction," in I. Buchanan and C. Colebrook (eds.), *Deleuze and Feminist Theory*, 1–17, Edinburgh: Edinburgh University Press.

Deleuze, G. (1994), *Difference and Repetition*, trans. Paul Patton, New York: Columbia University Press.

Deleuze, G., and C. Parnet (1977), *Dialogues*, trans. H. Tomlinson and B. Habberjam, New York: Columbia University Press.

Deleuze, G., and F. Guattari (1980), *A Thousand Plateaus: Capitalism and Schizophrenia*, trans. B. Massumi, Minneapolis: University of Minnesota Press.

Deleuze, G., and F. Guattari (1987), *A Thousand Plateaus: Capitalism and Schizophrenia*, trans. B. Massumi, Minneapolis: University of Minnesota Press.

Gilson, E. C. (2011), "Responsive Becoming: Ethics between Deleuze and Feminism," in N. Jun and D. W. Smith (eds.), *Deleuze and Ethics*, 63–88, Edinburgh: Edinburgh University Press.

Grosz, E. (2002), "A Politics of Imperceptibility: A Response to 'Anti-racism, Multiculturalism and the Ethics of Identification,'" *Philosophy & Social Criticism* 28 (4): 463–72.

Grosz, E. (2011), *Becoming Undone: Darwinian Reflections of Life, Politics, and Art*, Durham, NC: Duke University Press.

Kontturi, K., and M. Tiainen (2007), "Feminism, Art, Deleuze, and Darwin: An Interview with Elizabeth Grosz," *Nordic Journal of Women's Studies* 15 (4): 246–56.

Seigworth, G. J., and M. Gregg (eds.) (2010), *The Affect Theory Reader*, Durham, NC: Duke University Press.

Stark, H. (2016), *Feminist Theory after Deleuze*, London: Bloomsbury.

Woolf, V. ([1925] 2013), *Mrs. Dalloway*, ed. Jo-Ann Wallace, Toronto: Broadview, 2013.

CHAPTER 13
ALICE IN WONDERWATER: HYSTERIA, FEMININITY, AND ALLIANCE IN CLINICAL AESTHETICS
Fernanda Negrete

Artistic creation is a clinical undertaking for Deleuze. In his 1981 essay on Francis Bacon's paintings, he explicitly calls for an "aesthetic clinic" or a "clinical aesthetic" (Deleuze 2003: 51, 54), one that had been implied since 1967 when he proposed to examine Sacher-Masoch's writing in its own terms, as an original style where perverse desire takes on a singular form and name:

> It is no accident that the names of two writers were used as labels for these two perversions. The critical (in the literary sense) and the clinical (in the medical sense) may be destined to enter into a new relationship of mutual learning. Symptomatology is always a question of art; the clinical specificities of sadism and of masochism are not separable from the literary values peculiar to Sade and Masoch. (Deleuze 1989: 11)

While Deleuze's interest in perversion and psychosis have led to understanding the relevance of psychiatric references in terms of so-called deviant desire, the question of desire's connection to literary, and, more broadly, aesthetic values is not exclusive to these two psychic structures. Femininity, I contend, is the crucial, shared aspect that makes perversion, psychosis, and hysteria productive, and why becoming-woman in schizoanalysis initiates the transformative movement of all becomings (see Deleuze and Guattari 1987: 277; 279). While Braidotti (2011), Colebrook (2013), and Grosz (1993), have notably stressed both the potential of Deleuzian concepts for feminism as well as the limitations of becoming-woman as a name for the movement of dissipation for all subject-locations that does not preserve the specificity and potential of female sexuality, my reading suggests that the relevance and potential of becoming-woman can be better mobilized by relating it to desire's aesthetic-clinical stakes.

In *Logic of Sense* Deleuze discovers with Carroll, one of the "astonishing diagnosticians" (1990: 237), that "the work of art alone will respond" to the question "what is a little girl?" (289). To tackle this question, which recalls Freud's impasse with female sexuality, Deleuze remains close to psychoanalytic concepts and problems (e.g., the phallus, castration, erogenous zones, partial objects), while introducing the ideas of the event, surfaces, and sense as Alice's original solutions. To cite Braidotti, Deleuze embraces the "joyful laughter" of Alice proclaiming "it is all a pack of cards and the emperor is naked," a stance resonant with radical feminism (2011: 245–6).

Yet there is potential, for both the expansion of schizoanalysis and radical feminism, in the clinical dimension of the question of the little girl, which is bound up with the singularity of the work of art.[1] To illuminate this potential, I will explore *Wonderwater: Alice Offshore* (2004), a project in which American artist Roni Horn collected *the titles* of her photography, sculpture, and drawings throughout the years to place them, alphabetically, in a book, each becoming the heading of an otherwise blank page.[2] Horn then proposed that this book be freely annotated by four feminist artists who work in different media: Louise Bourgeois, Anne Carson, Hélène Cixous, and John Waters. Carson and Cixous are writers of both fiction (in English and French, respectively) and feminist literary criticism (of ancient Greek and modern English, respectively). Bourgeois's field is closest to Horn's, although the latter, born 1955, is a generation younger (Bourgeois's sculpture, installation, and graphic works appeared between the 1940s and 2010). Waters is a camp film director and an art collector. Through original feminist tactics, their collective writing brings hysteria and delirium into clinic-aesthetic focus, taking these relevant elements of schizoanalysis in unprecedented, uncodified directions, as indicated by the title's displacement of *Alice* from Carroll's Wonderland to Wonder*water*.

Deleuze already explores the relationship between the critical and the clinical and a specifically clinical potential of creation in *Nietzsche et la philosophie* (1963). His study adopts the idea of a "transvaluation of all values" as a key to creation and, decisively, to a different criterion for health than the one offered by medical discourse.[3] Such a criterion for health would be, as the citation on Masoch states, inextricable from aesthetic values that may be completely at odds with both social norms and pleasure.[4] Aesthetic values can only be transmitted in stylistic singularities, which are revolutionary, for they introduce into the world unprecedented "proper names" (Deleuze 2002: 79; 120–1). In the late *Essays Critical and Clinical*, Deleuze adds that "literature appears as an enterprise of health" insofar as the writer has "seen and heard things too big for him (*sic*), too strong for him, suffocating things, whose passage exhausts him, while nonetheless giving him the *becomings* that a dominant and substantial health would render impossible" (2005: 3) The clinical effects of art and literature consist, then, in the becomings they enable, triggering the transversal movement of desire that undermines identity and homeostasis. The health underlying a clinic that results in such uncontained flow of desire is decidedly unconcerned with reestablishing the quiet functioning of physiological systems and organs. Instead, the transvaluation of values affirms passages of intensities that continually transform bodies and environments. Like Freud, the schizoanalyst recognizes a positive value in delirium or delusion (*délire*).[5] Far from inanity, delirium, in both psychoanalysis and schizoanalysis, offers a glimpse at the unique sense of an unrecognized, real experience working in a body and a society. This is desire's raw material and its distinction from the calculations of an ego, which remain caught within its civilization's prescribed values.

For Deleuze and Guattari delirium is a productive process that shatters representation and reproduction to disclose desiring bodies, which, citing Antonin Artaud, they refer to as a Body without Organs (BwO).[6] It is relevant for clinical aesthetics that the body in question invokes a writer who had direct, distressing experiences with the psychiatric clinic, and who contested civilization's (e.g., psychiatry's) program for the body. Artaud denounces an American institutional usurpation of bodies as reproductive machines for the sake of capitalism (producing soldiers for the Cold War). To break free from this manipulation, the (male) body must follow a process that begins with emasculation. One should recall here, furthermore, that *becoming-woman*, the first becoming in the schizoanalytic ethics of desire aimed at "making oneself a BwO" (Deleuze and Guattari 1987), is first presented by Deleuze and Guattari through a reading of Judge Schreber's delirious account of feeling like a woman when looking in the mirror (1983: 18), which was originally analyzed by Freud in 1911 (i.e., the *Schreber Case*) (Freud 2003). The schizoanalysts forcefully argue against an imaginary interpretation of this specific experience, while stressing the fluidity of the schizo's "delirious/desiring code," by playing on the replacement of a single letter that turns French *désire* into *délire*, "delirium": "*Code du désire ou du délire*" (Deleuze and Guattari 1972: 21). Adding to this discourse of delirium as a kind of fluidity of desire, in *Francis Bacon* Deleuze adds a decisive factor in his redefinition of health: "the passage of the nervous wave" (2003: 49) that invests organs with singular, transitory functions in hysteria. Such a "wandering wave" is the hallmark of hysteria, which was named by Hippocrates as the trouble of the "wandering womb." The diagnosis evokes an experience in a female body that deviates from its biological and ideological codification.

If Schreber's becoming-woman, a delirium, allows us to escape the logic of representation and reproduction, the notion of a body traversed and animated by desire beyond biology and ideology is enabled by hysteria. Delirium and hysteria, then, offer a glimpse of the specific desire that drives both the psychoanalytic and aesthetic clinics, a feminine, elusive desire, we will see, much like an eternally "late" and fleeting White Rabbit drives Alice after it, down a rabbit hole into a delirious Wonderland in Carroll's novel. The feminine desire at stake for both the psycho- and the schizoanalytic clinics defies meaning, representation, and consciousness as the complex bedrock of identity and being, for which, as Colebrook affirms, man is the model (2000: 12).

But the "feminine" will function as neither an essence nor an opposing value to the "masculine" that might replace it; rather, it indicates a path of singularity that cannot be grasped with bio-organo-ideological parameters. One could argue that the "feminine" preserves a simple binary conception of sexuality, but simply rejecting "masculine" and "feminine" in favor of posthuman becoming is a sure way of limiting thought, if not of repressing and perpetuating the same old gender regime.[7] Yet Schreber's becoming-woman and the hysteric women who Charcot and Freud encountered present us less with a female identity than with singularities that cannot be identified, represented, assimilated. Precisely the challenge of receptiveness to such feminine desire is crucial to the emergence of the aesthetic clinic and its becomings. In Francis Bacon's paintings this receptiveness is what prompts Deleuze to think of the aesthetic clinic with hysteria, and while the schizoanalysts recognized hysteria's literary potential with Flaubert's *Madame Bovary* in mind, the aesthetic force of hysteria goes beyond the late nineteenth century.[8] Another look at "the curious place of women's writing" (Colebrook 2000: 5) remains relevant for grasping the consequences of clinical aesthetics today.[9] What are the clinical effects of displacing Alice—from Wonderland, where Deleuze meets her, to Wonderwater, where Horn imagines her—and of allowing her to wander, as Horn's subtitle indicates, "offshore"? We now turn to *Wonderwater*'s forceful deterritorialization by highlighting the key strategy of *alliances* in Horn's collaborative piece.

As mentioned, Louise Bourgeois, Anne Carson, Hélène Cixous, and John Waters respond to the collected titles of Roni Horn's artworks, each contributing their unique book to the resulting four-volume work of collective enunciation (featuring different colors for each book cover). In singular juxtapositions with drawing and processes of mad polysemy, homophony, echoing, and humor, writing through these feminine tactics is brought to breakdowns of sense that open a field of contagious sensation, inhabited by fluid bodily intensities and literary names (such as Blake, Empedokles, Flannery, Hölderlin, Kafka, Rousseau) that describe unique modes of desire.

An important function of women's writing in Colebrook's introduction to *Deleuze and Feminist Theory* is transformative, nonidentical "contagion and contamination" of tradition (2000: 5). How exactly does Alice undergo contamination and contagion in Horn's project? A good indication lies in the title *Wonderwater (Alice Offshore)*. Logically, this title is included within the book for the annotators.[10] Alice's name there is placed by Horn within parentheses, in the same way that *Untitleds* are followed by a parenthetical subtitle that distinguishes them from each other—for instance "*Untitled (Aretha)*" and "*Untitled (Flannery)*". This is especially useful within this book, where titles are separated from the visual pieces to which they refer, rather like the Cheshire Cat from its smile.[11] If we can expect words in parentheses to clarify the sense of the words that precede them,[12] Horn tells us Wonderwater is a destination Alice has gone off to explore; that she has departed to different adventures to those she encountered in Wonderland. But "offshore" is certainly far from a reassuring destination. Once a character closely followed through the looking glass in Carroll's novel, Alice in this twenty-first century artwork has moved offshore, off solid ground, then, and into an unbound watery space. At the same time, the parenthetical title quietly discloses *Wonderwater*'s makeup; if Wonderwater is Alice offshore, everything in Wonderwater contains this new, imperceptible state of Alice, who always experimented with growing gigantic and small with regard to her surroundings. So Alice is again deterritorialized and, undergoing a becoming-imperceptible, she functions in the 2004 collective project as a kind of threshold, or a potent element dissolved in wonderwater and permeating all words and spaces of the work.

The liquid element returns abundantly across Horn's artworks, so it's also everywhere in *Wonderwater*'s collection of titles. Water's solubility, formlessness, and fluidity offer the prime conditions for a heterogeneous experiment of enunciation in incessant becoming. For this reason, Horn writes, "Water is the master verb" (Horn 2004a: 141)[13] In this role, water sweeps away that (male) bedrock of identity and being. Words in the *Wonderwater* books take on these properties of water (the compound "wonderwater" is an instance of a hybrid effect of water's solubility), and they undergo metamorphoses under Horn's and each annotator's treatment, just as the annotators allow conjunctions of words that are not their own to inflect their experiments. John Waters, for instance, has a comic approach to the project. Only he systematically comments on every single title with very brief synopses that retroactively propose reading the titles as hypothetically belonging to films or books. His literal take on the titles is surprising and hilarious. For example, under "Water, Still" he writes, " 'John Waters' third autobiography told from beyond the grave" (Horn and Waters 2004d: 125). The participants are allies in diverse productions of sense that relinquish authority and authorship as an individual, ego-based, self-identical, and possessive instance.

Besides the four invited annotators, other names from the Western literary tradition may then bathe in Alice's strange Wonderwater; indeed, Kafka and Hölderlin actually swim together in a set of whimsical comic drawings Carson appends to her annotation of *Wonderwater*.[14] In addition to multiplying names, there is sonorous repetition that acts as a watery amplifier. Cixous's annotations play, in her characteristic style, on the multiplication of sense through French homophonies. As it turns out, *eau*, the French word for water, is particularly productive:

eau

o au haut aux oh

o l'eau !

(Horn and Cixous 2004c: 147)[15]

The noun for "water," the exclamation "oh", the adjective "high," and the French preposition "*à*" contracted with the singular and plural definite articles "*le*" and "*les*" all make the same vocal sound. These homophonies invite one to describe the gesture of Horn's project as an inaudible slip from the masculine noun *auteur*, with all the features of mastery related above to the notion of the author, to *h-e-au-teur-e*, where *eau* is included. In this manner exactly, the previously mentioned title "Water Is the Master Verb" makes Cixous invoke the many words in "*eau*," and even a French name whose ending also includes French water: Rousse*au*. She cites from Rousseau's *Confessions*, where he meditates on his love of water and its inspiring effect of admiration and prayer in him. His associations lead him to a memory of a humble old woman who didn't know any prayers and could only say "o," a mode of praying Rousseau embraces. Cixous simply marks the insistent presence of *l'eau* in its various spellings throughout the passage by presenting this phoneme in light gray, contrasting with the otherwise black-inked paragraph. Cixous follows with a brief comment where water and prayer sensually merge multiple oral registers:

What is a prayer?

It is the literal translation of tears.

It is the evaporation of solid words into a mist for the lips of God.

I have always loved l'eau in French.

I love its monosyllabic strength.

(Horn and Cixous 2004c: 146)

What I find relevant about these immersions of recognized figures in *Wonderwater* is that they are less interested in the consolidated figures recognized by Western literary tradition than in a close, untranslatable sensation in them. This sensation, a liminal experience to which Deleuze was forced to return via hysteria, has to do with something feminine. Carson and Cixous, for instance, respectively become Hölderlin and Kafka when they present their love affairs and letters throughout their texts. Fiction is put to work in this way again by Carson and Cixous to approach what Deleuze beautifully calls the vital, "profound and almost unliveable *Puissance*" beyond "the lived body" (2003: 42; 44), in Hölderlin's poetry and Kafka's stories, and also in their bodies. This vital, unliveable *puissance* resists mass commodification as well as capture by scholarly, authoritative commentary; it only seems transmissible in an aesthetic clinic, and it's what insistently surges up, each time uniquely, as feminine desire.

Carson, for instance, encounters it in Horn's title "Her, the Water, and Me," and in Empedokles as "Nestis." She emphasizes its effect, appropriate in wonderwater, of leaving readers endlessly *wondering*:

> What do you make of the fact that when Empedokles named his root clumps—Earth Air Fire Water—he used changing terms for them? Water, for example, is also called sea, ocean, rain and Nestis. The first three are plausible. No one knows what to make of Nestis. Scholars conjecture it is the name of a local Sicilian goddess (Empedokles lived in Sicily). But in standard Greek otherwise the word means "famine" or "fasting." (Horn and Carson 2004b: 57)

Water in this cosmology underlies everything in combinations with three other components (moved by "Love and Strife"), but even each of these roots takes on changing names, so conceiving them as permanent underlying elements is inaccurate. As a goddess, water is "she," and also a force that indicates fasting, a form of ascesis—which Deleuze viewed as "the condition of desire" (Deleuze and Parnet 2002: 100–1).[16] Sexuality and desire are thus relevant to the water in question. Carson cites Empedokles and proceeds to remark on his lesson in schizoanalysis *avant la lettre*, insisting on "wonder" as curiosity:

> Nestis who with her tears soaks mortal streaming.
>
> (Empedokles, fragment 63)

> Mortal streaming, odd phrase. Likely includes rivers and streams as well as sweat and semen. That Nestis uses her tears to keep all things wet makes one wonder about her sadness (a variant reading of the phrase gives, "Nestis dispenses to the mortal race bitter tears"). Makes one wonder if she is not some version of Persephone, who had a relation to both fasting and famine, and was worshipped fervently on Sicily (Empedokles may have met Persephone; he claims in one of his poems to have gone down to the underworld and come back alive). (Horn and Carson 2004b: 57)

Empedokles's water has, all at once, to do with geography, sex, pain, bitterness, mortality, and femininity. Carson notices body liquids that can flow according to something like sadness; she indirectly recalls Alice's pool of tears, where many creatures swim. Such water also makes curiosity flow beyond the pleasures of understanding and knowing, freeing Carson to ponder the encounter of Empedokles and Persephone in the underworld, and to include, as the last pronoun in Horn's tripartite title proposes, "me" in the following manner:

> The sorrow of Nestis's tears, or Persephone's tears if that is whose they are, moves around in me as I sit at my kitchen table reading bits of Empedokles on a cloudy afternoon, perhaps simply it is a sad time in my life—no, that isn't why Nestis gets to me. (Horn and Carson 2004b: 57)

"Me" emerges as an instance traversed and inhabited by a cluster of symptoms: this singular flow of sorrow as much as by "bits of Empedokles," sitting, and the cloudy weather's promise of more water. In line with the title "Her, the Water, and Me," "me" is treated like a haecceity; a "this-ness" rather than a "what-ness" (See Deleuze and Guattari 1987: 253–304). It is this strange nature of Nestis that allows her to connect to "me" beyond a possessive notion of life (as "my life" and its different times and moods) in isolation from everything else.

Empedokles's fragment and Carson's annotation for Horn's title bring forth a specific non-representable body, one that can be traversed, intensively moved by tears, sadness, written words, a cloudy afternoon. A hystericized body. Deleuze discusses hystericization in Bacon in terms of "Presence or insistence. Interminable Presence" (2003: 51): "Everywhere there is a presence acting directly on the nervous system, which makes representation, whether in place or at a distance, impossible" (51). We will return to the breakdown of representation but let us first look at the beginning of *Wonderwater* and compare its strategy to the aesthetic clinic Deleuze invokes. Horn's first title reads "19th-Century Water." Bourgeois, the first of the four annotators and a multimedia artist, responds with the keyword "HYSTERIA," thus setting the tone that will trigger the line of flight on which Alice may go offshore. For its part, Deleuze's formulation on the aesthetic clinic in his Bacon essay is immediately followed by this potential clinic's "advantage of not being a psychoanalysis" (51), yet it surprisingly appears in the context of thinking about painting in terms of hysteria. While traditional psychoanalytic practice shied from psychosis and restricted its field to neurosis, that is, to treating hysterics or obsessionals, the schizoanalysts claimed psychosis as exit from the Oedipal model, which limited desire or even lost touch with it while representing it in the family romance. For instance, they cite Freud's distinction of paranoia, which decomposes, from hysteria, which condenses, to stress the importance of the disjunctive function, and they understand Freud's attributing the hysterical condensation a relation to "more basic, primordial" (Deleuze and Guattari 1983: 13) material with regard to psychosis as a strategy to keep the psychotic delirium within the bounds of Oedipus. So, the fact that hysteria is assigned to Bacon's canvases and, beyond, to painting as a practice in general, invites attention to the specificity of hysteria, since Deleuze does not fully develop this. In the same chapter of the Bacon essay, Deleuze also stresses the distinction of the aesthetic clinic from psychiatry. Yet he simultaneously accepts the invitation in Bacon's canvases to think about painting and the body with the symptoms of hysteria—"the famous spastics and paralytics, the hyperesthetics or anesthetics" (Deleuze 2003: 49) precisely as described by Charcot, the inventor, in the late nineteenth century, of this illness whose distinctive trait was the absence of an organic lesion to account for the inexplicable, provisional sufferings that would fall upon predominantly female patients' distinct body parts, and the patients' splits with reality that revealed a knowledge about their sensorial experience that remained outside of consciousness. Importantly, such female hysterics are the starting point for Freud, then a student, to develop, as a clinician to hysteric women, the field of psychoanalysis, with an inaugural notion of the unconscious anchored in sexuality (which is not necessarily Oedipal) (see Van Haute and Geyskens 2012). While Deleuze tries to set the aesthetic clinic apart from psychoanalysis in this late essay on painting, the turn to hysteria attests to a close and relevant link between Deleuze's idea of the clinical and psychoanalysis, beyond the known criticism Deleuze engaged in to propose schizoanalysis with Guattari, who was then involved with psychoanalyst Jean Oury in the *La Borde* clinic for psychotic individuals.[17] Far from losing its edge or "regressing" to the Oedipal narrative, in the late return to a neurotic structure via Bacon, schizoanalysis recognizes hysteria's crucial role in the aesthetic clinic.

How do hysteria and the clinical fuel contemporary aesthetics? Psychoanalytic theory risks making reductive statements, as Deleuze contended, but one should never forget its attempt at conceptualizing and transmitting a rich clinical field that is always in process and exceeds theorization, given that each analytic treatment brings something uncharted to psychoanalysis, which can never work as a ready-made system of interpretation.[18] Consequently, the problems and figures of the unconscious simply cannot remain static and attuned to those Freud encountered at the turn of the twentieth century. In recent teaching for the *École freudienne du Québec* (EFQ), psychoanalyst Lucie Cantin addresses this very problem:

How to elaborate theoretically and clinically a generalization that does not efface the contribution and the relevance of these singular analytic trajectories that underlie [the elaboration of analytic knowledge] and for which it tries to account? Analytic knowledge establishes itself and develops with the clinic, with the real of the subject who lives in a given age and socio-historical context. (Cantin 2017: 23: my translation)

Cantin's claim does not rely on an ordinary historicism, in which the unconscious would only be the product of its already-assimilated contextual elements. Rather, "the real of the subject,"—a unique experience that has never been articulated yet bears relation to the context of its emergence—is the essential stuff that grounds and moves analytic knowledge, which, for its part, should be the attempt to account for this unheard-of stuff without erasing its singularity in trying to make it fit within available analytic terms.[19] In line with this argument, I propose to approach the aesthetic as an unconscious, experimental field of sensation that, by definition, cannot be totalized, and as the site that orients schizoanalysis, as a mode of analysis concerned with the production of desire. Therefore, just as psychoanalysis has its indispensable clinical dimension, the aesthetic clinic might be considered the clinical dimension of schizoanalysis, with all the innovations and challenges this theory and practice of desire, grounded in an experimental unconscious, pose to psychoanalysis (Deleuze and Guattari 1980: 348; Deleuze and Parnet 2002: 77–123).

Bourgeois, in *Wonderwater*, emphasizes hysteria's relevance to art, and vice versa, in her own and Horn's projects. She employs a combination of names of psychoanalysts, psychiatrists, musicians, and poets to make a drawing of "19th-Century Water" as a multiplicity of bright red waves flowing by, over two bottom lines made from the word "hysteria" and from words that refer to some of its symptoms. She deliberately does not separate doctors and artists, or even those known for being diagnosed with or treated for mental illness from the rest. Her approach resonates with Juliet Mitchell's view of hysteria (2000) in terms of lateral relationships and with a feminist view of Freud, Breuer, and the women in their *Studies* as creative co-participants (Dimen and Harris 2001). Furthermore, it recalls Deleuze when he examines literature and the arts in clinical terms and symptomatological figures in aesthetic terms. For hysteria itself reveals an intimate, long-standing connection between the clinical and the aesthetic that tells us something about both psychoanalysis and schizoanalysis. In both analytic projects the clinic is initiated by welcoming modes of creativity foreign to both the theoretical dimension and the tradition where these theories emerge. This is why Deleuze praised Freud's "genius" (noticing that "Oedipus and Hamlet inform us on the complex" and not inversely) and turned to Carroll, Proust, and Masoch as "clinicians of civilization" (1990: 237). Freud's work is "artistic," since he is one of the clinicians who "know how to renovate a symptomatological table" (237).[20]

Freud also recognized fundamental lessons about the unconscious and desire in literature and sculpture. Oedipus, of course, embodies one of these lessons, and Freud came to accord it a paradigmatic place in his account of human development, unfortunately at the expense of questions that femininity and psychosis raised beyond the scope of Oedipus, as he himself recognized.[21] So let us also consider that, to come into existence, the psychoanalytic clinic required the opening of a discipline (medicine) to a heterogeneous scene, where not recognized masterpieces but rather the body and word of hysteric female patients unlocked the production of the unconscious. Forced to break out of monological and genealogical methods, Freud explored an alternative mode of listening, reading, and writing by following these women's speech, and he acknowledged the connection between hysteria and artistic creation: "It was obvious that the forms assumed by the different neuroses echoed the most highly admired productions of our culture. Thus hysterics are undoubtedly imaginative artists, even if they express their phantasies mimetically in the main and without considering their intelligibility to other people" (Freud 1955: 257).

While Freud criticizes the hysterics' opaque style, he also recognizes their artistic and poetic force, one that pushes him beyond culturally accepted medical techniques to develop a new clinic that demands "an in-depth portrayal of the workings of the inner life, such as one expects to be given by novelists and poets," he explains in the early Elisabeth Von R. case (Freud and Breuer 2004: 165). Freud's admirable artistic work is, then, already and necessarily the product of an alliance with the hysterics' enigmatic expression, which fuels painting, as Deleuze's study on Bacon shows, as much as literature, and, more fundamentally, the aesthetic. Thus, hysteria's close affinities with art allow it to deterritorialize nineteenth-century psychiatric descriptive practices and treatment, giving rise to the psychoanalytic clinic. This concerns the aesthetic clinic too.

In *Logic of Sense,* Deleuze discusses the relationship between the novel and hysteria that the Viennese doctor investigated in his own writing of cases and also in terms of hysterics'' inclination to daydreaming (to which Freud himself was admittedly prone). Like Freud with Oedipus or Hamlet, Deleuze is interested in what can be learned from Alice about "sense," rather than in pathologizing Carroll. Deleuze does not merely separate the sick patient from the clinician or from the creator who has succeeded in sublimating his perversions, although he does see a difference between the work of art and a hysteric's "family romance" ("*roman familial*"), which does not attain the status of the work of art, as it reproduces the established roles that prevent it from bringing a proper name into the world, whereas the novel (*roman*) as a work of art creates an event (Deleuze 1990: 238) by employing the very forces of hysteria. This distinction does not oppose sublimation to pathology: it's not that hysterics necessarily remain entrapped in the Oedipal web, whereas artists have managed to escape Oedipus and hysteria at once. In fact, Freud's hysteric patients, such as Dora and Emmy whose bodies suffer from intractable pain, insistently show him that any attempt at pinning their desire down through Oedipus will fail.[22] In the aesthetic clinic, novelists are not necessarily recovered hysterics, and hysterics are not necessarily failed artists. Perhaps the very terminology of success and failure is inaccurate. The writer engaged in a creative project faces the task of breaking out of the Oedipal frame to harness forces beyond it for an original production of desire.[23] The latter may advance another form of enunciation, "make language stammer" (Deleuze and Guattari 1987: 98) as does *Wonderwater*, where Bourgeois makes writing and drawing collaborate.

Bourgeois further highlights bodily symptoms' aesthetic power. She dedicates four pages to "19th-Century Water." The first has the form of a poem in three stanzas. The first two capture an experience of fear triggered by the sensation of deadly silence:

I was always aware of a possible silence falling

like the cover of a tomb and engulfing me forever.

The silence overruns the room and I am afraid to hear

My heart beating; this danger coming from inside—

only a continual flow of words can push it aside,

if not control it. (Horn and Bourgeois 2004a: 8)

"Always" and "forever" favor a shift from the initial past tense to the second stanza's overwhelming present. Instead of the dreadful voices known to invade schizophrenics, here the dreadful agent is silence, revealing the sound of the listener's beating heart. The latter is activated, according to the ear, heightened by dangerous silence rather than by an organic function. We are not dealing with an organism here. To overcome this danger of eternal engulfment within the tension of "the room" and the body's inside too, the speaker requires neither a pacemaker nor a doctor, "only a continual flow of words." The third and last stanza approaches "19th-Century Water" in terms not just of words, but of sound and flows, in a powerful, sonorous, and also somewhat violent sensation that overturns the danger of silence:

Listen to chaos, waterfall, the Marne locks –

Beethoven, a river that carries rocks and trees,

the thunder rolling by.

(Horn and Bourgeois 2004a: 8)

Once a fluid musicality of water is suggested ("Listen," it says) we turn the page to find the previously mentioned field of famous names printed as wavy lines flowing across the next two pages: Charles Baudelaire, Sigmund Freud, Melanie Klein, Prosper Mérimée, Frédéric Chopin, George Sand, R.D. Laing, and many others, while two straight lines made up of words in all caps along the page's bottom form a kind of sediment. Of these twelve words, the first, "HYSTERIA," appears in bold, while the rest are printed in light red and refer to bodily symptoms (deafness, fainting, frigidness, insomnia, numbness, etc.). Unconcerned with protecting normalcy, the drawing advances a criterion of health marked by the aesthetic; the latter can neither discard Beethoven, of course, nor chaos, the plummeting force of the waterfall, the river that sweeps the destroyed landscape away, nor the rolling thunder. In a way, the account of these sensations of silence and nineteenth-century water evokes Beethoven's deafness and Romanticism (the Sixth Symphony, especially, with its "Scene by the brook," and "Thunder, Storm" movements). Combined with the emotions of fear and relief these sensations awaken, Bourgeois's text, like Carson's on Empedokles and Cixous's on Rousseau, awakens a bodily experience. In both cases a solubility of names that responds to Horn's gesture of multiplicity and collective authorship with *Wonderwater*, as well as with various titles and artworks of hers, is at work in the experiences they transmit.

When Deleuze considered writers and characters known to be diagnosed with some form of psychosis (Artaud, Nietzsche, Molloy), their extreme experiences were not simply cast aside from their creative work. These figures are actually not even constrained to psychosis in Deleuze's analyses. In the chapter of *Francis Bacon* "Hysteria," for instance, Deleuze argues for a unity of the senses at the limit of life by invoking, again, Artaud on the BodywithoutOrgans: "No mouth. No tongue. No teeth," and so on (2003, 45). The point is,

> The body is completely living, and yet nonorganic. Likewise sensation, when it acquires a body through the organism, takes on an excessive and spasmodic appearance, exceeding the bounds of organic activity. It is immediately conveyed in the flesh through the nervous wave or vital emotion. (Deleuze 2003: 45)

More important than abolishing bodily organs as such is destroying the organism, which locks bodies into ideological reproduction, as Artaud had explained. More important than the psychiatric diagnosis or the unconscious structure is what Deleuze called sensation. The schizoanalysts make this point already in *Anti-Oedipus*:

> An *I feel* at an even deeper level, which gives hallucinations their object and mental delirium its content. An "I feel that I am becoming a woman," "that I am becoming god," and so on, which is neither delirious nor hallucinatory, but will project the hallucination or interiorize the delirium. Delirium and hallucination are secondary in relation to the really primary emotion, which in the beginning only experiences intensities, becomings, passings. (Deleuze and Guattari 1983: 18–19)

Excess beyond the organism emerged specifically in hysteria when Charcot established the category (see Didi-Huberman 2004), and what matters to Deleuze is that Artaud conveyed the experience of this very excess, as did Bacon.[24] Indeed, Artaud and Bacon "meet on many points" (Deleuze 2003: 45). They also meet Bourgeois, who expands hysteria's specificity in multimedia art and writing.

In her annotation for "Dictionary of Water," Bourgeois includes the title of one of her own installations: *Precious Liquids*. A list of body fluids follows: bile, blood, ear lubricant, milk, pus, saliva, semen, snot, sweat, tears, and urine. *Precious Liquids* (1991) was purchased by the Modern Art Museum in Paris, and Bourgeois sent a note along with the work, where she wrote, "[I]ntense emotions become a material liquid, a precious liquor" (Bernadac 1996: 135). That these liquids as effects of intense emotions spill out of a body and defy any attempt at its unified image is relevant in Bourgeois's field of sculpture, drawing, and installation, because it betrays inadequacy of representation to deal with passages of desire through bodies. Hysteria makes this especially evident, as Deleuze points out in discussing the passage of the nervous wave that invests and withdraws from the hysteric body (2003: 48–9) In *Wonderwater*, as in her own art, Bourgeois recurrently deals with the body as various bodily fluids mobilized by sensation and desire. As mentioned, Carson also engages with sweat, semen, and tears. She also discusses black bile, which brings the different extreme experiences of Empedokles, Hölderlin, and Kafka to swim in a common fluid that "doesn't exist, although its operations have been theorized for millennia," (Horn and Carson 2004b: 43) and this because, while it doesn't exist, it names something real. The problem of sensation in terms of body fluids thus seems to be one of the constraints Horn's titles introduce, in spite of the very open-ended appearance of the experiment. The last of the four pages Bourgeois devotes to "19th-Century Water" features a single, large red spiral made of three sentences in large font curling inward, starting at the top left and moving down the right side of the page, turning the letters upside down at the bottom of the page to continue up the left side of the page and inward, to the final period placed at the center of the page: "Someone is pissing and it sounds true. Truth has a sound, look, and smell all its own. It cannot be made up" (Horn and Bourgeois 2004a: 11). The sonority of this flow, relating to the first text on silence, Beethoven, and water sounds in nature, is also rendered through the insistence of the letter *s* in these sentences, included in the onomatopoeic "piss," of French origin. Truth, in these statements, does not need to coincide with itself through the verb *to be*, the condition implied in the ordinary idiom "sounds true," which distances appearance from truth. A different idea of truth emerges, inextricable from the senses (here of hearing, sight, and smell) involved in operations that make it distinctive, which also gives insight to the logic guiding Bourgeois's annotations, where words and letters are inseparable from all the material determinations of lines, color, and space. Investigating the differential work of sensation in Bacon's bodies, Deleuze suggests the following possible, existential, or better, experiential connection of the senses: "Between a color, a taste, a touch, a smell, a noise, a weight, there would be an existential communication that would constitute the 'pathic' (nonrepresentative) moment of *the* sensation" (2003: 42) Bourgeois writes about truth as something aesthetic, nonrepresentative, and also uninterpretable, if interpretation distances from the hysteric excess of presence Deleuze highlights for the aesthetic clinic. Interpretation, according to Bourgeois, is "made up," whereas sensation, as Deleuze notices, names something primary, intensive, and liminal, "at the limit of the lived body" (Deleuze 2003: 44). Sculpture, installation, and drawing enabled Bourgeois to inhabit and communicate this limit; "Art is a guaranty of sanity," she wrote on late artworks such as *Precious Liquids* (1991). Sensation, in this precise sense, is the decisive factor of health in the aesthetic clinic, and what allows Carson to meditate on madness and its actions:

> Madness wanders. We call it error, and them deranged. Madness is something you "go." Yet when you are mad you may feel you are moving exactly on course. Ficino says of the melancholic:
> Black bile obliges thought to penetrate and explore the center of its objects, because black bile is itself akin to the center of the earth. (Ficino, *De vita triplici*, 1482: 1.4).
>
> *(Horn and Carson 2004b: 49)*

Here, Carson explicates the kind of movements through which madness is commonly described. Erring, breaking out of orderly rows, and "going" all point to wandering, "offshore" indeed. One might add Deleuze and Guattari's *délirer*, whose etymology is literally "to deviate from the furrow." Carson's text features a crucial shift to madness as an agent with its own trajectory, just as Ficino insists on the agency of black bile, its exploratory action and affinity with the center of the earth—a radical "Outside"

(Deleuze and Parnet 2002: 24; 36). The passage importantly acknowledges that this trajectory disrupts civilizations, such that two opposing pronouns become relevant: "we" and "them." But the passage shifts again, to "you," to account for the very schizoanalytic "*I feel*," that determines delusion and hallucination. On this plane of madness as an experience, the effect of the wandering course is no longer to distribute humans in paths of either correctness or error.

Wonderwater insists on the need for someone else—a listener, reader, viewer—in not just any relationship, but in one of alliance. This is another crucial function of "you" throughout *Wonderwater*, adopted, according to Cixous, from water:

> Before any century, when the earth was still alone, the water was already not alone: the breath of God airplaned upon the face of the waters. And water took pleasure
> "As far as water can remember the creative breath and I have been allied," says 19th century water. (Horn and Cixous 2004c: 7)

Alliance, which in *Wonderwater* implies contagion or hystericization, is nothing less than what enables the production of desire that concerns schizoanalysis. Inversely, as a mode of analysis that attends to productions of desire, schizoanalysis is receptive to the rhizomatic, polyvocal, and boundless wandering of *Wonderwater (Alice Offshore)*. A return to hysteria and delirium from this fluid, collective, and aesthetic perspective reveals one way in which feminism can continue transforming thought with a feminine "creative breath."

Notes

1. On the potential in American women's poetry to expand Deleuzian becoming-woman, see Lamm (2003).

2. The catalogue of her retrospective, *Roni Horn aka Roni Horn* (2009), gives a sense of her style—at once "sensual and conceptual," as art critic Briony Fer's essay therein points out— and of her address of queer identity, femininity, place and fluidity.

3. There's an important conversation between Deleuze and Klossowski regarding Nietzsche as a clinical case and the relevance of this perspective to his most radical ideas. Deleuze refers to Klossowski's take on Nietzsche throughout *Difference and Repetition* and *Logic of Sense*. See Klossowski ([1969] 1997), and chapter 5 in Kaufman (2003).

4. On this criterion of health, see Buchanan (2001).

5. In "Neurosis and Psychosis" Freud figures delusion "like a patch where originally a rent had appeared in the ego's relation to the external world" (Freud 1961: 19, 151).

6. This notion is expressed by Artaud most forcefully in the 1947 radio play *To Be Done with the Judgment of God* (1988).

7. Colebrook (2013) develops the argument well. Irigaray first resisted the danger of a feminine position's dissipation in becoming-woman, and Grosz insists on the advantages of bringing Irigaray and Deleuze into conversation (2005: 182).

8. It remains necessary to interrogate feminine desire in literature that engages it directly, and also beyond Carroll, Masoch, and other "symptomatologists" Deleuze appreciated. For a Deleuzian study of this corpus, see Tynan (2012); Buchanan also explicates the relationship between schizophrenia and literature in *Anti-Oedipus* (2008) (although Buchanan's claim that Deleuze and Guattari would view the cause of schizophrenia as organic (35–6) is at odds with my argument).

9. Colebrook (2013) returns to this place through Virginia Woolf, an inspiration for Deleuze and Guattari's concept of becoming-woman.

10. Her name only refers to a character within the book in John Waters's annotation of it, in a one-sentence-long fictive camp film synopsis: "A pedophile's obsession with a European schoolgirl" (Horn 2004 (4): 135). The other three annotators leave this page blank.

11. Kristeva (2012: 119–20) states that women are like "Cheshire Cats" to the voyeurs' eyes; either they see their head but not their being, speaking body, or their head disappears with the body, just when they try to behead them. In this sense, in Horn's project offering heads that can each acquire four different bodies is a feminist gesture.

12. Deleuze examines this in Carroll: "If we agree to think of a proposition as a name, it would then appear that every name which denotes an object may itself become the object of a new name that denotes its sense" (1990: 29). On Alice's hysterical discourse see Lopez (2003).

13. Like all of Horn's titles, this one appears in all four volumes, although the page numbers vary.

14. She names this comically "Kafka and Hö: River by River." Two human figures wearing suits with their name's initials on them dive into the water. In the last scene, a part of their heads emerges from the shared water line under a crescent moon. Movingly, the two characters are parallel rivers who end up merging into a common wonderwater and keep swimming.

15. The English translation features the original French text for the first two lines since the play on homophony is untranslatable. A literal translation would be: "water/oh to high to the oh/ Hey water!"

16. Deleuze here also associates "anorexia," as a specific desiring body refusing to be consumed by rejecting consumption, to sexuality and becoming-woman (Deleuze and Parnet 2002, 109–10).

17. Written before *Anti-Oedipus*, Deleuze's *Difference and Repetition* and *Logic of Sense* owe much to his reading of Freud's *Beyond the Pleasure Principle*. Moreover, Deleuze and Guattari never tire of insisting that their attack is not against the idea of the unconscious, but rather against its codification and subjection to norms (see Buchanan 2013). I'm therefore less interested in reproducing Deleuze's criticism of psychoanalysis than in approaching points of contact between psychoanalysis and schizoanalysis that may offer a more productive notion of hysteria's and the aesthetic clinic's relevance to schizoanalysis.

18. Guattari especially insists on this. See Sauvagnargues's "Symptoms are Birds Tapping at the Window" (2016: 153); and Guattari and Rolnik (2008: 327–30).

19. Thus, for the EFQ, and for Lacan since 1969, analysts can no longer rely on Oedipus to address the experience of the unconscious when "the family structure … is increasingly losing its sense and its function of ideological reproduction of the social link" and when psychosis, as Freud recognized, shows the limits of the Oedipal frame (Apollon 2017: 33). The analysts of the EFQ practice psychoanalysis with psychotic individuals since 1982. Their "subject" is not a self or ego, but rather the instance of what remains at odds with the ego and the social, to be produced in an analysis. Deleuze directed Apollon's dissertation on Voodoo and voices, published in 1976.

20. Here and in *Francis Bacon,* Deleuze uses the word "*tableau*," which Charcot employed and which means not only table, as "a display of information in columns," but it also "painting or picture." The English translators use, respectively, "table" and "picture" (Deleuze 2003: 48).

21. Civilization's normalizing powers have much more to do with Oedipus than with experiences of femininity and psychosis, so Oedipus certainly illuminates something about the social regime that led to our present situation.

22. Van Haute and Geyskens (2012) highlight Freud's hint at this when he discusses his failure to figure out his patient Dora's desire in *Fragment of a Case of Hysteria*, and Lacan's post-Oedipal turn in *The Other Side of Psychoanalysis*. Before them, Cixous highlights this in a play (1976). See also MacCannell (2000).

23. Deleuze warns against confusing the writer, the little girl, and the schizophrenic in *Logic of Sense*. While all three escape the limits of the family romance that the Oedipus complex represents, each one faces different becomings in language and body.

24. That Bacon was not hospitalized for mental illness, for instance, is not central to their affinities.

References

Apollon, W. (June 2017), "*La castration et le transfert. Enseignement*," *Correspondances* 17 (2): 31–40.

Artaud, A. (1988), "To Be Done with the Judgment of God," in S. Sontag (ed.), *Selected Writings*, Berkeley: University of California Press.

Bernadac, M. (1996), *Louise Bourgeois*, trans. D. Dusinberre, Paris: Flammarion.

Braidotti, R. (2011), *Nomadic Subjects: Embodiment and Sexual Difference in Contemporary Feminist Theory*, New York: Columbia University Press.

Buchanan, I. (2001), "Deleuze's Immanent Historicism," *Parallax* 7 (4): 29–39.

Buchanan, I. (2008), *Deleuze and Guattari's Anti-Oedipus*, London: Continuum.

Buchanan, I. (Summer 2013), "The Little Hans Assemblage," *Visual Arts Research* 39 (1): 9–17.

Cantin, L. (June 2017), "*L'absence de l'Autre, le sujet de la pulsion libre et sa quête intraitable*," *Correspondances* 17 (2): 23–9.

Cixous, H. (1976), *Portrait de Dora*, Paris: des femmes.

Colebrook, C. (2000), "Introduction," in I. Buchanan and C. Colebrook (eds.), *Deleuze and Feminist Theory*, Edinburgh: Edinburgh University Press.

Colebrook, C. (2013), "Modernism without Women: The Refusal of Becoming-Woman," *Deleuze Studies* 7 (4): 427–55.

Deleuze, G. (1989), *Coldness and Cruelty*, trans. J. McNeil, New York: Zone Books.

Deleuze, G. (1990), *The Logic of Sense*, trans. M. Lester, New York: Columbia University Press.

Deleuze, G. (2003), *Francis Bacon: The Logic of Sensation*, trans. D. W. Smith, New York: Continuum.

Deleuze, G. (2005), *Essays Critical and Clinical*, trans. M. A. Greco and D. W. Smith, Minneapolis: University of Minnesota Press.

Deleuze, G., and F. Guattari (1972), *Anti-Oedipe: Capitalisme et schizophrénie*, Paris: Les Éditions de Minuit.

Deleuze, G., and F. Guattari (1980), *Mille Plateaux*, Paris: Les Éditions de Minuit.

Deleuze, G., and F. Guattari (1983), *Anti-Oedipus: Capitalism and Schizophrenia*, trans. R. Hurley, M. Seem, and H. Lane, Minneapolis: University of Minnesota Press.

Deleuze, G., and F. Guattari (1987), *A Thousand Plateaus*, trans. B. Massumi, Minneapolis: University of Minnesota Press.

Deleuze, G., and C. Parnet (2002), *Dialogues II*, trans. H. Tomilson and B. Habberjam, New York: Continuum, 2002.

Didi-Huberman, G. (2004), *Invention of Hysteria: Charcot and the Photographic Iconography of the Salpêtrière*, trans. A. Hartz, Cambridge, MA: MIT Press.

Dimen, M., and A. Harris (2001), *Storms in Her Head: Freud and the Construction of Hysteria*, New York: Other Press, 2001.

Freud, S. (1955), "Preface to Reik's *Ritual*," trans. J. Strachey, *The Standard Edition of The Complete Psychological Works of Sigmund Freud* (1923–5) V17, London: Hogarth Press.

Freud, S. (1961), "Neurosis and Psychosis," in *The Standard Edition of The Complete Psychological Works of Sigmund Freud* (1923–5) V19, London: Hogarth Press.

Freud, S. (2003), *The Schreber Case*, trans. A. Webber, London: Penguin Classics.

Freud, S., and J. Breuer (2004), *Studies in Hysteria*, trans. N. Luckhurst, London: Penguin Classics.

Grosz, E. (1993), "A Thousand Tiny Sexes: Feminism and Rhizomatics," *Topoi* 12 (2): 167–79.

Grosz, E. (2005), *Time Travels: Feminism, Nature, Power*, Durham, NC: Duke University Press.

Guattari F., and S. Rolnik (2008), *Molecular Revolution in Brazil*, trans. K. Clapshow and B. Holmes, Los Angeles, CA: Semiotext(e).

Horn, R. (2004), *Wonderwater: Alice Offshore*, annotated by L. Bourgeois, A. Carson, H. Cixous, and J. Waters, Göttingen: Steidl.

Horn, R. (2009), *Roni Horn aka Roni Horn*, New York: Whitney Museum of American Art and Steidl.

Horn, R., and L. Bourgeois (2004a), *Wonderwater: Alice Offshore*, Volume 1, Göttingen: Steidl.

Horn, R., and A. Carson (2004b), *Wonderwater: Alice Offshore*, Volume 2, Göttingen: Steidl.

Horn, R., and H. Cixous (2004c), *Wonderwater: Alice Offshore*, Volume 3, Göttingen: Steidl.

Horn, R., and J. Waters (2004d), *Wonderwater: Alice Offshore*, Volume 4, Göttingen: Steidl.

Klossowski, P. ([1969] 1997), *Nietzsche and the Vicious Circle*, trans. D. W. Smith, Chicago: Chicago University Press.

Kristeva, J. (2012), *Visions Capitales*, Paris: Réunion des Musées Nationaux.

Lamm, K. (2003), "Writing Becoming-Woman: The Movement of Deleuzian Thought in Contemporary American Poetry," *theory@buffalo* 8: 42–67.

Lopez, A. (2003), "That Hysterical Discourse in Lewis Carroll's *Alice in Wonderland and Through the Looking-Glass*: Locating a Critical Subject within Carroll," *theory@buffalo* 8: 69–98.

MacCannell, J. F. (2000), *The Hysteric's Guide to the Future Female Subject*, Minneapolis: University of Minnesota Press.

Mitchell, J. (2000), *Mad Men and Medusas: Reclaiming Hysteria*, New York: Basic Books.

Sauvagnargues, A. (2016), "Symptoms are Birds Tapping at the Window," in *Artmachines: Deleuze, Guattari, Simondon*, trans. S. Verdeber and E. Holland, Edinburgh University Press.

Tynan, A. (2012), *Deleuze's Literary Clinic*, Edinburgh: Edinburgh University Press.

Van Haute, Philippe, and T. Geyskens (2012), *A Non-Oedipal Psychoanalysis? A Clinical Anthropology of Hysteria in the Work of Freud and Lacan*, Leuven: Leuven University Press.

CHAPTER 14
ASCETICISM AND IMPERSONALITY IN SPIRITUAL AVERSION FROM SCHIZOANALYSIS TO CHRIS KRAUS

Austin Sarfan

This essay is guided by Chris Kraus's literary and philosophical involvement with the schizoanalysis of *A Thousand Plateaus*. My main goal is to trace a consistency regarding the schizoanalytic conceptions of asceticism and impersonality emerging in *A Thousand Plateaus* and extending to Kraus's *Aliens & Anorexia*. Asceticism, that is, provisionally, a spiritual exercise of self-renunciation, produces a sense of impersonality by self-reduction, or desubjectification, in a process of estrangement effective in becoming, motivated by a principle of aversion (turning-away). As Deleuze says in a late interview, "In each of us there is, as it were, an ascesis, in part turned against ourselves" (Deleuze and Parnet 1987: 11). Asceticism and impersonality combine in Deleuze and Guattari's schizoanalytic model of artistic practice. Kraus uses such a conception of artistic practice, both ascetic and impersonal, guided also by Simone Weil's ascetic spirituality, in order to describe her own literary practice and to frame the biographies represented in her novel *Aliens & Anorexia*. In total this essay functions to demonstrate the conditions of a momentary spiritual alliance, around the late 1970s to early 1980s, between French theory (Deleuze and Guattari) and a schizoanalytic feminism in the American avant-garde (Kraus in New York).

A few works have managed to untangle the traditional logic of spiritual asceticism that is often confused with Deleuze's futurist innovation. Alain Badiou claims in *Deleuze: The Clamour of Being*, reading Deleuze as an heir to Henri Bergson, "that the condition of thought, for Deleuze, is ascetic" (Badiou 2000: 13). In a similar vein, Joshua Ramey's *The Hermetic Deleuze* embraces the asceticism of Deleuze's thought recognized by Badiou and examines Deleuze's relationship to the historical traditions of spiritual hermeticism in unusually revealing and expansive detail. The breadth of Ramey's presentation of Deleuze's thought within the hermetic spiritual tradition, rooted in antiquity, provides ground to further determining Deleuze's precise relationship to his historical contemporaries similarly attracted to spiritualism. In my view, what constitutes Deleuze's local and immediate involvement with the spiritualist trends of French philosophy is his singular focus on the movement of disorganization in spiritual aversion (turning-away), which builds on Bergson's descriptions of artistic conversion. In Deleuze's understanding of asceticism, which I consider to be avant-garde due to its emphasis on the creative disruption and aesthetic transformation realized by asceticism,[1] the artist attains style and intuits the molecular and cosmic following an ascetic reduction of the majoritarian and molar accomplished by spiritual aversion. In this sense, the ascetic reduction treats the majoritarian and molar as if it were like the block of undifferentiated matter from which one's life must be formally sculpted, following Socrates' injunction to the care of oneself recounted by Diogenes Laertius ([1925] 1976: 164–5).

Kraus engages with Deleuze and Guattari's schizoanalysis both throughout her own novels, which have been called "theoretical fictions," and in the context of her work for *Semiotext(e)*, where for two decades she edited the Native Agents series. From the authors that Kraus published in the series, who were American writers informed by the style of French theory, she says that she also learned how to write. Kraus says that the Native Agents series was created at *Semiotext(e)* in the 1980s in order to "retroactively deal with the women's movement, and feminism more broadly," which at that point had been absent from the schizoanalytic agenda of Semiotext(e) (Schwarz and Balsamo 1996). *Semiotext(e)*, since its founding in 1973 by Sylvère Lotringer, has played a key role in disseminating French theory, including schizoanalysis. Lotringer frames the journal as designed to subvert institutionality and to resonate with what was perceived as the American avant-garde, which was exemplified by the incendiary 1974 Schizo-culture conference organized in anticipation of Semiotext(e)'s first journal issue (Schwarz and Balsamo 1996; also Cusset 2008: 65–75). Publishing works concerning feminism, the later Native Agents series aimed to show the authentic "legacy of French theory" in America, illuminated by emerging "gay and women's writing," where the "theoretical issues" of French theory "were being worked on or over" (Schwarz and Balsamo 1996: 212). For example, Anne Rower's *If You're a Girl*, one of the first novels published in the series, portrays the New York scene in the 1970s and 1980s with a roguish reflexivity, ending with a meditation on the anti-Platonism of writing, learned through memories of Rower's time babysitting Timothy Leary's children. Kraus's work, while introducing and developing the logic of French theory, here set in relation to the schizoanalysis of *A Thousand Plateaus*, illuminates the conditions of a historical alliance between schizoanalytic asceticism and feminist aesthetics, insofar as both emphasize the production of impersonality in artistic practice.

1. Bergson and the Ascetic Artist

As Deleuze and Guattari admit, the concepts of the molar and the molecular are taken from Bergson. Because the asceticism attributed to the artist in schizoanalysis intervenes between what Deleuze and Guattari consider the molar and the molecular in Bergson, it is worth briefly sketching how asceticism already operates in Bergson's thought. Attention to Bergson's aesthetics, which emphasizes the shock of defamiliarization or estrangement accomplished in aesthetic perception, also enables the condensation of various avant-garde aesthetic theories which have evolved from it equally focused on disruption (see Robinson 2008: 51; Benjamin 1968: 157–8; Agamben 2007: 40–9).

For Bergson, the artist achieves an impersonal intuition of the molecular following their detachment from ordinary practical engagement. In ordinary life, the interests of our practical and personal engagements selectively determine our perception of the world. Bergson says: ordinary life "demands that we put on blinders, that we look neither to the right, nor to the left, nor behind us, but straight ahead in the direction we have to go"; consequently, perception "shows us less the things themselves than the use we can make of them" ([1946] 2007a: 113–14). Moreover, concepts and hence language express the logic of "molds," that is, fixed forms produced by the intelligence in contact with a given organization of matter practically necessary everyday life (Bergson [1911] 1998: xx, 195). On the other hand, the artistic life is devoid of ordinary personal attachment to social convention, motivated by an artistic asceticism, that is, a renunciation of the self's attachment to social goods. Describing artists, Bergson says, "When they look at a thing, they see it for itself, and not for themselves ... [T]hey are born *detached*" (Bergson [1946] 2007a: 114). The artist's detachment from everyday life enables the artist to achieve an immediate intuition of the aesthetic, estranged from habitual concepts. Intuition requires passing through an ascetic reduction of "currently-accepted ideas, theses which seemed evident, affirmations which had up to that time passed as scientific" (Bergson [1946] 2007b: 89)—otherwise said, a reduction of the "artificial schema we interpose between reality and us" (Bergson [1946] 2007a: 118). Impersonality is what remains sensible to the artist following the ascetic reduction of concepts in an artistic practice that accedes to originality. Through an intuition estranged from molds of the understanding derived from interest and habit, the detached and ascetic artist's impersonal and defamiliarizing vision of the world informs works of genius (111–14).

The ascetic intuition realized in the withdrawal of the artist facilitates the artist's sensitivity to the reality of molecular becoming. As Bergson says, the quality of sensible becoming "shocks the habits of thought and fits ill into the molds of language" ([1911] 1998: 314). Genius realizes the creation of an original form whose effective shock Bergson compares to the sense of spiritual conversion. The conversion accomplished by artistic genius opens perception to the sense of a qualitatively new form, to an original molecular arrangement liberated from the molds habitually informing cognition. In *The Two Sources of Morality and Religion*, Bergson, in the language of metallurgy, which remains central to Deleuze and Guattari and Kraus, distinguishes between merely intellectual reproduction, following the cast logic of molds, and an original genius of transformation. In reproduction, "the mind cold-hammers the materials, combining together ideas long since cast into words and which society supplies in a solid form"; in genius, "the solid materials supplied by intelligence first melt and mix, then solidify again into fresh ideas now shaped by the creative mind itself" (Bergson [1935] 1977: 34). Genius reduces molded material to its basic molecular organization and creates new forms by reorganizing the elements contained by the intellect's molds "long since cast." In opposition to the Platonic myth of conversion to transcendence from the cave, Bergson argues that artistic creativity illustrates an effectively immanent spiritual conversion of attention to sensible becoming (Bergson [1946] 2007a: 114–6; also Mossé-Bastide 1959: 275–96; Jankélévitch 2015: 237–46).

Such a molecular intuition realized through artistic practice, whose shocking disruption is comparable to a spiritual conversion, restores the dynamic sense of cosmic "universal becoming" to humanity (Bergson [1946] 2007a: 131). The aesthetic creativity of the artist reveals, through example, the perpetual creative transformation composing the molecular universe. In reality, the molar elements, informed by molds, dissociate into molecules, which dissociate into atoms, that finally dissociate into energy, pure "movements dashing back and forth in a constant vibration so that mobility becomes reality itself" (123). In creating new sensible forms, art brings attention to the perpetual transformation composing molecular reality. In *Two Sources of Morality and Religion*, Bergson compares the cosmic sense of universal becoming that is realized in the molecular transformations of original genius to the "line of flight" (of Zeno's arrow) that illustrates the dynamic and vital movement of life (Bergson [1935] 1977: 197; also, Jankélévitch 2015: 263ftn.31). Against Zeno's paradox that claims the theoretical impossibility of movement upon excessive analysis, the flight of the arrow, when simply shot, demonstrates movement as practical reality. In creation, the molecular transformations of the original genius reflect the perpetual lines of flight continuously opening up in the molecular compositions of the universe. Only through an ascetic reduction of molar understanding is the artistic genius able to intuit such a cosmic refrain, in order to develop new forms in communication with cosmic becoming.

2. Asceticism in Schizoanalysis

Deleuze and Guattari write, "From the viewpoint of micropolitics, a society is defined by its lines of flight, which are molecular. There is always something that flows or flees ... things that are attributed to a 'change in values,' the youth, women, the mad, etc." (Deleuze and Guattari 1987: 216). Flight has the form of an ascetic reduction, a transformation, involving a subtraction of the logic of the molar organization that inadequately contains the always imperceptible molecular whose forces are harnessed only by the artist (6). Following Bergson's insistence that originality requires an ascetic reduction of intellectual understanding to achieve an intuition capable of transforming the molecular, Deleuze and Guattari find in all stages of art history a *"freeing of the molecular"* that involves the cosmic in an artistic experiment (346).

The ascetic is a principal figure in Deleuze and Guattari's conception of artistic practice because it is fundamental to the artistic practice of becoming-minoritarian. Like Bergson's ascetic genius whose detachment from society facilitates creative reorganization of material, Deleuze and Guattari emphasize how the artist's becoming-minoritarian subjects the elements of the majoritarian to continuous variation. The figure of the ascetic is introduced by Deleuze and Guattari to convey an avant-garde strategy of revolutionary disruption. The disruption of representation and habit involved in becoming-minoritarian is expressed in the artist's style of relating to discourse. Describing how the artist must be "a foreigner, but in one's own tongue, not only when speaking a language other than one's own" in order to attain artistic style, Deleuze and Guattari conclude, "One attains this result only by sobriety, creative subtraction. Continuous variation has only ascetic lines, a touch of herb and pure water" (1987: 99).

The ascetic artist enters into proximity with ascetic elements, that is, elements that are freed by intuition from the static, fixed forms of the majoritarian, and that are unadulterated in their immediate relation to the earth. The ascetic reduction enacted in becoming-minoritarian, liberated from the fixations of the majoritarian, realizes the phenomenological sense of "autonomy": becoming free from the stasis of discourse, the consciousness of becoming-minoritarian reflects the ascetic ideal of authenticity that is fundamental to existential phenomenology (Deleuze and Guattari 1987: 106).[2] Yet, it is Bergson who remains vital: the continuous variation produced in artistic asceticism is "inseparable from a sensible intuition" (369). The difference between the ambulant science of the artisan which transforms beings, and the royal science of concepts that fixes beings, replicates the distinction between "intuition and intelligence in Bergson" (374). Thus, Deleuze and Guattari write, "The artisan is the itinerant, the ambulant. To follow the flow of matter is to itinerate, to ambulate. It is intuition in action" (409). Intuition in action, the artisan's practice is spiritual asceticism, reducing the organizations of the majoritarian that constrain matter in order to compose works following the flows of the liberated molecular. The cosmic artisan is the ascetic artist of Bergson.

The ascetic artist enjoys a special relationship to the earth that borders on the schizophrenic, insofar as asceticism enables communication with a molecular reality that traverses the earth. R. D. Laing's anti-psychiatric research on schizophrenia is key to the correspondence between the artist and the schizophrenic since Laing frames schizophrenia in terms of a spiritual conversion equivalent to desubjectification—involving spiritual dissolution of the personal ego (Laing 1972). The spiritual conversion of the schizophrenic realized in ego loss, according to Laing, constitutes the spiritual return of the human being to its authentic origin, producing a double estrangement: the schizophrenic is estranged from normal society in returning to the origin, while society is estranged from the origin in pretending to be normal (Laing 1967). In *Anti-Oedipus*, Deleuze and Guattari write, "R. D. Laing is entirely right in defining the schizophrenic process as a voyage of initiation, a transcendental experience of the loss of the Ego" (1983: 84). Both Laing's description of schizophrenia as spiritual initiation through ego loss and Deleuze and Guattari's embrace of it through the model of desubjectification exhibit a remarkable consistency with the general conclusion of Mircea Eliade's study of spiritual initiation, *The Mysteries of Birth and Rebirth*: the "classic pattern of initiation" requires the use of "ascetic training and spiritual exercises" to obtain "the neophyte's transmutation through a mystical death" (Eliade 1958: 107). The spiritual estrangement from society experienced by the ascetic requires the death of the socially normal person and an initiation into a reality normally unavailable.

The mysticism of this ascetic death, in turning away from oneself, features prominently in Deleuze and Guattari's insistence that the intuition of the artist as ascetic achieves an extraordinarily profound relationship to the religious-aesthetic forces of the earth. Referencing Eliade's work, Deleuze and Guattari claim "that religion, which is common to human beings and animals, occupies territory only because it depends on the raw aesthetic and territorializing factor as its necessary condition" (1987: 321). In deterritorialization, schizoanalytic asceticism uncovers the "intuition of the earth as a religious form" (548 ftn. 20) in contact with the immediate (raw) aesthetic of the earth, the genesis of quality, whose chaos may be disguised by organized society in the habits of "rites and religions, which are forces of the earth" (322). The ascetic intuition of the artist and the schizophrenic, through a desubjectification equivalent to personal death, intuitively harnesses the defamiliarized force of a raw aesthetic, which grounds an idiosyncratic, ascetic spirituality whose mysticism antagonizes the organized religions of society (Deleuze 2006; also Deleuze and Guattari 1983: 112, 269, 322, 342).[3] No longer disguised in terms of another world, schizoanalytic asceticism derives salvation from an immanent earth (Deleuze 2000: 127–9; also Wampole 2016: 250). Foreshadowing the final words of Deleuze's 1988 "Afterword" to *Bergsonism*, which maintains that Bergson's philosophy finds its most relevant contemporary application in psychiatric discourse (Deleuze 1981: 116–17), intuition freed from molar logic, likened to an ascetic reduction of the molar, remains key to the kind of schizophrenic experience at stake in this essay. The becoming-minoritarian enacted by schizoanalytic asceticism pursues a line of flight from the normal personality informed by group logic which conserves standards, toward an anomalous universe of microscopic variation following ego loss.

3. Spiritual Aversion and Asceticism

In *A Thousand Plateaus*, artistic asceticism and schizophrenic experience are both governed by an ascetic practice of disorganization, motivated by what could be called the principle of aversion that informs a schizoanalytic conception of spiritual exercise (Bogue 2001). According to Deleuze and Guattari, aversion (turning-away) counteracts and disorganizes the logic of imperial institutions which rely on signifiance ("the Signifier in person") (1987: 114–15) because aversion refuses the face that centralizes power in a fixed personality. As that toward which all imperially civilized subjects must turn, the personal face of the empire—whether the face of the imperial sovereign or Christ—is refused by the subject, equivalent to the betrayal of imperial power which every citizen must be allied with and obey (134, 137). Such betrayal leads one to wander into barbaric zones, to flee into deserts where one might encounter nomads beyond the empire, where "subterranean becomings-animal occur, becomings-molecular, nocturnal deterritorializations overspilling the limits of the signifying system" (115). Aversion from the face of imperial power therefore constitutes the initial spiritual movement of disorganization whose flight is supposed to disrupt the logic of centralized organizations fixing allegiance to imperial groups.

Deleuze and Guattari's understanding of the disorganizing effects of ascetic aversion is exhibited in their discussions of religion and empire in *A Thousand Plateaus*. Deleuze and Guattari describe traditional anchorite asceticism, or desert monasticism, as disrupting the organized church as a vector for human empire. Regarding the function of becoming-animal in anchorite asceticism, they write, "[T]he asceticism machine is in an anomalous position, on a line of flight, off to the side of the Church, and disputes the Church's pretension to set itself up as an imperial institution" (1987: 247).

Anchorites, often performing extraordinary feats in their withdrawal, demonstrate the powers available to the ascetic outside established human institutions, instead allied with nonhuman forces. As Peter Brown writes, anchorites perform a "solemn ritual of dissociation—of becoming the total stranger," in order to draw holy "powers from outside the human race: by going to live in the desert, in close identification with an animal kingdom that stood … for the opposite pole of all human society" (1971: 91–2). Yet, the function of aversion in flight from the imperial church is not limited to religion; it is "is applicable not only to the imperial despotic regime but to all subjected, arborescent, hierarchical, centered groups: political parties, literary movements, psychoanalytic associations, families, conjugal units, etc." (116). The common point is that groups justify their claims to power through fixed conceptions of the human subject, embodied in definite personalities. Impersonality, produced through ascetic aversion, hence disorganizes and disrupts the power of the iconic personality used to aggregate power following collective logic. Spiritual aversion motivates the most general movements of ascetic disruption of collectivized organization, introducing anomalies and escape routes dissecting limits (134).

Schizoanalytic asceticism communicates with the forces of the earth through averse deterritorialization, harnessing power through an elemental intuition of the earth that connects the ascetic to the cosmos, instead of being limited to a definite concept of the human being, incarnated by a particular personality. The becoming-animal initiated by the aversion of asceticism from theological organization has its terminal moment in the passage to the imperceptible cosmos, in the form of a becoming-everything. The ascetic reduction accomplished by the artist facilitates the passage to molecular intuition, into the cosmic. Deleuze and Guattari write, "Not everybody becomes everybody [and everything: *tout le monde*—Trans.], makes a becoming of everybody/everything. This requires much asceticism, much sobriety, much creative involution" (1987: 279). Aversion throws the ascetic into communication with an impersonal cosmos following its universal molecular composition. The ascetic reduction required in order to attain such a cosmic becoming everything is absolute: we must eliminate "everything that roots each of us (everybody) in ourselves, in our molarity. For everybody/everything is the molar aggregate, but *becoming everybody/everything* is another affair, one that brings into play the cosmos with its molecular components" (280). From the imperial face of Christ which subjectifies, aversion leads to the probe-head of desubjectification, or the desubjectified face, which is metallic, enduring to unite matter with energy in life (190). As Deleuze and Guattari write, "Not everything is metal, but metal is everywhere. Metal is the conductor of all matter. The machinic phylum is metallurgical, or at least has a metallic head, as its itinerant probe-head or guidance device" (411).[4] Desubjectification produces oneself as a probe-head, a metallic instrument or machine to explore the microscopic compositions of life. Against complex forms of justification used by groups to classify what is and is not a member of the collective, schizoanalytic asceticism pursues the simplest means to traverse the cosmos, that is, energetic becoming, represented by metal, to compose new alliances departing from human institutions and their imperial pretensions.

4. Desubjectification and Asceticism in Kraus

Kraus's writing attains impersonality through an ascetic desubjectification, an initiation into the elements of the earth that she ultimately associates with schizophrenia. Though I want to focus on *Aliens & Anorexia*, it is worth briefly showing how desubjectification is key to Kraus's first novel, *I Love Dick*. *I Love Dick* treats ironically the psychoanalytic conversion to significance of the phallus, whose face is expressed by the character Dick, an ascetic academic who has withdrawn into the desert. Writing a series of ultimately unanswered letters to the ascetic Dick, Kraus comes to realize her own ascetic authorship, but only after an experience of desubjectification, in which she becomes lost outside. After "walking erratically in jagged circles" in the woods near her home, she

> tried one more time to walk back the way I came but nothing looked familiar. Woods-woods-woods and frozen ground. I saw no way out, no animal markings, which in any case I didn't know how to read. So carefully I traced my way back again to the chainlink fence. I felt as though my eyes had moved outside my body. (Kraus [1998] 2006: 127)

This desubjectification toward the earth begins an increasingly schizophrenic and cosmic participation in the universe, through increasingly impersonal literary production. Immediately following her desubjectification, Kraus reflects on her newfound ability to write in the first person, which she has previously been unable to do. She writes, "[T]here's no fixed point of self but it exists & by writing you can somehow chart that movement. That maybe 1st person writing's just as fragmentary as more a-personal collage, it's just more serious: bringing change & fragmentation closer, bringing it down to where you really are" (Kraus [1998] 2006: 139). From this relation with the molecularly fragmented cosmos, Kraus's increasingly impersonal existence enters into expansive communication with the universe, first through molecular empathy with women whose artistic impersonality has never been contained by the molar or majoritarian (197, 210), and then through extended reflection on schizophrenic impersonality (254). In an interview, Kraus describes her writing the book in terms of producing schizophrenic experience. She says, "The real person who 'Dick' in *I Love Dick* was based on, had experienced a schizophrenic episode or two in his life. I wanted to try and enter this experience of schizophrenia he'd had, without attributing it to him ... So I thought, I'll become schizophrenic too" (Kraus Fall/Winter 2006). For Kraus, like Deleuze and Guattari, it is the impersonality of desubjectification in schizophrenia that is important: "The schizophrenic leaves the body, transcends himself, herself, outside any system of belief," Kraus writes in *I Love Dick* (Kraus [1998] 2006: 233). Following Deleuze and Guattari's *A Thousand Plateaus*, artistic creation enters into a zone of proximity with the molecular through an ascetic impersonality expressed in schizophrenia.

Kraus considers impersonality to be a defining feature of her writing, inherited and developed in the exchange between French theory, specifically Deleuze, and the New York avant-garde. Like Deleuze and Guattari, Kraus considers her use of impersonality to be strategic, elaborated in terms of an aversion from priestly organization, which is governed here by a majoritarian exclusion of a perceived anomaly: the becoming-everything of woman. Kraus sees such an exclusion already in the reception of Weil's work: "She was a crazy modernist like Artaud, Celine, Bataille, but as a female her 'I' has been pathologized—she can't get fucked, she's manipulative and anorexic, she's ugly and she dresses badly—her 'I' was never read as universal and transparent" (Kraus and Frimer 2006). In Kraus's view, her own work has similarly been labeled in popular criticism to limiting genres inflected by psychoanalytic or religious prejudice against women's writing, supposed to be merely memoir or confession. Asked about the confessional quality of her work, she responds, " 'Confessional' of what? *Personal confessions*? There's a great line from a book we published by Deleuze: *Life is not personal.* The word 'confessional' is not a good descriptor of my work … It's a very Catholic word, 'confession' " (Kraus and Frimer 2006).[5] Elsewhere, Kraus describes how female desubjectification, or impersonality, is considered impossible by critics: "There is no problem with female confession providing it is made within a repentant therapeutic narrative. But to examine things coolly, to thrust experience out of one's own brain and to put it on the table, is still too confrontational … It's the distancing of female experience that drives art critics crazy," that is, "presum[ing] to treat female experience universally" (Kraus 2004: 63). Kraus's distance from female experience in her own writing motivates her to disavow not only the generic labels of memoir or confession but also of feminism: "I'm not writing about feminism. I'm a woman writing about things," she says in response to a question about the common fate of women's art, "lumped together in the 'feminist' room" at the hands of "cultural gatekeepers" (Kraus and Epps 2016). As Maggie Nelson has shown, the refusal of the labels of feminism by women in the New York School avant-garde stems from a double bind that emerges in the pursuit of artistic originality (2007: 8–9), which I have partially illuminated in terms of an ascetic aversion to organization informing originary artistic practice. The disavowal of organization, here seen in Kraus's distancing of her work from generic labels, is the necessary consequence of a schizoanalytic asceticism that configures becoming impersonal as an effective process of spiritual aversion liberating perception from cognitive constraint.

Despite Kraus's disavowal of generic labels, the force of her aversion illustrates the terms of an alliance, in a schizoanalytic feminism, between schizoanalytic asceticism and a feminism whose aversion to organization aims to become revolutionary. Indeed, as Shulamith Firestone argues, in what Kraus says is one of her favorite texts (Kraus 2004: 60–1), artistic impersonality reflects a literary androgyny that is capable of "reflecting the human price of a sex-divided reality," given its unique ability to realize an impersonal vision that disorganizes the scope of gender (Firestone [1970] 2003: 152). Accordingly, the principle of aversion in schizoanalytic asceticism, leading to an impersonal desubjectification, forms an alliance between the revolutionary avant-garde and feminist revolution, aiming to realize androgynous impersonality socially and culturally: "[T]he end goal of feminist revolution must be … not just the elimination of male *privilege* but of the sex *distinction* itself: genital differences between human beings would no longer matter" (11).[6] The aversion of impersonality disorganizes not only religion but also gender; this is a consequence of the function of aversion central to schizoanalytic asceticism (Deleuze and Guattari 1987: 276). In Kraus's work, a line of flight proceeds away from feminism as a molar entity toward an impersonal becoming-universal, illuminating a feminism that schizoanalytically disrupts its own self-understanding to subvert the limits of the majoritarian through ascetic resistance in alliance with the cosmic.

5. Ascetic Impersonality: Anorexia and the Alien

Ultimately for Kraus, it is Weil's asceticism that comes to exemplify the schizophrenic impersonality that is described in *I Love Dick*.[7] Weil's asceticism and its inflection in Kraus's work provides opportunity to explore how asceticism poses a problem for the majoritarian logic which according to Kraus refuses to recognize impersonality when attained by a woman. According to Kraus, the illegibility of impersonality produces a form of ascetic experience whose cosmic reach exceeds that of the male-avant garde, motivating a spiritual exercise of anorexia that reformulates the spiritual function of fasting in the presence of the cosmic.

Kraus says, "I have this radical empathy, which Simone Weil talks about quite brilliantly herself. Weil went someplace way out past compassion … She had this thin membrane between herself and other people, not just individuals, but the state of the world" (Kraus and Indiana Fall/Winter 2006)· Such an empathy describes for Kraus how desubjectification enters into proximity with schizophrenia: "If you know no boundaries, you lose yourself in what you're experiencing, and that's a state very close to madness" (ibid.). Like schizoanalytic asceticism, Weil's spirituality reflects extreme aversion from society. "Society is the cave. The way out is solitude," Weil writes, interpreting the Platonic myth of conversion from the cave as an exercise in ascetic withdrawal (Weil [1952] 2002: 165). By renouncing society and its false goods, Weil enters into proximity with the renunciation she attributes to the cosmic divine. Weil writes, "Renunciation. Imitation of God's renunciation in creation. In a sense God renounces being everything. We should renounce being something. That is our only good" ([1952] 2002: 33). For Weil, an ascetic conversion of renunciation enables communication with the cosmos, realized in the spiritual exercise of decreation that aims toward impersonality. Decreation is an exercise in "destroy[ing] the self for the sake of the universe … to feel also the perpetual exchange of matter by which the human being bathes in the world" (142). In decreation, impersonality is realized in becoming habituated to the "universe, the seasons, the suns, the stars," so as to "feel the universe through each sensation" as if it were "the stick of a blind man" (141). Kraus considers decreation to aim at the same impersonality as the BodywithoutOrgans, which she relates to the spiritualized attention toward the everyday in New York School poetics (Kraus 2001: 304–5). More generally, Kraus's interpretation of Weil focuses on and develops the sense of empathetic feeling and sympathetic attachment proper to the schizoanalytic cosmic. In *Aliens & Anorexia*, Kraus uses Weil's exercise of decreation to frame the lives of an international band of revolutionaries and artists, such as Ulrike Meinhof, Paul Thek, and a pair of teenage girls named Gravity & Grace, whose stories, taking place in the 1970s, weave together forces of cosmic desire, affliction, and chance.

Weil's spirituality, following Kraus's interpretation of it, also illuminates the double bind of an avant-garde asceticism that is caught between the aversion proper to becoming-minoritarian and the exclusion enforced by majoritarian tradition. Kraus maintains that the majoritarian tradition of the male avant-garde under-appreciates the full extent of cosmic shock despite its pretension to exposing itself to the forces of the universe. In Kraus's view, the male-dominated avant-garde conducts experiments with cosmic forces from an insulated and privileged position of security, and, hence, deficiently senses the emotional and traumatic experience of the cosmos whose becoming violates form. Kraus writes that the avant-garde men of the twentieth century "were crocodiles in clubchairs, conductors of controlled experiments in chaos. In the interest of a greater science they were prepared to gouge out pieces of their own non-porous skin. Girls, on the other hand, are less reptilian" (Kraus [2000] 2013: 53). The asceticism of the male avant-garde hardly suffers the brunt of the forces of the cosmic insofar as the logic of the majoritarian continues to prop-up and propagate elite male genius. Kraus writes sardonically, "Throughout the 20th century, chance has repeatedly recurred as the basis of artistic practice among groups of highly educated men. Man Ray photographs Robert Desnos during the 'Nap Period' at the Surrealist Headquarters, a suite of rooms in a hotel owned by one of the Surrealists' dads" (52). As the male avant-garde chances to encounter the forces of the cosmos from an impenetrable and patriarchal citadel, ensconced by scaly armor, the exclusion of women ("those less reptilian") from the halls of tradition leaves them impoverished of its actual protections.

Exposure to the cosmos occurs not just by chance but in the sadness of a spiritual exercise that senses the perpetual affliction of elements in becoming.[8] Kraus considers sadness to be the "girl-equivalent to chance" (Kraus [2000] 2013: 119). Sadness results in impersonality: "Like chance, emotion is a current that dissolves the boundaries of a person's subjectivity" (120). Sadness connects the ascetic equally with the impersonal forces of the cosmos, whose trauma is lost on the chance of the male avant-garde. "A single moment of true sadness connects you instantly to all the suffering of the world" (155). The problem of gender in spirituality emerges in this context insofar as it regulates the legibility and illegibility of ascetic impersonality: "It's inconceivable that the female subject might ever simply try to *step outside* her body, because the only thing that's irreducible, still, in female life is gender" (163). A strategic use of impersonality, specifically in the use of cosmic sadness, or universal empathy, emerges in Kraus's interpretation of anorexia as spiritual exercise. Anorexia is aversion from universal suffering wrought on and by the universe. It is motivated by an intuition of the absurdity of the earthly organizations which viciously consume: "*Impossible* to drink coffee without thinking about the Inca laborers who picked it, transported from their villages in cattle trucks to work for fifty cents a day … *Impossible* to view the paintings at the Frick Museum without thinking about the murdered workers, gunned down outside while protesting child labor" (149). Yet, the totality of cosmic sadness exceeds the limits of this world. Crying from sadness, "[y]ou close your eyes and travel outwards through a vortex that draws you towards the saddest thing of all. And the saddest thing of all isn't anything but sadness. It's too big to see or name. Approaching it's like seeing God" (126). Cosmic sadness, reaching the point of mystical impersonality, overloads the impersonal body, so that one must turn away in aversion from empathetic shock: "Porousness equals malabsorption. The body is so fraught with information, it becomes impossible to process food" (159). As aversion from the cosmic sadness, anorexia illustrates a flight into nomadism, from the false nourishments of the universe: "To question food is to question everything. To question food is to recognize the impossibility of 'home'" (165). Anorexia as spiritual exercise here develops the sense of the cosmic following the principle of aversion in flight that Deleuze and Guattari describe in *A Thousand Plateaus*.

Aversion unifies the narrative of *Gravity & Grace*, that is, Kraus's short film, named after Weil's text, occupying the final third of the novel. In New Zealand, Gravity, a fictional avatar for Kraus, and her friend Grace, attend a long-prophesied alien encounter organized by the priestly Extraterrestrial Research Group (ERG), led by a mysterious, saintly man who channels the voice of the alien Sananda. While the man is conspicuously absent at the event he has prophesied, he has been speaking supernaturally through the various members of the group; together they all chant a song whose lyrics read: "*Zoom golly golly / God takes off like a jet!*" (Kraus [2000] 2013: 232). Soon, however, the inevitable conclusion dawns: both the man and the alien Sananda he channels have turned away from their promise of an extraterrestrial revolution. Aversion reigns, yet the failure of the Church of the ERG sends Gravity in flight to New York City.

Kraus writes, "During Gravity's first months in New York City, the most impressive people that she met were artists and so she becomes one, too" (Kraus [2000] 2013:235). Gravity's becoming artist consists of years of living in ascetic poverty and isolation. Drawing parallel with Kraus's own life, it would be during this time that Kraus-Gravity begins to refine her artistic intuition in the context of the New York School avant-garde. Kraus says of her life upon moving to New York City from New Zealand in 1978, "I lived in the same neighborhood as the poets. I was as poor as the poets. I went to all the readings and went out with *the* poets ... I really absorbed by osmosis a lot of the poet's rhetoric, the poet's way of seeing the world" (Kraus and Frimer 2006). In *Aliens & Anorexia*, the art which Gravity composes consists only of probe-heads, half-animal, half-metal: her welded sculptures are so many "miscegenated insects in aluminum" (Kraus [2000] 2013: 240). Kraus's ascetic artistic practice produces the metallic face of desubjectification united with the cosmic. Yet, the multiplicity of probe-heads, whose production is vital to Gravity's life, remain entirely illegible to the institution that would be responsible for representing her art. Meeting with Gravity to potentially arrange an exhibition of the pieces, the Senior Curator of the New Museum is consternated by the metallic insects. The meeting represents the inevitable resistance to ascetic impersonality that the majoritarian and molar consistently display toward the cosmic. This, then, is an encounter of schizoanalytic feminism, where an artisan's formed metal wanders into imperial, royal halls. The curator says, after admitting her surprise at Gravity's work, "I have a problem though, with the metal. It's so contrary to the notion of the feminine unformed … After all, you're a woman … And yet you haven't chosen to make an explicit feminist critique the way most of your contemporaries do … I see the sculptural medium as a serious problem in your work" (253). No wonder that, after this rejection, Gravity, in the novel's final lines, wishes only to flee in aversion toward the alien, the cosmic end of her work: "That Friday morning on Mulberry Street, Gravity is certain she's prepared to leave the world" (255).

Notes

1. On the avant-garde, see Bürger (1984) and Ziarek (2001); on disruption in modernism, see Gosetti-Ferencei (2007). See also, Foucault (2011): 183–9.

2. On asceticism in existential phenomenology, see Khawaja (2016).

3. For a historical analysis of spirituality in post-1968 French thought, see Bourg (2007).

4. The probe-head of desubjectification, a penetrating technology in alien abduction stories, harbors a subreption of the phallus. See also, Kraus, *Aliens & Anorexia* 39–40 where Kraus considers two kinds of alien abductions: one, religious, sexual, involving a female, the other, experimental, asexual, in a group.

5. Here, Kraus is referring, I think, to Deleuze and Parnet, "A Conversation: What is it? What is it for?," though I am unable locate an edition of this interview published by Semiotext(e).

6. On impersonality in Deleuze's modernism, see Colebrook (2013); On the alliance between a revolutionary avant-garde and feminism, see Sulemain ([1990] 2012). Cause for a good, asceticism as point of alliance between a revolutionary avant-garde and feminism reflects the orientation of ancient asceticism to social justice. See Ramelli (2017).

7. My reading of Weil has benefitted from Sharon Cameron's (2007) 'The Practice of Attention: Simone Weil's Performance of Impersonality.'

8. On a feminist sensibility to violence in the New York School avant-garde, see Nelson (2007: 210–12).

References

Agamben, G. (2007), *Infancy and History: On the Destruction of Experience*, London: Verso.

Badiou, A. (2000), *Deleuze and the Clamor of Being*, trans. L. Burchill, Minneapolis: University of Minnesota Press.

Benjamin, W. (1968), "On Some Motifs in Baudelaire," in H. Arendt (ed.), *Illuminations: Essays and Reflections*, trans. H. Zohn, New York: Schocken Books.

Bergson, H. ([1935] 1977), *The Two Sources of Morality and Religion*, trans. R. A. Audra and C. Brereton, Notre Dame, IN: University of Notre Dame Press.

Bergson, H. ([1911] 1998), *Creative Evolution*, trans. Arthur Mitchell, Mineola, NY: Dover Publications.

Bergson, H. ([1946] 2007a), "Philosophical Intuition," in *The Creative Mind: An Introduction to Metaphysics*, trans. M. L. Andison, 87–106, Mineola, NY: Dover Publications.

Bergson, H. ([1946] 2007b), "The Perception of Change," in *The Creative Mind: An Introduction to Metaphysics*, trans. M. L. Andison, 107–32, Mineola, NY: Dover Publications.

Bogue, R. (2001), "The Betrayal of God," in Mary Bryden (ed.), *Deleuze & Religion*, London: Routledge.

Bourg, J. (2007), *From Revolution to Ethics: May 1968 and Contemporary French Thought*, Montreal: McGill-Queen's University Press.

Brown, P. (1971), "The Rise and Function of the Holy Man in Late Antiquity," *Journal of Roman Studies* 61: 80–101.

Bürger, P. (1984), *Theory of the Avant-Garde*, Minneapolis: University of Minnesota Press.

Cameron, S. (2007), "The Practice of Attention: Simone Weil's Performance of Impersonality," *Impersonality: Seven Essays*, Chicago: University of Chicago Press.

Colebrook, C. (2013) "Modernism without Women: The Refusal of Becoming-Woman (and Post-Feminism)," *Deleuze Studies* 7 (3): 427–55.

Cusset, F. (2008), *French Theory: How Foucault, Derrida, Deleuze, & Co. Transformed the Intellectual Life of the United States*, trans. Jeff Fort, Minneapolis: University of Minnesota Press.

Deleuze, G. (1981), *Bergsonism*, trans. Hugh Tomlinson and Barbara Habberjam, New York: Zone Books.

Deleuze, G. (2000), *Logic of Sense*, ed. Constantin V. Boundas, trans. Mark Lester, New York: Columbia University Press.

Deleuze, G. (2006), *Nietzsche and Philosophy*, trans. Hugh Tomlinson, New York: Columbia University Press.

Deleuze, G., and F. Guattari (1983), *Anti-Oedipus: Capitalism and Schizophrenia*, trans. R. Hurley, M. Seem, and H. R. Lane, Minneapolis: University of Minneapolis Press, 1983.

Deleuze, G., and F. Guattari (1987), *A Thousand Plateaus: Capitalism and Schizophrenia*, trans. B. Massumi, Minneapolis: University of Minnesota Press.

Deleuze, G., and C. Parnet (1987), "A Conversation: What Is It? What Is It For?," *Dialogues II*, New York: Columbia University Press.

Eliade, M. (1958), *Rites and Symbols of Initiation: The Mysteries of Birth and Rebirth*, trans. W. R. Trask, New York: Harper & Row.

Firestone, S. ([1970] 2003), *The Dialectic of Sex: The Case for Feminist Revolution*, New York: Farrar, Straus and Giroux.

Foucault, M. (2011), *The Courage of Truth: The Government of Self and Others II: Lectures at the Collège de France 1983–1984*, ed. F. Gros, F. Ewald, A. Fontana, A. I. Davidson, New York: Picador.

Gosetti-Ferencei, J. A. (2007), *The Ecstatic Quotidian: Phenomenological Sightings in Modern Art and Literature*, University Park: Pennsylvania State University Press.

Jankélévitch, V. (2015), *Henri Bergson*, ed. A. Lefebvre and N. F. Schott, trans. Nils F. Schott, Durham, NC: Duke University Press.

Khawaja, N. (2016), *The Religion of Existence: Asceticism in Philosophy from Kierkegaard to Sartre*, Chicago: University of Chicago Press.

Kraus, C. (2001), "Ecceity, Smash and Grab, The Expanded I and Moment," in S. Lotringer and S. Cohen (eds.), *French Theory in America*, New York: Routledge.

Kraus, C. (2004), "Pay Attention," *Video Green: Los Angeles Art and the Triumph of Nothingness*, New York: Semiotext(e).

Kraus, C. ([1998] 2006), *I Love Dick*, Los Angeles, CA: Semiotext(e).

Kraus, C. ([2000] 2013), *Aliens & Anorexia*, Los Angeles, CA: Semiotext(e).

Kraus, C., and P. Epps (2016), "Chris Kraus on Her Radical 1997 Novel 'I Love Dick'," interview by Philomena Epp, *Dazed*, May 31, 2016, http://www.dazeddigital.com/artsandculture/article/31239/1/author-chris-kraus-on-her-radical-1997-novel-i-love-dick (accessed April 18, 2019).

Kraus, C., and D. Frimer (2006), "Chris Kraus in conversation with Denise Frimer," interview by Denise Frimer, *The Brooklyn Rail*, April 10, 2006, http://brooklynrail.org/2006/04/art/chris-kraus-in-conversation-with-denise-frimer (accessed April 18, 2019).

Kraus, C., and G. Indiana (2006), "Looking Back," interview by Gary Indiana, *Purple Diary*, Fall/Winter 2006, http://purple.fr/magazine/fw-2006-issue-6/chris-kraus/ (accessed April 18, 2019).

Laertius, D. ([1925] 1972), *Lives of Eminent Philosophers: Books 1–5*, trans. R. D. Hicks, Cambridge: Harvard University Press.

Laing, R. D. (1967), *The Politics of Experience*, New York: Pantheon Books.

Laing, R. D. (1972), "Metanoia: Some Experiences at Kingsley Hall, London," in Dr. H. M. Ruitenbeek (ed.), *Going Crazy: The Radical Therapy of R.D. Laing and Others*, New York: Bantam Books.

Mossé-Bastide, R. (1959), *Bergson et Plotin*, Paris: Presses Universitaires de France.

Nelson, M. (2007), *Women, the New York School, and Other True Abstractions*, Iowa City: University of Iowa Press.

Ramelli, I. L. E. (2017), *Social Justice and the Legitimacy of Slavery: The Role of Philosophical Asceticism from Ancient Judaism to Late Antiquity*, Oxford: Oxford University Press.

Robinson, D. (2008), *Estrangement and the Somatics of Literature: Tolstoy, Shklovsky, Brecht*, Baltimore, MD: Johns Hopkins University.

Schwarz, H., and A. Balsamo (1996), "Under the Sign of Semiotext(e): The Story According to Sylvere Lotringer and Chris Kraus," *Critique: Studies in Contemporary Fiction* 37 (3): 205–20.

Sulemain, S. R. ([1990] 2012), *Subversive Intent: Gender, Politics, and the Avant-Garde*, Cambridge: Harvard University Press.

Wampole, C. (2016), *Rootedness: The Ramifications of a Metaphor*, Chicago: University of Chicago Press.

Weil, S. ([1952] 2002), *Gravity and Grace*, trans. E. Crawford and M. von der Ruhr, London: Routledge.

Ziarek, K. (2001), *The Historicity of Experience: Modernity, the Avant Garde, and the Event*, Evanston: Northwestern University Press.

Figure 15.1 *"The Other side, Breakthrough," 2013, wood and varnish installation, Hollie Mackenzie 183 cm × 104 cm × 13 cm, wood and varnish. Photo taken by the artist.*

Through a feminist process of writing a labial language of difference into wood, the Other side of Breakthrough conveys the features of a female sexual imaginary by presenting a composition of the dynamics of fluids. Carving an alliance between Irigaray's labial language (1985) and Deleuze and Guattari's "a thousand tiny sexes" (2004), these labial drips pose a resistance to the gravity of our world in a desire for different kinds of gravity.

CHAPTER 15
A SCHIZO-REVOLUTIONARY LABIAL THEORY OF ARTISTIC PRACTICE
Hollie Mackenzie

This chapter is an invitation to participate in a feminist aesthetics of resistance that can challenge the capitalist and patriarchal systems of representation and thoroughly incite the practice of *becoming-woman*. I suggest that we can develop this feminist aesthetics of resistance by allying Deleuze and Guattari's (2013) notion of *schizo-revolutionary art* with Irigaray's (1985) concepts of the *indifferentiated woman* and the *labial lips*. Such an alliance has an enfolded purpose: (1) to formulate a new feminist and artistic *theorization* of resistance, and (2) to propose a different feminist artistic *practice* of resistance. This enfolded approach amounts to a *schizo-revolutionary labial theory of artistic practice* that produces not just political art nor an aesthetic approach within political theory, rather, an enfolded theory-practice of art and politics "without any possibility of distinguishing what is touching from what is touched" (Irigaray 1985b: 26); a *labial art-politics* (Mackenzie and MacKenzie 2014: 77).

For Deleuze (1994), thinking schizoanalytically can enable us to sense new ideas that are outside our normative images of thought. These ideas cannot be represented in thought but are nonetheless real as they become the structures that condition our experience in the world (156–67). Deleuze explains that we come to sense these ideas through experiencing an *encounter*. An encounter bears a problem which "perplexes" the subject and forces them to think (140). Thinking through this problem forces the subject to think of an idea, not to solve the problem but to transform it in order to bring about a new way of thinking and being. It is within this notion of the encounter that we can explore the potential of a schizo-revolutionary labial theory of art that can provide a resistance to the normative dogmatic and judgmental image of thought based on the phallogocentric system (Braidotti 1994: 101) and engender processes of transformation that can explore the emancipation of female imagination, pleasure, and expression.

1. An Ontological Conception of Art

According to Deleuze, the art "object" is not a recognizable object; rather, its primary aesthetic characteristic is that it is a fundamental encounter that "can only be sensed" (1994: 139). It is through experiencing the art's "precepts and affects" that an encounter with the art "object" is distinct from our experience of empirical objects (Deleuze and Guattari 1994: 164). This distinct experience is what Zepke calls a heterogeneous duration, which does not obey representational knowledge-claims, coherent narrative frames and/or linear temporalities (2008: 34). The art object therefore cannot be represented in thought but can be understood as an assemblage of sensory affects. Preserved within the artistic encounter, the percepts and affects condition the artistic experience and emit the problematic signs that perplexes the subject and forces them to think. The new ideas that are forced into thought engender a different way of thinking and acting, as they become the new structures that condition the subject's experience in the world. Understood in this way, this ontological conception of art has the revolutionary potential to transform the normative ideas of subjectivity and judgment that are aligned with the interests of patriarchy and capitalism (Mackenzie and MacKenzie 2014: 70).[1]

In describing the revolutionary potential of art, it is important to acknowledge that artistic flows can be captured by patriarchal and capitalist systems of representation. In Deleuze and Guattari's terms, there are always movements of reterritorialization that follow movements of deterritorialization that over code any difference produced, so as to (re-)submit it to the systems of representation. To the extent that this ontological conception of the artistic encounter can resist being dominated, subordinated, and appropriated by the patriarchal and capitalist systems of representation, I will argue that a feminist artistic practice can create lines of flights that can escape these dominant structures. This is not to say that feminist practices are outside of capitalism (or patriarchy)—they too can be subsumed through movements of reterritorialization. There is, nonetheless, a feminist critique embedded in such reterritorializations that incites us to continue a feminist artistic practice. By enlivening the feminine within the artistic process, art can move in processes of deterritorializations of the dominant structures.

Deleuze and Guattari explain that, when movements of deterritorialization take hold, machines are released that can open territorial assemblages to other assemblages. They describe this rupture "like a set of cutting edges that insert themselves into the assemblage undergoing deterritorialization and draw variations and mutations of it" (2004: 367). Within this rupturing process, these cutting edges create points of escape that connect the assemblage with the Cosmos, thereby opening it onto new possibilities. It is within this opening that the matters of expression enter into a process of passage and relay, during which the components from the territorial assemblage and the Cosmos become "parts and pieces of one another" (367). Within this movement of escape, the heterogeneous components express "a series of relations between a territory and its outside that ignores subject/object distinctions" (Zepke 2008: 35). Accordingly, the subject and the art object become indiscernible in this process in which they are all parts and pieces of one another. It is here that we can create lines of flights that can resist the authoritative nature of the individual artist and the commodification of the art object.

Even though the artist makes the expression, Deleuze and Guattari explain that the artist's expression is but a chancy formation of a domain (2004: 349). They delineate a territory in order to work through their experience of territorialization. Within this movement of territoriality, Deleuze and Guattari describe that the art produced is "not the privilege of human beings"; rather the artist is a participant in the movement that produces a *territorial mark* (349). Here, we can note Zepke's account of how the subject becomes a participating artist. Zepke's description of the artistic experience builds upon Deleuze's notion of the encounter by explaining that the subject can administer a "shock" after being forced to think (2008: 42). Using Guattari (1995), I will further explain that this shock is expressed by a "partial enunciation," which indicates the subject's transformation from a passive spectator into a participating artist or "cocreator" (14). It is important to note that both Guattari and Zepke speak of the participating artist or cocreator in order to delegitimize the sense of authority that resides within the traditional idea of the artist. In order to investigate what the subject finds shocking within the artistic encounter, it will be useful to turn to Guattari's description of "mutant" percepts and affects (1995: 91).

Within the experience of the artistic encounter, a mutant affect seizes the spectator, making them part of the artistic process, and sets the conditions for what can be sensed. In doing so, the artistic process becomes an experience of "affect as immanent evaluation, instead of judgment as transcendent value" (Deleuze 1989: 141). In this movement of deterritorialization, the affective evaluation also connects with the Cosmos through the points of escape, thereby enabling evaluation from the outside as well as from within. Through a partial access to the infinity of virtual possibilities of the Cosmos, the parts and pieces become lost with the cosmic forces in a movement of, what we will call, "iridescent chaos" (Cézanne 1978: 150). Within this iridescent chaos, the immanent evaluation provides a heterogeneous duration of evaluating "every being, every action and passion, even every value, in relation to the life which they involve" (Deleuze 1989: 141). The life involved is a mixture of the subject and the mutant affect; there is no way to recognize either as the subject and the art object have become indiscernible. However, what can be evaluated is what can be sensed, therefore the evaluation rests upon the experience related to the life of that mutant affect. This is what, then, makes art an experience with difference or otherness, or in other words, a shocking encounter.

Evaluating every-*thing* related to the life of that mutant affect does not mean that what is produced henceforth becomes all-knowing about that life. The access to the Cosmos is only partial, not complete, because there is still a partial connection to the territorial assemblage. This partial connection is important as it maintains our engagement in the world and is how we can engender change within it. There is a danger, however, of arbitrary selection. The cosmic forces that are available to enter into a process of passage and relay are content dependent upon the life of that mutant affect. Given that this evaluation is of every-thing, not every available cosmic force can be selected because of the risk of forming a "black hole" (Deleuze and Guattari 2004: 368). Therefore, I suggest the forces that can be selected are evaluated through experiencing their power to affect and be affected, in which this process of selection becomes a process that "asserts the affirmative, joyful affects over and above the negative ones" (Braidotti 2010: 307). This mode of selection is not judgmental, because it is immanent to the process. Moreover, it is not conceptual in which involves a determinative judgment, because we can never know in advance what new forces are selected nor can we predict the outcome of the regrouping.

We can instead understand this process of selection as the "combats-between" forces. As Deleuze claims, "it is combat that replaces judgment," and the "combat-between is the process through which a force enriches itself by seizing hold of other forces and joining itself to them in a new ensemble: a becoming" (Deleuze 1997: 132). It entails an approach that selects the affirmative forces within the process of combat-between, which is taking place in the movement of iridescent chaos, to enter into the process of passage and relay. This method of passage and relay consists of the ordering and disordering of the *readymade*; where new affirmative forces take the place of existing forces that have been evaluated as negative and will not bring anything new to the territorial assemblage. Here we can understand that the expression of a territorial mark does not end the process, but rather enriches the artistic ensemble so as to incite a new artistic encounter(s) or becoming(s).

Guattari describes this artistic process as the "function of enunciative appropriation of aesthetic form" (1995: 13), in which the mutant affect can engender a certain mode of aesthetic enunciation that becomes correlative to "a logic of non-discursive intensities" and to a "pathic incorporation-agglomeration of ... vectors of partial subjectivity" (22). A partial enunciation is therefore no longer specific to a semiotic register but can be expressed in other domains as enunciative substances of a machinic order (24).[2] The shock that is expressed by a partial enunciation becomes part of the machinic assemblage of enunciation, in which it cannot be recognized as being administered from the subject because it is a heterogeneous agglomeration. Guattari does however describe this machinic assemblage of enunciation as a machinic subjectivity, which "installs itself ... before and alongside the subject-object relation" (24). Therefore, positing the mutant affects and percepts as pre-personal components that can make possible a becoming of subject and art. It is in this sense that Guattari describes art as an event that produces "mutant centres of subjectivation," (1996: 200) from which new intensities are extorted and being is summoned to exist differently (1995: 96).

Zepke further describes this process as schizoanalytical, as it entails the " 'art' of making something ... escape from its 'self' " (2014: 32). This does not mean that the subject will die in a movement of deterritorialization, or that the work produced is nothing. Instead, it is an artistic process of escaping the systems of representation: to make something escape from its "self" as defined by normative models and images.[3] That is to say, what can be created can escape "the gravity of its self-evidence" and become something different (2008: 42). This schizoanalytical artistic practice is therefore a transformational process that can open up new possibilities for thinking and being. Moreover, it is an artistic process that can provide "the potential for revolution" (Deleuze and Guattari 2004: 388). Understanding artistic practice in this way will enable us to rethink what we mean by art generally speaking; or, more particularly, what we mean by art objects, the artist, and art practice. The art can be thought of as an experience of the artistic process; the artist as the "artist-as-process" (Cutler 2013: 356); and the artistic practice as *schizo-revolutionary*.[4] However, before we frame the schizo-revolutionary artistic practice as a feminist artistic practice, we must specify exactly what is at stake within this experience of the schizo-revolutionary artistic process as it is not always clear within poststructuralist accounts. I will argue that this specification can be achieved by understanding schizo-revolutionary artistic process as the *indifferenc/tiated organization of the Cosmos*.

2. Indifferenc/tiated Organization of the Cosmos

The term indifferenc/tiated includes both the C and the T because, as I will explain, the artistic process becomes the dynamic between the *differenciated* and *undifferentiated*. The indifferenc/tiated is not about organizing chaos into a differenciated order, or more precisely, subordinating any concept of *difference* to *the Same*.[5] Such an approach would suppress the forces of the Cosmos and end the process. This would be an approach privileged by the artist-as-chooser and would result in a "finished" art object. Neither is it about the organization of an undifferentiated order, in which the organization is incomprehensible or wholly *schizophrenic*. Such an approach can only happen outside of the refrain and could result in forming a black hole, which would do away with the artist and art object completely. Instead, I propose that it is a dynamic between the differenciated order and the undifferentiated chaos that has an organization to it through a selection of the, in principle, infinite possibilities of the Cosmos. This artistic organization works between the territory and the outside to organize the territorial assemblage as composed chaos (Deleuze and Guattari 1994: 204). This approach will develop Zepke's concept of the readymade by arguing that we need to bring the *made* out of the readymade; not in order to return to the artist-as-maker, but to posit that new existential territories are always ready-to-be-*made*.

The readymade described by Zepke is different to the readymade defined by Duchamp (1973). According to Duchamp art was produced for "the service of the mind" (1998: 274), to which any ordinary object could become a work of art if it is the artist's conceptual choice or "nomination" (1973: 32). Art, in this sense, becomes "complete anaesthesia"; where its affects (and aesthetics) are completely subtracted from art (141). Contrary to Duchamp's claim is Zepke's articulation of the readymade as "affectual" (2008: 36). Through its aesthetic excess, Zepke describes this affectual readymade as a "war machine of a politics of sensation" (36). This aesthetic excess provides the available materials from the territory with which to make an artistic encounter. Not in the sense that any of the territory's available materials can be elevated to the status of art, as would be Duchamp's version of the readymade. Rather, the territory's materials are ready-to-be-made. In this sense, the territory is always a readymade.

As the selected cosmic forces cannot be represented, the artistic problem becomes one of harnessing them in a territorial mark. This brings us back to the movement of territoriality, which for Deleuze and Guattari involves the process of "*a reorganization of functions and a regrouping of forces*" (2004: 353). In order to preserve the cosmic forces as affects, we can approach the indifferenc/tiated organization by working with the territory as readymade to mark the cosmic forces as appropriative qualities. It is only through preserving the affects of the cosmic forces that we can introduce difference into the territorial assemblage in order to engender change within the world. Deleuze and Guattari explain this process of marking as borrowing weapons in order to yield vision or sensation (1994: 204). This process raises the "lived perceptions to the percept and lived affections to the affect" (170). They describe this operation as "the moment the artist connects material with forces of consistency or consolidation" in order to form a synthesizer of "the molecular and the cosmic, material and force" (2004: 379–80). Here, we could think the synthesizer is a "force of the Cosmos" and as such, it can "make thought travel" (379). Following this, the synthesizer is what; makes the artistic encounter "something in the world that forces us to think" (Deleuze 1994: 139).

Harnessed in the territorial assemblage, the cosmic forces become "directional components" (Deleuze and Guattari 2004: 344–5). These enrich the readymade by resolving the combat without suppressing the cosmic forces or ending the process. Consequently, they become the force of the Cosmos that blows otherness through the system and opens up the virtuality of the readymade. This changes the direction in the ordering and disordering of the readymade which makes possible transformations from one territory to another. It is in this sense that "the readymade is in constant contact with a multiplicity of possible futures" (Zepke 2008: 35).

It is when a territorial mark is made that the indifferenc/tiated organization moves from *indifferentiated* to *indifferenciated*, and it is only this expression that can incite a becoming of art and subject. Moreover, the process of marking delineates a new existential territory, producing a complex ontological crystallization of the virtuality opened up in the readymade. That is to say, a territorial mark marks a transition from a virtual artistic organization as indifferentiated, to an actualized artistic organization as indifferenciated. In doing so, the territorial assemblage is (re)organized, in which the directional components transform into "dimensional components" and become expressive (Deleuze and Guattari 2004: 345). This transformative artistic process is what produces art as "an event that actualises a set of virtualities and in so doing expresses a possible world" (O'Sullivan 2006: 130).

However, this does not mean that the process is thereby complete. There is always a reterritorializing attack by patriarchal and capitalist systems of representation, which subsumes the artistic ensemble. It is therefore necessary to continue this artistic process as indifferenc/tiated in order to endlessly renew the artistic organization. The upshot is that the territorial mark expresses a "double enunciation" (Guattari 1995: 55), which delineates a new existential territory *and* the infinite possibilities of the Cosmos incorporeal in the virtuality of that affectual readymade. This can produce schisms within the artistic organization, in which some of the dimensional components can always give way to "components of passage" (Deleuze and Guattari 2004: 345) that can incite new processes of passage and relay and with it, new possibilities of difference. These particular dimensional components have remained functional and transitory because they are tied to a type of action (347).[6] Their functions, when territorialized, adopt a new practical pace that can suddenly draw a line of deterritorialization (354–9). I will argue that these dimensional components are feminine as they can enliven a process of deterritorialization in which components of passage and relay produce an "innovative opening of the territory onto the female, or the group" (358).

Consequently, a work of art is never "finished" because it is always in the process of escaping and becoming different. The nature of the indifferenc/tiated artistic process can now be thought of as a mixed two-way process of working within the ordering and disordering of the readymade. To this extent, new existential territories can continually be constructed from the affectual readymade through its untiring renewal (Guattari 1995: 56). Therefore, this indifferenc/tiated artistic process can also be thought of as a process of working within the ordering and disordering of possible worlds. Accordingly, the value of what is produced will never be subsumed within capitalist and patriarchal structures because these have already been left behind in the creation of "a possible world" (O'Sullivan 2006: 130).

We can now understand this artistic practice as a methodology of writing within, rather than about, the structures that condition our experience. As I have expressed elsewhere, this "art" can be thought of as *learning the art of expressing ideas as problems* (Mackenzie and MacKenzie 2014: 71). This methodology of expressing ideas as problems enables us a way of sensing these ideas by preserving them as problems in artistic encounters. Moreover, it becomes an artistic process of learning that can produce new images of thought in order to engage with the ideas that structure our experience. By transforming our way of thinking to engage with these ideas, we also transform the way we experience and engage with the world. The new images of thought produced, therefore, create a "new mode of life that contains within itself the conditions of its own sustainability" (77). It is this "revolutionary style of life" (Zepke 2014: 31) that enables escapes to the outside, but only to return with the possibility of bringing something new with which to express a different world. Upon this return, we face the reterritorializing habits of mind that aim to re-present reality to itself by equating the ideas to a preestablished normative model (Braidotti 1994: 101). Given the pervasiveness of patriarchal forms of thought, this artistic process could be applied as a feminist methodology of writing within the patriarchal structures that condition our thought. Understood in this way, one of the tasks of feminist art as a practice of resistance is to learn how to think schizoanalytically (in order to think difference).

3. Labial Theory of Artistic Process

In order to explore the ways in which this schizo-revolutionary artistic process can be sustained as a form of feminist resistance that can engender *becomings-woman*, it is necessary to consider what it means to think from within the *labial*.[7] By employing this expression within theory, we invoke the work of Irigaray (1985a, 1985b, 1993). As the normative image of thought is centered around the phallic signifier, Irigaray explores the labial as the potential for different forms of expression that can produce different modes of thinking and being. Moreover, it is in the feminine that Irigaray invests "the sole force that can break the eternal return of the Same and its classical Others"

(Braidotti 2011: 283). To this extent, thinking from within the labial could break our reterritorializing habits of mind.

It is important to note that labial machines can be located on *all* bodies: on the face, female genitals, and cuts (Riordan 2011: 86–7). Therefore, *everybody* can connect to the intensities of the feminine (85). A feminist artistic practice is not *only* for women, but also for everybody, to create new lines of flight that will "lead to the withdrawal of their cultural *Phallus*" (Boothroyd 1996: 67). Exploring the labial as the potential for different forms of expression does not entail "producing a discourse of which woman would be the object or the subject" (Irigaray 1985b: 135), or creating representations of the feminine subject in order to "know" the nature of woman, or to claim that there is one. Instead it is an exploration for different forms of expression that can produce different modes of thinking and being that are not subjugated to the phallic signifier.[8]

With the purpose of developing a labial theory of artistic practice that is schizo-revolutionary, I will now situate the mutant affect as *labial affect* in order to draw an alliance between processes of becoming-woman and Irigaray's explicitly feminist project. In considering a labial affect seizes the spectator, the artistic process they become part of can be thought of as feminist. Within the experience of this feminist artistic encounter, what can be sensed is conditioned by the labial affect. In following the initial poststructuralist framing, the escape onto the Cosmos, by way of deterritorialization, produces a movement of iridescent chaos in which new cosmic forces can be selected. As the immanent evaluation rests upon the experience related to the labial affect, the new forces that are available to select can be understood as *labial cosmic forces*.

Having already posited particular dimensional components as feminine; I will further argue they are labial because they are tied to that sexual action (Deleuze and Guattari 2004: 347). This could also explain why Deleuze and Guattari use the term "female" when describing the operation that opens the territory onto the Cosmos (358). The process of selection within a feminist artistic process can therefore be thought of as "sexual selection" (Grosz 2008: 33). According to Grosz, sexual selection produces and explores excesses "for no reason other than their possibilities for intensification, their appeal" (33). Moreover, the cosmic forces that are available to select in this excess are found as "pleasurable and intensifying qualities that can be used to adorn both territory and body" (102). This excess can therefore be allied to the aesthetic excess described by Zepke that makes the affectual readymade a "war machine of a politics of sensation" (2008: 36). To this extent, this process of sexual selection becomes about selecting forces by experiencing their power to intensify pleasure.

Given that the immanent evaluation is of every-*thing* related to the life of that labial affect, not every labial cosmic force can be selected because of the risk of the experience being too intense. This could result in blocking the cosmic paths by putting the "life [of that labial affect] at risk for the sake of intensification, for the sake of sensation itself" (Grosz 2008: 63). In the event that the cosmic paths are blocked, the cosmic forces that have been selected will no longer be cosmic. By losing their cosmic difference, these forces become negative and will not bring anything new to the territorial assemblage.

Such an approach could be considered as differenciated because it suppresses the possibility of difference offered by the labial cosmic forces for the sake of a pleasurable and intense climax that ends the process.

According to Irigaray's critique of the logic of the Same, I argue that this approach could also be thought of as phallocentric: not only does it subjugate the labial cosmic forces for the sake of the *one* climax, as a result it reproduces the same.[9] That is not to say, however, that the only way to experience the labial cosmic forces fully is to completely escape. This would enable the subject and art object to escape "the gravity of its self-evidence" (Zepke 2008: 42) as defined by patriarchal and capitalist systems of representation and be fully immersed with the life of that labial affect, but this would ultimately risk the life of the subject and art object. Such an approach could be considered as undifferentiated, because it would entail the creation of a black hole (of death) or artistic qualities that are incomprehensible.

Instead, this process of sexual selection can be explored through a method of combats-between labial cosmic forces. This approach to female pleasure does not entail a "choice" between "clitoral activity and vaginal passivity," but instead moves between the multiple different "caresses" that can invoke "the hystericization of her entire body" (Irigaray 1985b: 28). Moreover, this process of combats-between overturns the judgment that her body sex is "zero," because she *has sex organs more or less everywhere*" (28). Moving between her multiple sex organs avoids focusing on one sex organ that ends the process in *one* climax, and instead explores her body sex as "a thousand tiny sexes" (Deleuze and Guattari 2004: 235) which can continue and enrich the process. To this extent, we can understand this method of combats-between as *caresses-between*, in which the immanent evaluation draws the affirmative labial cosmic forces together in a "close embrace" of a combat of sexual energies (Deleuze and Guattari 2004: 354). This close embrace enriches the artistic ensemble so as to incite a new feminist artistic encounter(s) or becoming(s)-woman.

4. A Labial Formula for a Schizo-Revolutionary Artistic Process

Having described the opening of the territory onto the Cosmos as opening onto the female, we can now further liken the partial access of the labial machine to the partial access to the Cosmos by describing that labial machines can only be partially accessed because they are partially hidden inside the body. Both provide a partial access to the (in principle) infinity of virtual possibilities of the Cosmos, or, in relation to a labial affect, the (in principle) infinity of virtual possibilities of the female. Furthermore, the labial machine, like the Cosmos, provides an escape from the patriarchal and capitalist systems of representation because it presents *"the horror of nothing to see"* (Irigaray 1985b: 26). By escaping the territories of representation, the labial machine becomes a destratified space: a *smooth space*. Moreover, this smooth space could be described as "the smooth labial space of pure difference" (Mackenzie and MacKenzie 2014: 74). To this extent, everybody can find in their labial machines a movement of escape from their "self," from *within*. Accordingly, this labial theory of artistic process can provide a practical application of Deleuze and Guattari's formula for schizophrenia.

As there is no single model of female sexuality, it is through her sexual multiplicity that the/a woman is indifferentiated (Irigaray 1985a: 227). Neither open (undifferentiated) nor closed (differenciated), her morphology is indefinite and undefined (indifferentiated) (229). Lost in the movement of escape within a labial machine, the subject and the art object become indiscernible because they are in her "zone of … indifferentiation where one can no longer be distinguished from *a* woman, *an* animal, or *a* molecule" (Deleuze 1997: 1). It is in this space of pure difference that provides the momentary experience of *being a woman*, and it is from this experience that can incite a becoming-woman. A way of thinking through this process of becoming-woman is by embodying it in the idea of the "self-caressing" labial lips (Irigaray 1985b: 24).

Labias are different in that their folds are plural, have no center, and are different in and of themselves. The "two lips" of the labia are in fact "*neither one nor two*" and this "keeps woman in touch with herself, but without any possibility of distinguishing what is touching from what is touched" (Irigaray 1985b: 26). It is taking place "all the time" because the two lips are in "continuous contact" (24). By sacrificing no lip over the other, no one of her pleasures to another, she is able to identify herself with none of them in particular, but rather always an ever-folding becoming "*of never being simply one*" (31). Without knowing (never "knowing"), she is already "several," but these are identities that cannot be dispersed because the other within her is already becoming something else (31).

The lips are in a ceaseless exchange with each other, each expressing a continuous differential enactment of singularities that are enunciated involuntarily: "She steps ever so slightly aside from herself with a murmur, an exclamation, a whisper, a sentence left unfinished … When she returns, it is to set off again from elsewhere. From another point of pleasure, or of pain" (Irigaray 1985b: 29). Each singular expression is unable to be distinguished from which lip it was expressed, therefore what is enunciated can only be partial. That is not to say that two (or more) partial enunciations expressed together, as a unit, can make *one* whole (something that can be understood within the phallic symbolic order). For they are contiguous and what they express is not the same. What is expressed between them has an enfolded meaning, an "*other meaning*" (29) that expresses a difference. It is these enfolded partial enunciation(s) that make her "whimsical, incomprehensible, agitated, capricious … leaving 'him' unable to discern the coherence of any meaning" (28–9). This labial language of difference cannot be understood by the phallic symbolic order because it speaks from the smooth labial space that is outside of the patriarchal territories of representation. Instead, it can be understood as belonging to an enfolded "logic of non-discursive [sexual] intensities" and "vectors of partial [female] subjectivity" (Guattari 1995: 22). To the extent that the labial lips are *in touch* with the infinite possibilities of the female, they can be thought of as already in touch with the infinite possibilities of the Cosmos. The difference they express can therefore be considered *cosmic*. Understood in this way, it is through her self-caressing lips that she can set "off in all directions," (Irigaray 1985b: 29) toward a "multiplicity of possible futures" (Zepke 2008: 35).

The process of becoming occurs in the smooth labial space, but "all progress is made by and in the striated space" (Deleuze and Guattari 2004: 536–7). The partial access of the labial machine is only partial because there is still a partial connection to the rest of the body. This can be described as the connection to the striated space as it is how we maintain an engagement in the world and engender change within it. The striated space is rendered homogeneous through its "parallel forces" "striating all of space in all of its directions" by "formalizing all the other dimensions" according to the "*center of gravity*" (Deleuze and Guattari 2004: 408). In other words, the directional components selected from the smooth labial space are transformed into expressive dimensional components in the striated space. This necessary operation preserves the labial affect(s) of the labial cosmic forces and introduces a labial cosmic difference into the territorial assemblage. It is within the process of marking that delineates the transformation of her morphology as indifferentiated to indifferenciated and incites a becoming-*woman*. By expressing a labial cosmic difference, her morphology becomes definite and defined *as* difference. Her morphological difference is not, cannot, be understood by patriarchal forms of thought in so far as it is *difference*.

Although this is a necessary operation, it can run risks of closure or stoppage (Deleuze and Guattari 2004: 536). That is to say, parallel forces can work in accordance with patriarchal and capitalist structures to the extent that they discontinue the change of direction in the ordering and disordering of the readymade, by formalizing the labial cosmic forces according to a center that is fixed upon the logic of capital and the phallic as ultimate signifiers. To this extent, any difference or progress produced from the smooth labial space will be reterritorialized in the triumph of phallogocentrism and the law of capital (411), thereby reproducing the female body in the territories of representation that judge and re-present her in models and images designed by and for men (Grosz 1989: xx). This is the necessary structural operation of the phallogocentric system: to represent her difference as other, subjugated and pejorative (Braidotti 1994: 80).

However, what is "troublesome" in the patriarchal and capitalist systems of representation is that "[s]he is morphologically dubious" (Braidotti 1994: 80). There are always opportunities for openings on the striated space, as the "geography of her pleasure is far more diversified, more multiple in its differences, more complex, more subtle, than is commonly imagined" (Irigaray 1985b: 28). These opportunities are produced as the territorialized function(s), in the labial dimensional components, change pace and enliven processes of deterritorializations which create openings, or in other words, smooth patches in the striated space. Enlivening the feminine process releases labial machines that open the territory onto the female, in which the smooth labial space can reconquer the properties of contact that free it from the parallelism between the patriarchal and capitalist structures (Deleuze and Guattari 2004: 411). In this movement of escape, she becomes lost in her zone of indifferentiation, in which she experiences being a woman *again (and again …)*. Through a process of caressing-*within*, she is able to (re-)discover her labial cosmic difference and introduces it into a new assemblage. In a movement of territorialization, she reclaims her morphological difference by expressing it as affirmative, joyful, and empowering (Braidotti 2010: 306–7). This territorial mark not only expresses the indifferentiated woman as indifferenciated, that incites a becoming-woman, but it also delineates the transformation from one assemblage to another that is "the becoming-imperceptible of women becoming-women" (Mackenzie and MacKenzie 2014: 74). Understood in this way, her territorial mark expresses an enfolded enunciation. Accordingly, the process of becoming in the reimparted smooth labial space becomes an enfolded becoming of (at least) two: the *becoming-imperceptible* of *women becoming-women*.

We can now understand this artistic practice as a feminist methodology of creating within the patriarachal structures that condition our experience. Moreover, it is a feminist artistic practice of resistance that reveals her libidinal energy as the source of her creativity and ethical relation to the world (Olkowski 2007: 11). The indifferenciated woman is still indifferentiated, because her morphology is always in the process of becoming other. What she produces can never be "finished" because her expression is in a continuous process of touching within. Her territorial mark, therefore, is an expression of a point in the artistic process of becoming-woman that is always becoming (within). Moreover, it is an expression of a point in which she was/is able to (re-)discover herself away from the phallic signifier. Consequently, what she produces can never be owned because there is no patriarchal image that can recognize its enfolded meaning. She cannot be asked to repeat herself because she has already returned (to the indifferentiated) within herself. When asked who she is, or more precisely to explain her indifferenciation, she "can only reply: Nothing [(differenciated)]. Everything [(undifferentiated)]" (Irigaray 1985b: 29).[10] Accordingly, the value of what she expresses will never be subsumed within capitalist and patriarchal structures because it is a line of flight that leaves them behind in the creation of "a possible world" (O'Sullivan 2006: 130). To this extent, the indifferent/ciated woman *is* a line of flight (Deleuze and Guattari 2004: 305). She does not, and cannot, belong to the models and images given to her by and for men because she is enfolded: she is both indifferentiated and indifferenciated, Nothing and Everything, finite and infinite, within and outside. She is different; she is other; she is sublime; she is becoming; she *is* cosmic.

5. Conclusion: A Labial Artistic Formula for Thinking Schizoanalytically

This labial formula for a schizo-revolutionary artistic process can therefore engender new feminist artistic encounters that can force us to think differently about women, for women, (men and others) becoming-women, and as women, (men and others) becoming-women. In working through what makes these feminist artistic encounters something in the world that forces us to think, we can turn to Irigaray's description of artistic process in which she explains the operation of connecting the territorial materials with the labial cosmic forces as "the meeting point of the properties of physical matter and an elaboration of sexualised subjective identity" (Irigaray 1993: 153). This operation therefore forms a synthesizer that is a force of the labial cosmic difference, and to this extent can "make thought travel" beyond the patriarchal forms of thought.

Moreover, the preserved labial affects and percepts emit problematic signs that are outside the patriarchal images of thought because they bear the enfolded meaning that make feminist art an encounter with the labial cosmic difference.

In order to engage with its enfolded meaning, a new enfolded image(s) of thought is forced into thought that can think of two, for two. This enfolded image(s) of thought provides us with a two-way enfolded basis for thinking the relationship between the indifferentiated and indifferenciated (and the differenciated and undifferentiated). It is a mode of thinking that continually recognizes one's own boundaries but also surpasses them (Olkowski 2007: 11). Thinking in this way allows us to experience the world through a perspective that is *à deux*, in which we can consider ourselves indifferentiated, unfinished, and always becoming (Olkowski 2007: 97–8). Understood in this way, these feminist artistic encounters can transform ideas of subjectivity and judgment aligned with the interests of patriarchy and capitalism and create new enfolded images of thought that are better suited to a life lived *à deux*. This feminist artistic practice of resistance, therefore, becomes an artistic process of learning a labial formula for thinking schizoanalytically.

The nature of a schizo-revolutionary labial theory of artistic practice can now be summarised as an on-going, never-complete, ever-folding, labial revolution of learning, creation and becoming. By enlivening the feminine within the artistic process, art can move in processes of deterritorializations of the capitalist and patriarchal systems of representation toward possibilities of becoming-woman. By exploring the emancipation of the female imagination, pleasure, and expression through art, we can produce different ways of thinking and being that will allow us to experience the world through a perspective that is *à deux*. I suggest that it is engaging in a feminist aesthetics of resistance that we can establish "a non-nihilistic ethical future" for women, men and others (Boothroyd 1996: 77). The feminist artistic encounters, processes and practices that are produced amount to neither a set object or subject, but rather, *a labial art-politics* (Mackenzie and MacKenzie 2014: 77): an enfolded practice of art and politics "without any possibility of distinguishing what is touching from what is touched" (Irigaray 1985b: 26).

Notes

1. For further details of this normative subjectivity and judgment, see Deleuze and Guattari's (2004) description of the majority or molar formation; the logic of the Same by Irigaray (1985a); and Braidotti's description of the dominant subject (2011).

2. Guattari describe these domains as extra-linguistic, nonhuman, biological, technological, aesthetic, etc.

3. See Chapter 10 of this book in which Sarfan describes this process of escaping from the self as the ascetic practice of desubjectification, or impersonality, through aversion (turning away from the self), also in defiance of normative models.

4. See Zepke (2014) for a description of schizo-revolutionary artistic practice.

5. In describing this approach of reducing difference to the same, I am suggesting that the operation of the differenciated order is based upon Irigaray's description of the logic of the *Same* (Irigaray 1985a: 74).

6. Deleuze and Guattari describe these actions as sexuality, aggressiveness, and flight.

7. For excellent overviews of the connection between Irigaray's explicitly feminist project and Deleuze and Guattari's philosophy of difference, see Braidotti (1994), Grosz (1994), Lorraine (1999), Olkowski (2000), and Colebrook (2000).

8. See Chapter 4 of this book, where Lorraine also sees sex and gender as a way of reworking the subject toward more productive figurations.

9. By italicizing *one*, I refer to the way Irigaray describes the male organ: "The *one* of form, of the individual, of the (male) sexual organ, of the proper name, of the proper meaning … supplants, while separating and dividing, that contact of *at least two* (lips) which keeps woman in touch with herself, but without any possibility of distinguishing what is touching from what is touched" (1985a: 26).

10. A connection could be made to Sarfan's articulation (Chapter 10) of becoming-woman as a form of *becoming-everything* that opens perception onto the infinite possibilities of the Cosmos.

References

Boothroyd, D. (1996), "Labial Feminism: Body Against Body with Luce Irigaray," *Parallax* 2 (2): 361–86.

Braidotti, R. (1994), *Nomadic Subjects: Embodiment and Sexual Difference in Contemporary Feminist Theory*, New York: Columbia University Press.

Braidotti, R. (2010), "Woman," in A. Parr (ed.), *The Deleuze Dictionary*, 306–8, Edinburgh: Edinburgh University Press.

Braidotti, R. (2011), *Nomadic Theory: The Portable Rosi Braidotti*, New York: Columbia University Press.

Cézanne, Paul (1978), *Conversations avec Paul Cézanne*, Paris: Macula.

Colebrook, C. (2000), "Is Sexual Difference a Problem?," in I. Buchanan and C. Colebrook (eds.), *Deleuze and Feminist Theory*, 110–27, Edinburgh: Edinburgh University Press.

Cutler, A. (2013), "Museum of Now," in B. Dillet, I. MacKenzie, and R. Porter (eds.), *The Edinburgh Companion to Poststructuralism*, 352–67, Edinburgh: Edinburgh University Press.

Deleuze, G. (1989), *Cinema 2: The Time-Image*, trans. H. Tomlinson and R. Galeta, London: Athlone Press.

Deleuze, G. (1994), *Difference and Repetition*, trans. P. Patton, London: Athlone Press.

Deleuze, G. (1997), *Essays Critical and Clinical*, trans. D. W. Smith and M. A. Greco, Minneapolis: University of Minnesota Press.

Deleuze, G., and F. Guattari (1994), *What Is Philosophy?*, trans. H. Tomlinson and G. Burchell, London: Verso.

Deleuze, G., and F. Guattari (2004), *A Thousand Plateaus: Capitalism and Schizophrenia*, trans. B. Massumi, London: Continuum.

Duchamp, M. (1973), *The Writings of Marcel Duchamp*, M. Sanouillet and E. Peterson (eds.), New York: Da Capo Press.

Duchamp, M. (1998), as quoted in H. H. Arnason and Marla F. Prather, *History of Modern Art: Painting, Sculpture, Architecture, Photography*, 4th ed., New York: Harry N. Abrams.

Grosz, E. (1989), *Sexual Subversions. Three French Feminists*, Sydney: Allen & Unwin.

Grosz, E. (1994), *Volatile Bodies: Toward a Corporeal Feminism*, Indiana: Indiana University Press.

Grosz, E. (2008), *Chaos, Territory, Art: Deleuze and the Framing of the Earth*, New York: Columbia University Press.

Guattari, F. (1995), *Chaosmosis, an Ethico-Aesthetic Paradigm*, trans. P. Bains and J. Pefanis, Sydney: Power Publications.

Guattari, F. (1996), "Subjectivities: for Better and for Worse," in G. Genoso (ed.), *The Guattari Reader*, 193–203, Oxford: Basil Blackwell.

Irigaray, L. (1993), *Sexes and Genealogies*, New York: Columbia University Press.

Irigaray, L. (1985a), *Speculum of the Other Woman*, New York: Cornell University Press.

Irigaray, L. (1985b), *This Sex Which Is Not One*, New York: Cornell University Press.

Lorraine, T. (1999), *Irigaray and Deleuze: Experiments in Visceral Philosophy*, New York: Cornell University Press.

Mackenzie, H., and I. MacKenzie (2014), "A Labial Art-Politics," *Contention: The Multidisciplinary Journal of Social Protest* 2 (1): 69–78.

Olkowski, D. (2000), "Body, Knowledge and Becoming-Woman: Morpho-logic in Deleuze and Irigaray," in I. Buchanan and C. Colebrook (eds.), *Deleuze and Feminist Theory*, 86–109, Edinburgh: Edinburgh University Press.

Olkowski, D. (2007), "Beyond Narcissism: Women and Civilization," in H. Fielding, G. Hiltmann, D. Olkowski, and A. Reichold (eds.), *The Other: Feminist Reflections in Ethics*, 71–101, New York: Palgrave Macmillan.

O'Sullivan, S. (2006), *Art Encounters Deleuze and Guattari: Thought Beyond Representation*, Hampshire: Palgrave Macmillan.

Riordan, G. (2011), "Haemosexuality," in F. Beckman (ed.), *Deleuze and Sex*, 69–88, Edinburgh: Edinburgh University Press.

Zepke, S. (2008), "The Readymade: Art as the Refrain of Life," in S. O'Sullivan and S. Zepke (eds.), *Deleuze, Guattari and the Production of the New*, 33–44, London: Continuum.

Zepke, S. (2014), "Schizo–Revolutionary Art: Deleuze, Guattari and Communization Theory," in I. Buchanan and L. Collins (eds.), *Deleuze and the Schizoanalysis of Visual Art*, 31–53, London: Bloomsbury.

NOTES ON CONTRIBUTORS

Cheri Lynne Carr is Associate Professor in Philosophy at CUNY LaGuardia. A graduate of the University of Memphis, her research is primarily in Ethics, Feminism, Philosophy for Children, and Post-Structuralism. Her recently published book, *Deleuze's Kantian Ethos: Critique as a Way of Life*, explores the potential for a new form of ethical life based on the ideal of critique as the self-perpetuating evaluation of values (Edinburgh, 2018).

Amy Chan Kit-Sze is Associate Professor in the English Department at Hong Kong Shue Yan University. She is the coeditor of *World Weavers: Globalization, Science Fiction, and the Cybernetic Revolution* (2005), *Science Fiction and the Prediction of the Future* (2011), *Technovisuality: Cultural Re-enchantment and the Experience of Technology* (2015), and *Deleuze and the Humanities* (2017).

Katja Čičigoj is a philosopher completing her PhD at Justus-Liebig University, Giessen and a former visiting researcher at CRMEP, Kingston University, London and CPCT, Goldsmiths, London, focusing on feminist philosophy, critical theory, and contemporary European philosophy. She is currently translating and writing a scholarly introduction to Shulamith Firestone's *The Dialectic of Sex*.

Claire Colebrook is Edwin Erle Sparks Professor in English, Philosophy, and Women's and Gender Studies at Penn State University. She has written books and articles on contemporary European philosophy, literary history, gender studies, queer theory, visual culture, and feminist philosophy. Her most recent book is *Twilight of the Anthropocene Idols* (coauthored with Tom Cohen and J. Hillis Miller).

Erinn Cunniff Gilson is Associate Professor in Philosophy at Skidmore College, Saratoga Springs, New York. Drawing both on feminist theory and twentieth-century European philosophy, she teaches about and researches a diverse range of ethical and political issues, with particular interest in the concept of vulnerability, food justice, and racial and sexual justice. Recent publications include *The Ethics of Vulnerability* (Routledge 2014), "Vulnerability and Victimization: Rethinking Key Concepts in Feminist Discourses on Sexual Violence" in *Signs* (2016), and the entry on "Continental Feminist Ethics" in Kim Q. Hall and Ásta Kristjana Sveinsdóttir's forthcoming *The Oxford Handbook of Feminist Philosophy*.

Jeanne Hamilton is an artist, university lecturer, and translator based in Germany. A graduate of the School of the Art Institute of Chicago (BFA-Multi-Media) and Central European University, Budapest (MA-Gender Studies), her art focuses on feminist theories of embodiment, sexual being and representation as well as biography, history, and socio-political phenomena.

Fredrica Introne is an artist, former attorney, and competitive Brazilian jiu jitsu athlete. Her work focuses on the grace and violence of physical struggle.

Mihee Jeon is an interdisciplinary artist and independent curator currently based in Seoul, South Korea. After graduating with her Fine Arts degree in London, she developed her unique approach of socially engaged artworks. Her artistic aim is to address a deep human understanding in the manner of art.

Nir Kedem is Assistant Professor in Cultural Studies in the Department of Cultural Studies, Creation and Production at Sapir Academic College, Israel, and lectures in literature, queer theory, and film at Tel Aviv University. He is currently working on his first scholarly monograph, titled *A Deleuzian Critique of Queer Thought: Overcoming Sexuality*, to be published by Edinburgh University Press in 2019. His work on Deleuzian strategies of reading and queer translation is forthcoming in *Poetics Today* and *Symplokē*.

Timothy Laurie is a scholarly teaching fellow in the School of Communication at the University of Technology Sydney. His research interests include gender studies, continental philosophy, cultural theory, and studies in popular culture.

Tamsin Lorraine is Professor in Philosophy at Swarthmore College. Her work includes the books *Irigaray and Deleuze: Experiments in Visceral Philosophy* and *Deleuze and Guattari's Immanent Ethics: Theory, Subjectivity, and Duration*.

Celiese Lypka is a PhD candidate in the Department of English at the University of Calgary, specializing in women's writing, modernist literature, feminist theory, and the theoretical framework of Gilles Deleuze and Félix Guattari. Her current research investigates productive modes of anxious femininity found within modernist texts.

Hollie Mackenzie is an artist and a PhD candidate in Social and Political Thought at the University of Kent (UK). Her publications explore a feminist philosophy of labial art-politics and critical pedagogy. Hollie has received multiple art awards and a teaching prize for her creative and experimental pedagogy (2018). She was the lead artist for the *MA in Politics, Art and Resistance* (University of Kent) in the *Fairground* at Tate Exchange, Tate Modern (2017).

Fernanda Negrete is Assistant Professor in French at the University at Buffalo. She has published essays on aesthetics, women's experimental literature, contemporary art, Deleuze, and psychoanalysis in *ARTMargins, CR: The New Centennial Review, Mosaic, Humanities, Samuel Beckett Today/Aujourd'hui*, and *Entorno a la imaginación*.

Chrysanthi Nigianni is a lecturer in the Psychosocial studies at Goldsmiths, University of London. She has written on the topics of ethics, aesthetics, politics, and the body. She is the coeditor of *Undutiful Daughters: New Directions in Feminist Thought and Practice* (with H. Gunkel and F. Söderbäck, Palgrave McMillan Press, 2012), *Deleuze and Queer*

Theory (with M. Storr, Edinburgh University Press, 2009), and 'Deleuzian Politics?' (with J. Gilbert, 2010)—a Special Issue of *New Formations: A Journal of Culture/Theory/Politics*. She is a trainee in psychoanalytic psychotherapy at the Site for Contemporary Psychoanalysis.

Macarena Rioseco is Associate Lecturer at Lancaster University, UK and obtained her PhD in Art at Lancaster University, Institute of Contemporary Arts.

Heidi Samuelson earned her PhD in philosophy from the University of Memphis in 2012. She currently works as an editor based out of Chicago. Her current research and most recent presentations have been on feminist economics.

Austin Sarfan is a PhD student in Literature at Duke University, with research interests in modernism and the history of the emotions.

Janae Sholtz is Associate Professor in Philosophy and the Coordinator of Women's and Gender Studies at Alvernia University. Author of *The Invention of a People, Heidegger and Deleuze on Art and the Political* (Edinburgh, 2015) and articles on topics ranging from Deleuzian dramatization, the avant-garde and aesthetico-political resistance, and the Anthropocene; her research focuses on continental philosophy, aesthetics, social and political philosophy, and feminist theory.

Hannah Stark is Senior Lecturer in English at the University of Tasmania. She is the author of *Feminist Theory after Deleuze* (Bloomsbury) and the coeditor of *Deleuze and the Non/Human* (Palgrave Macmillan).

Audronė Žukauskaitė is Chief Researcher in the Lithuanian Culture Research Institute. Her recent publications include the monographs *Gilles Deleuze and Felix Guattari's Philosophy: The Logic of Multiplicity* (in Lithuanian, 2011), and *From Biopolitics to Biophilosophy* (in Lithuanian, 2016). She also coedited (with S. E. Wilmer) *Deleuze and Beckett* (Palgrave Macmillan, 2015), and *Resisting Biopolitics: Philosophical, Political and Performative Strategies* (Routledge, 2016). Her research interests include contemporary philosophy, biopolitics, biophilosophy, and posthumanism.

INDEX

Index

Index

Index

Index

Index

Index